THE BIRDS OF KENT

A review of their status and distribution

This book is dedicated to the memory of

Richard Constantine Homes (1913–1978)

and

Dr. Jeffery Graham Harrison O.B.E. (1922–1978)

THE BIRDS OF KENT

A Review of Their Status and Distribution

Edited by
D. W. Taylor, D. L. Davenport and J. J. M. Flegg

Published by
The Kent Ornithological Society

ISBN 0 9507418 0 9

First published in 1981 by the Kent Ornithological Society,
Hon. Secretary: I. C. Castle
'Winnats', Whitehill Road, Meopham, Kent DA13 0NS

Text set in 10/12pt Linotron Palatino, printed and bound in Great Britain by The Pitman Press, Bath

Acknowledgements

The Kent Ornithological Society expresses its appreciation and gratitude to the following for their help in the production of this book:

Texts

J. A. Allen
R. E. C. Collins
D. L. Davenport
J. J. M. Flegg
B. H. Green
J. G. Harrison
W. G. Harvey
A. C. B. Henderson
C. H. Hindle
R. C. Homes
J. N. Hollyer
G. F. A. Munns
D. F. Musson
E. R. Parrinder
R. Smith
R. C. Stone
D. W. Taylor
C. E. Wheeler
L. F. Woollard

Artwork

I. C. Castle
K. J. Derrett
N. Tardivel
D. W. Taylor

Typing & Distribution

S. A. Webb

Illustrations

I. C. Castle	pp. 22–31t, 234b
R. J. Chandler	pp. 235, 237t, 239t, 240b, 241b
R. K. Coles	pp. 232t, 233, 236t
A. J. M. Fletcher	p. 238b
P. J. Grant	pp. 193,197, 210, 214
D. F. Harle	pp. frontispiece, 6–20, 35, 65, 89, 117, 127, 175, 254, 261, 342, 373
G. C. D. Harrison	p. 230b
P. F. Harrison	pp. 31b, 231, 232b, 234t, 240t
B. Hawkes	pp. 230t, 236b, 237b, 238t, 239t, 241t
C. J. Hodgson	pp. vii, 3, 72, 111, 125, 130, 273, 317, 397, 407
J. N. Hollyer	pp. 47, 323
T. R. Perkins	pp. 49, 52, 281, 363
M. W. Woodcock	pp. 40, 134, 145, 265, 309, 376
M. J. Woods	pp. title page, 105, 180, 228

Contents

Acknowledgements	v
Introduction	1
The Breeding Bird Survey	3
The Kent Environment	6
Systematic List	32
Appendix I Category D Species	420
Appendix II The Hastings Rarities	422
References	426
Index of English Names	429
List of Subscribers	435

Introduction

Most birdwatchers, within and outside the county boundary, would agree that Kent is one of the premier counties in Britain for birds, not least because both inland and on the extensive coastline, the habitat is rich and diverse. It is now nearly 30 years since there was a book on the birds of Kent, the last being written by Dr. James Harrison in 1953. Before Harrison had been a series of scholarly volumes, including R. J. Bolston, C. W. Shepherd and E. Bartlett's *The Birds of Kent* (1907), and the extremely useful *A History of the Birds of Kent* by Dr. Norman F. Ticehurst (1909). On a more parochial basis were such works as Walter Prentis's *Notes on the Birds of Rainham* (1894), *The Birds of the Dartford District* by W. J. Davis (1904), and more recently Harrison's own *Handlist of the Birds of the Sevenoaks or Western District of Kent* (1942) and E. H. Gillham and R. C. Homes's *The Birds of the North Kent Marshes* (1950).

James Harrison published at the start of the great post-war upsurge in the popularity of birdwatching as a hobby. He could not have foreseen the growth of enthusiasm that has provided far more comprehensive records, from all over the county, than were available to him. Such was the enthusiasm for collaboration and for a centralised system of recording that in 1952 the Kent Ornithological Society was formed, with the continuing documentation of the county's birds as one of its major objectives. Even the founder members of the KOS could hardly have imagined that the Society's strength in fieldwork would allow a Breeding Season Survey on a scale that has produced the finely-detailed and fascinating maps in this book.

A wealth of information on bird numbers, distribution and ecology, from 25 years of recording, is presented in these pages, but such are the changes in the environment—natural and man-made—that this is a story that will never be fully told. The record books must remain open, the birdwatchers alert, both to enjoy their birds and to document the changes, arrivals and departures from the scene yet to come. Even history is not necessarily unchanging! Harrison gives details of many rare birds seen or obtained in the general area of Hastings (including a large number from Kent) around the turn of the century. The validity of some of these was questioned following a detailed investigation in 1962, and in the light of this, these 'Hastings Rarities' (as they became popularly known) are omitted from the main text but listed in Appendix II.

This new *Birds of Kent* differs from its predecessors: it has to, if only because of the sheer amount of information available. That information on the birds of the county has been gathered, over the years, by thousands of birdwatchers, many watching on their own, others joining in co-operative censuses or surveys, or helping in the work of the two Bird Observatories, at Dungeness and Sandwich Bay. Each year, this mass of data is collated and condensed by a team of Area Recorders and published in the *Kent Bird Report.* Records of less usual species are considered for acceptance by the KOS Editorial and Records Committee, and where appropriate, by the National Rarities Committee.

The idea that a new *Birds of Kent* was due was stimulated by several factors, including the obvious need to bring Harrison up to date, the silver jubilee of the KOS and the completion of the Breeding Bird Survey. Because of the mass of information that had to be sifted, the tasks of compiling it were shared among a number of authors. They, and the photographers and artists whose work embellishes the text, all live, or birdwatch in Kent, as does Dr. Bryn Green, of Wye College, University of London, who has written the physiographic introduction to the county. Thus this is a book on the birds of Kent, based on the fieldwork of the birdwatchers of Kent, and written by some of those birdwatchers. In most cases it was possible to allocate species to authors with a relevant personal interest in them, and although each has been written within the same broad format, it is hoped that the variety of approaches will add to the attraction of the book.

The tasks of editing the texts and compiling the actual book have been undertaken by a small editorial group. Initially the chairman was R. C. (Dick) Homes, followed by Dr. Jeffery Harrison. One of the greatest sadnesses is that neither lived to see the end-product of their enthusiasm and drive, for without them it is unlikely the embryo of ideas for this book would have hatched, let alone fledged into this elegant volume. I succeeded Jeffery Harrison as chairman, and it is my pleasure to express heartfelt appreciation of the enormous amount of work undertaken by my colleagues to ensure the successful completion of a Herculean task. Don Taylor and David Davenport have been primarily concerned with texts, maps and histograms, whilst Ian Castle, besides providing much of the landscape photography, has been responsible for the logistic and administrative detail concerned with preparing such a varied mass of material for publication. Our special thanks to Shirley Webb who typed the manuscripts and stoically handled the secretarial side of mailing and distribution. Finally, we are indebted to The Pitman Press for their help in making this an attractive and informative production.

J. J. M. Flegg

The Breeding Bird Survey

The Breeding Bird Survey, initiated by the Editorial and Records Committee of the Kent Ornithological Society, was originally planned to run for five years from 1967–71, but for various reasons the period was extended to seven years spanning 1967–73.

On a county scale, there are obvious benefits to be derived from the use of as small a survey area as possible when relating distribution to habitat—manpower permitting. Recording began in 1967 on a 1-kilometre square basis, noting confirmed breeding only. This proved not only too ambitious, but unrealistic, and a decision was made to adopt the tetrad as the unit area, a 2 × 2-kilometres square formed by the even-numbered lines of the Ordnance Survey national grid system. The presence, probability and confirmation of breeding for each species was recorded, using the same categories established by the British Trust for Ornithology for the national survey, which was based on the 10-kilometre square. This resulted in the publication in 1976 of *The Atlas of Breeding Birds in Britain and Ireland* compiled by J. T. R. Sharrock.

There was close liaison between the national and local schemes, and organisers were appointed for each of the fifty-two 10-kilometre squares, or part squares (there are forty-five with 10–25 tetrads) that cover the county. All tetrads containing even the smallest amount of coastline were included, but along the boundaries with Sussex and Greater London only squares containing more than half their area within Kent were included. This resulted in a total of 1,000 tetrads.

Our own survey, based on the tetrad, produced a distribution pattern on a scale twenty-five times more detailed than the national Atlas, and though the coverage was a little patchy, the results provide a more complete picture of our breeding birds than ever before. One of the most valuable aspects of this survey is that it provides a base-line against which future comparisons can be made.

During 1967–73 over 39,500 records were filed and eventually plotted on the distribution maps which feature in this book. A total of 135 species was recorded, 127 of which were proved to breed. Hundreds of KOS members took part, putting in varying amounts of time and effort. We hope that the publication of these maps will be just reward for their labours.

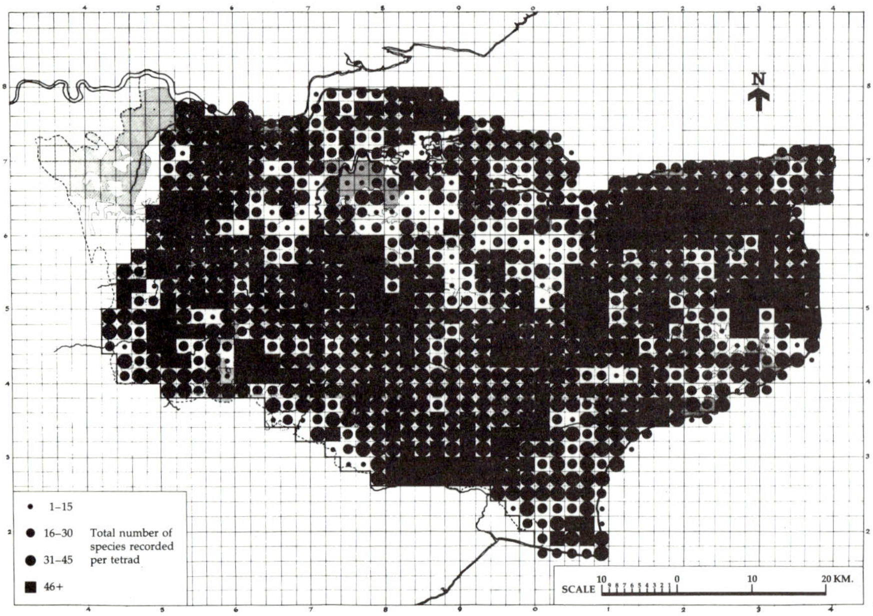

Coverage achieved during Breeding Bird Survey 1967–73

The distribution of effort was clearly uneven, with the least well covered areas scattered along the Downs and to the southwest along the border with Sussex. This should be borne in mind when studying the distribution maps. However, an average of 40 species per tetrad indicates that the overall coverage was quite good. Some tetrads with a wide variety of habitat provided nest sites for over 80 species, the highest total being 88 in TR16V, the Westbere square in the Stour Valley. On marshland areas, with little cover, totals in excess of 30 are realistic, but most tetrads include some variety of habitat, even in built-up areas, and up to 50 species, or more, could normally be expected.

The codes used in completing the record cards, given in ascending order of importance from least to most definite evidence of breeding, were as follows:

Possible Breeding (shown by a small dot)

Bird recorded in breeding season in possible nesting habitat, but no other indication of breeding.

Probable Breeding (shown by a medium dot)

S Singing male present, or breeding calls heard on more than one date in same place.
T Bird, or pair, apparently holding territory.
D Courtship and display, agitated behaviour or anxiety calls from adults suggesting probable presence of nest or young nearby; or brood-patch on trapped female.
N Visiting probable nest site.
B Nest Building, including excavating nest hole.

Confirmed Breeding (shown by a large dot)

DD Distraction display or injury feigning.
UN Used nest found.
FL Recently fledged young.
FS Adult carrying faecal sac.
FY Adult(s) with food for young.
ON Adult(s) entering or leaving nest site in circumstances indicating occupied nest.
NE Nest and eggs, or bird sitting and not disturbed, or eggshells found away from nest.
NY Nest with young, or downy young of ducks, gamebirds, waders, etc.

The Kent Environment

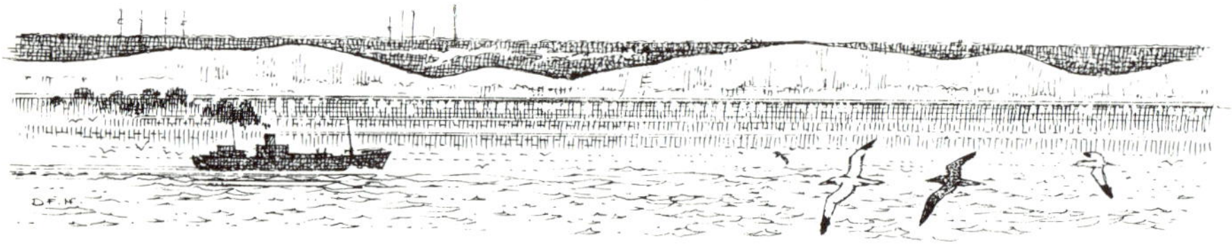

A varied geology, long sea coastline, and a history of different agricultural and sylvicultural land uses have conspired to generate a wide range of natural and semi-natural habitats in the Kentish countryside. The position of the county in the climatically amenable south-easternmost part of the British Isles, with its proximity to the rich continental flora and fauna, has populated these habitats with diverse plant and animal communities including several species which are rare or absent from other parts of the country. Like other groups, its avifauna is rich and contains some species of predominantly continental distribution which just gain a slender foothold in the British Isles in Kent. These same physical, and especially climatic characteristics, together with the nearness of London, make Kent equally attractive to man and his enterprises. Urban expansion, industry, seaports, new roads, mineral extraction, and perhaps above all modern agricultural intensification, have begun to erode the natural fabric of the countryside at an alarming pace. But not all this new development has been for the worse. Reservoirs and wet gravel pits have, for example, greatly enlarged the extent of open freshwater habitats, for natural lakes and their associated species are otherwise rare in Kent. Furthermore, the attrition of wildlife habitats is now being countered by the acquisition and management of reserves by a number of active conservation organisations. The Kentish environment is thus in a state of change. Probably it has ever been so, and our present avifauna is the product of these changes.

Climate

Kent has a warmer and dryer climate than most other parts of the British Isles. The mean annual air temperature corrected to sea level is between 10°C and 10.6°C, and the mean annual rainfall is almost everywhere below 770 mm. January is generally the coldest month with mean temperatures of around 4°C and July the warmest with mean temperatures of about 17°C. Rainfall is fairly evenly distributed throughout the year, most falling in October, November, December and January. These averages conceal surprisingly marked differences in climate between different parts of the county. The high ground of the Downs and other Wealden ridges is substantially cooler and wetter than the rest of the county. The highest rainfall is at Bedgebury with 825 mm, but parts of Sheppey have less than 530 mm, and much of the north Kent coast and Romney Marsh have less than 640 mm. Most coastal districts are also substantially cooler in the summer and warmer in the winter than inland. This amelioration of temperature extremes by the heat stored in the sea is nowhere as marked as under the oceanic climates of western Britain, but in an area of predominantly continental climate is of significance in adding over a month to the length of the growing season. This relative freedom from frost in the winter in coastal areas is also perhaps of direct relevance to many birds, particularly those forced southwards and westwards by severe weather on the Continent.

Geology and Topography

Primarily it is the geological template which determines the nature of the environment. It is the exposure of different rock types and their hardness which largely directs erosion and the resulting relief of the land and course of its rivers. It is their chemistry which dictates which plants can grow and soil and vegetation develop. It is vegetation which provides food and shelter for birds and other animals and largely determines the nature of the habitat and the species which populate it.

The rocks exposed in Kent are sedimentary deposits laid down in the Cretaceous and Tertiary periods. The earlier Cretaceous series constitute the northern half of what remains of an anticlinal dome or ridge which extends from Hampshire into Northern France. This Wealden anticline was raised at the time of the earth movements which built the Alps some 70–25 million years ago and has been subsequently eroded right down to the oldest rocks at its core. These are the Hastings Beds—predominantly fairly resistant sandstones which constitute the High Weald stretching in Kent from Penshurst to Tenterden as a series of ridges rising to nearly 150 metres near Tunbridge Wells. Surrounding the High Weald, the more readily-eroded Weald Clay forms a low-lying broad flat vale, less than 30 metres above sea level. It is bounded to the north by the ridge of harder rocks of the Lower Greensand climbing gently from Folkestone to Toy's Hill, where it reaches over 240 metres. Beyond is the vale of Homesdale, that narrow exposure of the Gault clay lying between the Lower Greensand and the prominent Chalk escarpment of the North Downs, which stretches from Folkestone to the highest point in the county at Westerham Hill, 251 metres above sea level. The remains of the Wealden dome thus form in Kent a series of parallel ridges and vales, the oldest rocks in the central High Weald and the youngest, the Chalk, around the periphery. In Sussex the Kentish pattern is repeated in mirror image to the coastal escarpment of the South Downs.

In Kent the dipslope of the North Downs reaches the coast only in Thanet. The lower dipslope of the Chalk is elsewhere overlain by the Tertiary sediments of the London Basin. The oldest of these, the Thanet, Woolwich and Oldhaven Beds, are predominantly sands which form a narrow belt of fertile soils running from Sandwich to the London suburbs. Over most of the Isle of Sheppey, the Grain Peninsula and the area between Canterbury and Whitstable they are in turn overlain by the London Clay which forms a series of plateaux and low hills, typified by the Blean.

No part of Kent was glaciated, but more recent superficial deposits cloak the solid geology in some parts of the county. The crest of the Downs and all the upper dipslope, save only the dry valleys which run down it is covered in Clay-with-Flints and other more sandy, loesslike, plateau drift deposits. The valleys of the Darent, Medway and Stour contain alluvium and terrace gravels. They all breach the Chalk in a northerly course, likely imposed by their origin on the flanks of the Wealden Dome. Alluvium and terrace gravels also border the Thames from Erith to Cliffe. The most extensive of the superficial deposits are the estuarine alluvium and coastal sand and shingle. Marine action has deposited large sand and shingle spits across the mouth of the Rother between Rye and Hythe and across the mouth of the Stour from Deal to Sandwich. In the slack water behind these spits and also in the mouth of

the Medway and Swale, sheltered by the Isle of Sheppey, extensive sedimentation of alluvial silts and muds has occurred. These marine deposits forming the 'soft' part of the coastline occur where the more readily erodable rocks like the Weald and London clays are exposed to the action of the sea, where bays and inlets with flat coastal scenery are produced. Where the harder Chalk reaches the coast around Thanet and between Deal and Folkestone, it forms impressive cliffs with wave-cut beaches and rock pools at their foot.

Land Use History

We know from the analysis of pollen and other plant remains in peat deposits that before man began to make a substantial impact on the environment in Mesolithic and, more especially, Neolithic times nearly all of Kent, hill and vale, was covered in mixed deciduous forest. The climate then may have been dry enough to restrict the growth of trees on the better drained soils of the sand and chalk escarpments which perhaps, bore some open heath and grassland. Megalithic remains in Kent, such as Kits Coty near Aylesford, are mostly in these situations. However, the Clay-with-Flints over most of the North Downs dip-slope probably provided a more congenial soil for trees than the thinner cappings of the South Downs and, because it was more afforested, presented a less attractive entry into the county than the more open southern ridge. There is certainly less archaeological evidence of early man on the North Downs than on the South. So birds of open habitats like the Kestrel, Lapwing and Skylark were almost certainly then much rarer in Kent than today, and confined to the sand dunes and other open habitats of the coast. Much of what is now Romney Marsh was then saltmarsh, reedswamp and fen, and the river valleys and poorly-drained clay vales would have been vast, impenetrable swampy alder and willow-dominated carr woodland and fen where cranes, pelicans and Sea Eagles likely bred. They certainly did in similar situations in other parts of the country. Remains of the Dalmatian Pelican and Crane are known from deposits of this age and the Sea Eagle, or earn, is commemorated even in Saxon times in place names like Yarner Wood and Yarnscombe in Devon and Arnecliffe in Yorkshire.

It is from this natural cover of forest and fen that man has carved the present landscape. Early clearance was of the more easily worked, less luxuriant woodland of the thin soils of the Chalk and sandstone escarpments. These were cultivated as arable by Neolithic and, later, Celtic iron age peoples, but reverted to pasture when the Saxon and Jutish settlers and their more efficient tools began to clear the thicker tangle of the valley woodlands. It was the products of open sheep walks such as these on which the prosperity of Kent, and England, was based right until the industrial revolution. They provided open habitats of enormous extent, suitable for birds of the steppe like Wheatears and perhaps Quail and Great Bustard. The coastal marshlands were progressively 'inned' and drained for the same purpose from Roman times onwards. Settlements were concentrated on the chalk, particularly at the foot of the escarpment of the Downs, and on the Greensand ridge. Only gradually were clearings opened up in the vast wood or 'weald' which covered the clay vales. The first clearances or 'dens' were made by men from the ridge villages for timber and grazings. Tenterden was the dene of Thanet. The wealden and hill forests were steadily cleared for agriculture and by charcoal burners providing the fuel for the wealden iron smelting, which until the discovery of coal was the main centre of the industry in the country. The settlements gradually pushed back the forest and in some places the only remains of the original tree cover now survives in woods and copses and hedgerows where parish boundaries from adjacent settlements met. But the difficulty of clearing the claylands of the Weald was great and the forest resisted clearance much longer than most of the woodland cover in the country. Even now Kent and Sussex are the most wooded counties in Britain.

The fields cleared from the Wealden forest were mostly small and directly enclosed by hedges. Large open field systems typical of most of the country until the parliamentary enclosures of the late eighteenth and early nineteenth century were not common in Kent, though such hedgeless, 'champion' countryside seems always to have been characteristic of Thanet. Much of the unenclosed heathland and downland was held in common for the exercise of grazing and other common rights. Some of these 'commons' of the poorer soils, particularly the series on the Greensand ridge in West Kent, still survive, but most have been unused for the last half century or so and in the absence of grazing have scrubbed over with bracken, gorse and birch, forming secondary woodland.

Farmland

Kent is now predominantly an agricultural county and most of the landscape is under a vegetation cover created and maintained by agriculture. As the 'Garden of England' the county is renowned for its horticultural products, particularly the fruit and hops grown on the favourable loamy soils of the superficial deposits on the North Downs dipslope between Canterbury and the Medway towns. Also important is the Wealden fruit belt, south of Maidstone, which extends over the deep and fertile soils of that part of the Greensand, across the Weald clay vale, more tractable here because of superficial lower deposits of alluvium and brickearth, and onto the High Weald. This is a countryside of orchards, mainly apples and pears and declining cherries; and hop gardens, all characteristically enclosed by tall windbreaks of poplar, alder, or conifer. It is the land of the Bullfinch, here a Schedule 2 species controlled for its depredations of fruit buds. The modern orchards with their small, heavily pruned trees are not as congenial a habitat for birds as the traditional orchards, particularly of the sweet cherries with their old and gnarled trees with Wrynecks nesting in the holes; nor are the new windbreaks so suitable for nesting finches as the thorns they have replaced. The fruit countryside, however, does still bear a good deal of woodland where the soils are poor or the topography difficult.

The good soils of superficial deposits of the Downs in East Kent and in West Kent between the Medway towns and London are also devoted in large part to horticultural production, here mainly of soft fruit and vegetables. There are other important market gardening areas on Romney Marsh where potatoes and, increasingly, bulbs are a major crop, and also on the better soils of the Grain peninsula. These areas are perhaps the most intensively cultivated in the county and little natural cover remains. Some birds, however, seem to favour the open conditions in more isolated areas.

Despite the county's renown for fruit, justified in its having half the orchards and hops of England and Wales, arable cultivation, mainly of wheat and barley, occupies a much greater part of the agricultural acreage, nearly a third in 1970, compared with about a tenth under top fruit or hops and less than a tenth under market gardening. Thanet and the dipslope of the Downs to the south is the cornland par excellence, but there is much growing of cereals elsewhere on the Downs and on the Lower Greensand. Increasingly, drainage is enabling much of the traditional grassland to be converted to arable. The change is most advanced in the alluvial marshlands of Romney Marsh, North Kent and the Lower Stour Valley, but inroads are also being made even into the wet clays of the Low Weald. Modern arable cultivation with its big machines needs large fields and creates a bleak landscape with its hedgerow removal, canalised waterways, and plethora of agricultural chemicals which eliminate many species from those fragments of natural habitat which do survive. However, some birds like Golden Plover continue to use old haunts even when changed in this way, particularly if conversion has been sympathetic in leaving some of the former habitats. Grey geese now find the winter cereals attractive and seem to do little harm, indeed perhaps benefit the crops by stimulating tillering.

The richest wildlife habitats on agricultural land in Kent are the permanent grasslands which still survive largely unimproved for agriculture. Most of the Weald and Gault clay vales are devoted to dairying, or sheep, with some beef cattle in places. The fields are small with thick hedges and almost every field has its pond with fringing reedmace, and Moorhen and Reed Bunting. It is the country of the Snipe and Lapwing. Even these grasslands are subject to agricultural intensification nowadays, involving the use of chemical sprays and fertiliser, or even drainage ploughing and reseeding to short term leys, and this makes them a less attractive habitat to birds like Redshank, which prefer the old wet rushy fields, unfortunately now anathema to the farmer. The same changes are taking place in the rich bird habitats of the coastal marshes.

Natural and Semi-natural Habitats

Since modern agriculture leaves little room for any but the most adaptable wildlife, the most important habitats for most birds are now those areas which survive largely outside the agricultural system, like woodlands and open waters, or those, like grazing marshlands and chalk grasslands, which are still maintained by traditional unintensive practices.

Woodlands

Once completely covering Kent, woodlands now occupy only some 12% of the area of the county. As such it is still one of the most wooded counties in the country, but not all this woodland represents the remains of the fragmentation of the original forest cover; much has been planted relatively recently. There are three main kinds of woodland in the county.

Primary woodlands are the relicts of the primeval woodland where there has been continuous tree cover of native species on the site. Most have been managed for timber production, commonly in Kent as coppice-with-standards. Despite this their long establishment makes them by far the most species-rich woodlands, and the only ones in which some typical woodland plants and animals still occur. The original forest cover in Kent was of mixed deciduous woodland with common oak probably the dominant tree in the clay vales and plateaux; sessile oak and beech on the greensand ridge; common oak, beech and ash on the chalk; and alder, black poplar and willows on the wet alluvial soils of the valleys. Limes were much commoner than today judging by their pollen in peat deposits like those at Hothfield, and hornbeam and wild service trees were likely important species on the clays as they still are today. Most of this woodland which still survives is on the High Weald, the high western part of the Greensand ridge, the escarpment face of the Downs and on the Blean, all areas where difficult topography has prevented clearance and the use of the land for agriculture.

Surviving examples of the woodland of the more fertile soils, and particularly of the riverine alder and willow forest, are rare in the county.

Many woodland birds depend on the mixed aged structure of primary woodlands, with old trees and dead wood, and the distribution of species like the Great Spotted Woodpecker reflects very well that of primary woodlands. Other species like the Nightingale favour, and perhaps in the case of some like the Redstart, depend upon this kind of woodland. Coppice management is important to Nightingales in providing glades and scrub cover where they reach much higher breeding densities than in high forest. The old pollards of wood pasture and boundary trees are likewise important to many hole-nesting species.

Secondary woodlands occurring over land once cleared and used for agriculture are both natural and planted. Successional woodlands have arisen spontaneously, replacing heathland and downland once kept open by the grazing and burning regimes used to keep the unenclosed, and often common, grazing lands in good heart. Some may be very old but much of the woodland of the Greensand ridge, particularly the chart country around Sevenoaks, was open heather heathland forty or fifty years ago. Abandoned by agriculture and relinquished by rabbits after myxomatosis, it quickly scrubbed over with bracken, gorse and birch and is now well on the way to climax woodland with oak well established. Similar changes have taken place on the Chalk where large sections of the escarpment are now covered in thorn, yew, whitebeam and ash woodland which has developed from open grassland in the relatively recent past. In their earlier stages such natural secondary woodlands are very rich bird habitats because of the great variety of niches their complex structure of tree, scrub and open grassland provides. They provide a typical habitat for the Linnet and Yellowhammer, Green Woodpecker and Tree Pipit, and it was these situations which the Red-backed Shrike and Woodlark once favoured. As the woodlands mature, so this richness fades, but as they are rarely managed, it is likely that a rich avifauna, perhaps comparable with that of the primary woodlands, will ultimately reappear.

Plantations are also mostly recent for there was little planting of woodland in this country until the seventeenth and eighteenth centuries, when the more enlightened landowners began to realise that the constant attrition of woodland was endangering the nation's key resource for buildings and ships. Subsequently there was a movement both to plant up new ground for commercial, sporting and landscape reasons, and to re-plant existing woodland with more productive species. The main forestry plantations in Kent are the Forestry Commission holdings at Challock, Orlestone, Shipbourne and Bedgebury which cover about 5,000 hectares, though smaller private woodlands managed under Commission schemes on aggregate cover three times this area. The sweet chestnut introduced from southern Europe formed much of the earlier planting and large areas of this species are still managed as coppice. More recently conifers, mostly Douglas fir, Corsican pine, Scots pine, Norway spruce and western hemlock have predominated, though now that the amenity role of forestry is acccepted, hardwoods, mainly oak and beech nursed by larch and other conifers, are again being planted. The plantations consist typically of compartments of single species separated by wide rides. Compartments are generally clear felled or coppiced and the open, often heathy, areas thus created, although transitional, are important habitats for species like the Nightjar in the absence of other heathland in the county. Many of the large plantations include or link up with more natural secondary or primary woodlands to form extensive tracts of varied forest cover. Canterbury is almost encircled by woodland. These extensive Kentish woodlands contain all the members to be expected of the British woodland avifauna save only the large raptors, which they could easily sustain if the persecution, and perhaps overuse of pesticides, which presently inhibits their spread from adjacent counties and the Continent were relaxed, and were a more broken canopy, higher in places, to be available.

Parkland

Kent is rich in castles, fine houses and large estates surrounded by parks laid out in the informal manner of Kent, Brown and Repton. Much is now farmed as arable but some, like Knowle, still retain their deer-grazed pastures and landscaped tree plantings which are a typical habitat of birds like the Green Woodpecker needing the combination of old trees and open grassland. The construction of lakes by damming streams was often a feature of such landscaping and the water bodies thus created provide important habitats for waterfowl in a county with few natural open waters.

Wetlands—Open Waters

Natural freshwater lakes and ponds are scarce in unglaciated Kent, but man-made water bodies of several kinds provide a good range of wetland habitats. Many of the lakes in the great parks constructed primarily for landscape purposes by damming streams are now so well colonised by vegetation that their artificial origin is often unsuspected. This is equally true of the thousands of small cattle ponds, with their Snipe and Moorhens, which almost every field contains in parts of the Low Weald. More recently the excavation of alluvial gravels in the river valleys, particularly of the Darent and Stour, has created extensive new bodies of water, as has the flooding of land for water supply and river-regulating reservoirs like Bough Beech and Bewl Bridge.

With their colonisation by the natural process of hydroseral succession, plant and then associated animal communities have developed as the invertebrates, fish and birds follow the plants which feed and shelter them. Many of these man-made lakes now have rich submerged and floating waterweed floras, limited emergent reed-swamp of bulrush, reedmace and reed, and sometimes well developed alder and willow carr and fen communities which represent the end point of the hydrosere. The best examples of the few natural lakes thus colonised are the small Oppen Pits at Dungeness. Tufted Duck, Pochard, Mallard, Coot and Canada Geese populations have prospered greatly as a result of this new habitat and nationwide some species like the Great Crested Grebe have perhaps been rescued from rarity largely as a result.

This spread of suitable wetland habitat has also likely been a factor in the recent re-colonisation of this country by Savi's Warbler and colonisation by Cetti's Warbler, both species first breeding in Kent, and in this case dependent on freshmarsh formed following subsidence in the Kent coalfield. Like them, and many other species, the Great Reed Warbler has a continental distribution right up to the Channel and since it requires similar habitat may perhaps be expected as well. Natural colonisation of open waters is a slow process and can be readily accelerated by planting the appropriate native species. In this way, and by creating suitable niches for particular species, by for example grading shorelines for waders or leaving secure islands for nesting duck or terns, very rich bird populations can be built up as has been achieved on the Wildfowl Trust/WAGBI Reserve at Sevenoaks and the RSPB Reserve at Dungeness.

These new habitats are of particular importance because they help compensate for the loss of natural wetlands through drainage. Little natural or semi-natural marsh or fen now remains along the river valleys except in their estuarine reaches where extensive grazing marsh still survives, particularly on Sheppey and around the mainland adjacent to the Swale and Medway. Romney Marsh and the Wantsum Channel marshes were once vast complexes of saltmarsh, fen and bog where the waterfowl darkened the sky, but now relatively little remains even of grazing marsh and only the relict flora and fauna of the dykes gives some idea of their former glory. Much of the Kent grazing marsh behind the sea walls would develop reedswamp if not so well drained and it is to be hoped that it will be possible to manage some of the newly acquired reserves on Sheppey in this way. Extensive reedbeds are scarce in Kent. The best developed are those of the colliery subsidence areas in East Kent, particularly the National Nature Reserve at Stodmarsh where Bearded Tits and Bitterns breed and Marsh Harrier formerly did so. The new, rather deep, gravel pit and reservoir lakes do not substitute for this kind of shallow-water wetland. Species like the Marsh Harrier which require very extensive tracts, maybe at least 120 hectares of reed, to sustain a brood successfully, are never likely to colonise them.

Rivers

Much of Kent is occupied by the outcrop of the Chalk which by virtue of its porosity is mostly devoid of streams and rivers except for the seasonal bournes and the Stour, Medway and Darent. In addition to the wet gravel pits now excavated in their valleys, the springs which mark their course through the Chalk have long been utilised to feed water-cress beds, which are also important bird habitats. Teal, Grey Wagtail and Water Rail often favour them. The Gault and Weald Clay country is well watered, with streams generally draining the adjacent high ground of the Chalk or Greensand. Kingfishers are not uncommon after a series of mild winters and Yellow Wagtail and Grey Heron are to be found alongside most. Some still retain marshy tracts with small streams and ponds where Green Sandpipers occur in winter.

Coastlands—Foreshore

The seemingly sterile tidal sand and mudflats of the Thames, Medway, Swale, Stour and Romney Marsh are teeming with invertebrate life beneath the surface. In the winter these bivalves, marine worms and snails form the principal food of great flocks of Dunlin, Sanderling, Knot, Grey Plover, Bar-tailed Godwits and Curlew. Oystercatcher and Turnstone favour the mussel beds and rockier parts of the shore and Brent Geese and Wigeon feed on the flannel weed and especially eel

grass. Eel grass is now spreading again in the Swale and Medway after the disease which greatly reduced its extent and the population of the Brent Goose, before the war. Higher up the shore where exposure to the tides is less, land plants can colonise in sheltered situations and saltmarsh develops. In Kent the best areas of saltmarsh are on the Sheppey shore of the Swale, in the Medway estuary, and in Pegwell Bay. The first colonisers of the mud are usually the hybrid cord grass and various glassworts. However, actively-growing early stages in the saltmarsh succession are not common in Kent. In the Swale and Medway the seaward edge of the marsh is often truncated in a small cliff, and middle-marsh communities with sea lavender, sea aster and sea purslane from the greater part of the marsh. Upper-marsh communities are also scarce, having frequently been eliminated by the construction of sea walls. Fragments of similar brackish-water communities often survive in the dykes or the grazing marshes behind them. Saltmarsh plants and their seeds are important items in the diet of some wildfowl like Teal, and where red fescue and sea poa swards still survive in the upper-marsh levels they are used as high tide grazing-areas by Brent Geese and Wigeon. Some isolated tracts of saltmarsh in the Medway and Swale have breeding colonies of Black-headed Gulls and Common Terns.

Grazing Marsh

Most of Romney Marsh, the Wantsum Channel and the land between the sea walls and higher ground on Sheppey, the Cliffe-Grain peninsula and in the Medway was once saltmarsh. Long isolated from the sea by the sea walls it has been converted to freshwater marshland used traditionally for sheep and cattle rearing. Under pasture the saltmarsh rills often still survive as water-tracks and the marshland is also intersected by more regular drainage dykes. The pasture consists mostly of the commoner meadow grasses with rushes and sedges in the rougher fields. The dykes and larger fleets contain submerged, floating, and emergent-aquatics of the brackish water hydrosere. Water crowfoots are typical of the floating-leaved species and sea club rush, reed

and reedmace characteristic emergents. The pastures are typically flooded in the winter and form high-tide feeding and roosting areas for the great flocks of waders and wildfowl which commute between them and the foreshore, while Hen Harriers, Short-eared Owls, the occasional Merlin, Peregrine and Rough-legged Buzzard feed on them and the rodents of the long grass. Lapwing, Redshank, Snipe, Skylark, Meadow Pipit, Yellow Wagtail and others breed in rougher parts, as recently have Short-eared Owls in really tall grass areas where grazing has been abandoned. Garganey breed in small numbers, but only rarely the Black-tailed Godwit, so characteristic of similar areas just across the sea in the Netherlands. The fringing vegetation of the dykes is the nesting habitat for Little Grebe, Coot, Moorhen, Mallard, Shoveler and Pochard, and for Sedge and Reed Warblers and Reed Bunting. Unhappily much of this grazing marsh is now being drained and converted to arable and the disappearance of nesting cover from the fields and from the steep-sided and regularly cleaned and eutrophicated dykes is nearly always a consequence.

Beaches

Long sandy beaches border the eastern shore of Romney Marsh, east Sheppey and the coast of Sandwich Bay between Deal and Ramsgate. There are smaller sandy beaches in the Chalk coves around Thanet, and shingle beaches stretch along the North Kent coast around Whitstable and Herne Bay. There is also shingle at Folkestone and Hythe and pre-eminently it constitutes the enormous spit at Dungeness. Beaches are few in the mudflats of the North Kent Marshes but there are some small shell-shingle and sand beaches made up almost entirely of cockle and mussel shells from the animals living out on the foreshore. Most of these beaches are heavily used for recreation in the summer, and areas where shore-breeding birds like Ringed Plover and Little Tern can safely breed are now few. The most important localities are Dungeness, Sandwich and the North Kent Marshes.

The spit at Dungeness is much more than a shingle beach. Its enormous size, aridity and sparse vegetation of lichen and dwarf broom

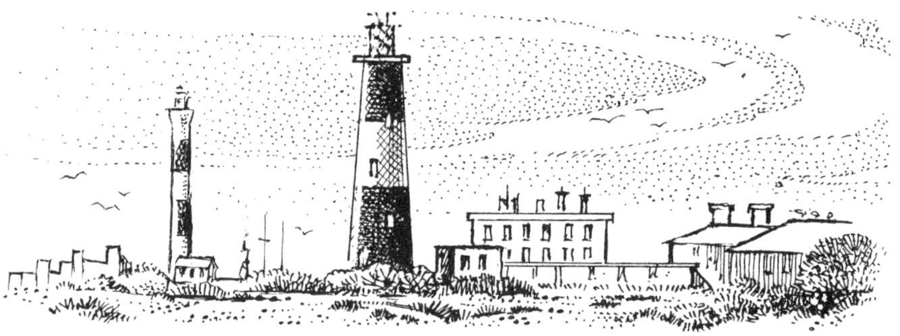

make it the nearest thing we have in this country to a desert. Indeed, birds of the steppe and desert like the Wheatear and until recently the Stone Curlew, are typical breeding species. Its nearness to the Continent and position, jutting out into the deep water of the Channel, makes it an important migration and sea passage point, and recently the wet gravel pits have added considerably to its birds. So, despite their devastating visual intrusion, have the nuclear power stations. Kestrels now breed on the pylons and Black Redstarts amongst the buildings, while the cooling water outflow is a constant food source for gulls and terns.

Cliffs

Coastal cliffs in Kent are mainly of Chalk. London Clay forms unstable, rapidly-eroding cliffs around Minster on Sheppey and around Herne Bay which are too unconsolidated to be suitable for breeding sea birds, although fascinatingly rich in bird fossils. The Lower Greensand outcrop at Folkestone is all built up, as is much of the Chalk around the Thanet coast. The highest and wildest cliff habitats in Kent are those of the Chalk between Folkestone and Deal. Between Folkestone and Dover the Chalk is slumped over the Gault to form the spectacular landslips and screes of Folkestone Warren, well vegetated with grass and scrub at the foot and in places on the cliff face. North of the Warren the cliffs fall sheer to the shore. Cliff-nesting sea birds other than gulls are not now common in south-east England. Kittiwakes have their only Kent colony on the cliffs north of Dover and Fulmars breed here and on Thanet. There are regrettably no longer any of the auks, or of more recent extinction, Peregrines, which once bred on these cliffs in some numbers. Black Redstart and Stonechat do, however, still breed in the old embattlements and scrub along the cliff tops.

Dry Grassland and Heathland

Once quite widespread, calcareous grassland on the chalk scarps and fixed dunes, and heathlands on the High Weald rocks, Lower Greensand and Tertiary sands, are now amongst the scarcest habitats in the

county. They have been lost both to agricultural enclosure and improvement and paradoxically, to agricultural abandonment leading to their scrubbing over and passing to woodland. Skylarks, Meadow Pipits, Kestrels and Cukoos are the typical birds of the dry grasslands, though on the South Downs at least Wheatears were once so common that shepherds trapped them in the rabbit burrows in which they nested and sold them in their thousands to be eaten as a delicacy in Brighton. Hothfield common, near Ashford, is now virtually the only remaining open heather heathland in the county, but even here bracken, gorse and birch invasion is well advanced. Dartford Heath, once the home of the Dartford Warbler which still features on the crest of the town's hospitals, has almost gone, and with the heathlands thus lost, their typical birds are increasingly rare. Stonechat and Whinchat are now only rare coastal breeders in the county and the Hobby extremely rare. Happily, Nightjars have found woodland clearings a suitable substitute.

Protection

Lying between London and that part of the British coastline nearest to the rest of the European Community, Kent habitats must inevitably come under pressures particularly for communications to and from the Continent and their associated developments. Urban expansion around London and elsewhere, and agricultural changes are also likely to continue to threaten what remains. The County Structure Plan and Regional Plans for the South East recognise these pressures, and conservation of the Kent landscape and its wildlife figure prominently in them. Past experience shows, however, that only acquisition and management as reserves or other protected areas is really effective in maintaining the natural and semi-natural environment. There are five National Nature Reserves in Kent managed by the Nature Conservancy Council: Blean Woods, Hamstreet Woods, Wye and Crundale Downs and the East Swale; and three Local Nature Reserves: Hothfield Common, Lydden Down and the South Swale. In addition to these statutory reserves the National Trust, the Kent Trust for Nature Conservation, the

Royal Society for the Protection of Birds, the Wildfowl Trust and the Wildfowler's Association of Great Britain and Northern Ireland also manage substantial areas as nature reserves. There are nonetheless many important areas for wildlife which remain unprotected. Kent has a particular national responsibility to protect them since it lies astride a main route of colonisation for species expanding their range into this country from the Continent. Some which have recently done so like Cetti's Warbler, have already been mentioned. Examination of European distribution maps shows a number of species which breed regularly a mere fifty kilometres away. Given sufficient of the the right habitats they might well do so here.

Shellness, Sheppey. The old blockhouse is an ideal observation point for autumn seabird movements, and for watching the thousands of waders roosting, during winter high tides, on the shell-spit of Shellness Point in the background.

page 22

River Swale—the foreshore, looking northwest to Harty Ferry on Sheppey. The mudflats are excellent for waders and Brent Geese, while the seeds left on the shellbanks in winter provide food for Shore Lark, Twite and Snow Bunting.

Cliffe pools, with the Thames in the background. Created by the extraction of clay for cement manufacture, during the last decade many of the pools have been infilled with dredgings from the river.

page 23

Northward Hill, overlooking the North Kent Marshes to the Thames. This predominantly oak wood (an RSPB Reserve and National Nature Reserve) on the steeply sloping London clay holds the biggest heronry in Great Britain. In recent years, the rough grazing marshland has largely been drained and turned over to arable fields.

Funton, near Lower Halstow. Sheltered waters and mudflats combine in the Medway estuary to attract a wealth of wildfowl and waders.

page 24

Stoke lagoon, near Allhallows. Shallow brackish water and extensive areas of mud are favoured by waders and wildfowl.

Elmley, Sheppey. A typical fleet in the grazing marsh behind the sea wall. This marshland holds many grey geese in winter and attracts Rough-legged Buzzards. Some of the area is now an RSPB Reserve.

page 25

Westbere—trees and scrub on drier ground amongst the reed beds increase habitat diversity and thus the ornithological attraction of the area.

Stodmarsh—a view over the Stour valley lakes, created by land subsidence following coal mining, with the River Stour itself in the foreground.

page 26

Stodmarsh—the reed-fringed lakes of the National Nature Reserve. Some of the reed beds are very extensive and house, among others, Bearded Tits and Savi's Warblers.

Dungeness—the lakes of the RSPB Reserve looking towards the twin masses of the nuclear power stations. Gravel extraction is to a detailed plan, providing as wide a range of habitats as possible.

page 27

A.R.C. pits, Lydd. Although the machinery in the background is still functional, the islands attract breeding gulls and terns in summer and the deep water holds many grebes and wildfowl in winter.

The chalk cliff at Langdon, part of the famous 'White Cliffs of Dover'—once inhabited by Peregrines, now a nesting site for Fulmars and Kittiwakes.

page 28

North Downs at Wye, near Ashford. In many areas, intrusion of scrub or arable farming has destroyed the nature of the Downs. Sheep grazing is essential if the grassland is to retain its typical plants and animals.

Sweet chestnut coppice with oak standards, a form of woodland management typical of lowland Kent. The chestnut is cut back to stools at ground level every 10–25 years, creating a cycle of growth stages favouring, amongst others, Nightingale and Nightjar.

page 29

Birling Edge, near Snodland. Beech woodland typical of the scarp slope of the Downs—one of the habitats of the Wood Warbler in Kent.

Sevenoaks gravel pit—the supreme example of a reserve created by planned excavation and an ecologically based planting programme to produce excellent waterfowl and wader habitat in urban surroundings.

Trottiscliffe—a Sand Martin colony in a sand pit, typical of many in the exposed Greensand belt, running east–west through Kent beneath the chalk of the Downs.

Bough Beech, near Tonbridge, typical of the 'new generation' of flooded valley reservoirs, adding greatly to the bird life of the region.

page 31

Bough Beech reservoir—the shallows provide rich feeding and the gently shelving banks ample loafing areas for waterfowl.

Systematic List of Species

The systematic list follows the sequence and scientific nomenclature of Dr. K. H. Voous as in *List of Recent Holarctic Bird Species* (1977).

Under the brief summary of status for the review period 1952–76, 'very rare' means less than 10 records; 'rare' 10–24 records; 'scarce' generally 25–49 records; and 'occasional' usually 50–100 records over the whole period. In only a few instances has the status materially changed since 1976. A summary of the previous accounts written by Ticehurst (1909) and Harrison (1953) normally follows, but when there is no historical comment the reader can assume that there has been little if any change in status.

Histograms and tables have been used extensively and when analysing winters, records for January and February 1977 have been included for the sake of completeness. Wintering wader records are summarised by giving the means for three 8-year periods, omitting 1952/53 data for convenience.

Divers

Gavia spp.

There are two periods in the year when large numbers of divers occur, in winter between November and early March, and in spring between March and May. Those in winter may occur anywhere round the coast and most are known to be Red-throated Divers. However, in spring a good proportion of the other two species occurs, and as a result many are left unidentified. It is therefore necessary to discuss the spring passage in more detail to take these unidentified birds into account and put the numbers of all three species in proper perspective.

The spring passage consists entirely of birds flying up-Channel past Dungeness. The only numerical reference made to this by Harrison concerns 50 Red-throated Divers passing in ten minutes on 13th April 1940. Between 1952–76 the total numbers of divers flying east at Dungeness in a whole spring never exceeded 400, although it must be emphasised that at that time there was relatively little seawatching in March. [This is in marked contrast to the spring passages of 1977 and 1978, when there were in excess of 1,100 and 1,600 divers respectively. Eds.] An analysis of the movements at Dungeness has shown that the rate of passage in March, which almost exclusively involves Red-throated Divers, is greater than in either April or May, when the two larger species tend to occur. Generally the largest numbers occur between the second week of March and the second week of May, when up to 60 a day may be seen.

Red-throated Diver

Gavia stellata

Regular passage migrant and common winter visitor, rare in summer.

Harrison regarded this as an abundant bird around the coast, usually appearing between mid-September and mid-March, and listed records between 31st August–8th May. For Dungeness, he gave counts of 50 in ten minutes on spring passage and 300 in a day in winter.

In recent years there have been a few midsummer records. The spring passage usually ends in the first week of June and there are no June records later than the 19th. However, there are July records for the 9th and 11th and August records for the 3rd, 4th, 8th, 10th and 28th, all concerning single birds, though there are none since 1968.

The autumn passage normally starts in September, but numbers are very small until a general influx occurs, usually in November, but not until December in some years. Thereafter, Red-throated Divers are widespread off all coasts during the winter, but least recorded on the east coast between Hythe and Thanet, generally only occurring there in single figures. The largest numbers have normally been seen off Dungeness, with counts of a hundred or more as follows: 200 west in 45 minutes on 25th January 1953, 314 west in 90 minutes on 11th January 1955, 230 west in 90 minutes on 6th February 1955, and about 100 on 26th December 1958, 26th January and 7th February 1961, and 10th January 1962. It is probable that these sort of numbers still occur annually, as counts of up to 75 are still frequent and seawatching coverage there is at its poorest between December and February.

On the north coast counts of 20–60 have been recorded between Reculver and Allhallows on various dates between 7th November–27th March, with larger numbers as follows: 100 at Herne Bay on 20th February 1962, 152 east there in 20 minutes on 20th March 1965, 142 at Shellness on 27th December 1969, 120 again at Shellness on 6th January 1974, with a flock of 75 there on 20th January 1974. Despite the fact that all the largest counts in this area are comparatively recent, there is good evidence of a recent decrease in the upper reaches of the Thames estuary. Between 1955 and 1960 there were records of 10–30 wintering on Cliffe Pools, but only ones and twos have occurred there since. There are also many winters when the largest counts on the north coast only amount to 10 or 20 birds.

The recent increases in numbers seen on spring passage at Dungeness are thought to be due to fuller coverage. Continuous seawatching in early May began in 1972, and has since been brought forward progressively through April and into March. It is now known that peak counts of 22 in a day up to 1974 were insignificant and that up to 60 may occur at any time between the second week of March and the second week of May.

Inland sightings are relatively scarce, with one to three records every other year on average, and a total of forty during the period under review. However, in 1976 there was an exceptional total of nine records. They all occurred between 30th November–22nd April.

Black-throated Diver

Gavia arctica

Regular autumn and winter visitor in small numbers, most numerous on spring passage.

Harrison considered this a species of somewhat erratic appearance, occurring mainly between November and March. The records he cites refer to the period 6th September–11th April, but Ticehurst includes one obtained on 2nd June 1842.

In recent years it has been recorded between 9th September–3rd June. By far the largest numbers have been seen on spring migration moving up-Channel off Dungeness, particularly in the second half of April, when there have been counts of up to 40 in a day. There has been an average of about 40 per spring since 1966, with a maximum during the period under review of 89 in 1972.

There have also been, on average, about four autumn and winter records per year at Dungeness, involving up to five birds in a day. Elsewhere there has been an average of about four coastal records of up to five birds each year, two-thirds of them in the Thames and Swale estuaries.

Inland records are very rare. Between 2nd February and 7th April 1956 there were singles at Mote Park, Eastwell Park, East Peckham and Leybourne. One remained at Eccles from 25th March–15th May 1962, with a second one there in the autumn from 21st–29th October. At

Westbere singles were present from 29th January–5th February 1972 and from 5th–12th December 1976.

Great Northern Diver

Gavia immer

An uncommon visitor in autumn and winter, occurring more often in spring, when it is now seen annually.

The few records listed by Harrison, who considered it a rare and irregular visitor, fall between October and April, apart from one at Dungeness on 17th September 1938.

By far the largest numbers now occur on spring passage at Dungeness, where it has been seen annually since 1966, particularly between the last week of March and the second week of May. Most occur in the last three weeks of April, with up to 11 in a day. There has been an average of about 15 per spring since 1966, with a maximum, during the period under review, of 44 in 1971. The latest spring record is 30th May.

There is a total of 25 autumn and winter records from Dungeness involving one or two birds, the earliest on 22nd September. During the same period there are 25 records from the Thames and Swale and 15 other coastal records, the extreme dates being 18th September and 28th April. Apart from three off Herne Bay on 9th February 1961, these all refer to ones and twos.

There are only four inland records of singles at Leybourne on 18th January 1959, at Sevenoaks from 26th December 1961 to 2nd January 1962, at Farningham Road on 1st December 1965 and at Westbere from 1st–23rd November 1975.

White-billed Diver

Gavia adamsii

Very rare vagrant.

The only record of this species concerns an immature bird that was found dead near Sittingbourne in November 1969. It was eventually identified from photographs.

Little Grebe

Tachybaptus ruficollis

Widespread resident.

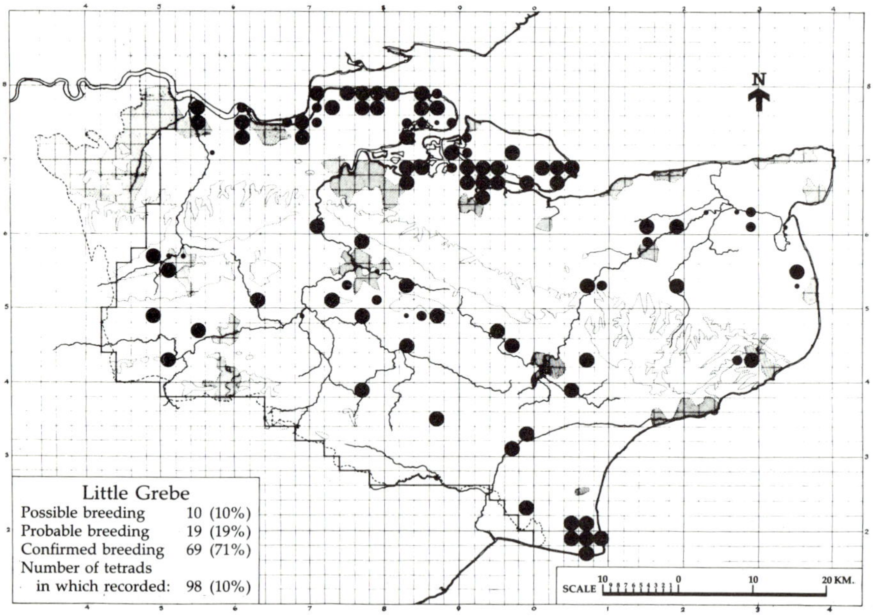

The Little Grebe breeds most commonly on the coastal marshes in north Kent, in dykes, fleets and small pools with luxuriant vegetation. Inland the nest sites are concentrated along the river valleys, but quite small farm ponds and mature well-vegetated gravel workings, such as those at Dungeness, are frequently used.

There is little actual evidence of migration, apart from isolated reports of birds found stranded well away from water, or seen on the open sea, but at Dungeness one was killed at the lighthouse on 7th August 1953, and the small numbers that appear in the Observatory area show annual peaks during August–October and again in April.

The best-recorded aspect of this species' behaviour is the autumn and winter flocking, when it is far less shy. By far the largest flock occurs on Cliffe Pools, where 150 were seen in December 1959. More systematic counts since 1971 show that at least 180 have been seen there each winter, with maxima of 245 in 1975 and 315 in 1976. Peak numbers generally occur in November. It would be very interesting to know the extent of the breeding range from which these birds are drawn. With 19 pairs on 121 hectares of the Cliffe Marsh in 1976, it is conceivable that this large flock could be representative of the Thames marshes breeding population, though it seems more likely that it contains some winter visitors from further afield, possibly even from the Continent.

Further up the Thames there were 130 at Northfleet in November 1959, but there are no records of flocks there in subsequent winters. Small numbers can sometimes be seen in the tidal creeks of the Medway and flocks of 20–40 favour the small coastal lagoons at Kingsnorth, Stoke, Murston and Capel Fleet during August–February. In the Dungeness area similar flocks have been seen on Walland Marsh and at Lade in September.

Inland, up to 61 have occurred at Bough Beech, with the highest numbers there usually in September. Flocks of 20 or more have also been seen at Mote Park, Leybourne and Lullingstone.

Great Crested Grebe

Podiceps cristatus

Common resident on suitable open fresh waters, larger numbers on coast and estuaries in winter.

Ticehurst wrote that this was solely an autumn and winter visitor, and almost entirely a salt-water species. Harrison describes the first breeding records and the subsequent increases in the breeding and wintering populations. He records winter flocks of 150 off Sheppey in 1939 and 300

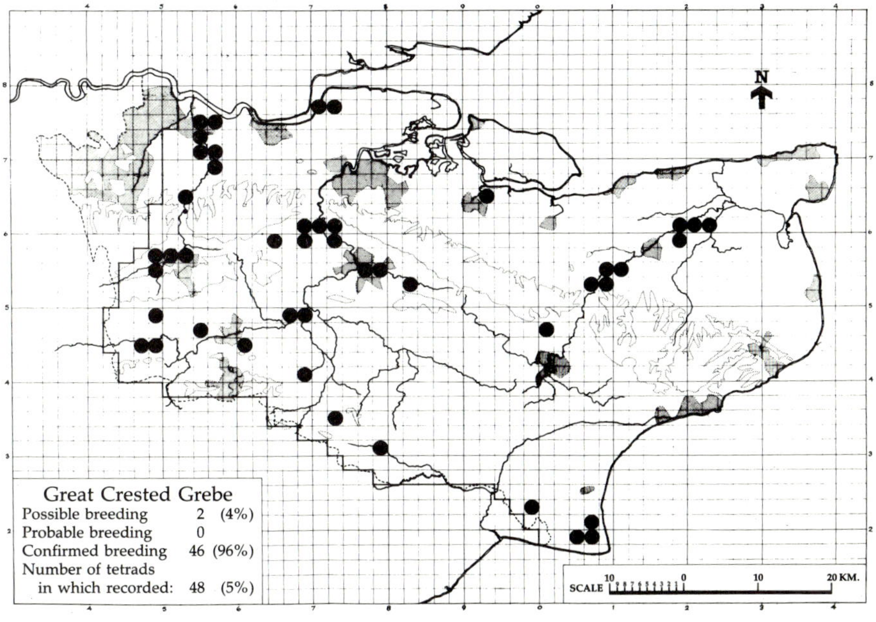

off Greatstone in 1946. The first breeding took place at Hever in 1911 and by 1933 a survey published in *British Birds* gave the Kent population as 29 pairs.

Two recent surveys in midsummer have put the population at 102 adults in 1965 and 202 adults in 1975. Man-made reservoirs, gravel, clay and sand workings now provide the majority of the breeding sites, especially in the west of the county, where in 1975 the largest concentrations were 23 on the gravel pits between Darenth and Horton Kirby, 18 in the Leybourne/New Hythe area, 16 each on Sevenoaks Reserve and Bough Beech reservoir, and 12 at Hever. Another 70 birds in the east of the county were concentrated mainly on the lakes in the Stour Valley between Fordwich and Stodmarsh. Only a few pairs bred on the marshes in the north of the county or on the gravel pits in the Dungeness area.

Apart from 26 off Allhallows on 20th March 1955, there are no other records of large parties on the tidal Thames, although the brackish Cliffe Pools supports a wintering population of up to 20 birds. The tidal creeks of the Medway are far more sheltered, and the area between Motney Hill and Ham Green in particular has regularly held up to 70 in winter, with peaks of 250 in November 1961 and 102 in January 1966. It is also normal for about 30 to winter off Sheppey, although much larger numbers occurred there between 1958 and 1961, with peaks of 100, 208, and 110 in three winters, mostly off Shellness and Warden Point. In 1966 a flock of 400 was seen off Leysdown in February.

Further east, at Reculver, large flocks occurred between 1967–1971, with counts of 150, 275, 350 and 250 in four winters, although in most years it would be unusual to see more than 30 there. Further east still, up to 70 often occur off Thanet or Sandwich Bay. This area, too, went through a short period when much larger flocks wintered. At Sandwich Bay there were 120 in January 1962, 250 in February 1964, and 300 in January 1965, while in January 1969 a flock of 400 was seen off Birchington, undoubtedly the same flock that was seen at Reculver earlier the same month.

Another important wintering area is Dungeness, with flocks of up to 70 at sea between there and Greatstone, and occasionally further north to St. Mary's Bay. Much larger flocks have also been recorded in this area, with 130 in March 1954, 220 in December 1954, 200 in January 1956 and 340 in January 1961.

Large flocks were therefore recorded regularly in winter round the Kentish coast between 1954–1971, but for some reason these large numbers have not occurred subsequently.

The breeding areas usually support a winter population roughly equal to the numbers that breed, although in 1970 there were much larger numbers at Bough Beech in the autumn, with 70 in August and 94 in September.

Red-necked Grebe

Podiceps grisegena

Uncommon winter visitor.

Both Ticehurst and Harrison describe this species as an uncommon winter visitor and its present-day status remains the same. It is now probably the rarest of the grebes in Kent.

Favoured localities for all three rare grebes are the estuaries of the Thames, Medway, Swale and Stour, while an equal number are also seen in the vicinity of Dungeness. Coastal lakes in these same areas are equally important.

During 1952–76 there was an average of six Red-necked Grebe records per year, including seventeen inland records, with the extreme dates being 21st August and 7th May. Most records refer to singles occurring between October and March, but there is some evidence of passage in November and April, as it is in these two months that small parties have occasionally been seen. On the south side of the Medway there were six in November 1961, three of which remained until January 1962, three on 3rd April 1963 and three in November 1972. At Dungeness there were three on 22nd November 1967 and parties of three and two in April 1976. This species was most numerous in the arctic winter of 1962/63, when 11 live and 11 dead birds were recorded between December–February.

Slavonian Grebe

Podiceps auritus

Uncommon winter visitor.

Between 1952–76 there was an average of seven records per year, including a total of 27 inland records. The Slavonian Grebe is encountered more frequently than either the Red-necked or Black-necked Grebe, not only because it has occurred slightly more often, but by virtue of the fact that it frequently stays in the same locality longer, occasionally for periods of up to two months. Nevertheless, the majority of records concern individuals and, unlike the other rare grebes, there are no records of parties larger than three. The extreme dates are 29th August and 4th May, although all but five of the records occurred between October–April. In recent years there has been some evidence of spring migration in April, especially at Dungeness.

Black-necked Grebe

Podiceps nigricollis

Uncommon winter visitor, more evident on passage than the other rare grebes. Has bred in recent times.

Ticehurst found this by far the rarest of the grebes, although Harrison was able to record an increase, including a flock of ten in Dover Harbour in March 1947.

This species summered on Walland Marsh in three successive years. In 1964 there were records between 31st May–4th October, with three adults in June and later a pair was seen with three young. In 1965 only one adult was present, between 6th May–11th June. Breeding was reported again in 1966, when two adults were seen with four young. Meanwhile at Stoke two adults with one young were seen on 2nd August 1969 and there is a possibility they could have bred in that area unobserved.

Otherwise, between 1952–76, there was an average of six records per year, including a total of 25 inland records. Although most frequent in mid-winter between December and February, this species occurs much earlier in autumn than either of the other rare grebes. There are four July records away from the breeding area, with the earliest on the 20th, and rather more in August and September. The majority of records refer to individuals, although small flocks have occurred. There were 12 in the Medway on 27th September 1952, nine in the Swale and three in the Thames on 31st October–1st November 1963, and six were seen in the Swale on 13th March 1955.

Recently, with the increase in seawatching, it has been shown that there is a spring passage at Dungeness in April, when flocks of up to four have been seen.

Fulmar

Fulmarus glacialis

Resident, scare in winter, more numerous in summer.

Harrison lists only six records between 1878–1912, including two inland. From 1938–47 four more were found dead around the coast, with the first sight record, one off Littlestone as recently as 30th May 1948.

In 1952 one was found dead, well inland, at Seal on 18th October and three were seen off the Kentish Knock lightship on 25th October. In 1953 singles were seen off Dungeness on 31st March and inland flying over East Malling on 22nd October. The most significant event that year was the presence of prospecting birds on the coast at Kingsdown on 10th April and St. Margaret's Bay between 27th May–17th June.

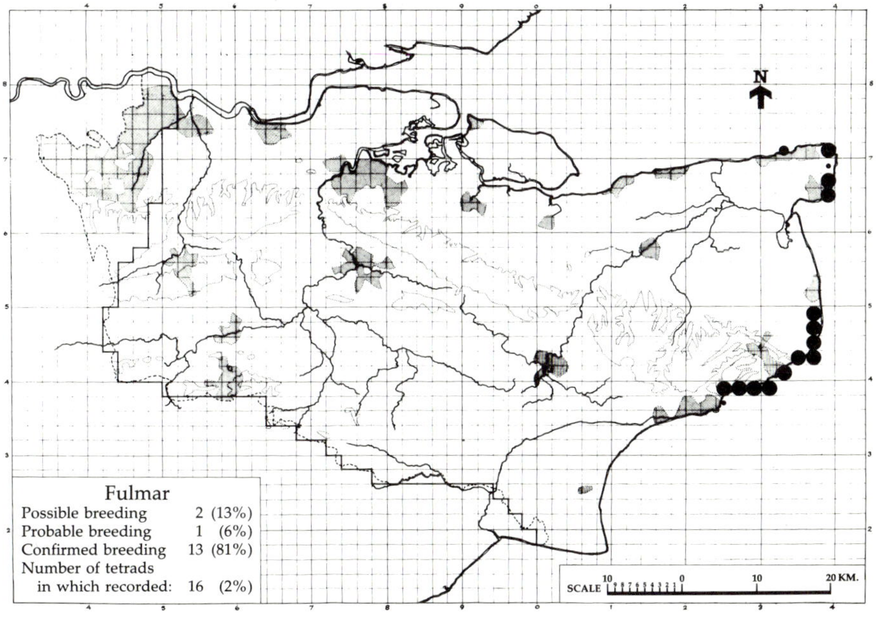

Since then numbers have increased, not only in the breeding areas, but around the coast generally. Ones and twos were seen prospecting the cliffs between Folkestone and Kingsdown again in 1954, 1955 and 1957, after which they increased quickly to 50 by 1962. Breeding was first confirmed in 1966 at St. Margaret's and Dover, where several males were seen feeding females sitting on eggs at eleven different sites. The population along these cliffs seems to have stabilised at around 25 pairs. Meanwhile on Thanet, singles were seen prospecting the cliffs in 1965, increasing to eight in 1967, with young first seen in 1973. By 1976 there were 12 pairs breeding there. The breeding colonies are usually deserted by late August.

At Sandwich Bay, which is situated between these two breeding areas, there were 80 on 4th August 1966, possibly the whole of the local breeding population feeding together.

Elsewhere on the coast, Dungeness is the best place to see this species, with good numbers from March–August, and up to 40 a day, especially in May. It is rarest on the north coast, west of Thanet into the Thames estuary, although recently it has also increased here, with up to four in a day, especially in April–June, since 1970.

The Fulmar is generally uncommon between September–February, apart from the breeding birds, which begin to return from early December. It is conspicuously absent from the large seabird movements which take place every autumn between August–November.

Two recent inland records concern individuals flying over Stodmarsh on 23rd August 1969 and Sellindge on 23rd May 1971.

Cory's Shearwater

Calonectris diomedea

Very rare vagrant.

Two were seen off Sheppey on 14th November 1954. Between 1966–72 there were five spring records between 13th April–15th May of one or two birds in four years, with four off Dungeness and one off Sandwich Bay. In addition, singles were seen off Sandwich Bay on 19th September 1967 and off North Foreland on 17th November 1971.

Great Shearwater

Puffinus gravis

Very rare vagrant.

Harrison gives details of three records. One was found alive at Ramsgate on 29th October 1890, one seen off Dungeness on 30th August 1915, and one found dead near Dungeness on 21st November 1938.

In recent years, one was seen over the Thames at Cliffe on 16th August 1953, another found dead at Sandwich Bay on 24th February 1963, and a third seen off Foreness on 22nd October 1968.

Sooty Shearwater

Puffinus griseus

Scarce autumn migrant.

The records listed by Harrison concern singles seen in autumn off Dover in 1912, Folkestone in 1948 and Swalecliffe in 1950, while at Dungeness 13 flew southwest in one hour on 20th October 1913, and a flock of 14 was seen on 23rd September 1915.

There were no records between 1950–62, but since then Sooty Shearwaters have been seen almost annually, with a total of 36 records involving 85 birds occurring between 5th August–21st November. One was also seen off Dungeness on 8th April 1976.

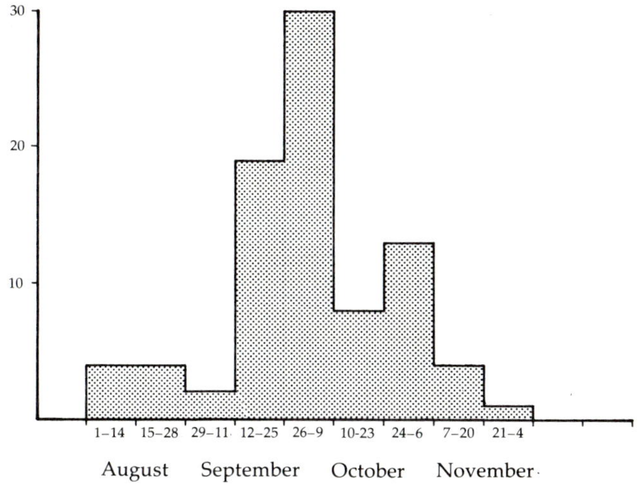

Fortnightly distribution of Sooty Shearwaters 1963–76

Of these, 60% occurred off Dungeness and 25% off Shellness, with the rest around the north coast between Deal and Allhallows. Nearly half of the records involved two-five birds and on 27th September 1975 a total of 17 flew southwest off Dungeness. Peak years were 1971, 1975 and 1976, with 16, 22 and 23 respectively.

Good days for this species are often predictable; they appear in heavy cloud and rainy conditions, associated with N–NE winds for Shellness and S–SW winds for Dungeness.

Manx Shearwater

Puffinus puffinus

Regular spring, summer and autumn visitor.

Harrison lists a few coastal records of one-four birds for August–October and two inland reports of singles stranded in a Dartford street on 24th September 1887 and near Tenterden on 10th August 1898.

Between 1952–76, a total of 210 was recorded, with annual means of just three up to 1969 and 30 for the period 1970–76. Systematic seawatching in recent years has produced an interesting pattern of records.

	J	F	M	A	M	J	J	A	S	O	N	D
Manx Shearwater												
P.p puffinus				2	27	22	3	17	123	10	4	2
Balearic Shearwater												
P.p. mauretanicus		1		2		1	19	18	14	1	3	

Monthly distribution of Manx Shearwaters 1952–76

The May–June peaks occur off Dungeness, with a day-maximum of 11 on 28th May 1972. The marked September peak is more widespread around the coast, with two-thirds of the birds involved off the northern coastline between Deal and the Thames, and the remainder off Dungeness.

The majority of the records refer to individuals, but a few small parties have been seen. Off Thanet on 24th September 1974 there were three flocks totalling 39, while off Dungeness there were totals of 16 on 11th September 1970 and 15 on 27th September 1975.

There have been no recent inland records, though one was seen on Cliffe pools on 11th September 1975.

Balearic Shearwater

Puffinus puffinus mauretanicus

Scarce autumn visitor.

Ticehurst notes just one, found dead inland at Wingham about 1865.

One was seen in 1954, and records have been almost annual since 1960. A total of 59 birds has been recorded, with the monthly distribution shown in the accompanying table. The majority occurred between 2nd July–14th September, with about 80% off Dungeness, including 16 on 2nd July and six on 14th September 1972, but most records refer to one-four birds.

Storm Petrel

Hydrobates pelagicus

Rare autumn visitor.

Most of the early records included by Harrison referred to storm-driven birds in late October and November, with the exception of singles in December 1924 at Dungeness, on 16th February 1929 at Pegwell Bay and on 9th September 1951 in the Thames. Inland, singles were found at Tunstall and Lenham.

	Sept.	Oct.		Nov.		Dec.		Totals
	12–25	26–9	10–23	24–6	7–20	21–4	5–18	
Storm Petrel			10	4	6		3	23
Leach's Petrel	4	5	3	7	16	3	1	39
Petrel species	2	2	6	5	2	2		19

Fortnightly distribution of Storm and Leach's Petrels 1952–76

Of the autumn records tabulated here, which occurred between 11th October–15th December, 12 were seen off Shellness, four in the Thames, with one up-river as far as Gravesend, and the others off Thanet, at Dover and Dungeness. Most records concern one or two birds, the only larger numbers have occurred during or just after NW gales, with two at both North Foreland and Shellness on 21st October 1970, and three at Shellness on 10th November 1971.

The only records outside the autumn period are of one found dead at Dungeness on 3rd April 1960, and one at Stodmarsh on 9th January 1967. The only other inland record concerns one found dead in Maidstone on 17th October 1964.

Leach's Petrel

Oceanodroma leucorhoa

Scarce autumn visitor.

The records listed by Harrison occurred between 22nd September–1st December, with the exception of one found dead at Seasalter on 14th January 1915. The only sight record appears to be one in Pegwell Bay on 23rd September 1922. Inland, four singles were found near Tonbridge, at Maidstone, Horsmonden and Lyminge on various November dates between 1853–1931.

In the 'wreck' of this species in 1952 there were five Kentish records, four of which died, between 28th October–30th November. On the first date one was found dying at Tunbridge Wells, the only inland record in recent years.

The extreme dates for the records shown in the accompanying table under Storm Petrel are 14th September–5th December, with the addition of one in the Medway Estuary on 16th January 1966.

Three were attracted to Dungeness lighthouse in the early years of the period under review, with another offshore there, one stranded at Folkestone, and one dead at Sandwich Bay. The remaining records, mostly concerning one or two birds, all occurred along the north coast from Thanet to the Thames, with 15 in the mouth of the Swale and 12 in the Thames. Larger numbers have been seen in NE gales, with three at Shellness on 26th September 1957, and four at Allhallows and two at Egypt Bay on 11th November 1962. There were also two at Shellness and singles at both Cliffe and Allhallows on 9th November 1975.

Gannet

Sula bassana

Passage migrant, most numerous in autumn.

Ticehurst considered this species to be a winter visitor, but Harrison noted records in all months, with an increase in numbers during the first half of this century, though no double-figure counts were recorded. He also refers to three inland records of dead or stranded birds.

The first large movement, involving 130 in an hour off Dungeness was recorded on 24th October 1960. Since the mid-sixties, there has been a considerable increase in the numbers of Gannets seen. This is partly as a result of an increase in systematic seawatching, but also undoubtedly linked with the increase in the Gannet population, particularly on the Bass Rock and at Bempton, on the east coast of Britain.

	J	F	M	A	M	J	J	A	S	O	N	D
Thanet/Thames	25	12	5	30	26	26	9	40	100	200	300	5
Dungeness	30	5	18	21	39	12	43	90	125	375	97	70

Peak monthly counts of Gannets 1952–76

The Gannet is least common between December–March, 70 at Dungeness on 21st December 1962 being exceptional. Day-totals of 20–30 have been recorded in only five winters, and only once on the north coast, where it is not unusual for none to be seen.

There is a small spring movement in April–May, but peak counts of 20–40 are still unusual. Numbers remain low during June–July, with exceptional counts of 26 off Reculver on 30th June 1968 and 43 off Dungeness on 21st July 1962.

During the autumn months there is a general increase round the coast. In August and early September there are fairly frequent counts of up to 30 on the north coast and up to 50 at Dungeness. However, the autumn migration is most marked from mid-September to mid-November, when large westerly movements of 100–250 have occurred fairly regularly, with higher counts of 300 off Shellness on 17th November 1969 and 375 off Dungeness on 1st October 1973. In most years the peak counts occur in October, though northerly gales during November may produce large numbers in the Thames estuary.

A number of inland records include birds found exhausted at Sevenoaks, Leigh, Horsmonden, Stockbury, Lenham and Aylesford, all between September–December. In addition, singles have been seen flying well inland over Mereworth on 13th November 1965, and, more surprisingly, over Bough Beech on 4th June 1972, while six were seen a short distance inland over Sarre on 29th October 1974.

Cormorant

Phalacrocorax carbo

Winter visitor, with non-breeding birds present throughout the summer.

Harrison writes of an enormous increase in the numbers of Cormorants reported around the Kent coast during the first half of this century, with winter flocks of 100–200 in the Thames and Medway in the 1940s. At Stodmarsh, in 1947, five nests were built in dead willows, eggs were laid, but the colony was raided. This is the only authenticated breeding record for the county, though there were claims of cliff nesting earlier this century.

Largest numbers are still recorded between October–March, and though Cormorants are relatively scarce during May–August, there were counts of 50 at Cliffe in May 1976 and 40 at Sheerness in August 1974.

The Medway estuary remains the most favoured locality, with counts of 140 in the mid-sixties and a norm around 50–70. Further up-river, flocks of 15–20 are regularly seen at New Hythe or Leybourne, with an exceptional peak there of 65 in January 1975. Winter flocks in the mouth of the Swale and on Cliffe pools vary between 30–50, with maximum counts of 65 and 62 respectively.

In the Stour Valley, from Stodmarsh to Westbere, the winter population usually varies between 30–50, with a peak count of 76 in March 1956, while on the east coast between Thanet and Dover counts of 30–40 are usual, with a maximum of 59 at Sandwich Bay in October 1976. Similarly, the gravel pits in the Dungeness area support a wintering population of 20–30, with a peak of 45 in March 1974. A few also winter on Walland Marsh, usually attracted by flooded drainage ditches.

Two localities well inland are also visited regularly. Since the early fifties there have been parties of around 10 wintering at Hever, increasing to 25 in 1974. Close by, on the new Bough Beech reservoir, similar numbers now occur, with records in all months. Otherwise, inland reports are relatively few.

Examples of the Continental race *P.c. sinensis*, which is more migratory, have been obtained, but there is a possibility of confusion in the field with old birds of the nominate race, which may also show silvery-white head feathers.

Shag

Phalacrocorax aristotelis

Winter visitor.

Harrison includes a record of a pair nesting in a cave between Dover and St. Margaret's Bay in 1928 and 1929, but there is no other evidence of breeding. He writes of more frequent records during the thirties and forties, with a few at inland localities, and parties of up to seven around the coast. He also includes a report of twelve or more in the Swale estuary in 1945, and a recovery there of a bird ringed on the Bass Rock.

An analysis of the 1952–76 records shows that the Shag is a regular visitor between September–March, usually less numerous in April and August, and particularly scarce in June-July, when singles have been seen on just six dates, plus an exceptional party of five off Abbot's Cliff

(Folkestone) on 9th June 1962. The numbers, however, vary considerably from year to year, from a handful of birds in some years to peaks of nearly 50 in 1960 and 1962, followed by about 35 in 1974 and 1976. Most records refer to individuals, although small parties were seen in sixteen years. These larger numbers occur most frequently on the east coast, particularly in Ramsgate harbour. In peak years there may be increased numbers in spring, as in 1962 when there were six at both Dover and Ramsgate in April; or as a result of a marked autumn influx in stormy weather, as in 1974 when there was a total of 16 at five localities between 6th–9th September.

There have been about twenty inland records, most concerning singles, and some involving exhausted, storm-driven birds. Three were seen at Sevenoaks on 15th–16th March 1962 and four at Bough Beech on 9th September 1974.

Three immatures, found dead in different years at Dungeness, Sevenoaks and Leybourne in February–April, had all been ringed as pulli on the Farne Islands.

Bittern

Botaurus stellaris

Resident, in very small numbers, and winter visitor.

Ticehurst found no evidence of breeding and regarded this species as quite a widespread winter visitor. According to Harrison this status remained true until the mid-thirties. There were several unconfirmed reports of Bitterns nesting from 1935, in the Stour Valley and at Cottington Court (Deal), with first evidence from the Stodmarsh area in 1947. In the severe winter of 1947 up to seven were seen at Cottington Court.

From 1952–57 there were regular records from the Stour Valley, though mainly in winter, with booming heard only in 1954. Since 1958 Bitterns have probably bred annually. The population built up from one-four pairs in 1958–61, to five-ten pairs in 1962–68, with peaks of ten in 1962 and nine in 1968. Since then the population had declined to three-four pairs in 1969–72 and only one-two pairs in 1973–76. These are maxima based on booming males and breeding has only been proved in a few years.

The main reason for the decline has probably been the loss of suitable reed beds. Three have dried out, or been infilled, and parts of others have become too dense, or overgrown with scrub.

Away from the Stour Valley, Bitterns are essentially winter visitors, and may turn up in relatively small areas of reeds, in dykes and small ponds, and in gravel pits. There is probably a small wintering population of up to six birds scattered throughout Kent, though this increases in severe winters. In such conditions they may occur almost anywhere and mortality may be high, at least eight died in early 1963.

There are eleven early-autumn records, from late July to mid-September, mostly from the marshes bordering the Swale. These may represent post-breeding dispersal from the Stour Valley, or further afield.

[American Bittern]

Botaurus lentiginosus

Ticehurst gives two records, but neither was fully substantiated.

Little Bittern

Ixobrychus minutus

Rare visitor.

Ticehurst comments on frequent references to this species in the nineteenth century, but without precise data. Harrison reports that between 1929–47 there were regular occurrences at Cottington Court (Deal) and, though breeding has been claimed, no published evidence has been forthcoming.

Between 1958–76 there are fifteen records in eleven years, including three each in 1964 and 1976, with the following monthly distribution:

J	F	M	A	M	J	J	A	S	O	N	D
				9	1	1	3		1		

The extreme dates are 2nd May–11th June and 23rd July–25th August, with one at Sevenoaks on the remarkably late date of 17th October 1976. Most refer to single adult males, with two at Westbere on 6th May 1973. Two of the August records were immatures. Nine records were from the Stour Valley, two at Dungeness, and singles at Cliffe, Chetney, Yalding and Sevenoaks.

Night Heron

Nycticorax nycticorax

Rare vagrant.

Harrison gives a number of nineteenth century records, suggesting that it may have been a regular visitor to some parts of north Kent. In May 1947 and 1951 singles were seen on Romney Marsh.

Between 1953–74 there were ten records in nine years, of which seven were in the period 1968–74. The records are from widespread localities, with five between 2nd April–27th June and three between 23rd July–2nd October. Outside these dates one was found dead at Mersham (Ashford) on 2nd February 1958 and another was present at Sheerness from 16th October–11th November 1953. The latter and two other immatures, at Cranbrook from 6th August–6th September 1955 and Stodmarsh from 23rd July–23rd September 1969, represent the longest stays. Most reports refer to sightings on one or two days only.

Squacco Heron

Ardeola ralloides

Ticehurst found two early records, one for Romney Marsh around 1847 and another, shot in Bedgebury Park, on 20th May 1867.

[Cattle Egret]

Bubulcus ibis

One present at Wittersham between 22nd July–16th August 1974 was considered to be an escape.

Little Egret

Egretta garzetta

Rare vagrant.

A total of 12 has been recorded in eight years between 1957–76, with nine between 4th May–23rd June and three from 30th July–3rd September. The first was at Murston on 3rd September 1957 and most refer to sightings on single days, but there was one unusually long stay in the Swale and Medway estuaries from 6th–21st June 1970. Half the reports are from the North Kent Marshes, with four in the Stour Valley and two at Dungeness.

Grey Heron

Ardea cinerea

Resident and partial migrant.

Ticehurst remarks that of the two flourishing and well-protected heronries in the county, that at Chilham was the oldest known in Britain. He cited the Kirkby's Inquest manuscript (1280–93) of the reign of Edward I, which mentions the Chilham heronry as situated in the 'Hundredum de ffeleberghe', a wood still called Felborough Beeches. In Ticehurst's time, Chilham held 70–110 nests, with an average of about 90, whereas the other heronry he mentioned, Cobham Park, held 40–50. Ticehurst also mentions occasional breeding attempts elsewhere, including the Oppen Pits at Dungeness and a large wood 'abutting the Cooling Marshes.'

Doubtless this last reference was the start of the movement of the heronry from the ash trees at Cobham Park to the oak, and later elm at High Halstow. Gillham and Homes note the first Halstow pair as originating from Cobham in 1900. By 1928, and the first BTO Heronry Census, there were 65 pairs, and by 1938 a total of 146. The severe winters of the early 1940s reduced these numbers to 67 in 1945.

Harrison mentions the comings and goings of several comparatively tiny heronries in places like Eastwell Park and Mote Park, but also documents the origin of the Ashenden colony around 1915, rising to 30 nests by 1935, after which it was thought to have moved to Potmans Heath, Wittersham, in 1941. The heronry at Lympne Castle he records as of eight nests in 1948.

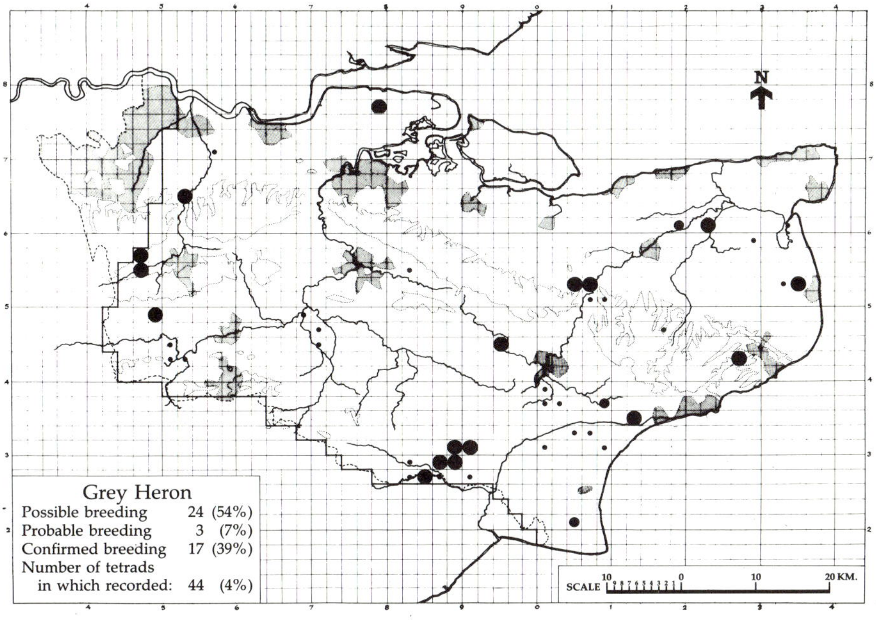

Between 1952–76, small heronries of one-five pairs existed briefly in at least 16 localities, but the bulk of the breeding population was to be found in the five major sites tabulated.

	High Halstow	Chilham	Lympne	Wittersham	Ashenden
1952	113	91	25	14	
1953	114				
1954	129	91	33	4	
1955	127		33	9	11
1956	87			7	4
1957	92	108	31	9	4
1958	110		13	11	3
1959	100	86	16	felled	10
1960	104	70	8		10
1961	121	67	8		13
1962	106	15			
1963	56			1	13
1964	80	22		1	17
1965	87			4	19
1966	103	29	12	5	16
1967	145	42		5	11
1968	149	44	4	3	20
1969	148		11		36
1970	148	10	21		
1971	150	32	38		30
1972	167	46			22
1973	174		22		22
1974	178		22		20
1975	183	2	19		17
1976	185	25	15		12

A continuation of the interchange noted by Harrison between Wittersham and Ashenden is apparent. Clearly the four smaller colonies hold fluctuating numbers, perhaps declining slightly overall. The colony at Northward Hill, High Halstow, is in marked contrast. It seems to have been just about the largest British heronry in 1954, and since 1972 has been considerably bigger than any other. There seems to be a ceiling to the British heron population at about 4,000 pairs (Reynolds, 1979) and the reduction at High Halstow between 1962–63 fits well with the national figure of about 50%. Recovery was slow, as would be expected compared with smaller, more fecund birds, but seems to have continued well, increasing steadily through the 1970s towards the apparent county ceiling of about 250 pairs. The colony was originally in oaks, but as nearby elms grew taller in the 1950s, gradually moved into the elms. In 1970 Dutch elm disease struck, quickly killing the elms. As dead trees collapsed or were felled, so the heronry gradually returned, safely and with its growth unhindered, to the oaks.

In the breeding season birds may commute many kilometres to suitable feeding grounds, High Halstow birds reaching the Swale marshes and the Darent Valley. Outside the breeding season individuals or small groups may be found feeding on suitable waters anywhere in the county. In summer flocks of juveniles and adults may gather near to the heronries, but otherwise large groups are scarce. Exceptions are 24 along Windmill Creek on 28th August 1972 and 40 at the same place a year later. These gatherings presumably reflect a localised abundance of food.

Kentish ringed young Grey Herons have been recovered in the home counties, as far north as Yorkshire and west to Worcester in the winter after ringing, and several have been killed in various parts of northern France. Birds ringed as nestlings in Holland and Sweden, as well as elsewhere in Britain, have been recovered in the county.

Purple Heron

Ardea purpurea

Scarce summer visitor, annual since 1966.

Harrison lists just ten records since 1838, but during the period under review the Purple Heron has become a regular visitor. Between 1958–76 a total of 38 birds was recorded, with the following monthly distribution:

J	F	M	A	M	J	J	A	S	O	N	D
		1	7	12	5	3	8	2			

The extreme dates are 31st March 1971 and 30th September 1969. The spring records, which predominate, fall mainly between late April and early June, with ten in the Stour Valley, five at Sandwich Bay, four each at Dungeness and on the North Kent Marshes, and two elsewhere. The autumn records are more evenly distributed, including some well inland, with a high proportion of immatures and a tendency for longer stays. Three have remained for over ten days, including one at Sandwich Bay from 31st August–30th September 1969.

In spring more adults are seen, and although only a small proportion stay for more than two days, there was one at Stodmarsh from 25th April–19th May 1971, the peak year, with four other spring records. On 19th May 1974 two were seen together at Stodmarsh. The favoured habitat is reed beds, with open lagoons, and it is possible that the regularity of spring records in the Stour Valley may presage breeding.

Black Stork

Ciconia nigra

Very rare vagrant.

Ticehurst gives details of four records between 1846–84.

Apart from a probable escape in the Canterbury and Dover areas in September–November 1957, the only recent record is of an immature on Romney Marsh on 7th August 1958, which subsequently moved into Sussex and stayed until 14th September.

White Stork

Ciconia ciconia

Rare visitor.

Ticehurst gives details of ten records and Harrison adds three more between 1909–21, with one in east Kent from 31st July–4th August 1939.

In four years between 1960–76 at least 14 birds were recorded. In 1960 there was an adult and an immature in the Stour Valley between 24th–29th May. In 1967 there were records from six localities between 14th April–3rd May, probably involving three birds. In 1971 there were two at three localities between 3rd–29th May, while in 1976 there were spring records from five localities between 30th April–8th June, involving at least three birds. That autumn there were four at three sites between 30th July–14th September.

The pattern of records indicates that small influxes occur at irregular intervals. Most individuals stay for several days and wander widely, so assessment of the actual numbers involved is often difficult. Arable and low-lying pasture, particularly on the Romney Marsh and lower Stour Valley have been the favoured haunts.

Glossy Ibis

Plegadis falcinellus

Very rare vagrant.

Harrison gives five Kent records between 1830–1916, including a party of four on the Rother Levels in September 1903.

One was seen at Swanscombe from 11th April–12th May 1974, and a second, which appeared at Stodmarsh on 14th December 1975, was still present at the end of 1978. Such a long stay is unprecedented in Britain. This bird roosted in the Stodmarsh reed beds and spent much of its time feeding on water snails in shallow dykes in the Stour Valley, although regularly visiting the Swale between May–September.

Spoonbill

Platalea leucorodia

Annual visitor in very small numbers, usually during the summer months.

There is circumstantial evidence that Spoonbills may have bred in the old heronry at Cobham in the sixteenth century. Certainly they were regular, perhaps annual visitors in the nineteenth century and Harrison includes numerous reports, mainly in spring and autumn, from the

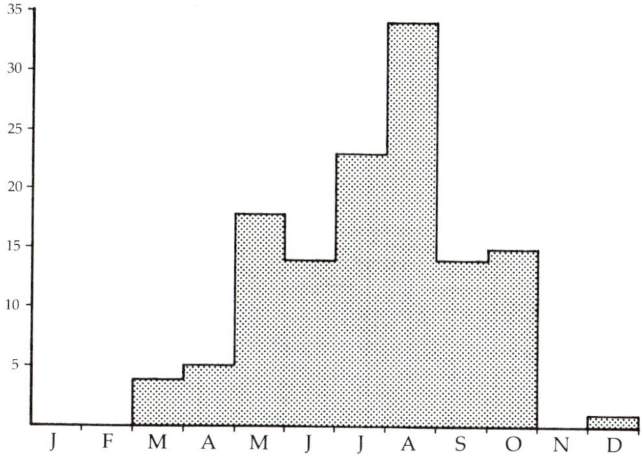

Monthly distribution of Spoonbills 1952–76

Romney Marsh area, the lower Stour Valley and the North Kent Marshes, during the first half of this century. One, ringed as a nestling in Noord, Holland in June 1912, was recovered two months later in Kent.

Since 1952 there have been over eighty records concerning at least 130 individuals, spanning every month and every year except 1963.

The accompanying histogram shows the absolute minimum numbers of Spoonbills seen with, in the case of prolonged stays, the record included only in the month of arrival. The October total is perhaps exaggerated by the inclusion of a flock of 10, the largest recorded in recent years, which remained in the Swale between 8th–12th October 1957. Otherwise, the preponderance of summer arrivals, between May–September, is clearly shown. Outside this period, one was found dead on Sheppey on 17th November 1956, another seen at Grove Ferry on 26th December 1962, and finally, one wintered at various localities on the North Kent Marshes and in the Stour Valley from 30th October 1973–14th June 1974. This last record represents by far the longest stay of any individual, most reports referring to single days, or short periods of a week or two.

Although most records concern individuals, twos and threes have been seen on about twenty occasions. In addition five adults were seen at Stoke on 26th May 1958, nine flew west at Dungeness on 29th August 1961, with six east there the next day, probably involving some of the same birds. In June 1976 there were separate parties of three adults at Stodmarsh and four immatures at Cooling.

Mute Swan

Cygnus olor

Resident and occasional winter visitor.

Both Ticehurst and Harrison suggest the possibility of immigrants from the Continent occurring in winter. The latter cites winter flocks of up to 40 on Romney Marsh and 130 in the Stour Valley. Gillham and Homes wrote of the Mute Swan breeding sparingly in north Kent, with only around six pairs on the Thames marshes and a few on Sheppey, where the largest winter flock was 18 in the severe weather of early 1947.

Mute Swans will breed on almost any type of freshwater with submerged vegetation, ranging from ponds and gravel pits to lakes and reservoirs. As the map shows, they nest commonly along the river valleys and on the low-lying coastal marshes. A census in 1961 produced about 160 pairs with nests, but excluded part of north and all south Kent, so it is likely that the breeding population then was between 180–200 pairs, perhaps more.

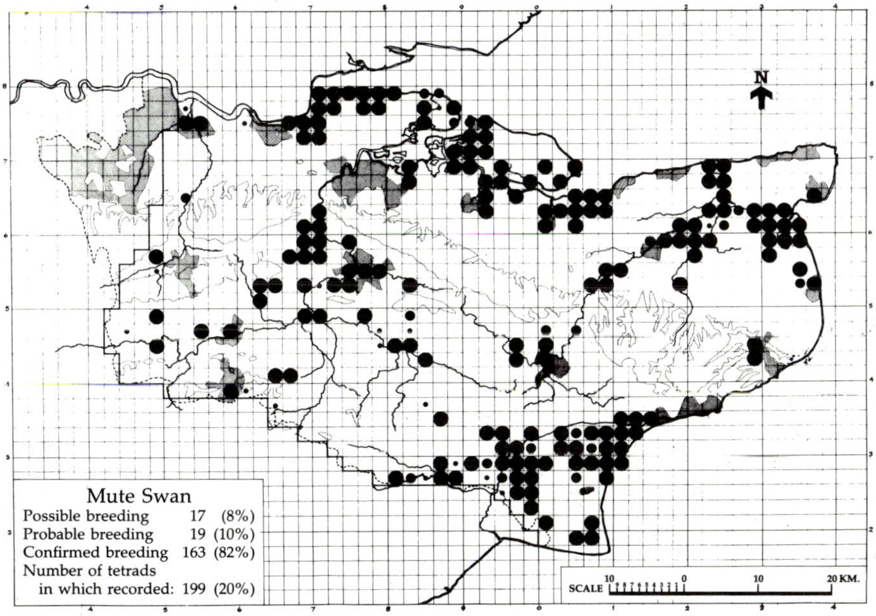

Non-breeding birds form into sizeable flocks during the summer months and counts of around 100 have been recorded in the Stour Valley, between Westbere and Stodmarsh, in 1959 and again in the 1970s. In south Kent there was another flock of around 100 on Walland Marsh in 1959, with 82 on the Dungeness Reserve in 1971. In north Kent the non-breeding flocks tend to be smaller, in the region of 30–40 on both Sheppey and the Thames marshes.

Winter flock sizes vary considerably from year to year, counts of 40–60 being regular, with the largest in the region of 200 on the Rother Levels and Walland Marsh in 1960 and 1967 respectively. Peak counts at other sites where large flocks are frequently seen are 120 at Stodmarsh in 1959, 100 at Cliffe in 1973, 89 at Sheerness during the severe weather in early 1963, and 78 on the Medway at Burham in 1965.

It is now known that some wintering Mute Swans are immigrants from the Continent. One ringed on the Medway at Maidstone in February 1963 was recovered at Mecklenberg, East Germany in October 1966. Various coastal reports also suggest immigration. At Sandwich Bay flocks of five and 19 flew north on 29th October and 31st December 1974 respectively, while four flew in from the northeast at North Foreland on 13th October 1975. The following year there were several more coastal observations, including three on the sea off Kingsdown in

January and another three off Thanet on 18th October. A further seven also flew north off Sandwich Bay on 2nd November. It may sometimes be possible to recognise immigrant Mute Swans in the field, as they tend to behave like other 'wild' swans, being more wary and easily put to flight. There is clearly still much to be learned about the status of this species in Kent.

Bewick's Swan

Cygnus columbianus

Annual winter visitor and passage migrant.

Ticehurst considered this species to be one of the rarest hard weather visitors, citing just one flock at Dungeness in about 1844. Harrison refers to another flock in the Thames Estuary in 1871, but apart from odd records of singles being shot, there were no more until 16th March 1946, when 14 were seen in east Kent. In the severe weather of 1947 there were up to 14 on Walland Marsh and another five in east Kent between 5th January–8th February. Further singles were seen in 1949–51.

One was seen in 1952, four in 1953, but none in 1954. Since 1955 the Bewick's Swan has become an annual winter visitor in increasing numbers, now averaging over 100 each winter. This reflects the massive increases which have also taken place on the Fenland Washes and at Slimbridge, probably reflecting changes on their wintering grounds on the Ijsselmeer in Holland.

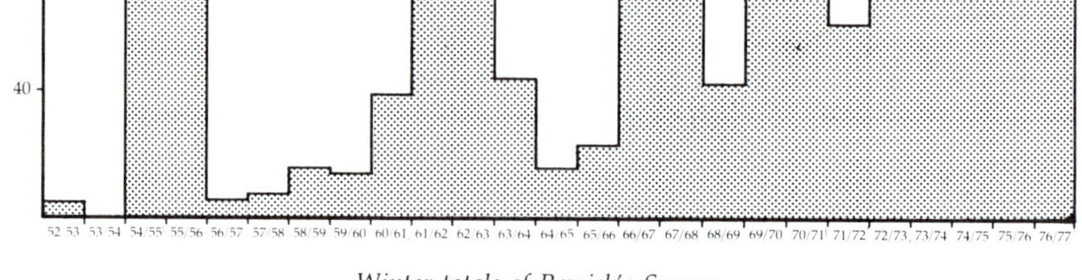

Winter totals of Bewick's Swans

Although a large number of records refer to hard-weather migrants in mid-winter, flocks may occur at any time between October–April, and an increasing number are now being seen on spring and autumn migration. The extreme dates are 18th October and 28th April. A flock of 65, on Walland Marsh between 24th–28th March 1976, is the largest so far recorded in the county and was obviously on return passage. Autumn migrants have been seen arriving on the north coast in a number of years, normally in cold north winds, the weather conditions associated with movements of seabirds and other wildfowl. On 1st December 1973 a flock of 40 flew up the Swale and later joined another eight birds at Cliffe, while on 30th October 1974 a flock of 50 flew up-river past Allhallows.

There are now two regular sites for wintering flocks, on the Isle of Grain, and on the Rother Levels or Walland Marsh, averaging 14 and 21 birds respectively. Flocks also occur regularly, and occasionally over-winter, elsewhere on the Thames and Sheppey marshes, at Sandwich Bay and in the Stour Valley. Smaller numbers have also appeared on inland waters along the Medway and Darent Valleys and at Bough Beech.

Whooper Swan

Cygnus cygnus

Almost-annual winter visitor and passage migrant.

Harrison considered this species an irregular winter visitor and spring passage migrant, most numerous in severe winters, the largest flocks recorded by him being 48 at Stodmarsh in 1942 and 49 on the Rother Levels in 1945. The highest numbers invariably occurred in February and in the severe winter of 1947 at least 50 were present.

The status of the Whooper Swan has remained unchanged during a period which has seen the Bewick's Swan increase from a great rarity to a regular winter visitor. The vast majority of the records during 1952–76 refer to parties of six or less, with records in all but four of the twenty-five winters, and an annual average of four records totalling 10 birds. In addition there have been fourteen flocks of 11–29.

In 1956 a flock of 12 flew west over Thanet on 20th February and there were 23 at Stodmarsh on 4th–5th March, with 11 on Sheppey on 2nd April. By far the largest numbers, however, occurred in the arctic weather of early 1963, when there were nineteen records of one–seven birds, totalling 42, plus flocks of 25 between Westbere and Grove from

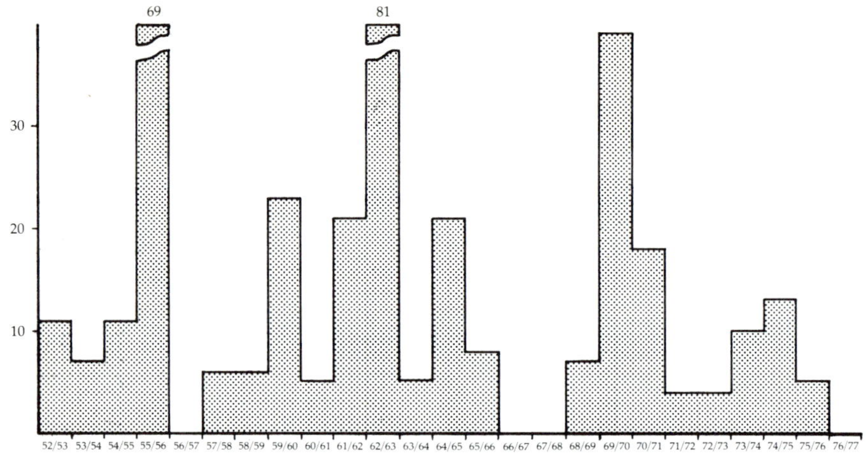

Winter totals of Whooper Swans

20th January–24th March, and 14 at Chilham in January–February. These last two flocks are almost the only records of genuine wintering in the county, the vast majority of records referring to single dates only.

There have been six records in October, with the earliest on the 6th, and six in April, with one bird remaining at Stodmarsh to 10th May 1963.

A few have been seen on inland waters along the Medway and Darent Valleys, and at Bough Beech reservoir, but this seems very much a bird of the coastal marshes.

Bean Goose

Anser fabalis

An occasional winter visitor, usually in small numbers.

Ticehurst described this species as the commonest of the grey geese, but expressed the opinion that the Bean and Pink-footed Goose were very often confused. Harrison considered the Bean Goose to be the rarest goose and lists less than ten records since 1930. The largest flock was 20, but most records concerned one–seven birds between 22nd October and early April, most commonly occurring during spells of hard weather. All those examined closely referred to the Forest race *A.f. fabalis*. It is probable that there has been a major change of status.

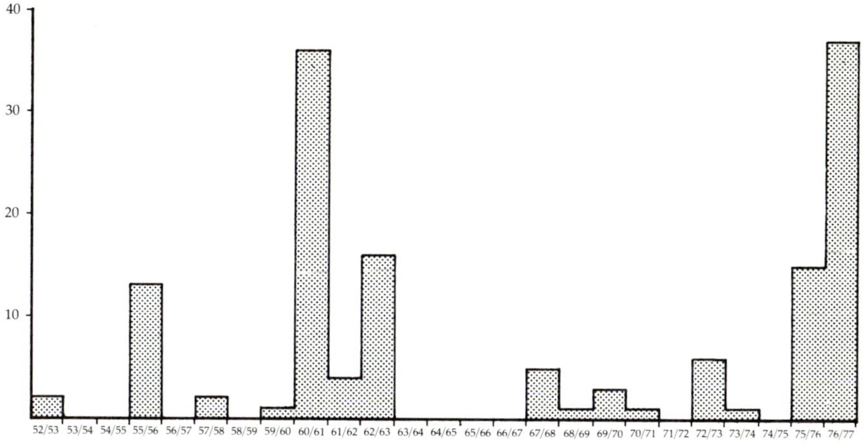

Winter totals of Bean Geese

A total of 143 birds has been recorded in 15 of the 25 winters under review, with the following monthly distribution.

J	F	M	A	M	J	J	A	S	O	N	D
43	73	20								1	6

The extreme dates are 9th November and 27th March. The vast majority of records concern one–six birds, and two-thirds emanate from the North Kent Marshes, with 66 birds by the Thames and 25 on Sheppey. Most of the records from east Kent are in the Stour Valley between Grove and Sandwich Bay. Flocks of 34 on 18th February 1961 and 11 on 31st January 1976 were both on the Thames marshes, with 13 at Reculver on 3rd January 1977 and 12 on Sheppey on 5th March 1977.

Inland, 12 were seen grazing in a clover field at Langley on 27th February 1956.

Only once has the Tundra race *A.f. rossicus* been positively identified, when three were seen at Cooling on 24th February 1976. All others seen sufficiently well referred to the Forest race *A.f. fabalis*.

Pink-footed Goose

Anser brachyrhynchus

Passage migrant and winter visitor in variable but usually small numbers.

The Pink-foot was described by Ticehurst as the rarest of the grey geese, and Harrison considered it to be of irregular occurrence. During the spells of inclement weather flocks of up to 40 were recorded and there were exceptional numbers in January–March 1940, with a flock of 200 in early March on the Thames marshes.

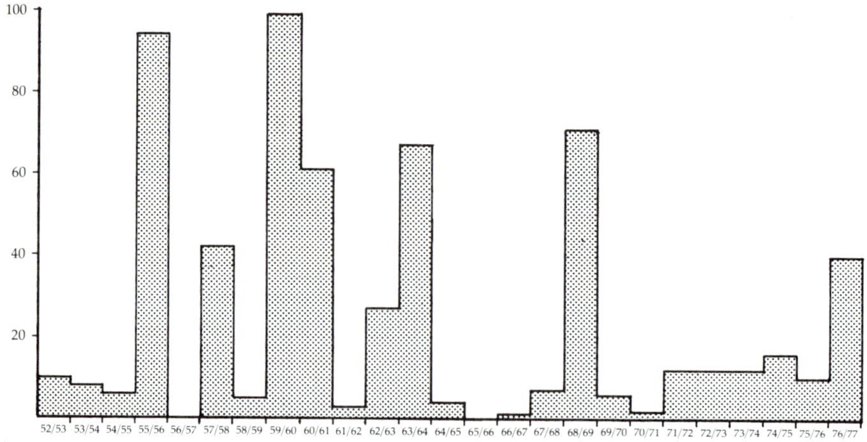

Winter totals of Pink-footed Geese

A total of 615 has been recorded in the three main haunts during the period under review, with 59% on the North Kent Marshes, 23% in the Stour Valley and Thanet region, and 18% on Romney Marsh and Dungeness. A flock of 53 on Chislet Marshes on 7th February 1960 is the largest recorded and there have been three flocks of 40–50 on the North Kent Marshes between 1st January–3rd March.

The vast majority of records have occurred between 14th September–23rd April, with wintering birds present from late December to early March. The monthly totals are summarised below:

J	F	M	A	M	J	J	A	S	O	N	D
195	267	24	9					35	25	18	48

The September total consists of a flock of 28 on the Thames marshes on 24th September 1976, six in the Stour Valley from 14th–28th September 1974 and one in the same area on 25th September 1954. The October total is made up of two migrant flocks, 17 off Dungeness on 21st October 1962 and eight off Sandwich Bay on 30th October 1974. The November total also consists of migrant groups off Dungeness and Thanet.

Spring passage records are scarce. Off Dungeness passage has been recorded between 25th March–23rd April, with one–ten on five dates in the review period. What was probably a pricked bird was present on Walland Marsh from 21st April–11th June 1962 and another remained on the Thames marshes from 16th April–19th May 1963.

There are very few inland records and some are considered to be escapes. However, there were five at Sevenoaks on 9th February 1973 and two at New Hythe on 17th March 1974.

It is possible to speculate on the origin of Kentish Pink-feet. It is known that some birds of the Icelandic population do occur, for a bird ringed on the Scottish wintering grounds was later shot on the Isle of Sheppey. However, most of those seen on the North Kent Marshes have been in company with White-fronted Geese, which suggests that they are more likely to be of the Spitzbergen population, which winters in the Low Countries and Northern France, and where the two species also intermingle. With the Spitzbergen population increasing in the Low Countries, this goose could well increase further in Kent.

White-fronted Goose

Anser albifrons

Regular winter visitor and passage migrant.

Numbers have increased considerably since the turn of the century, when Ticehurst considered the White-fronted Goose to be a moderately common winter visitor, but less numerous than the Bean Goose. According to Gillham and Homes, numbers did not begin to increase until the mid-forties, when 250 were seen on the Thames marshes, followed by 500 in the severe winter of 1947.

During the period under review, the number of White-fronted Geese wintering regularly on the Thames and Sheppey marshes increased substantially from around 600 in the early 1950s to over 1,600 between 1968/69–1972/73. This area is now one of the four most important wintering sites in Britain.

Numbers increase considerably when there is severe weather on the Continent. In 1956 about 1,000 were present on the Thames marshes for a month, with a peak count of 1,500 in early March, while in 1963 there were 1,000 on the Thames marshes again and 450 on Sheppey in mid-January. In December 1976 severe weather in Holland brought an influx of 1,900 to these two haunts for a brief period. The highest count for Sheppey is 1,120 in February 1971.

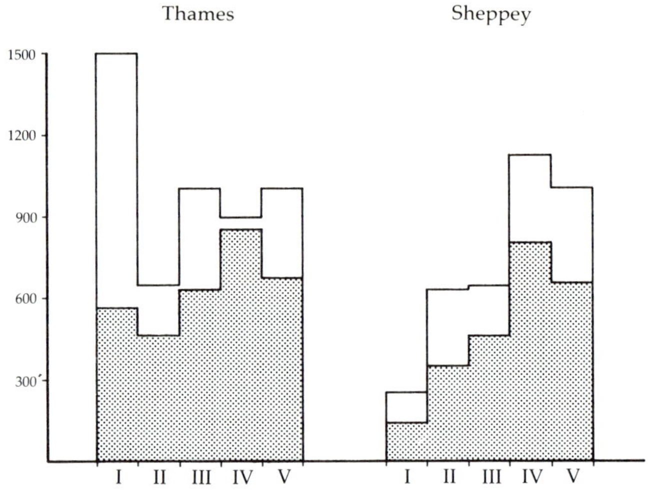

Regular and peak populations of White-fronted Geese in five five-winter periods

In autumn the first arrivals from the east are usually seen in November, but small flocks occasionally occur in October, with two records in September of which a skein of 45 flying west at Cliffe on 14th September 1976 is the earlier. On two occasions flocks have been seen flying down the Thames from the west, having presumably overshot their destination. High counts in November probably involve passage birds, while the main arrival of winter flocks often coincides with periods of cold weather in December, or occasionally in early January. The fact that peak numbers in January–February may not be maintained for more than a short period suggests that there may be some mid-winter movement between the different wintering areas in Britain and on the Continent, depending on local conditions. There is certainly some interchange between the Thames and Sheppey flocks, with small gaggles occasionally feeding in the Medway, particularly on Chetney.

The main departure to the east or northeast usually occurs between 21st–31st March, with a few birds lingering into April. The latest records concern singles at Harty on 2nd May 1956, at Cliffe on 4th May 1974, and at Sandwich Bay from 10th April–27th May 1975. In addition one was present at Cliffe from 19th May to early August 1956.

Elsewhere in Kent the majority of reports usually concern passage birds, but during severe weather flocks may remain for short periods in suitable habitat. In 1956, during February, 30–70 were present along the Medway Valley between Maidstone and Tonbridge, with 54 in the Stour Valley and 57 on Walland Marsh. In February 1963 there were 150 in the Stour Valley and 120 on Walland Marsh, while earlier, on 6th January, there were four flocks of 100–350 on the east Kent lowlands, giving a total of 900 in all. In 1968 another marked passage was observed between 28th–31st December, with 258 at Sandwich Bay, 150 at Stodmarsh, 110 at Herne Bay, 237 at Dymchurch, and smaller numbers elsewhere. Not infrequently skeins of migrants may be seen over inland Kent, flying southwest in mid-winter and northeast in spring.

The agricultural changes on the Thames and Sheppey marshes give cause for concern, though the White-fronts appear to be adapting to the change. The favoured winter habitat has been, and probably still is, grazed pasture, with shallow flashes of flood water, but since the early seventies winter wheat has been grazed more extensively.

A uniformly melanistic bird was seen on the Thames and Sheppey marshes in January and February 1966 respectively, with two more on the Thames marshes in January 1969 and one there again the following January.

Greylag Goose

Anser anser

Winter visitor and passage migrant. Resident feral population.

Early records of this species are poorly documented, but the first refers to eight on Romney Marsh in April 1925. Thereafter Harrison gives several more spring and autumn records for south Kent and the first winter record for north Kent in January 1937. In the severe weather of 1947 about 60 were seen on the Thames marshes.

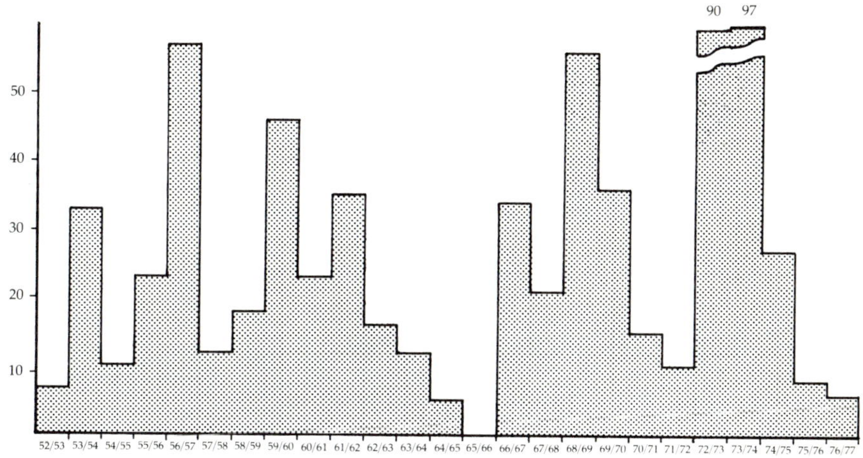

Winter totals of immigrant Greylag Geese

The Greylag Goose has become an almost annual winter visitor and passage migrant, with nearly 700 birds now recorded. Some of the winter parties have remained for up to nine weeks, these are included only under the month of arrival in the following table, which shows the monthly totals. The extreme dates are 1st October–11th May.

J	F	M	A	M	J	J	A	S	O	N	D
235	99	50	11	1					88	46	166

Of these birds 80% were seen on the North Kent Marshes, with over half on Sheppey and a third by the Thames. Flocks of 15–30 have been seen in five winters, with peak counts of 40 on the Thames and south Swale on 4th January and 4th October 1973 respectively, and 50 on Sheppey in December 1972.

With the exception of a flock of 25 on 31st January 1954, there have been very few records for Romney Marsh, while the majority of the east Kent observations concern spring and autumn migrants, notably 18 on the Worth marshes on 1st October 1966, up to 14 at Sandwich Bay from 2nd–17th March 1968, and 18 flying north off Sandwich Bay on 29th October 1974, during a massive movement of wildfowl.

Five of the north Kent records, including the 40 in October 1973, involved birds showing pink on their bills, typical of the population that winters in the Low Countries and further south to the Iberian peninsula.

In 1963 WAGBI introduced Greylags on the Sevenoaks Reserve and a very successful breeding population has developed in west Kent. By 1975 there were 21 pairs breeding and the feral population had reached 220. These birds tend to divide into the Darent Valley flock, based on Sevenoaks, and the Medway Valley flock, based on Hayesden.

In 1968 twelve birds were introduced at Dungeness, where one–three pairs now breed annually, and where there was a peak count of 37 in May 1974. In 1969 another 29 were released at Westbere and one–three pairs now breed in the Stour Valley, where there were 35 in September 1974.

Since 1955 a successful feral breeding population has been established at Le Zwin, Belgium, with other colonies in Holland. In order to encourage further movements between north Kent and the Low Countries WAGBI also established a reserve on the south Medway, releasing 33 birds in 1970. Three years later a further 29 birds were released, this time brought over from Belgium. So far three of these have been recaptured in Belgium, with one shot in Holland and two in Denmark. In 1976 ten pairs bred and there were 145 in August. Some of these birds now feed on the Sheppey and Thames marshes, and further releases have been made on the Isle of Grain. These introduced Greylags now seem well established in Kent, and the north Kent population may well attract more birds from the Continent to winter.

Snow Goose

Anser caerulescens

Possible vagrant.

The true status of the Snow Goose is impossible to determine because of the frequency of escapes from British and European waterfowl collections.

The 26 records are evenly divided between the north and east Kent coastal areas and the inland waters of west Kent, with two records from Dungeness. Six, being first seen in summer, must surely have been feral, but some of the others might have been genuine vagrants, including a party of six which flew north off Sandwich Bay on 14th September 1971. Of those that were identified racially one was a Greater *A.c. atlanticus* and nine were Lesser *A.c. caerulescens.*

Canada Goose

Branta canadensis

Introduced resident, increasing in numbers.

Ticehurst gives a few records attributed to escapes, but by the 1940s Harrison was able to cite several records of feral birds, including a party of 15 at Eastwell Park in July 1939 and 36 on the North Kent Marshes in February 1940.

Breeding birds are now quite widespread throughout the Weald, with small populations in the Stour Valley and at Dungeness, nesting beside reservoirs with natural margins, flooded gravel pits, rural ponds, town lakes and slow-flowing rivers.

There were no records for 1952–54. One was seen near Maidstone in May 1955, with six at Eastwell Park in the severe weather of 1956, followed by one in the Swale in May. A few pairs were introduced on the Sevenoaks Reserve in 1956, another pair at Leybourne in 1959, and 21 birds on the Dungeness Reserve in 1964. Other feral populations began breeding in the Stour Valley in 1971 and on the Medway in 1974.

On the Dungeness Reserve the numbers have remained fairly stable since 1970, reaching a peak of 74 in 1972, while in the Stour Valley there were 40 by 1975. The spread into north Kent has been slow, as the Canada Goose favours freshwater lakes rather than estuaries and brackish marshes. There were odd records in the late fifties, with one

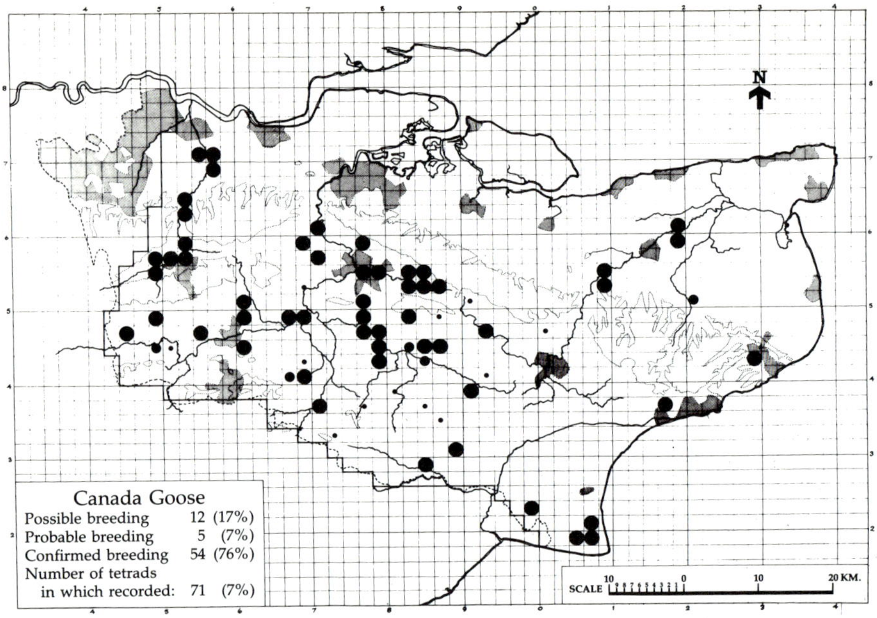

pair breeding near Faversham, followed by two pairs at Murston in 1963. By the mid-seventies there were about 10 on both the Sheppey and Thames marshes, and up to 30 in the Medway.

The main populations are centred around Sevenoaks and Maidstone, with the grassy slopes of the new reservoirs now providing attractive feeding areas. The Sevenoaks population increased from 12 birds in 1956 to a peak of 354 in September 1969. Since 1971, there are peak counts of 450 at Leybourne, 367 at Bough Beech, 266 at Mote Park and 200 at Leeds Castle. Parties flight regularly between these last two sites and eastwards to Chilston Park. The largest numbers are invariably recorded in September, but by November each autumn the principal flocks have dispersed. Ringing recoveries show that there is some interchange between Sevenoaks, Leybourne and Mote Park and the total population in these areas was estimated at around 600 in September 1971 and in 1976. These increased numbers seem higher than could possibly be accounted for as a result of local breeding, and both the June population, when the birds are moulting, and the mid-winter numbers appear to be lower. An accurate census in addition to further ringing may resolve some of these unanswered questions. One ringed in Lincolnshire and recovered at Sevenoaks suggests that some may migrate.

In 1976, from 9th October until the end of the year, one showing the characteristics of the Cackling Canada Goose *B.c. minima* was present at Bewl Bridge reservoir, probably an escape from captivity.

Barnacle Goose

Branta leucopsis

Scarce winter visitor.

Ticehurst describes the Barnacle Goose as a rare winter visitor and Harrison cites only a few records, including a flock of about 40 in the Swale during 1914–18, 12 in the Medway in December 1923, and one–seven in several winters during the 1940s in north and east Kent.

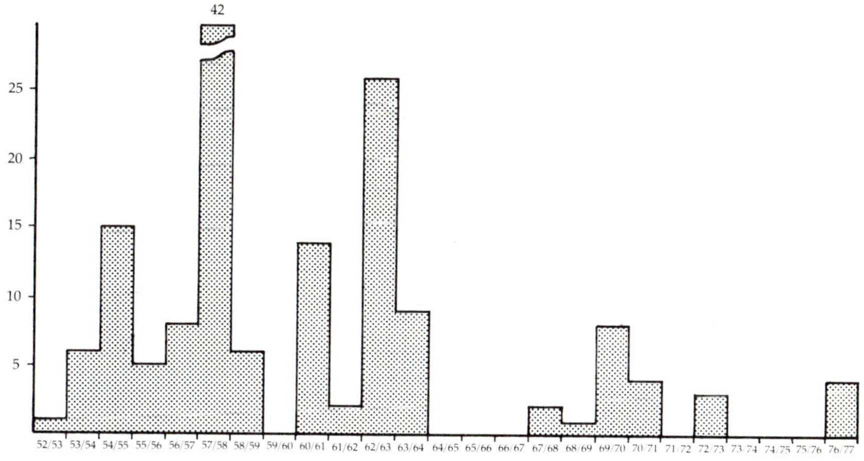

Winter totals of Barnacle Geese

The majority of the small parties that remained for periods of a few days to a month or so associated with White-fronts grazing coastal pastures. One, however, seen on the Swale in January–February 1971, kept company with Brent and fed on the *Zostera*. Nearly 80% of the total birds seen were on the North Kent Marshes; with eight records for the Swale totalling 64 birds, four records totalling 30 on the Thames and five records totalling 27 in the Medway. The largest flocks were 24 on the marshes at Kingsferry on 20th January 1958 and 21 at Capel Fleet between 24th–28th February 1963.

In east Kent the largest party was eight at Sandwich Bay on 15th December 1963, with one–six in nine other winters, totalling 30, including a migrating flock of three off North Foreland on 21st October 1970. In south Kent there is just one record of a migrant flying west off Dungeness on 13th November 1969.

On 24th February 1956, five flew low over the Medway near Maidstone in company with a flock of 70 White-fronts. It is surprising that so few were seen during this cold winter, as over 50 were seen in Sussex in February.

J	F	M	A	M	J	J	A	S	O	N	D
52	73	2	2						3	14	10

Monthly distribution of Barnacle Geese 1952–76

The peak numbers in January–February suggest that these are birds normally wintering in Holland, driven out by severe weather on the Continent. A few of the February parties in north Kent have remained into March, with the latest on the 26th, while at Sandwich Bay two were also seen on 28th April 1961.

Since 1966 there have been increasingly widespread reports of feral birds in all months of the year. In three successive years from 1971 two–four appeared on the Sevenoaks Reserve between late June–late September, staying to complete their moult. In 1975 two pairs bred in Eastwell Park and the young were free-winged, while a flock of up to 11 remained in the Stour Valley from that November until January 1976, with another flock of 20 there between August–November 1976.

Brent Goose

Branta bernicla

A regular winter visitor and passage migrant.

Ticehurst wrote of immense flocks visiting the Thames, Medway and Swale in severe weather, flocks which were uncounted, and which were to decline rapidly in the 1930s, when a mycetozoan disease destroyed many of the *Zostera* (eel-grass) beds, their main food. Harrison noted that by 1938 the maximum was only 250, but the nadir was reached in 1946–47, when the peak counts were only 18 on the Swale, 20 on the Thames and 13 on the Medway. Since then, from a world population estimated at under 10,000, a remarkable recovery has occurred, to an estimated 100,000 in 1975/76. The Swale and Medway are the most important wintering grounds in Kent.

Seven had returned to the Medway by 30th August 1976, but otherwise there are no autumn records earlier than 12th September, and the first birds are more usually seen in the last week of the month or the

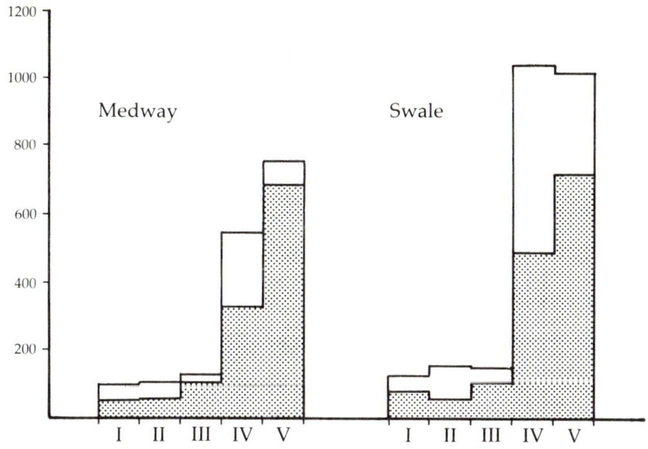

Regular and peak winter populations of Brent Geese in five five-winter periods

first half of October. Migrants occur in large numbers in late October and early November, with up to 500 in a day in the Thames and Swale estuaries. In 1975 and 1976 this passage was most exceptional: in 1975 there were 650 on the Thames on 2nd November, 730 on the Thames and 700 on the Swale on 8th November, and 1,000 on the Thames and 800 on the Swale on 9th November. In 1976 there were 1,050 on the Thames on 30th October and 860 there on 13th November. Passage of smaller numbers continues in these two areas in late November and early December.

In 1970, a northward autumn movement off Thanet and Sandwich Bay was discovered. It has subsequently proved to be regular, and is thought to consist of birds which have overshot Essex and are working their way back, as it is most marked in strong NW winds. The largest number using this route was 420 on 10th November 1971. In addition a smaller westerly movement is noted off Dungeness in autumn, with a maximum of 250 in a day.

The large autumn passage in 1975 and 1976 involved two overland routes. These routes are westwards up the Thames, or south to southwest over the North Kent Marshes and across inland Kent. Skeins seen over inland Kent in 1975 included 140 over Headcorn on 18th October, 120 over Staplehurst and 130 plus 80 over Langley on 8th November, 46 over Bough Beech on 9th November and 110 over Headcorn on 14th November. In 1976, 60 were seen over Langley on 30th October and 250 plus 130 over Lamberhurst on 17th December. Brent grounded inland have always been rare, but since the new migration route was established a few have been seen at Sevenoaks, Bough Beech, New Hythe and Naccolt. There is no evidence of a return migration overland, except for one or two grounded at Sevenoaks and Bough Beech in early spring.

Easterly return passage is noted at Dungeness from early March to mid-May, but the numbers seen are variable and seem mainly to be dependent on the amount of seawatching coverage there during the peak period, which is the last three weeks of March. The highest day-total was 560 on 15th March 1971 and the most intensive, prolonged passage involved a total of 1,360 on five dates between 15th–21st March 1976. The main departures from the Medway and Swale also occur in March, while one in the Swale on 8th June 1973 was the latest recorded.

A few mid-summer records have occurred, including singles at Folkestone on 24th June 1962 and presumably the same bird at the Wicks on 24th–26th June, an injured bird on the Swale until 23rd July 1961 and one there on 25th July 1963.

Two individuals, ringed with large 'Darvic' rings, identified in Kent after being caught at Foulness, Essex, have been seen later on Texel in Holland and on the German Friesian Island of Föhr during spring migration.

The main foods now are regenerating *Zostera* on the Swale and Thames, various green seaweeds and saltmarsh grasses on the Medway, and both winter wheat and pasture grasses inland of the sea walls. Family parties of adults with young tend to avoid the lower-protein green seaweeds, which are eaten by second-year immature birds, so that the Medway has become an important pairing-off ground for this age group.

One Pacific Brent Goose *B.b. nigricans* was identified in the Medway Estuary on several occasions with Dark-breasted Brents in February 1974. This is the only Kent record, but several have occurred in Essex.

Records of the Pale-breasted Brent *B.b. hrota* are irregular. Harrison describes five between 1929 and 1946, involving 30 individuals between 9th October–14th May, with a maximum flock size of 16. The locations of the eleven sightings between 1952–76 are shown below with the numbers involved in brackets.

Thames	Medway	Swale	Sandwich Bay	Dungeness
1(8)	2(16)	3(21)	4(20)	1(1)

The extreme dates are 9th December–17th March. The monthly distribution of records, with the bird numbers in brackets, is as follows:

J	F	M	A	M	J	J	A	S	O	N	D
1(2)	3(4)	1(15)									6(45)

Flocks of 15 were seen at Chetney on 17th March 1956 and at Shellness on 29th December 1971, with 16 at Sandwich Bay on 10th December 1967. There is no real indication as to whether these birds are from Spitzbergen or North America.

Egyptian Goose

Alopochen aegyptiacus

Ticehurst mentioned that numerous examples of this species were shot, presumably all escapes from captivity. Harrison cites one on Cliffe Marsh on 8th–9th April 1937.

Recorded annually since 1970, when one was present at Stodmarsh between 1st May–6th June. In 1973 a pair was present at Chilham between February–November, while three pairs summered in 1975. The majority of these birds probably originate from the feral East Anglian population.

Ducks

The regular winter populations of duck on the three estuaries in the north, in the Stour Valley and on Romney Marsh are shown in a series of histograms for each species. The figures are derived, where possible, from the average of the highest counts for each month December–February, and these in turn have been averaged over five seasons. By limiting the range to the three winter months, rather than the three highest counts from the seven months September–March, transitory migrant populations of such species as Shoveler are effectively omitted. This is important, because it is the regular counts that give the best indication of the holding capacity of any wetlands, and as such they are of greater significance than the peak counts.

In the histograms, the Stour refers to the whole of the valley east of Sturry, including Stodmarsh and Pegwell Bay. Romney refers to the peninsula southeast of the Royal Military Canal, including parts of the Rother Levels and the gravel pits at Dungeness. The Roman numerals at the foot of each column represent the following five-winter periods:

I—1952/53–1956/57
II—1957/58–1961/62
III—1962/63–1966/67
IV—1967/68–1971/72
V—1972/73–1976/77

or, in the case of autumn peaks, the following five-year periods:

I—1952–56
II—1957–61
III—1962–66
IV—1967–71
V—1972–76

At the International Conference on the Conservation of Wetlands and Waterfowl, held in West Germany in 1974, it was agreed that any wetland in northwest Europe which held either a total of 10,000 head of waterfowl, or 1% of any one species, was to be designated as being of international importance. During the period under review the Medway has replaced the Thames as being the most important wetland area in Kent, and is now of prime international importance, regularly holding over 1% of four duck species, Shelduck, Wigeon, Teal and Pintail, as well as of Brent Goose, and on occasions Shoveler. In addition, it has regularly held in excess of 10,000 wintering waterfowl since 1969.

Some of the decreases on the Thames marshes, particularly for Shelduck, Pintail and Teal, may be explained by the increasing numbers of wildfowl which have been using the Inner Thames in Greater London since the late sixties. This shift upriver is attributed to the amount of food available in the mud now that there is effective pollution control in the Thames (Harrison & Grant, 1976).

A survey of the breeding wildfowl of the North Kent Marshes was conducted between 1961–64 (Hudson, 1967).

Ruddy Shelduck

Tadorna ferruginea

Possible vagrant.

A duck was obtained at Newenden in April 1885 and a drake was shot on the Medway Estuary in the 1890s. Another was shot there on 17th August 1943 and the fourth record concerns one at Cliffe from 30th April 1950 for a month.

In recent years an adult female was present at Swanscombe on 28th April 1967 and later seen at Chetney, Stoke and High Halstow until 22nd May. At least four were recorded in 1973. One, which spent much of its stay on the Inner Thames, was seen at Cliffe on 20th February and 22nd September and again between 19th January–28th April 1974. One was also seen in the Stour Valley from 11th–14th August 1973, another at Dungeness on the 1st, 2nd and 29th December and another at Motney Hill on 2nd December. A pair present near Pembury on 18th April 1974 were probably escapes, and this possibility cannot be ruled out in Ruddy Shelduck records, though some may refer to genuine vagrants. The most recent record was of a duck seen at Swanscombe on 16th May 1976.

Shelduck

Tadorna tadorna

Locally common breeding species, winter visitor and passage migrant.

A considerable increase in the breeding population and in wintering numbers occurred during the first half of this century. Ticehurst quoted as exceptional one winter flock of 200, while Gillham and Homes recorded counts of 3,000 on the Thames by 1950. Breeding has been recorded since the turn of the century on the North Kent Marshes, since 1920 on Romney Marsh and since 1925 at Sandwich Bay and in the Stour Valley.

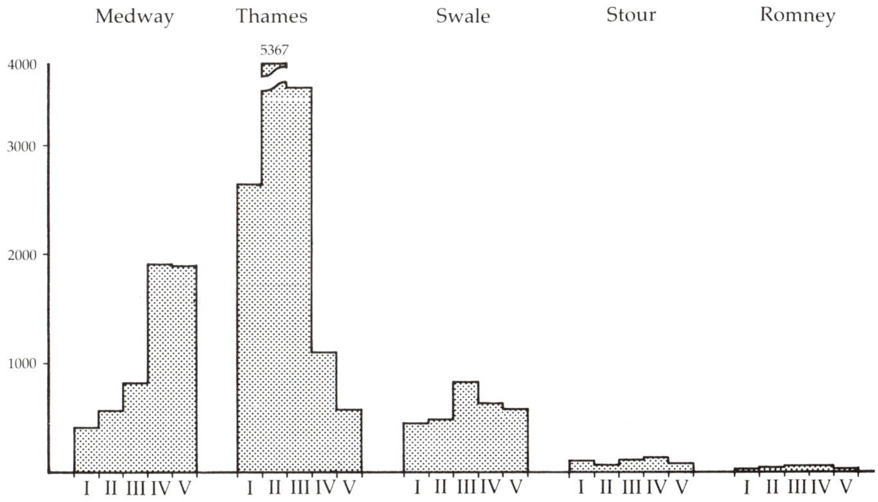

Regular winter populations of Shelduck

Peak counts for this period include 10,000 on the Thames in both February 1960 and 1963, 3,400 in the Medway in February 1972, and 2,500 in the Swale in December 1963. The largest counts in the mouth of the Stour are 400 and 435 in December 1970 and 1973 respectively, while on Romney Marsh just over 100 were present in January 1967 and February 1970.

The preferred winter food of the Shelduck in Kent is the laver spire shell, found in the intertidal zone. During the arctic spell of 1962/63, when the intertidal zone was frozen, at least 400 Shelduck were found dead round the Kent coast, a large percentage being females.

The winter population on the North Kent Marshes decreased by around 2,000 in the late 1960s, a decline corresponding closely with the colonisation of the inner Thames following pollution control. By 1970 about 1,500 were present on the Swanscombe–Dartford stretch, attracted by the *Tubifex* worms on which they were feeding. With the decline of *Tubifex*, following increasing oxygen saturation, Shelduck have also decreased substantially here. Smaller numbers have moved into the Medway and Darent valleys, with winter peaks of 50 at Cuxton and 33 at New Hythe in the 1970s. Others now visit the new reservoirs at Bough Beech and Bewl Bridge regularly, with up to 16 at the former site.

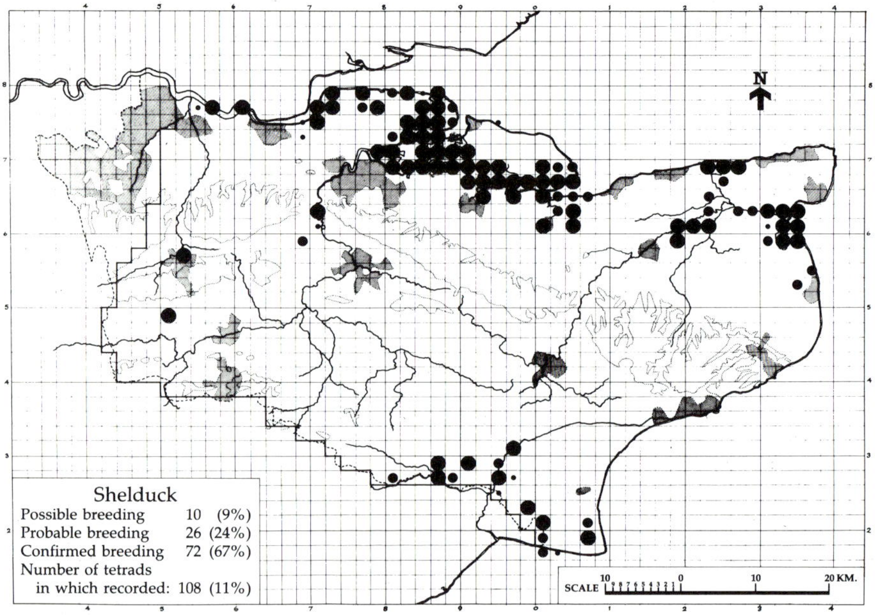

The North Kent Marshes are the stronghold of the breeding population. Numbers are difficult to assess accurately, but the Medway Island censuses show an increase from 18 pairs in 1955 to 74 in 1972 and 96 in 1977. This increase in the saltings population may partly be explained by the shift to alternative nest sites. The drastic reduction in rabbit burrows around the shores of the estuary in the early 1960s caused a marked redistribution of breeding Shelduck throughout the North Kent Marshes. Then the population on the marshes was in the region of 200 nesting pairs, with totals of 77 on the Swale, 66 in the Medway, and 65 along the Thames in 1961. Prior to the breeding survey, pairs occasionally nested successfully south of Sittingbourne in the Doddington and Stockbury areas. Along the Medway Valley breeding has been recorded since 1955 and in 1973 one pair bred well inland near Bough Beech and another pair attempted nesting at Sevenoaks.

A prolonged study of the breeding biology of Shelduck on the Isle of Sheppey has, in particular, demonstrated the tendency for this species to assemble and nest in discrete breeding communes. It is also common for two or more ducks to lay their entire clutches in one nest, and the ducklings are often collected together in large creches comprising several broods (Hori, 1964a, 1964b, 1965, 1969).

Later in the summer these creches merge and flocks of 100–150 juveniles in the charge of a few adults are not unusual. In July 1967 one such flock on Windmill Creek included 400 juveniles.

Flocks of up to 500 non-breeding Shelduck summer on the Thames marshes, with smaller numbers on the Medway and Swale. These and most of the breeding population undertake a moult-migration to the Heligoland Bight from late June, leaving a few adults in charge of the 'nurseries' mentioned above. By mid-September most of the young have also gone.

The wintering birds return in late autumn and in mild winters the peak may not be reached until early February. There is evidence of others moving to and from the west past Dungeness, and one bird, ringed at Harty in October 1961, was recovered in northern France just two months later. Other ringing recoveries confirm the moult-migration to and from the Heligoland Bight.

Mandarin

Aix galericulata

The Mandarin is now established as a breeding resident in southeast England. First recorded in Kent in the 1920s, it now occurs annually in small numbers.

The published records since 1971 show that Mandarins have been seen most frequently on inland waters in west Kent and along the river Len, twice at Sandwich Bay, once at Margate and once at Dungeness.

Reports from the Len valley in central Kent probably refer to feral birds originating from the Leeds Castle collection. One pair nested successfully at nearby East Sutton in 1967.

Wigeon

Anas penelope

Common winter visitor and passage migrant. Has bred.

Ticehurst could find no evidence of breeding, but Harrison documents several instances of successful nesting, both on the North Kent Marshes and on Romney Marsh.

The greatest change in distribution and status has been brought about by widespread drainage. Both Romney Marsh and the marshes of the lower Stour used to hold winter and migrant populations of several thousands according to Harrison, but the peak counts there during the period under review were 1,200 at the Wicks in March 1956 and 1,500 on Grove Marshes in December 1961. On the credit side, however, far larger numbers now occur on the North Kent Marshes, particularly in the Medway.

The highest counts in this period were 15,000 on the Thames marshes in February 1956 and over 10,000 in the same area in January 1969 and on Elmley in January 1977. The peak count for the Medway was 9,456 in January 1974.

The first autumn migrants usually arrive in mid-August and since the late 1960s have concentrated earlier, and in larger numbers, in the Medway, with a flock of 1,500 there by 27th September 1970. The main arrival occurs from late October to mid-November and a small passage can occasionally be observed at Dungeness at this time. Further large increases may occur in January during severe weather on the Continent. In mild winters, many leave early. On 6th–7th February 1972, for example, at least 1,000 were seen leaving northeast towards Holland from the Medway.

The winter flocks have generally dispersed by mid-March, but a late peak may occur as the lingering winter flocks are supplemented by spring migrants. Some individuals remain into May and summer birds are reported in most years, with breeding suspected in several seasons. The only proven nesting records concern single pairs on Sheppey in 1956 and in 1963, when a pair also bred on Walland Marsh, and in the Medway in 1971 and 1976.

Inland records show that a few birds arrive in Kent from early June on mid-summer dispersal, lone drakes actually passing through their flightless eclipse moult at Sevenoaks in 1968 and 1974. Small inland waters, including gravel pits, also attract a few birds in the winter months and 20–30 have occasionally been seen at Eastwell Park, Sevenoaks and in the Medway Valley at New Hythe. The new large reservoirs at Bough Beech and Bewl Bridge, with their grassy banks, have attracted migrant and wintering flocks, with peaks of 85 at the former in February 1972, 70 at Bewl Bridge in February 1976, with 250 there the following February.

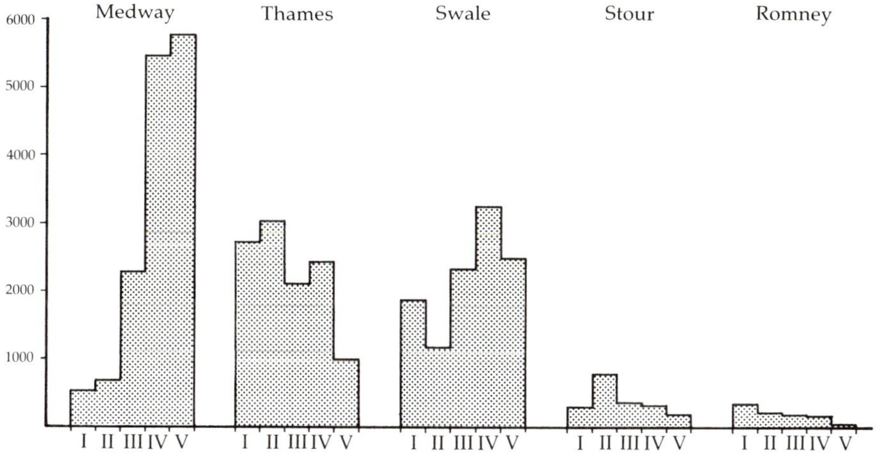

Regular winter populations of Wigeon

Autumn foods in north Kent consist mainly of green seaweeds, marsh samphire and crache seeds from the intertidal saltmarshes, together with eel-grasses. In mid-winter Wigeon move to fresh and brackish marshes to feed on various grasses, fennel-leaved podweed and winter wheat, then concentrate on the 'early bite' grasses in spring. At Stodmarsh, they often eat the tuberous roots of mare's tail. Everywhere they are always attracted to flooded pasture, a steadily decreasing habitat in Kent.

The population structure shows that Kent holds about 2.5 adult drakes for each adult duck, whereas in first year birds the sexes are in approximately equal numbers. Differential migration is a phenomenon which was accentuated by the severe weather in 1962/63, when the ducks emigrated, the remaining flocks containing three drakes to one duck.

One ringed on Chetney in February 1963 was recovered in Spain in December 1972, about 80 km north of the Cota Donana. Another, ringed a day later at the same locality, was recovered in late May of the same year at Salekhard (Tumen) USSR, on the Arctic Circle 66° 30'N 66° 40'E.

American Wigeon

Anas americana

Very rare vagrant.

A drake, shot at Monkton, Thanet on 15th March 1917, is in Maidstone Museum.

A young drake was identified on Windmill Creek on 28th October 1961, and an adult drake was seen on Stoke Lagoon on 27th April 1968.

Gadwall

Anas strepera

Winter visitor, passage migrant and local breeding species.

At the turn of the century Ticehurst considered the Gadwall a rare autumn and winter migrant, but it became more regular, particularly in the thirties and forties. Harrison wrote of successful breeding in the Stour Valley between 1939–42 and on the Thames marshes in 1946–47, but the only sizeable count was 20 on Romney Marsh in December 1946.

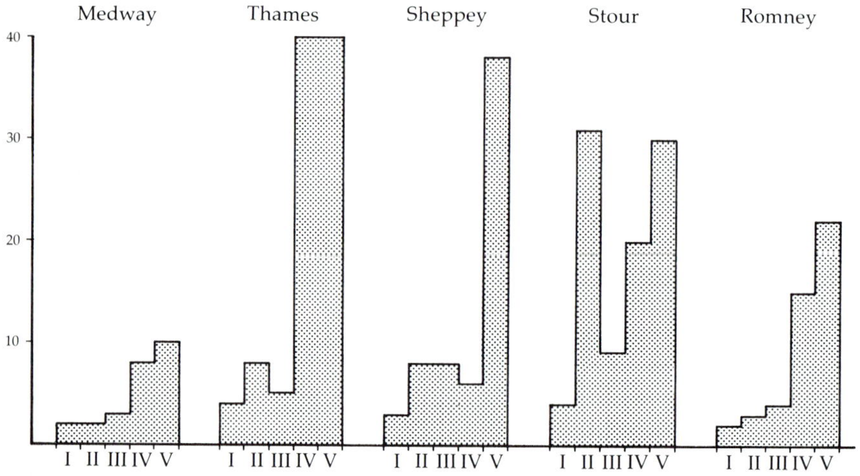

Autumn/winter peak counts of Gadwall

A marked increase has taken place since the late sixties. This may partly be explained by the presence of a feral population originating from the Sevenoaks Reserve, but it is interesting to note that increases have also been recorded in East Anglia and in Sussex. In December 1969, for example, when the first count of 40 was recorded at Cliffe Pools, there was a peak count of 43 in Chichester Harbour. It seems likely that the numbers are supplemented by immigrants from the Continent and an observation of six flying into the Thames off Allhallows on 22nd September 1973, with two more a week later, is of interest.

Between 1965–72 over 100 WAGBI bred birds were ringed and released at Sevenoaks, six of which have been recovered in France and one in N.W. Germany, showing that some, at least, may migrate. Others remain in the Sevenoaks area, where autumn counts of 20–25 have become regular since 1967, with up to 14 at Bough Beech and 12 at Leigh. At Cliffe Pools 22 were seen in December 1967, increasing to 27 in January, with 40 in December 1969 and again in October 1972. On Sheppey the numbers recorded increased to 16 in September 1976, with 38 in February 1977. In the Stour Valley the exceptional total of 31 in January 1961 occurred when the fields at Grove Ferry were flooded, attracting large numbers of dabbling duck, otherwise there were 20 there in January 1972 and 30 by March 1976. On the Dungeness Reserve the numbers have also increased, with 15 in November 1971 and 22 by March 1977.

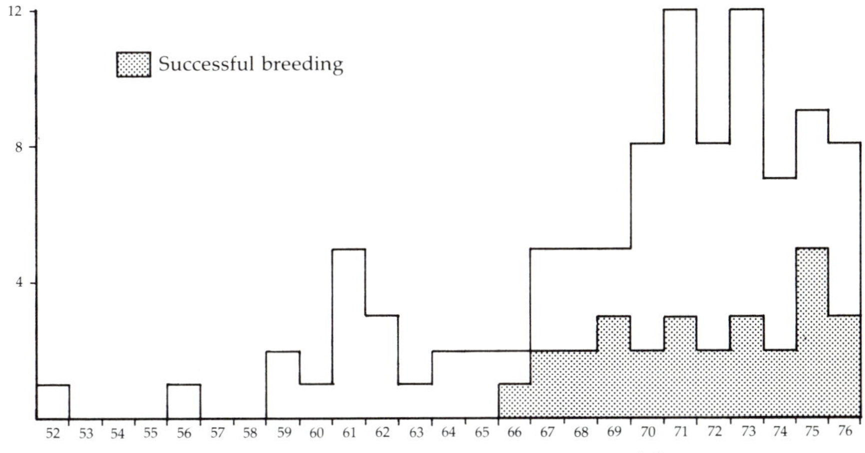

Pairs of Gadwall summering and breeding successfully

Up to four pairs now summer regularly on the Sevenoaks Reserve, with one or two pairs breeding successfully almost annually since 1967. In the Stour Valley, pairs have summered regularly since the late fifties, with one pair breeding successfully in 1966 and five pairs in 1975. Similarly, in north Kent breeding has been proved occasionally since 1969, most frequently on the Thames marshes, but also on Sheppey and in the Medway Estuary on Chetney and at Kingsnorth.

Teal

Anas crecca

Common winter visitor and passage migrant, scarce and local breeding species.

Gillham and Homes noted 2,000 on the Thames in 1946 as exceptional, so there is little doubt that a marked increase has occurred in the north of the county, but numbers in the Stour Valley and on Romney Marsh have certainly declined as a result of drainage. The number of nesting pairs on Romney Marsh has also shown a marked decline since Ticehurst's time.

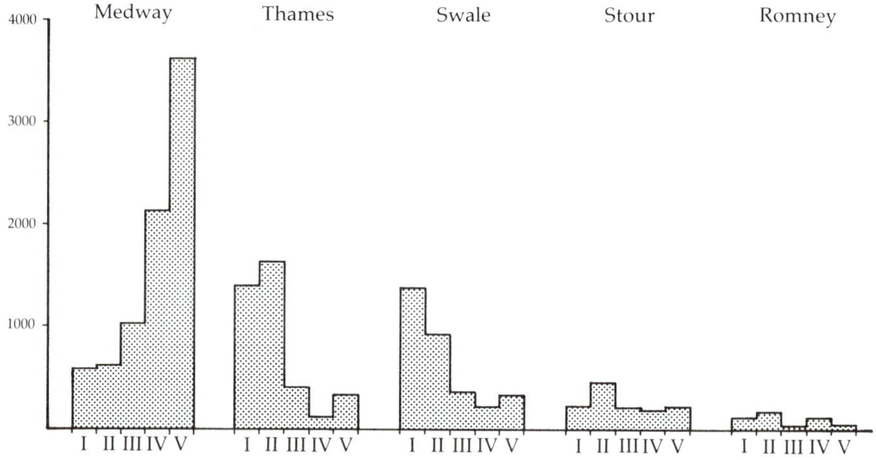

Regular winter populations of Teal

The peak counts for the different areas include 5,460 in the Medway in December 1973, and one flock of at least 4,000 on Chetney in December 1969. These were feeding on less than ten hectares of shallowly flooded marsh samphire, the seeds of which are a favoured food item of Teal. On the Thames there are counts of 3,000 for December 1955 and January 1958, with similar numbers in the Swale in January 1957 and 1962, while in the Stour Valley there were 1,000 in January–February 1961 and again in January 1962. There were exceptional numbers on Romney Marsh in January–February 1952, with 1,000 on Walland Marsh and 500 on the Rother Levels, but no winter counts since then have approached these figures.

The histogram showing the population changes largely obscures the marked fall in numbers of this species experienced throughout Britain between 1964/65–1967/68. In 1967/68 the peak count for the North Kent Marshes reached a low of only 1,200.

It seems likely that the substantial increase during the 1970s in the Medway, which is now the most important estuarine area in Britain for this species, may be explained by the displacement of Teal from the new Dutch polder of South Flevoland as it gradually dried out. This also happened in the late 1950s when East Flevoland was pumped dry.

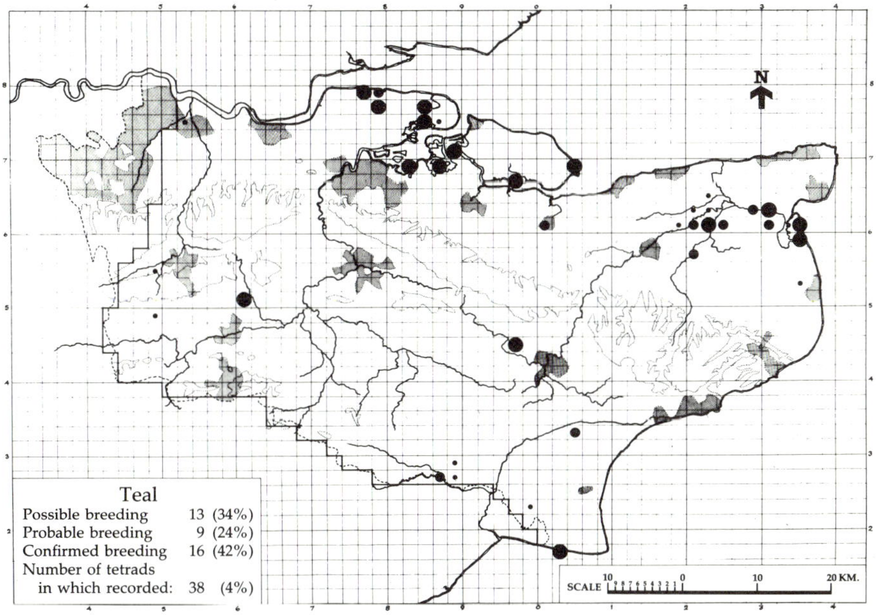

The map clearly shows the concentration of breeding records in the North Kent Marshes and Stour Valley. In north Kent, breeding has been recorded annually since 1959, with an estimate of 10–15 pairs in that year, but confirmation of nesting is difficult and reports from elsewhere are irregular, making the size of the breeding population difficult to ascertain. However, it is probable that between 10–25 pairs breed in Kent each year.

Non-breeding birds have been recorded from late May into early July at various regularly watched inland waters since the 1960s. By late July small flocks are recorded in coastal localities. Numbers then increase steadily throughout the autumn and peak counts in November invariably include passage migrants. On 8th November 1975 there was an exceptional movement into the Thames, involving 1,290 flying west off Allhallows, with 510 the next day. Hard weather may bring a further influx, but freezing conditions in Kent may also produce a mass exodus.

In mild winters some birds may leave in late February, but the main passage is usually in late March and early April. Occasionally this can be quite marked, with increased numbers occurring in widespread localities. At Dungeness there was an exceptional passage on 31st March 1971, when 576 flew up-Channel. There is little indication of offshore passage here normally, but numbers on the gravel pits in the area often peak during spring and autumn passage.

Inland, gravel pits, reservoirs, marshy river valleys and flooded pastures all attract varying numbers, with winter counts in excess of 200 at Bough Beech and in the Medway Valley at Burham, with 100 at Bewl Bridge and 80 in the Len Valley at Leeds and the Loose Valley at Langley. There are also widespread reports of smaller numbers, primarily during the winter months.

Ringing recoveries indicate considerable movement between the Baltic countries and Kent, with others moving further west and south. Notably, a juvenile drake ringed in the Camargue in December 1964 was recovered the following November in the Stour Valley.

Green-winged Teal

Anas crecca carolinensis

A drake, showing the characteristics of this American race, was seen on Walland Marsh on 21st March 1961, and over the border in Sussex between 19th–22nd.

Mallard

Anas platyrhynchos

Widespread breeding species, numerous as a winter visitor and passage migrant.

Though the Mallard breeds widely throughout the county, the map clearly shows its absence from the Downs and Thanet. Accurate estimates of the breeding population are difficult to obtain. The censuses of the Medway Islands show fluctuations between 37 pairs in 1955 and 94 in 1967. The breeding survey in the early 1960s suggested a total of 540 pairs for the North Kent Marshes, with 290 on Sheppey, 150 in the Medway and 100 on the Thames. In 1969 the estimate for the whole of the Medway Estuary had increased to 270 pairs. Other counts include 200 pairs in the Stour Valley between Fordwich and Grove in 1975, and a total of 115 pairs breeding at the Sevenoaks Reserve, Bough Beech reservoir and Hever Lake in 1976.

Most Mallard moult on their breeding grounds, favouring the dense cover of reed-fringed fleets, ponds and lakes. For a brief period in the

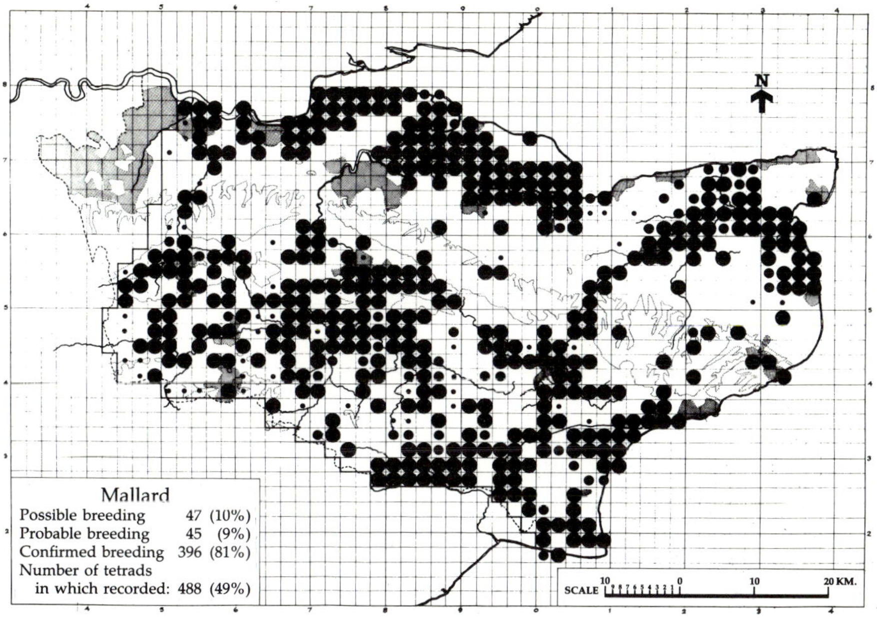

late 1960s Barksore Marsh became a regular moulting ground, with a peak of 350 drakes in late June 1970, probably representing the majority of the Medway and Swale nesting population.

Post-breeding flocks generally reach a peak in late August or early September, but remain widely dispersed and many are uncounted. The regular population of Mallard in Kent during the early autumn is 7–8,000, but in 1974 there were 7,100 on the North Kent Marshes alone, which compares favourably with the estimate of 8,000 for 1951 (Harrison). Stodmarsh is the centre for the Stour Valley population, where up

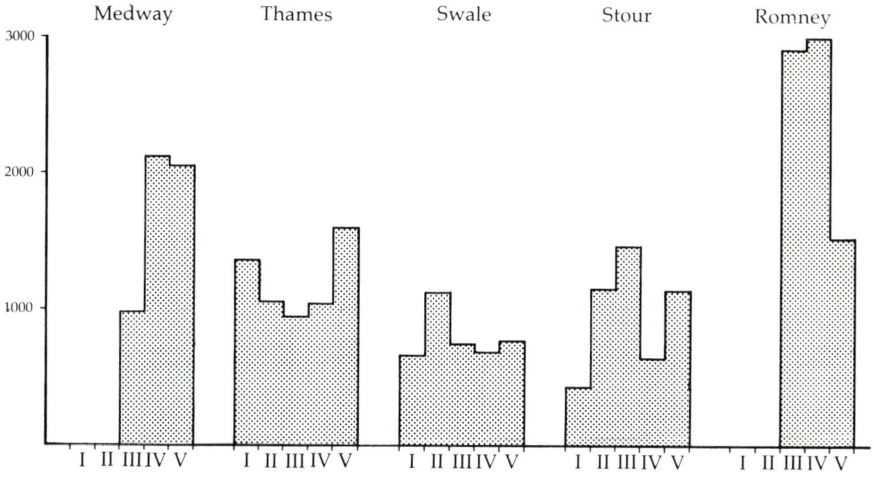

Regular post-breeding populations of Mallard

to 2,000 have occurred following good summers, while in the 1970s up to 800 were also present on the Wantsum Marshes between Reculver and Birchington. Romney Marsh has been less well censused, but there was a maximum of 4,600 there in 1967. Following the severe drought in 1976, numbers were low in most areas, with only 2,200 on the North Kent Marshes. However, on the four major inland waters in the west of the county there was a count of 1,260 in 1976, where the regular post breeding population is in the region of 960.

Numbers decline in October, with some birds probably migrating to the Continent, as suggested by recoveries of WAGBI-ringed birds released in the wild, which have been widely reported from the Low Countries, Denmark and France.

Migrants, mainly from the Baltic, start arriving in Kent from November onwards, depending on the severity of the weather, but the population in winter is usually smaller than in early autumn, with 4–5,000 birds regularly wintering in the county.

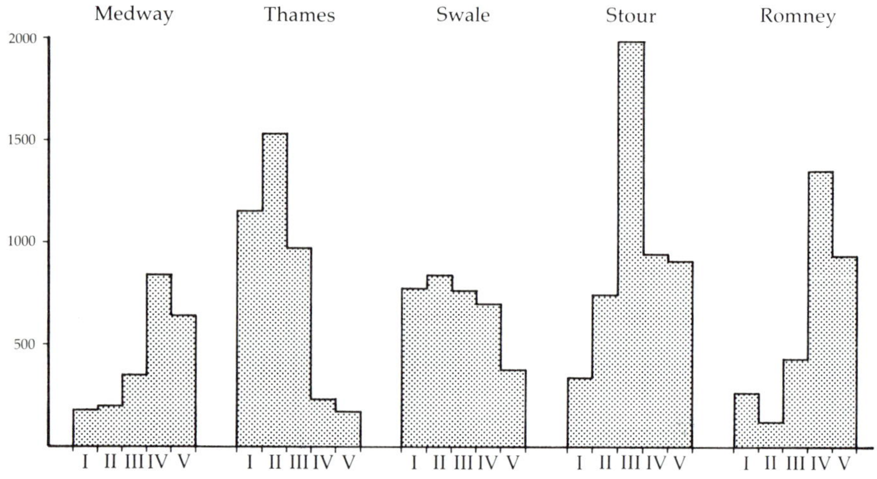

Regular winter populations of Mallard

Maximum counts include 1,600 in the Medway in January 1971, 3,000 on the Thames in January 1968 and the Swale in February 1967, 3,200 in the Stour Valley in February 1963 and on the Dungeness gravel pits in January 1971. In west Kent, where two large reservoirs have been flooded since 1969, the regular winter population has increased to 950, with a peak total of nearly 2,000 on five principal waters in December 1976. The winter flocks usually disperse rapidly during February.

Wing analyses of Mallard shot on Romney Marsh strongly indicate that there is a differential migration of first winter birds from the Continent. In 1976/77 a sample of 386 wings showed that the percentage of young in September was about 70, rising to nearly 90% in February (Harrison, 1978).

The Mallard is omniverous, prime foods being cereals in autumn, particularly barley, followed by acorns, seeds of sedges and other emergent plants. Alder and silver birch seeds are taken in mid-winter. In the severe weather of 1962/63 Mallard were taking mussels and shore crabs on the Medway, which accounts for the very low starvation mortality that winter compared with more specialised feeders like Shelduck and Wigeon.

Black Duck

Anas rubripes

Very rare vagrant.

One, probably a drake, was present at Stoke from 18th–25th March 1967.

Pintail

Anas acuta

Regular winter visitor and passage migrant. Breeds occasionally.

This duck has undoubtedly increased, particularly in north Kent, where around the turn of the century Ticehurst considered flocks of 30 noteworthy. By the late forties Harrison was recording 300 on the Thames marshes. The highest counts elsewhere were 400 at Cottington in October 1941 and 150 on Romney Marsh in January 1948, but counts of that order have not been recorded in these areas since. There are relatively few early records of breeding, with one or two pairs on Romney Marsh in several years between 1910–1948, in the Stour Valley between 1928–1951, and in north Kent since 1947.

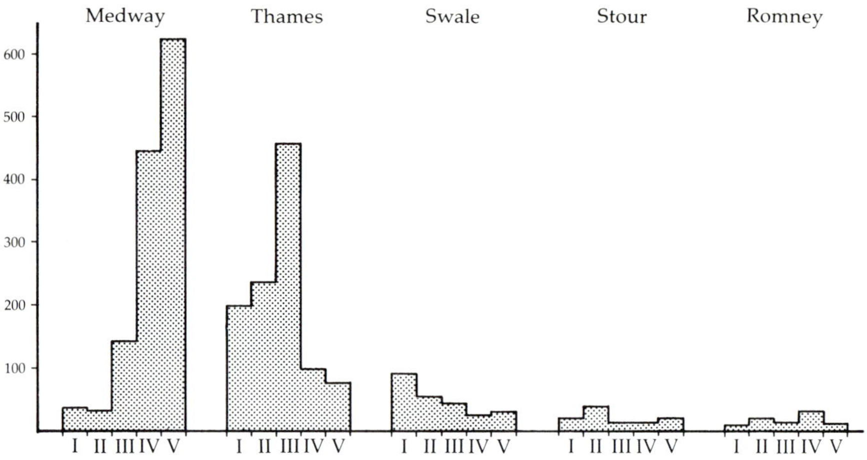

Regular winter populations of Pintail

Peak counts include 1,400 on the Thames in February 1963, 1,250 in the Medway in January 1972, 200 in the Swale in January 1954, 1955 and 1961, 80 in the Stour Valley in February 1961 and 1962, and 36 on the Rother Levels in February 1968.

The recent decline on the Thames marshes can partly be explained by the increased numbers that are able to winter further up-river, as a result of recent pollution controls. The increase in the Medway is unexplained, though the Pintail's favoured food, laver spire shell, is more abundant here than anywhere else in Kent. Seeds of seablite and marsh samphire also feature in the diet.

As with Teal, a marked, but short-lived decline occurred between 1964/65–1966/67, when the peak winter counts for the North Kent Marshes dropped from a high of 1,629 in February 1963 to 232 in February 1967, returning to 1,570 in January 1972.

During 1952–76 breeding was proved only on the North Kent Marshes, with six pairs in 1952, but none in the following year, when disastrous salt water flooding left the marshes highly unsuitable for breeding duck. One–five pairs bred annually between 1957–67 and single pairs in 1971, 1972 and 1974. Summering individuals were also recorded there in several other years, and occasionally in the Stour Valley and on Romney Marsh.

Small migrant flocks in July, particularly at inland localities, may involve birds on midsummer dispersal, but autumn migrants are occasionally observed from late August, with increased numbers during October–November moving into the Thames or through the Channel. At Allhallows on 29th September 1973 several flocks totalling 268 flew west into the Thames, where a flock of 400 in November 1974 were probably also migrants bound for the inner Thames.

Return passage commences in late February in mild winters, and migrant flocks create short-lived peaks, mainly in east or south Kent in March, with a few stragglers remaining into May.

Inland, the Pintail is still relatively scarce, though in west Kent there has been a marked increase in records, particularly since the flooding of Bough Beech reservoir, where up to 10 now occur, mainly during the winter months. A flock of 12 was also seen there on 27th August 1973. At nearby Sevenoaks there was a remarkable influx in July 1974, with 10 on the 9th and 14 on the 17th, but the highest inland count concerns a flock of 17 flying east over Tonbridge on 27th December 1968.

Garganey

Anas querquedula

Now a scarce summer visitor and passage migrant, breeding annually in small numbers.

Harrison recorded an increase during the first half of this century, following the prohibition of spring shooting. The highest count was 100 in east Kent in July 1937 and the extreme dates 3rd February 1945 and 25th November 1938. As a breeding species the increase was quite

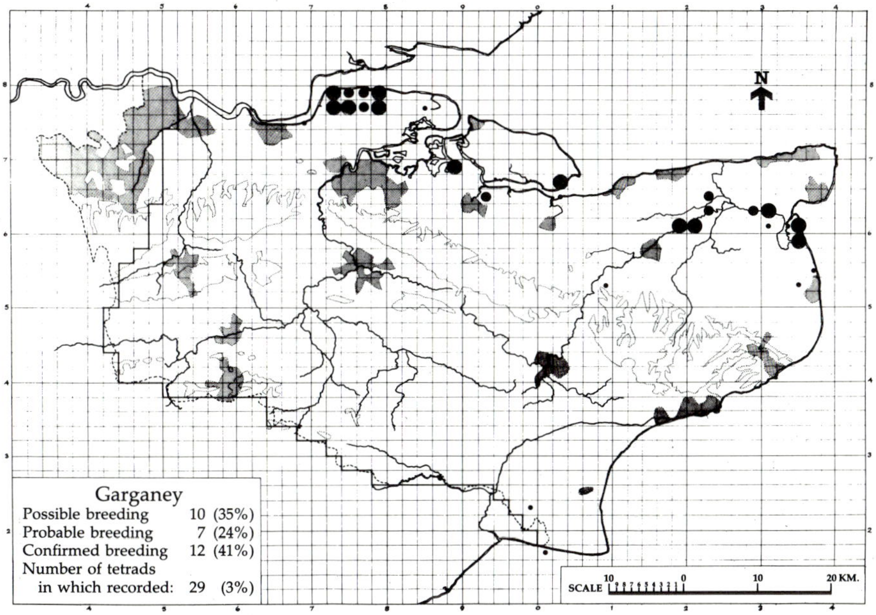

marked. Ticehurst estimated seven or eight pairs on Romney Marsh in 1909, after which the Garganey became more widespread there. During the thirties they also became established in the Stour Valley and on the North Kent Marshes. Gillham and Homes estimated around 20 pairs on the Thames marshes in the late forties.

Garganey favour shallow fresh or brackish pools for feeding and nest in tall grass close to well sheltered reedy lagoons and fleets. Being hidden away in vegetation for much of the breeding season, it is a difficult species to study and nesting pairs may well be overlooked.

Following the disastrous floods in 1953, the number of nesting pairs on the North Kent Marshes declined dramatically, but by the early sixties 13–18 pairs were nesting annually, with 11 pairs on Sheppey in 1961 and 1963, and a peak of 12 pairs on the Thames marshes in 1965. At least 16 pairs were also present in the Stour Valley in 1962 and 1963. In the same period up to four pairs were known to breed on Romney Marsh, but since then the numbers have declined again overall, but particularly on Sheppey, where only one or two pairs now breed. In 1975 there were only nine pairs on the North Kent Marshes, including three on Chetney, and only four pairs in the Stour Valley.

The Garganey is an early migrant, one at the Wicks on 19th February 1957 being the earliest recorded in recent years. The first arrival dates normally range between 26th February–20th March, with the mean around 8th March, while the main influx occurs between mid-March and early April. Small parties of up to 20 occasionally occur, though there was an exceptional count of 120 at Stodmarsh on 7th April 1952. Since 1970, however, two-figure counts at any one locality have become very rare.

An analysis of autumn flock sizes also reveals a decline since the 1960s. The flocks in July and August may give some indication of

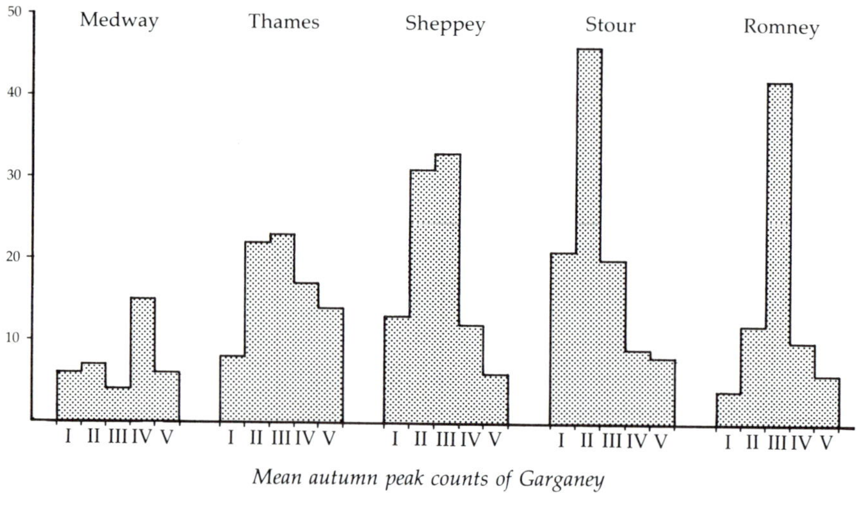

Mean autumn peak counts of Garganey

breeding success, but this may be confused by the presence of passage migrants, as some begin to reappear as early as mid-June.

The Medway has never attracted many Garganey, though a flock of 20 was seen on Chetney on 1st September 1969. On the Thames marshes the peak count was 50 in August 1964, while there were 60 on Sheppey in August 1963, but no more than seven have been seen there since 1968. In the Stour Valley, the flooded fields at Grove Ferry attracted exceptional numbers in 1961, with a peak count of 150 on 6th July, otherwise the largest flock there was 37 in June 1963. In the same year 80 were seen on Romney Marsh during August. Numbers drop rapidly during September and the latest dates usually range between 16th September–22nd October, with the mean around 1st October. A pricked bird, seen on Walland Marsh on 13th November 1966, is the latest recorded in recent years.

Inland, numbers seen have increased since the flooding of the two new reservoirs in west Kent, where spring and autumn migrants are now reported annually. At Sevenoaks Reserve there was a remarkable record of seven pairs in one party on 25th March 1970. Normally only one–four birds are seen on these three waters, and occasionally elsewhere along the Medway and Darent valleys.

Blue-winged Teal

Anas discors

Very rare vagrant.

A full-plumaged drake was seen on flood water at Sandwich Bay on 14th April 1970.

Shoveler

Anas clypeata

Regular breeding species, winter visitor and passage migrant.

Ticehurst considered the Shoveler more numerous in summer than in winter at the turn of the century. On Romney Marsh he noted an increase in the number of breeding pairs to about 10 in 1905. Gillham and Homes considered it a common breeding species, particularly on the Grain peninsula, where they estimated 50–80 nesting pairs, with winter flocks of up to 300. Harrison also noted several inland records, particularly on spring migration.

Although there is a significant wintering population, flocks of over 300 are relatively scarce during December–February. The peak annual counts may well be in November or March, when passage migrants are also present.

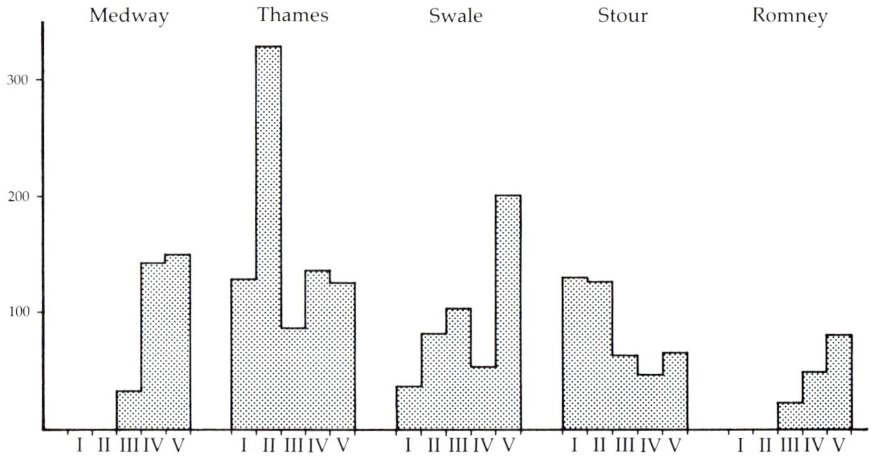

Regular winter populations of Shoveler

The quite exceptional counts at Grove Ferry from mid-February to mid-March 1961 have been excluded from the histogram. At that time, the fields between Grove Ferry and Stodmarsh were flooded, and a peak count of 2,000 was recorded on 19th February, with 1,000 still present on 19th March.

The highest winter counts for other principal localities include 650 on the Thames in February 1959, 484 flying west into the Swale on 29th January 1961, and 420 in the Medway in January 1971. During 1952–62 there were few counts for the Medway and Romney Marsh and a marked increase has occurred in both these areas, with flocks of over 100 now wintering on the new gravel pits on Dungeness Reserve. The Swale too is attracting larger winter flocks at Shellness and Elmley.

Accurate estimates of nesting populations are difficult to obtain, but the breeding survey for the North Kent Marshes in 1961–64 suggested a total in the region of 100 pairs, almost equally divided between the Thames and the Swale. Another 20–30 pairs have been recorded breeding annually in the Stour Valley, but there are few records for Romney Marsh apart from one pair in 1954 and two in 1965.

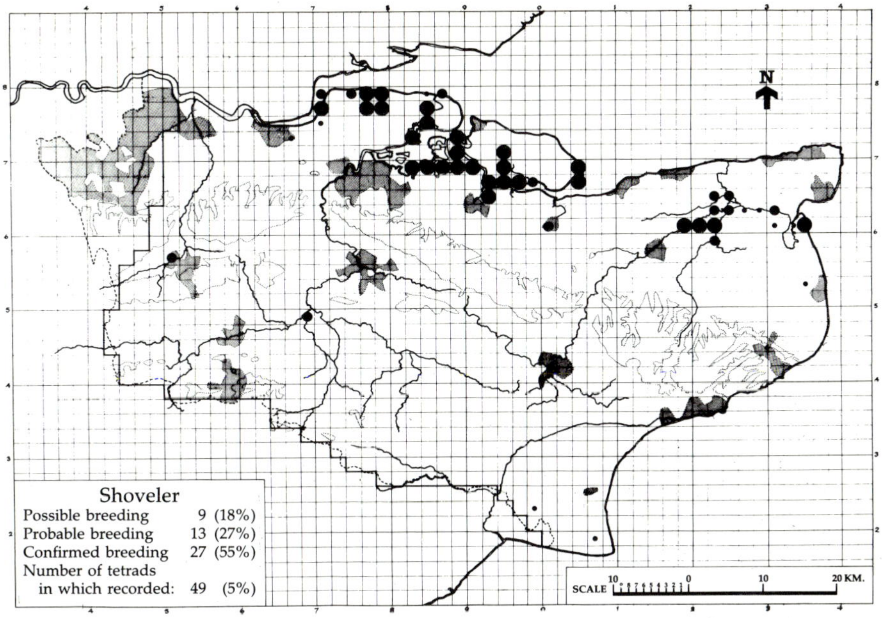

Shoveler show a preference for nesting in rough grass alongside fleets and ditches, rather than sea purslane, which is the dominant vegetation over much of the saltings in the Medway. Consequently relatively few pairs breed in that estuary, except on the grazing marsh on Chetney, where the population reached 27 pairs in 1971, before the northern end of the peninsula was drained. In wet springs, such as 1975, increased numbers may nest. On Chetney there were 20 pairs, compared with only one in 1973, while on the Thames 12 pairs nested in 121 hectares of winter wheat, having taken up territories beside pools of standing water in the crop.

Drake Shovelers flock during June and approximately 100 out of a flock of 120 at High Halstow on 15th June 1964 might conceivably have represented almost the entire drake population of the North Kent Marshes. After flocking the drakes apparently move out of the breeding areas and are largely absent from late summer flocks, which begin to increase in late July and by early August may total 100–200 in each of the three estuaries in the north and in the Stour Valley. Numbers swell again during October–November, with the arrival of passage migrants and winter visitors.

Spring migration may be more marked. At Dungeness a small passage is usually recorded offshore between mid-March and early May, with an exceptional movement of 927 on 31st March 1971. Annual maxima of 150 on Dungeness Reserve in 1975 and 120 at the Wicks in 1962 were, not unexpectedly, also in March, while an increase on the Thames marshes from 100 in early March to 450 on 21st March 1967 typifies the increase in numbers during spring migration.

Increased numbers have also been reported from inland localities in the last five years of the review period, with maxima of 35 at Bough Beech reservoir in October 1973, 20 at Leybourne in February 1976 and 14 at Sevenoaks in March 1973. A few occur occasionally on small lakes and gravel pits throughout the county, particularly on passage in March and during mid-summer dispersal in July–August.

Two, ringed as pulli in Holland, were recovered one month and two months later on 1st September 1955 and 1967 respectively in the Swale, while another, also ringed as a pullus in Midlothian in June 1955, was recovered on the Medway in January 1957.

Red-crested Pochard

Netta rufina

Rare visitor.

Harrison lists just two records. A duck was shot from a party of 18 on the Thames in 1853 and a drake was identified amongst a party seen with Pochard at Cottington Court on 28th November 1935.

Between 1961 and 1976 at least twenty individuals were recorded, but it is probable that a number of these were escapes. Fourteen were seen between 15th October–24th February, three between 13th March–6th May and a further three between 16th July–2nd August. Twelve occurred at coastal localities, six on inland waters in west Kent, and two at Stodmarsh.

It is evident from the dates that some may well be genuine immigrants from the Continent. In support of this, a drake was seen flying offshore at Sandwich Bay among a massive movement of wildfowl on 29th October 1974. Another arrived at Sevenoaks with immigrant Pochard from the east on 31st July 1975, at a time when the latter are known to arrive from N.W. Europe. In autumn 1971 at least fifteen were reported in England, eight between 10th–14th November, including one at Dungeness.

Pochard

Aythya ferina

Locally common resident and winter visitor.

Harrison reported the first breeding on the Thames marshes in 1907, with up to five pairs at Stoke and three pairs at High Halstow subsequently. A single pair bred on Walland Marsh in 1908, while in the Stodmarsh area breeding was first reported in 1934, with a population of up to 25 pairs in the early 1940s. In winter the highest numbers recorded by Harrison were 105 at Cliffe in January 1939, 100 at Stodmarsh in November 1940, and 700 on the Thames near Higham in the severe weather of February 1947.

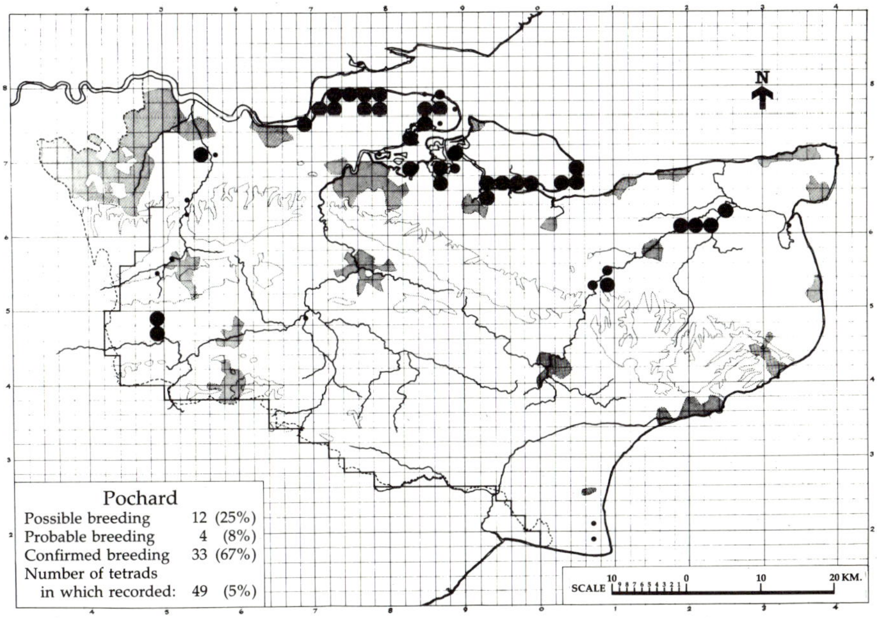

The breeding population has continued to expand, apparently reaching a ceiling in the 1960s, when the maximum number on the North Kent Marshes was probably about 60 pairs. In the main breeding areas on the Thames marshes there were peaks of 20 pairs at Stoke in 1956 and 28 pairs between Cliffe and St. Mary's Bay in 1965, but there was apparently a general shift from Stoke towards Cooling in the late 1960s. On Sheppey, breeding was first recorded in 1956, reaching a peak of 24 pairs in 1964. On the south side of the Swale there are records from 1961, and part of a subsequent decrease on Sheppey can be explained by the regular presence of six pairs at Murston since then. On the Medway up to six pairs have bred regularly on Chetney since 1961, with up to four pairs at Kingsnorth since 1969 and two pairs on Barksore since 1971. In the Stodmarsh area there have been reports of 12–18 pairs in some years, although there is no evidence that more than seven pairs have actually bred in any one year. Elsewhere single pairs have bred at four inland sites during the 1970s, but there are no recent reports from Walland Marsh.

The accompanying table shows how winter flocks have spread to all suitable freshwater sites. The wintering population has increased from an average of 400 in the mid-fifties to over 1,900 in the mid-seventies.

	First season	Mean winter peak	Normal maximum
Cliffe Pools		354	730
Fordwich/Stodmarsh		137	350
Leybourne/New Hythe	1953/54	116	350
Grain/Kingsnorth	1955/56	115	165
Capel/Windmill	1958/59	85	200
Dungeness Pits	1959/60	229	450
Sevenoaks	1962/63	44	65
Stonar (Sandwich)	1962/63	46	125
Bough Beech	1969/70	154	385
Bewl Bridge	1975/76	475	700

Major wintering flocks of Pochard 1952/53–1976/77

During the 1970s peak numbers have tended to occur in November, and the largest flock ever recorded in the county of 1,000 occurred at Dungeness in November 1974. Elsewhere the maximum was 950 on the Thames at Cliffe in the severe weather of February 1963. On the breeding fleets of the North Kent Marshes peak numbers usually occur in March, and there was an exceptional flock of 360 at Stoke in March 1962.

Relatively few Pochard have been seen on passage, by far the largest numbers involving 100 flying up the Swale at Shellness on 31st October 1963 and 90 flying up the Thames at Cliffe on 11th November 1971.

Ring-necked Duck

Aythya collaris

Very rare vagrant.

The first Kent record was an adult drake at Stodmarsh on 9th April 1972. [Spring records on inland waters in Britain and Ireland have been almost annual since 1959, and there were three other Kent records in 1977; all adult drakes, two in spring and one in autumn. Eds.]

Ferruginous Duck

Aythya nyroca

Very rare vagrant.

There are just three confirmed sight records, all involving drakes. A first-winter bird at Dungeness from 8th November–4th December 1960, an adult at Leybourne on 8th December 1968, and an adult at Bough Beech on 3rd November 1974.

Because of the identification problems caused by *Aythya* hybrids, the five records in Harrison can no longer be definitely assigned to this species. Since 1968, five hybrids have been reported from the Stour Valley, Leybourne and Cliffe.

Tufted Duck

Aythya fuligula

Locally common resident and winter visitor.

A considerable increase in numbers, at all times of the year, has taken place during the 25 years under review. This is a continuation of the events described by Harrison, who recorded that the then-new pits at Cliffe had produced exceptional counts of 105 in January 1939 and 500 in February 1947, while there were isolated breeding records of single pairs at Stodmarsh in 1935, Sevenoaks in 1936 and Tonbridge in 1950. The lack of natural lakes in Kent means that this steady increase can be attributed largely to the provision of man-made sites.

Regular breeding occurred first at various sites in the west of the county. Single pairs bred at Penshurst in 1952, Chevening in 1954 and Sevenoaks again in 1958, with between five and 14 pairs at Leigh from 1957–63. Significant new colonisations included the first breeding on Sheppey in 1962 and at Stoke and Leybourne in 1964, with regular breeding along the Darent Valley from 1965, at Sevenoaks from 1966, the Thames marshes from 1967, Dungeness Reserve from 1968, Bough Beech from 1969, Chilham from 1972 and Walland Marsh from 1974. All these areas now regularly hold three–eight pairs, with up to 13 pairs at Sevenoaks and Dungeness, while one or two pairs also breed at several other small freshwater sites. These records show a rapid expansion from

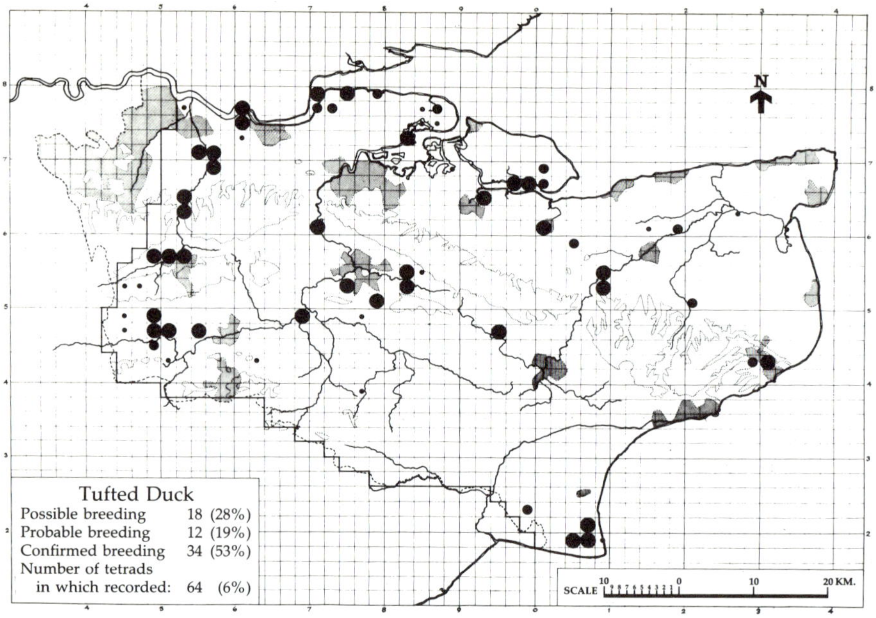

none in the early 1950s to a regular breeding population of about 70 pairs by the early 1970s.

Apparently there is also a larger population of non-breeding pairs and during the 1970s there were counts of 22 pairs at Leeds, 26 pairs on Dungeness Reserve, 18 pairs between Fordwich and Stodmarsh, and 35 pairs between Chilham and Chartham.

The accompanying table shows how winter flocks have spread to new and existing freshwater lakes and gravel pits. The winter population has increased from about 300 in the mid-1950s to over 1,500 in the mid-1970s.

	First season	Mean winter peak	Normal maximum
Cliffe Pools		392	800
Fordwich/Stodmarsh		55	150
Sevenoaks	1961/62	67	120
Leybourne/New Hythe	1962/63	86	215
Sundridge	1964/65	51	85
Dungeness Pits	1964/65	149	300
Grain/Kingsnorth	1968/69	74	150
Bough Beech	1969/70	147	220
Stonar (Sandwich)	1969/70	56	100
Chilham	1969/70	46	80
Bewl Bridge	1975/76	240	300

Major wintering flocks of Tufted Duck 1952/53–1976/77

The largest single flock of 1,300 occurred on the Thames near Cliffe Pools in February 1963, during almost arctic conditions, and the highest count for Stodmarsh also occurred at that time.

The moult migration of drakes is a recent phenomenon which was first observed at Sevenoaks. Between 1972–76 the average August population in the county totalled 415 birds, most of which were in three flocks averaging 75 at Sevenoaks, 110 at Bough Beech and 155 at Dungeness. Those at Sevenoaks and Bough Beech are known to contain almost 80% adult drakes, which use the waters as moulting areas.

Scaup

Aythya marila

Winter visitor in variable numbers.

Though recorded in all months, the Scaup is essentially a winter visitor, most prevalent in severe weather. Harrison describes exceptional cold weather numbers of 800–1,000 at Sandwich Bay in 1940, about 110 off the south coast in 1939, with flocks of around 50 in north Kent in January/February 1939 and 1947.

Although most Kent Scaup probably originate in N.W. Europe, the only ringing recovery, at Whitstable in February 1940, was of one ringed in Iceland on 26th June 1939.

The North Kent Marshes are generally the most favoured wintering grounds, the main areas being Cliffe Pools, the shallow reaches of the eastern Swale, the sheltered creeks of the south Medway, and Kingsnorth settling lagoons on the north Medway. The latter have already been virtually back-filled and Cliffe Pools partly so, thus Scaup are likely to decrease in these two localities. Small flocks are recorded occasionally offshore around Thanet, Sandwich Bay and Dungeness, though the peak numbers there in the early 1970s mainly occurred on the gravel pits.

Numbers in the three severe winters of 1953/54, 1955/56 and 1962/63 were sufficiently exceptional to be worth recording more fully. In 1953/54 at least 400 were present in late January and early February, with 300 remaining until mid-March. The movement of flocks between the Thames and Thanet made the overall numbers difficult to ascertain, but there were counts of 300 at Swalecliffe and 50 off Thanet in February, 250 at Cliffe in March, but only 10 at Dungeness. In 1955/56 the influx was almost entirely confined to north Kent, with 550 on Cliffe Pools from 12th February, and 150 still present in late March. Elsewhere the peak was only 17 off Deal and Minnis Bay. In 1962/63 the numbers were larger and the flocks more widespread, with 120 off Dungeness from late December, and peak counts of 700 at Cliffe and 400 at Ramsgate in January, 80 in the Medway in February, and 30–60 on the Thames, in the Swale, off Reculver and Herne Bay, and at Sandwich Bay.

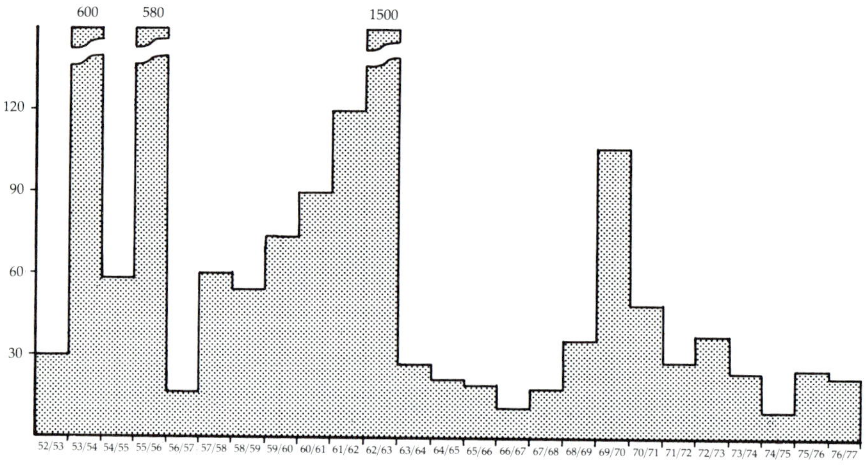

Winter totals of Scaup

The winter visitors have usually departed by early April, but occasionally a few stragglers linger into May, while in 1956 one drake stayed until 5th June. There is little evidence of passage, but groups of three flew east off Dungeness on 10th April 1976 and 12th April 1968. The first winter visitors are usually seen in October or early November. A flock of 300 at Shellness on 31st October 1963 was unprecedented.

The Scaup is relatively scarce inland, though it has occurred annually since 1968. Most records are from Sevenoaks and Bough Beech, where there were five on 14th April 1973. There is a remarkable total of 11 late summer records from these two localities since 1972, between 22nd June–9th September, the majority being adult drakes, including a party of six at Sevenoaks on 8th August 1976. In coastal localities there have been about 20 summer records since 1952, between 11th June–22nd September, including an exceptional flock of 32, mostly drakes, off Shellness on 29th August 1954.

Eider

Somateria mollissima

Passage migrant and winter visitor, smaller numbers occurring in summer.

Ticehurst regarded the Eider as a very rare visitor to the estuaries and seacoast of Kent, but Harrison recorded an increase during the forties, with up to 13 wintering at Sandwich Bay in 1949.

Since 1952 the Eider has been reported regularly, all the year round, records reaching a peak in the period 1958–69, when it was not unusual for flocks of 30–80 to spend two-three months wintering in the Swale, or off Thanet. There were peak counts of 109 in February–March 1958 and 150 in January–February 1963 off Thanet, with the largest flock of 206 in the Swale on 3rd January 1964. About 50 also wintered in the Medway in early 1962 and 1963. Although Eiders still occur regularly in winter, the numbers are lower, with only occasional reports of 30–50.

There is a fairly regular spring passage in April and early May, when day-totals of up to 65 have been seen at Dungeness, while at the same season there are isolated records of 150 off Thanet between 2nd–7th May 1960 and 100 in the Swale on 18th April 1968.

This species is least often recorded during June–September, though flocks of 30–40 have been seen, some spending most or all of this summer period in the mouth of the Swale, or off Thanet and Sandwich Bay.

In autumn migrant flocks of 30–70 have been seen all round the coast, with the peak passage in November. This is the only time of year when good numbers are reported in the Thames.

The only inland record is of six at Sevenoaks on 2nd January 1963, during the severe weather.

King Eider

Somateria spectabilis

Very rare vagrant.

A first winter drake was identified off Shellness, Sheppey on 27th December 1955.

Long-tailed Duck

Clangula hyemalis

Regular winter visitor and passage migrant in small numbers.

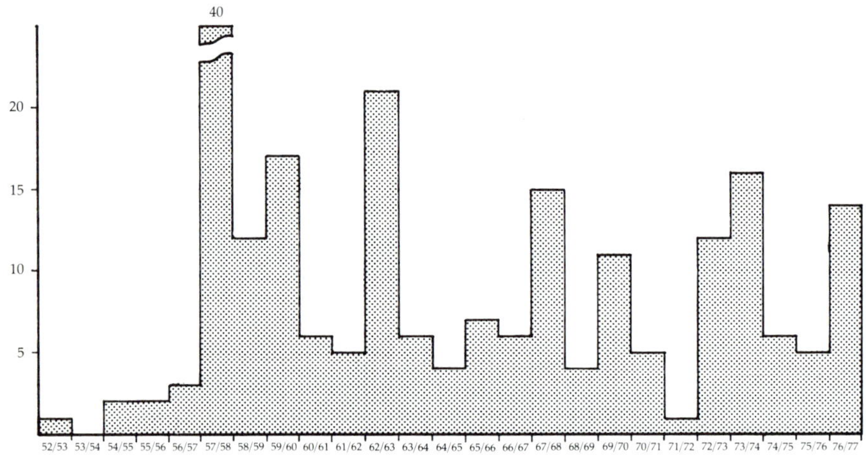

Winter totals of Long-tailed Ducks

Although the majority of records refer to ones and twos around the coast, there are several reports of larger parties. The largest influx occurred in October–November 1957, when there were 14 records totalling 30 birds, including parties of five and seven on the Thames on 9th and 23rd November respectively. Other large parties on the Thames included six on 15th March 1959, eight on 7th November 1959 and seven on 11th December 1962, while off Dungeness there were seven on 28th March 1970.

	J	F	M	A	M	J	J	A	S	O	N	D
Number of records	27	9	7	12	2	2				23	53	18
Number of birds	40	11	19	14	2	2				25	100	27

Monthly distribution of Long-tailed Ducks 1952–76

The table shows that numbers are greatest between October and January, with the autumn migration, from mid-October to the end of November, providing the bulk of the records. Apart from singles on the 4th and 6th October, there are no others earlier than the 19th of that month.

The Thames and Swale estuaries and the Dungeness area account for over 75% of all records. Those seen over the sea usually refer to single dates, although two wintered on the Medway off Motney Hill between 19th November 1971–11th March 1972. Those birds that occur on lakes or pits near the coast frequently remain for long periods. There was a pair on the ARC pit at Dungeness between 20th November 1970–31st May 1971 and one there from 28th October 1971–12th May 1972. Another bird, which arrived at Grain on 30th October 1976, eventually stayed there until 13th July 1977, the only record for that month. Both the June records refer to Dungeness, with one on the pits between 20th–29th June 1965 and one flying east at sea on 1st June 1974.

Inland, singles have been recorded at Leigh, Sundridge and Bough Beech on six occasions, all arriving between 11th–28th November, and staying for periods of up to 15 days.

Common Scoter

Melanitta nigra

Numerous passage migrant, with smaller numbers in winter and summer.

Harrison wrote of several thousand wintering on the east and south coasts of the county, particularly west of Dungeness in Rye Bay. He also cited records of 1,000 at Reculver in winter and 2,000 off Dymchurch on 1st July 1938.

There was obviously a marked change in status at the beginning of the period under review, and these large summer and winter flocks no longer occur. The only records which give any reflection of past numbers are of up to 2,000 in Rye Bay in the last quarter of 1952, while at Dungeness flocks of 3,000 and 1,200 flew west on 5th July 1956, followed by a total of 2,600 the next day.

Nowadays any winter count exceeding 100 is noteworthy and flocks of 150 in the Thames, 250 at Herne Bay, 500 at Ramsgate and 250 at Hythe in the hard weather of early 1963, represent a particularly good winter. In this context a flock of 1,000 off Sandwich Bay on 19th–20th December 1965 was quite exceptional.

By far the largest numbers are now seen on spring passage, flying up-Channel past Dungeness, where counts over 1,000 occur on several dates each spring between 18th March–7th May. A period of adverse weather often precipitates a sudden surge of movement, as soon as the wind shifts to southerly, either in bright clear weather, or when it is wet and windy, as with the arrival of a warm front. The peak number recorded under such conditions was 8,000 in three hours on 17th April 1962. A comparable spring passage occurs at Cap Gris Nez on the French coast, but in autumn these large numbers migrate exclusively down the French side of the Channel.

The population reaches it's lowest level in June and such flocks that do occur in that month are usually seen in the Dungeness area, with a maximum of 250 off Lade in 1965. Numbers show an increase between July–September, and the peak flock sizes in these three months are 500, 750 and 900 respectively, on the north coast between Thanet and Sheppey.

This species is most generally widespread and numerous round the Kent coast on autumn passage and flocks of up to 750 are fairly regular in October–November. The largest numbers occur on the north coast in NE winds, either in poor visibility, or in strong winds, with peaks of 1,200 at both Allhallows on 9th November 1957 and Shellness on 12th October 1965. At this time of year up to 600 have been seen on the Thames as far up-river as Cliffe.

There are inland records for every month except December, one-third of them in April and most of the remainder being between July–November. All but two of the 27 records have occurred since 1969, when the new reservoir at Bough Beech became the largest inland water in Kent. Elsewhere, there are only four records for Leybourne/New Hythe, two each at Sevenoaks and Sundridge, and one at Stodmarsh. The largest parties were four at Stodmarsh on 18th April 1964, while at Bough Beech there were four on 1st June 1969, five on 11th May 1970 and seven on 30th April 1976. The two parties in April coincided with the peak spring passage of several thousand birds offshore at Dungeness.

Velvet Scoter

Melanitta fusca

Passage migrant and occasional winter visitor.

Large flocks used to winter, and Harrison writes of an increase earlier this century, giving details of up to 6,000 scoter in Rye Bay in the winter of 1934/35, *of which about half were this species*! Such large numbers are unheard of today, when any count in double-figures warrants special interest. It would be particularly interesting to know the reason for this change.

During 1952–76 there were only 48 records of 10 or more, of which 30 were in the Dungeness area and 18 between Sandwich Bay and Allhallows. Over 75% were on spring or autumn passage and the rest in winter. There are relatively few records for June–September.

The main autumn migration lasts from mid-October to late November and is especially marked along the north coast in NE gales, with peaks of 55 and 29 off Herne Bay on 10th and 11th November 1962.

In the freezing winter of 1956, parties of 20–30 were present in the Swale and off Thanet and Sandwich Bay, between 28th February–10th March. Normally, however, relatively few remain through the winter months and a peak count of 36 off the Wicks on 12th February 1966 was an isolated record.

Regular seawatching at Dungeness in recent years has shown that this species is most numerous on spring passage, with day-totals of up to 47 in April and 65 in May, and a maximum of 165 on 12th May 1974. It is worth noting that the numbers occurring off the Kent coast are insignificant compared with those that migrate along the French side of the Channel, both in spring and autumn.

Inland, the Velvet Scoter is very rare, and records are restricted to singles seen at Leybourne on 6th March 1965, Sundridge on 8th January and Hever on 26th November 1972, and Bough Beech between 22nd–30th November 1975.

Goldeneye

Bucephala clangula

Winter visitor.

There has been no apparent change in status, and by far the most important wintering area is still the network of creeks in the Medway Estuary, particularly Stangate, Half Acre and East Hoo Creeks. The three other regular wintering sites, Cliffe Pools, Dungeness gravel pits and Bough Beech reservoir are all recently man-made. Bewl Bridge reservoir, too, is likely to become a regular wintering haunt.

The population in the Medway varies little, with an average of 57 between 1952–76, including 100 and 107 in 1971 and 1974. However, even larger numbers occurred in Half Acre Creek in the hard winters of 1956 and 1963, with peaks of 154 on 27th February and 131 on 23rd

February respectively. At Cliffe, Dungeness and Bough Beech, the average winter totals between 1972–76 were 15, 16 and 11 respectively, thus giving a normal winter population of 100 at these four principal localities.

Elsewhere round the coast the Goldeneye's preference for sheltered creeks makes it a scarce visitor, except perhaps in the Swale, where up to 25 have been seen, and at Sandwich, where up to 11 may occur, either offshore or on Stonar Lake.

This species may occur on any suitable inland water, and is recorded almost annually at Sevenoaks, Leybourne/New Hythe and in the Stour Valley, with occasional counts of up to six and unusual peaks of 14 at Westbere in February 1956 and 18 at New Hythe in March 1969.

The mean departure date is 17th April, though in four years since 1971 one or two have stayed until early May. Apart from occasional pricked birds, the only genuine summering record concerns a drake on the ARC pit at Dungeness in 1975, which stayed to moult and was still present in September. A drake was also seen on Windmill Creek on 4th August 1961 and one or two were present on the Oppen pits at Dungeness from 17th August 1956 into November, but there are no other records for June–September. The mean date for autumn arrivals is 21st October, with the earliest on 1st October 1971.

Smew

Mergus albellus

Scarce annual winter visitor, larger parties occurring in hard winters.

Harrison considered the Smew to be an irregular winter visitor, usually in very small numbers, and gives peaks of 17 at Yalding in 1940 and 10 in the Medway in 1947.

The highest numbers have occurred, as would be expected, in severe winters, with the peak consistently in January and February. One at Cliffe on 29th October 1974 was exceptionally early. There have been November records in just six years, and no autumn records at all in five years. A few wintering birds remain into March and in eight years there have been records of one–three during April, with the latest on the 20th on three occasions. Some of these, particularly those seen flying up-Channel off Dungeness, presumably refer to migrants. An adult drake at Fordwich on 17th May 1956 was probably sick or injured.

The most-frequented localities are Cliffe Pools and the lakes between Fordwich and Stodmarsh, while small numbers are now occurring

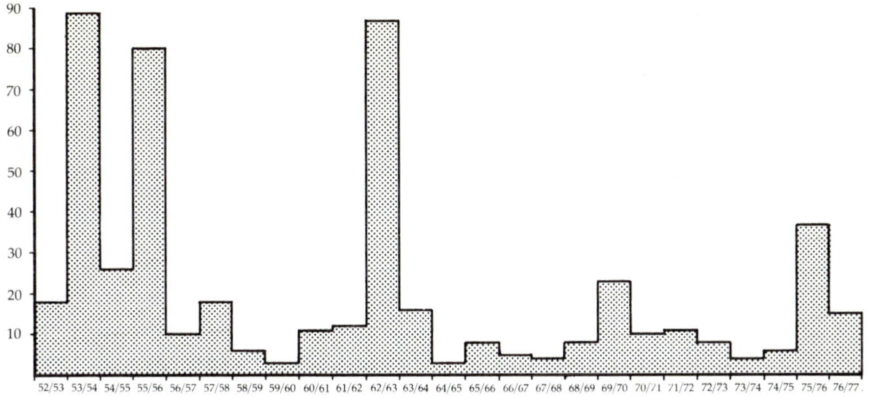

Winter totals of Smew

regularly on the Dungeness gravel pits, at Sevenoaks and Bough Beech reservoir. In hard winters small parties may occur anywhere on unfrozen coastal waters and inland lakes.

In 1953/54 the peak numbers occurred between 30th January–22nd February. On the Stour there were 14 at Sandwich on 30th January, while at Stodmarsh there were 21, including 15 adult drakes on 14th February and 30, including eight adult drakes on the 21st. At Cliffe there were 17, including four adult drakes between 13th–19th February. In 1955/56 the influx occurred in early February. There were several flocks of 8–12, with the largest flock of 35 at Cliffe on 4th February, which included an exceptional number of 28 adult drakes. In 1962/63 the first birds arrived in late December, with seven at Westbere on the 31st. During January–February parties of 8–12 were seen at Cliffe, Greenborough, Leybourne, Tonbridge and Sevenoaks. Since that winter numbers have been particularly low, with a peak of 10 at Dungeness on 5th January 1970 and a small influx from 31st January 1976, with up to five at eight different localities, six at Cliffe and another 10 at Dungeness.

Adult drakes are rare in normal winters and usually comprise only a quarter of the total in hard winters. Thus a flock of 12, flying over the Thames at Cliffe on 22nd December 1957, was most unusual.

Red-breasted Merganser

Mergus serrator

Regular winter visitor and passage migrant.

Harrison stated that the Swale was the most frequented wintering area and also cites an exceptional record of about 200 off Sandgate on 29th February 1940.

The main wintering areas are the three estuaries in the north of the county. The table below shows an overall decrease of 56% during the period under review, a decrease most evident on the Thames, which is apparently unsuitable as a wintering area, and where most peak counts now refer to autumn passage migrants. The Swale is still the most favoured estuary.

	1952/53–1963/64		1964/65–1975/76	
	Mean Winter Peaks	Max.	Mean Winter Peaks	Max.
Thames	54	180	12	39
Medway	29	60	25	58
Swale	104	155	46	100

Red-breasted Merganser numbers in north Kent

Peaks of 100–180 were recorded in two winters on the Thames at Cliffe Pools, and in seven winters on the Swale until 1964/65, since when there have been no flocks greater than 60. The largest numbers occurred in the severe winter of 1955/56, with 180 on the Thames, 24 on the Medway and 120 on the Swale.

Flocks of up to 40 have been seen from the mouth of the Swale eastwards to Reculver, while elsewhere round the east and south coasts, small flocks of up to 20 occur occasionally during the winter months.

This species is not normally recorded between May–September, although there are seven–ten records for each of the months of June, July and August. Most wintering birds arrive during November–December and leave during February–March.

Recent close study of the spring seabird passage of Dungeness has shown this species to be most numerous between late March and early May, with a peak total of 540 in the spring of 1976. Daily totals of 50–110 have been recorded between 30th March–1st May, and passage tends to be most concentrated in the second and third weeks of April.

Inland records are unusual, totalling less than thirty during 1952–76. Most of these are from the Stour Valley inland to Ashford, the Medway Valley, Bough Beech and Sevenoaks. By far the largest numbers of

Mergansers occurred in the severe winters. Between 18th February–22nd March 1956 there were four at East Peckham, nine at Mote Park and eight at Leybourne, while in January 1963 at least six were seen at Sevenoaks.

Goosander

Mergus merganser

Annual winter visitor and passage migrant in variable numbers.

There has been no apparent change in status this century. The only record of large numbers quoted by Harrison referred to 30, including 10 adult drakes, at Stodmarsh in February 1942.

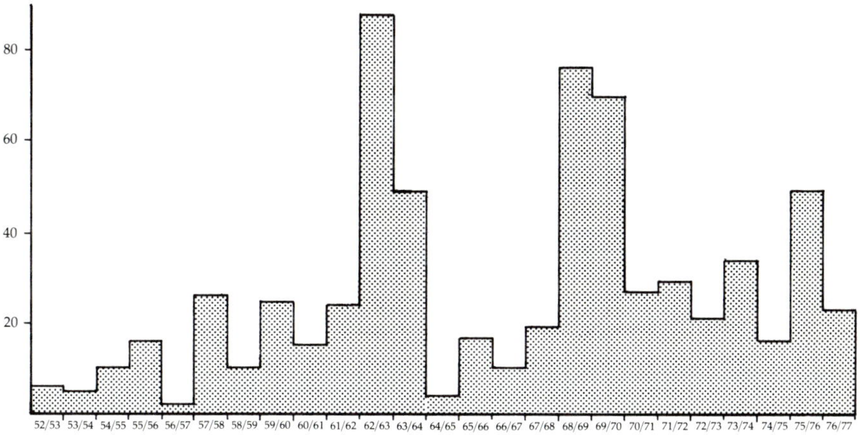

Winter totals of Goosander

There has been an average of 25 birds each winter, with the peak numbers in the severe winter of 1962/63, when there was a total of 88, including flocks of 10 at Dungeness and 32 at Sevenoaks in the last week of December. The total of 76 in the winter of 1968/69 included flocks of 10 at Stodmarsh and 22 at Dungeness, either side of the New Year. The total of 70 in the following winter included a passage of 14 birds during 26th November–2nd December, while good numbers present later on included a flock of 21 at Dungeness on 6th January 1970.

Apart from singles on 5th October 1958 and 11th October 1952, there are no other reports earlier than the 22nd of that month. In some years, as suggested above, there is a noticeable passage during November–December, when small parties have been seen arriving on the north and east coasts, although the maximum was 14 arriving at Shellness on 31st October 1963.

The main wintering sites are the pits at Dungeness and inland waters in the west of the county, although parties of more than 10 have not appeared in any winters other than the three detailed above.

Numbers usually decrease rapidly during February–March, and in some years there is a tiny return passage during March–April. There have been only four May records, all in 1955 and 1956, with the latest on 22nd May 1956.

Ruddy Duck

Oxyura jamaicensis

Rare winter visitor.

The first county record was a duck or immature drake at Bough Beech from 7th–17th November 1970. One was seen at Dungeness from 8th December 1974–23rd February 1975, another at Bough Beech from 28th November 1976 and a fourth at Mote Park on 31st December 1976.

[This species is colonising southern England from breeding stock, probably originating as escapes from the Wildfowl Trust's collection at Slimbridge, thus records may be expected to increase. Four birds were present in both January and December 1977. Eds.]

Honey Buzzard

Pernis apivorus

Rare passage migrant.

Ticehurst noted a marked immigration in the autumn of 1881, but otherwise considered the Honey Buzzard a rare visitor. There has been little change in this status, except that sightings have become more regular in recent years.

Three individuals were seen between 1953–55, but there were no more records until 1966. Since then 15 have been reported in eight of the eleven years, with maxima of four birds in 1968 and three in 1976. The extreme dates for the spring and autumn passage are 18th May–18th June and 3rd July–10th October respectively. The monthly occurrences of the 18 birds seen during the period under review are as follows:

J	F	M	A	M	J	J	A	S	O	N	D
				3	5	2	2	5	1		

One, killed by flying into overhead wires at Leysdown in July 1973, had been ringed as a nestling on 6th August 1967 in Schleswig Holstein, West Germany.

Black Kite

Milvus migrans

Very rare vagrant.

It was not until 8th May 1976 that this species was first recorded in Kent, when a single bird, being harassed by a Carrion Crow, flew north over Luddesdown.

Red Kite

Milvus milvus

Rare vagrant.

Ticehurst writes of the Red Kite breeding in Kent until the beginning of the nineteenth century and mentions a number of individuals shot, but there are no records for the first half of this century.

One at Grove Ferry on 27th May 1953 was the first of 13 records in recent years, and the monthly distribution is as follows:

J	F	M	A	M	J	J	A	S	O	N	D
		1	1	2	1		2	1	2	2	1

Two of the early spring records were at Dungeness, four occurred at Sandwich Bay, with others at Stodmarsh, Canterbury, Bough Beech and East Malling. The extreme dates are 13th March–21st June and 13th August–21st December.

One, found dead on the railway line near Wrotham on 13th August 1970, had been ringed as a nestling in mid-Wales in June of that year. A second immature was found dead in Eastwell Park in September 1972.

White-tailed Eagle

Haliaeetus albicilla

A scarce winter visitor in the nineteenth century, when Ticehurst was able to locate records of about 30 birds. It has only been recorded twice this century, according to Harrison, one being shot at Surrenden Dering on 29th October 1920, and a second killed near Dover on 7th March 1932.

Marsh Harrier

Circus aeruginosus

Annual passage migrant in increasing numbers. Occasionally present during winter and summer.

This species was a casual visitor to Kent according to Ticehurst, with few records in the nineteenth century. Harrison suggests that numbers appear to have increased during the first half of this century, although until the 1950s, even though an almost annual visitor, it was by no means as common as it is today. However, the only breeding records for the county occurred within this period. In 1942 a pair nested successfully on Preston marshes and in 1946 another pair attempted to breed on the Stour marshes, but had their eggs taken.

Numbers in the 1950s were generally rather higher than in subsequent years, with more summering birds and larger numbers in autumn. In 1954 two summered on Walland Marsh, with up to three there in August–September. Up to three were also present on the Thames and Sheppey marshes in other autumns.

Spring passage usually takes place between late April and early June and typically involves about five records of single birds. However, in 1975 and 1976 the spring passage was far heavier than in any previous years. In 1975 there were up to three at Stodmarsh and four at Sandwich Bay, with two on the Thames marshes, which subsequently summered. The spring total involved about sixteen different birds, while in 1976 the total was about eleven, including one which summered on Sheppey.

Autumn passage usually lasts from late July – late September and it is not uncommon for birds to spend most or all of this period feeding in one area, particularly on Sheppey, where up to three can be seen in many autumns. Ones and twos are also more frequently reported than in spring from the Thames marshes, Stodmarsh, Sandwich Bay and the Dungeness area. Occasionally stragglers are recorded in October and November.

Winter records are sparse, with one–two present during sixteen December–January periods. All the records concern singles, with the majority in the Stour Valley and on Sheppey, and on Walland Marsh during the early 1950s.

Inland records away from the Stour Valley and Walland Marsh are rare. Singles have been seen at Leybourne and over Stockbury in January, over Bough Beech reservoir in two consecutive years during May, over Tonbridge in mid-July and along the Medway near Tonbridge in late November.

Hen Harrier

Circus cyaneus

Regular passage migrant and winter visitor.

The Hen Harrier nested in Kent up to the last half of the nineteenth century, when it was an irregular and infrequent autumn and winter visitor according to Ticehurst.

It is only since the middle of this century that autumn and winter numbers have increased so that it can now be classed as a regular passage migrant and an almost common winter visitor in suitable areas, notably Sheppey, the Thames marshes and Stour Valley. Adult males have always been far less common than ring-tails.

In most recent winters there have been four birds on Sheppey and one or two each on the Thames and Medway marshes, at Reculver, Stodmarsh and Sandwich Bay, and in the Dungeness area, thus giving a normal winter population of about twelve birds. However, these numbers can fluctuate and four wintered on the Thames marshes in 1975/76. In addition the occasional discovery of roosts has shown that the total numbers present in any one particular area can be larger than would be detected by normal daytime observations. Between 1953–55 there was a regular roost of up to six on Walland Marsh, which rather surprisingly consisted of two–four males and only two females. [Other roosts of similar size have been discovered on Sheppey and at Stodmarsh since 1977, while the Walland roost was reoccupied in 1978. Eds.]

Between 1952–55 there were a number of spring records as late as 28th May and autumn records as early as 15th August. In retrospect these dates are exceptional when compared with more recent records, as the final spring dates are usually in the last week of April. Stragglers have been seen in May and there was an unusually late bird at Sandwich Bay on 24th–25th May 1975. The first autumn migrants are seen during the last two weeks of September and the first week of October, but on 25th August 1965 an immature was already present on Sheppey. The only summer record in recent times refers to an adult male at Windmill Creek on 2nd July 1961.

Montagu's Harrier

Circus pygargus

Passage migrant in very small numbers, now rarely recorded during the summer months.

There are a number of records of what appear to be wintering birds prior to 1952, although confusion with the previous species seems to be a possibility. Ticehurst records this species as breeding regularly in the marshes of north Kent, the open parts of Blean Woods, on the North Downs and probably on Romney Marsh up to the end of the last century. In more recent times Harrison cites three breeding records, at Adisham in 1945 and 1949 and at Cottington Court in 1948.

In the period under review one pair bred unsuccessfully at Sandwich Bay in 1952 and another pair was present at Stodmarsh for six weeks in 1954. In 1963 a male summered on the Swale marshes and a pair spent a month at Stodmarsh.

Between 1952–76 there were, on average, four–five records each year, with a maximum of eleven in 1964, none in 1961 and only one in 1973. The extreme dates are 4th April and 5th October, but passage is most concentrated in May and again between late July and early September.

There are a number of old records of melanistic birds, but in the last twenty-five years the only one is of a male at Sandwich Bay on 23rd–24th May 1970.

Goshawk

Accipiter gentilis

Rare vagrant.

Harrison cites five definite records and only one this century on 7th October 1950.

The true status of this species is masked by the undoubted presence of some falconers' escapes, but the following table of monthly occurrences supports the view that the Goshawk is a rare passage migrant and winter visitor to Kent:

J	F	M	A	M	J	J	A	S	O	N	D
1			2		2			1	3	2	1

Additional support comes from the location of the majority of records on the north and east coasts of the county at Northward Hill and Sandwich Bay. The 12 recent records occurred in nine years, with the majority on single dates, though there were several sightings of what was presumably the same bird at Northward Hill between 29th January–4th March 1967.

Sparrowhawk

Accipiter nisus

Rare breeding species; passage migrant and winter visitor.

Harrison considered the Sparrowhawk to be a common breeding bird in most of the wooded districts of the county, and as recently as 1946 Gillham and Homes recorded eight nests found within a mile radius of Sittingbourne.

The pattern has changed considerably in recent years. The Sparrowhawk has probably suffered more at the hands of man than any other species on the county list, and undoubtedly one of the most serious threats has been pesticide contamination during the 1950s and early 1960s, although keepering and woodland clearance will also have played a part. At this time numbers reached an all-time low and there was no confirmation of successful breeding between 1953–74, although pairs were present in various localities throughout several breeding seasons. Even during the Breeding Bird Survey, between 1967–73, probable breeding was recorded in only two tetrads and possible breeding in a further seventeen. In 1975 confirmation was at last received of six pairs nesting, successfully raising a total of 18 young. It must, however, be added that breeding information for birds of prey is often reluctantly divulged, and the picture may not be quite as black as this account suggests.

There have been almost annual records of migrant, sometimes exhausted birds observed on the coasts in autumn, and individuals have also been recorded from lightships off the Kent coast. With greater observer coverage during recent years, records have naturally increased, although some of the increase may, hopefully, be due to the better control of pesticide usage. In 1975, for instance, a good autumn passage was noted: at Sandwich Bay one–three were recorded almost daily from 11th–22nd September, with three singles again in mid-October, while at Dungeness one or two were seen on nine dates between 10th October–10th November. The earliest records of presumed migrants concern birds seen at the end of July, and passage continues through to November. Return movements are less obvious but recorded between March and May.

The Continental origin of some wintering Sparrowhawks is confirmed by several ringing recoveries. Single females ringed at Loosduinan, Holland on 28th October 1953 and 1st November 1954 were recovered at Tenterden on 12th December 1955 and near Ashford on 23rd February 1955 respectively. An adult male ringed at Assebroek, Belgium on 20th October 1966 was found dead at Snodland in January 1968.

Buzzard

Buteo buteo

An annual visitor in varying numbers in winter, spring and summer, and more numerously in autumn.

Harrison records that the Buzzard became extinct as a breeding bird in the county near the end of the eighteenth or at the beginning of the nineteenth century, but the number of summer reports in recent years suggest that it may return to breed.

Spring passage begins in March, with a slight increase in records during April, but only a few stragglers in May. These movements are small, never more than three–four birds in any year, and occasionally none, as happened between 1960–63. By comparison, the autumn passage is more regular, although numbers fluctuate between the one or two of 1962 and 1973, and up to ten, as in 1958 and 1976. Although the majority of these records come from the north and east of the county, individuals are regularly seen on passage inland.

Wintering appears to consist mainly of birds, possible cold weather wanderers, entering Kent in January, rather than of autumn birds remaining throughout. December sightings are very rare, with only seven records, all between 1952–67.

Buzzards are notoriously difficult species to identify satisfactorily, particularly at a distance, or in adverse light conditions, so unidentified buzzards are frequently reported. Over 70 have been seen in the last twenty-five years and it is probable that the majority of these relate to this species.

A bird showing the characteristics of the Steppe Buzzard *B.b. vulpinus* frequented the Reculver/Chislet area from 12th January–20th April 1975.

Rough-legged Buzzard

Buteo lagopus

Irregular winter visitor and passage migrant.

There has been little change in status, except that the invasions during the period under review have been on a larger scale.

When wintering in Kent this species has a predilection for wilder, flatter country, particularly around Dungeness, on Sheppey and on the marshes of north and east Kent, where it has been recorded taking rabbits.

In recent years there have been three unprecedented influxes during the winters of 1966/67, 1973/74 and 1974/75. There were no reports until 1957 and from then until 1976, excluding the invasion years, there have been one or two records in eight winters, with early autumn migrants on 18th August 1975 and 24th August 1957, and the latest overwintering bird remaining until 25th April 1971.

In 1966 the first arrivals were singles at Sandwich Bay on 15th and 26th October, with two at Dungeness and one at Cliffe on the 29th. On Sheppey there were five on 9th November, with two each at Dungeness, Stodmarsh and Chetney and one on the Thames marshes in November–December, bringing the total to at least 14. Six remained to winter, with the last two migrants at Dungeness on 13th April 1967.

The invasion of autumn 1973 was more spectacular, with the first bird at Cliffe on 14th October and a marked passage of 13 birds between 17th–20th October, including four at Dungeness on the 17th, three at Nagden on the 18th and two at Reculver on the 20th. On Sheppey there were eight on 8th November, while elsewhere there were only three singles, bringing the total to about 25. Only six remained to winter, with the last migrant at Reculver on 23rd April 1974.

Another large invasion in autumn 1974 started with one at Dungeness from 22nd October, followed by a marked passage of about 16 birds between 24th–27th October, including three at Sandwich Bay on the 24th, three at Dungeness on the 25th and six at Sandwich Bay on the 26th. During November there were three on Sheppey and four between Ash and Sandwich, with singles at eight other localities, bringing the total to about 32. Peaks of four on Sheppey and five at Sandwich Bay on 31st December included late passage migrants, with seven birds wintering on this occasion, a few remaining until 19th April, with an exceptionally late individual, presumably a migrant, on 24th May 1975.

Golden Eagle

Aquila chrysaetos

Very rare vagrant.

One was shot at Whitehill, Ramsgate on 6th December 1895.

The only other authenticated record concerns one that was seen well at Yantlet Lagoon on 23rd August 1964. From the plumage description it was considered to be in its third or fourth year.

Osprey

Pandion haliaetus

Regular passage migrant.

Harrison records this species as an irregular autumn visitor with even fewer occurrences in spring. The increase in records in recent years shown by the histogram may be linked with the re-establishment of breeding pairs in Scotland, or with changes in the northwest European population.

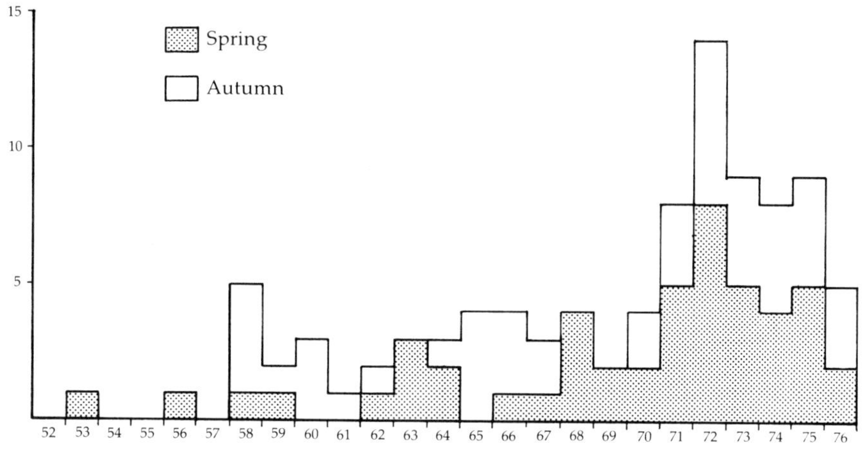

Annual totals of Ospreys

Passage usually takes place during April–May, and again in August–September. The extreme dates are 23rd March 1974 at Sevenoaks and 29th October 1964 at Leeds Castle.

Ospreys are seen most frequently at inland gravel pits and reservoirs, particularly in the west of the county in the upper reaches of the Medway valley, and only rarely on the coast. The three most frequented localities are Bough Beech, Sevenoaks and Stodmarsh/Westbere, each with an average of two birds a year during the 1970s.

Lesser Kestrel

Falco naumanni

Ticehurst records one caught near Dover in May 1877.

Kestrel

Falco tinnunculus

Widespread resident.

The Kestrel is most common in the more open areas of the county, but is also found nesting in towns and woodland. Numbers are augmented in spring, autumn and winter by Continental immigrants and birds from northern Britain.

Particularly large numbers of Kestrels were present in Kent in 1956–58 due to an abundance of Short-tailed Field Voles *Microtus agrestis*. On 17th August 1956, on Sheppey, 17 were seen in the air together and 15 were present at Sandwich Bay on 23rd September 1958.

Pesticide poisoning, which had such a disastrous effect on the British Sparrowhawk and Peregrine populations in the fifties, also took its toll on the Kestrel. There was a dramatic collapse in numbers in Kent so that by 1961 only four pairs were reported breeding. In 1962, even though records of this species were particularly requested, none was reported breeding anywhere in the county, although there were a number of records for January–April and August–December. An improvement was noted by 1964, but out of the 30 breeding-season reports only a quarter were known to have even attempted nesting. This improvement continued during the following three years and by 1968 the species had virtually re-established itself, making full use of the new motorway

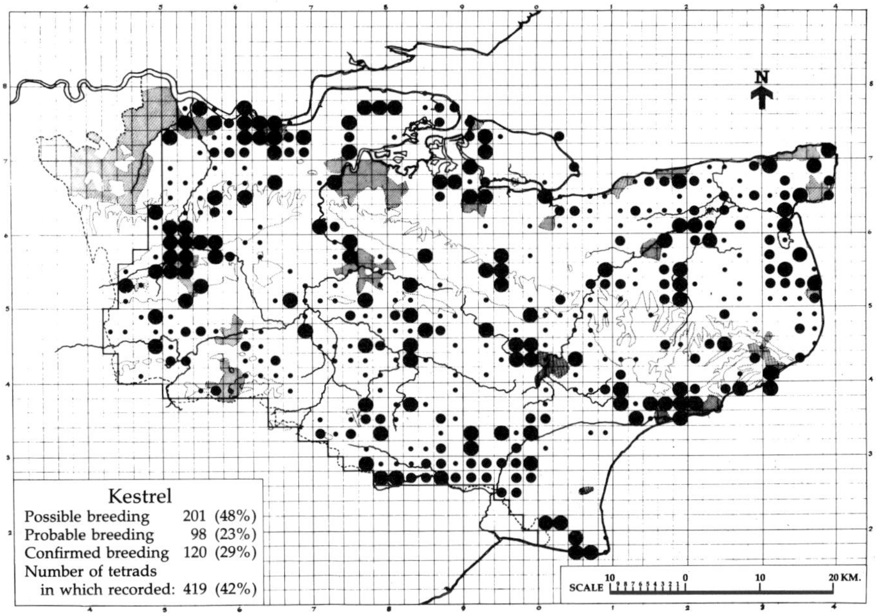

verges for feeding and exploiting urban environments for feeding and breeding.

Observations of what are considered to be passage birds continue to increase. Between late August and early October numbers at both Observatories may reach peaks of about a dozen, while singles have been seen flying west up the Thames, both in spring and autumn, and at Shellness a few are regularly seen flying south each autumn.

Ringing has produced some answers to the question of movements undertaken by this species. Most interesting is the recovery of four Dungeness birds in France, three of which were ringed as pulli. The adult was recovered furthest south, in Charente at 45° 5′N 0° 18′E. Some of the birds which enter Kent in autumn, either on passage or to winter, appear to originate from northern Europe, as shown by the recovery of three birds ringed in Belgium and one in Holland. Others originate further north in Britain (Snow, 1968).

[American Kestrel]

Falco sparverius

One present at Dungeness between 4th June 1966–19th April 1967 was remarkably tame and presumed to be an escape.

Red-footed Falcon

Falco vespertinus

Rare spring vagrant.

Ticehurst notes reliable spring records for 1862 and 1907.

During the last 25 years there have been 15 records, all of singles, with only one in autumn, an immature at Capel Fleet on 18th–19th August 1973. Of the spring records, seven fell between 1959–1964 and the other seven between 1970–1974, with no more than two in any year.

The extreme dates of the spring migrants are 17th April–10th July, with six records in the Sandwich Bay area, five around Dungeness, one at Reculver and the other two inland at Sevenoaks. Eleven of these fourteen birds arrived between 23rd May–21st June, with two in April and one in July. Six of the records refer to individual stays of seven to twenty days, with the remainder seen on one date only. Three were adult males, three immature males, and the other eight females.

Merlin

Falco columbarius

Regular winter visitor and passage migrant.

The status of this species appears to have changed little over the years.

The earliest reports usually occur during the last week of September or early October, but occasionally individuals have been seen as early as July: there are just four July–August records, all from the south of the county. An adult male was caught at Littlestone on 1st July 1958 and singles were seen in the Dungeness area on 25th July 1954, 19th and 25th August 1964 and 25th August 1963. Frequently, October produces more records than any other month, when the autumn migrants are supplemented by the wintering population. The last records usually occur in late March or early April, but there are three records for May. Singles were seen at Dungeness on 1st May 1971, at Westgate on 2nd May 1954, and at Brookland on 8th May 1964. The only later date is recorded by Gillham and Homes on 16th May 1946.

The vast majority of observations are from coastal farmland and marsh areas, notably the Thames, Medway and Sheppey Marshes, Sandwich Bay, the Stour Valley and the Dungeness Area. The normal wintering population consists of one or two birds in each of these six areas. Very few are reported from inland localities, though the Downs may well attract wintering birds.

Hobby

Falco subbuteo

Summer visitor and passage migrant, breeding occasionally.

Ticehurst considered the Hobby to be a summer visitor in small numbers, breeding irregularly. Harrison produced no confirmation of breeding, but a number of summer records suggested that pairs could have nested in the old and more secluded woodland areas of the county.

During the period under review, confirmation of breeding was received for 1967, when two pairs were successful, and in 1974 and 1975, when single pairs nested at two different localities. Pairs have summered in at least nine years since 1960, which augurs well for the future of this species as a Kentish breeding bird.

The marked increase in the number of annual records, in particular during the 1970s, is shown clearly by the following histogram.

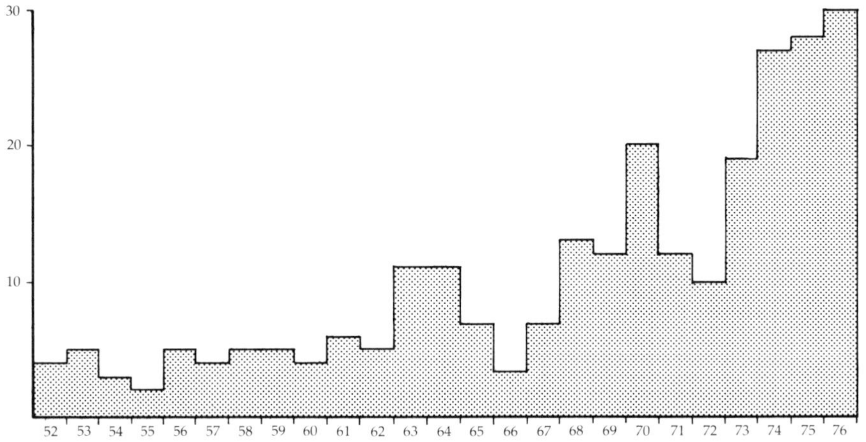

Annual totals of Hobbys

The earliest record is exceptional and concerns a female at Bedgebury on 26th February 1961, but the first arrivals do not normally appear until May. Singles on 12th and 13th April are the earliest of less than a dozen records for that month. Passage continues throughout May and into June, with peak numbers occurring between 20th–31st May. A few autumn migrants are seen in late July and early August, with a small peak in mid-September. There have been only 15 October records, eight of which occurred after the long, hot summer of 1976; all but three were before the 11th. The latest records are singles at Harty on 11th November 1955 and at Wittersham and Dungeness on 15th December 1971.

Spring migrants are occasionally seen coming in off the sea at both Dungeness and Sandwich Bay, while in 1971 there was an unusual record of a tired bird at Shellness (Sheppey) on 9th October, which rested on a mussel-bed for half an hour before flying inland.

Peregrine

Falco peregrinus

Passage migrant and rare winter visitor. Formerly bred.

In the periods covered by Ticehurst and Harrison the Peregrine bred regularly on the chalk cliffs between Kingsdown and Folkestone. There had, however, been some apparent change in status, from being an autumn visitor in the nineteenth century to becoming a regular passage migrant and winter visitor during the first half of this century. The Scandinavian origin of some of these birds was shown by the recovery of three Swedish ringed birds between 1935–1947. Nine pairs bred annually in well established eyries (see map) up to and including 1939. During the war years, when observations were discontinued, the birds were considered a hazard to carrier pigeons and were shot by order of the War Office. In 1946 only three pairs were present, two east of Dover, and all bred.

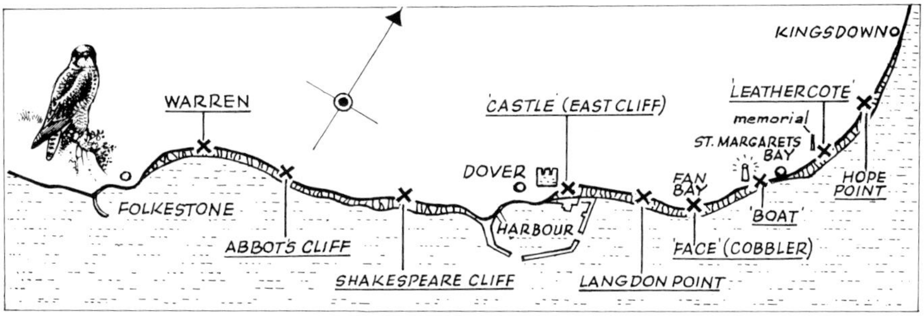

Traditional sites of Peregrine eyries

The successful breeding of three pairs continued until 1960, but in 1961 all eyries were unoccupied. This decline followed a national trend, attributed to the effects of various persistent organo-chlorine pesticides. During the same period, there was also a decline in the numbers of records of passage migrants and winter visitors. There were 20–25 annually until 1957, dropping to 12 by 1962. There were only eight records in 1963 and 1964, seven in 1967, but otherwise only two–five in the remaining years to 1976.

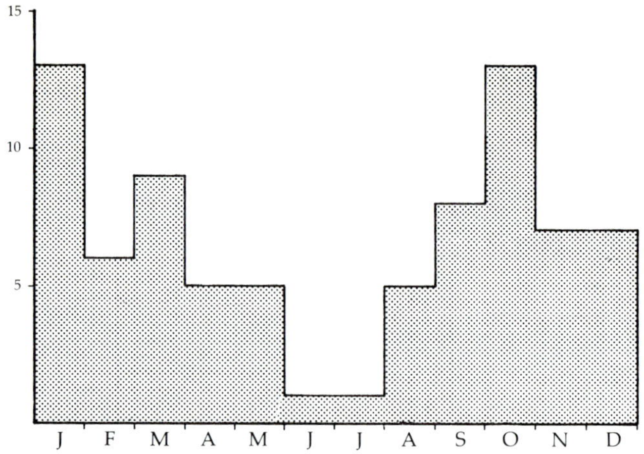

Monthly distribution of Peregrines 1961–76

Although birds do still occur in the winter months, very few now remain to overwinter. The majority of the records refer to single birds seen on or over coastal marshland, particularly in the north of the county. The Peregrine is only rarely seen inland.

Red-legged Partridge

Alectoris rufa

Resident.

The introduction of this species into Kent remains obscure. Ticehurst considered that reports along the east coast prior to 1845 might possibly refer to Continental immigrants, as the Red-legged Partridge did not become established until the latter half of the nineteenth century, and then in the northwest of the county. From there it spread southeastwards, being generally distributed by the turn of the century. However, evidence of genuine migration is thin. Harrison considered the Red-legged Partridge to be abundant, but nowhere as numerous as the Grey Partridge, except on parts of the Hoo peninsula.

Compared with the Grey Partridge the Red-legged is thinly distributed, and relatively scarce northeast of the Downs, with a noticeable absence from Sheppey and Thanet during the Breeding Survey. There are occasional reports from Thanet, and since 1973 ones and twos have been seen on Sheppey. The stronghold is still the Hoo peninsula, but the situtation there is confused by the release of game-farm stocks, including the closely related Chukar *A. chukar* and *chukar* x *rufa* hybrids. Some of these have successfully bred there in the wild.

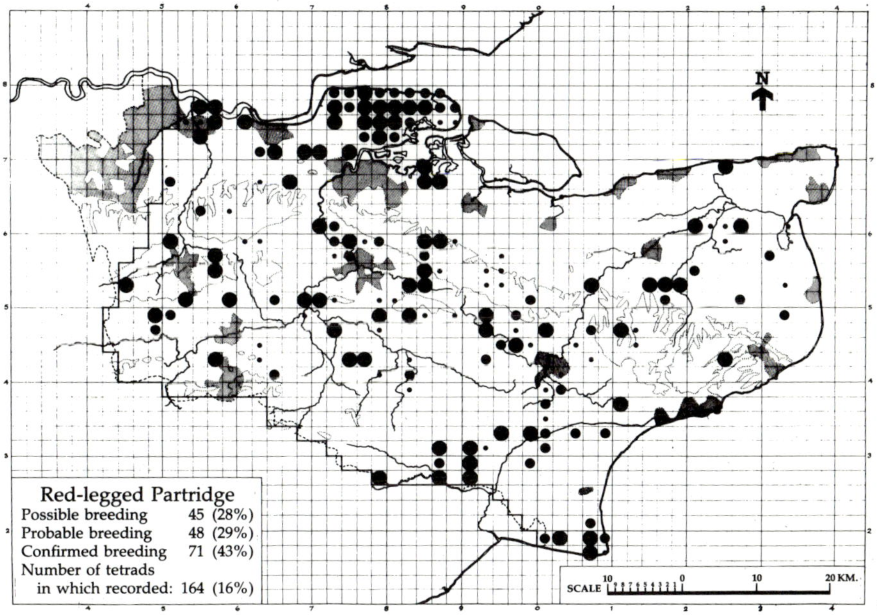

Though generally favouring drier sites, the Red-legged Partridge has spread onto parts of the Weald and into the Stour Valley. The shingle wastes of Dungeness have for many years attracted a resident population. There were 10 pairs on the Reserve there in the 1950s, but only one pair in 1963. However, there were up to four pairs again in the 1970s.

Coveys of 10–20 are most frequently recorded in the north and west of the county. The maximum counts were of 30 at Collier Street in the Weald in November 1971 and at St. Mary's Hoo in February 1975.

Grey Partridge

Perdix perdix

Widespread resident.

Ticehurst wrote of the Grey Partridge as numerous and increasing. Both he and Harrison considered the species well distributed, occurring on the upland areas and on the cultivation interspersed in the woodlands, as well as on the low-lying districts and marshlands.

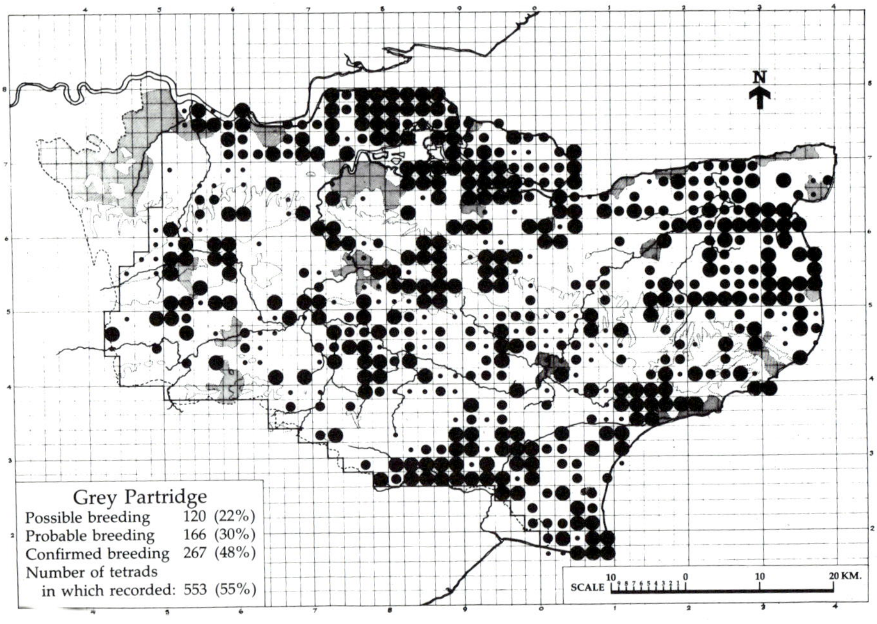

The general distribution of the Grey Partridge has probably changed little. The species shows a preference for cultivated areas, where good hedgerows and other marginal cover remain, including the most modest smallholdings and allotments. They are also to be found on open grassland and marshes, and even on sand dunes and shingle with some scrub. The apparently thin distribution along the Downs can be accounted for by poor coverage during the survey, but the absence of records in the Weald along the southwestern county boundary is difficult to explain.

Few estimates of population densities have been recorded, but it is likely that numbers have declined in Kent, as in other parts of Britain (Sharrock, 1976).

Coveys of 30–60 are occasionally reported in autumn and winter, particularly from coastal farmland, while in January 1971 and 1972 there were counts of 80 at Sandwich Bay and Elmley, and 115 at Capel Fleet. There was also an estimate of 300 on Chetney Marsh in October 1968.

Quail

Coturnix coturnix

Scarce summer visitor, breeding occasionally.

Ticehurst wrote that the Quail had bred at one time or another in every part of the county. Towards the end of the nineteenth century, the numbers declined and Harrison records only sporadic breeding, mostly in the east and south. There was an increase in reports during the 1940s, and 1947 was the first of four recent invasion years. Harrison also includes three records referring to wintering birds.

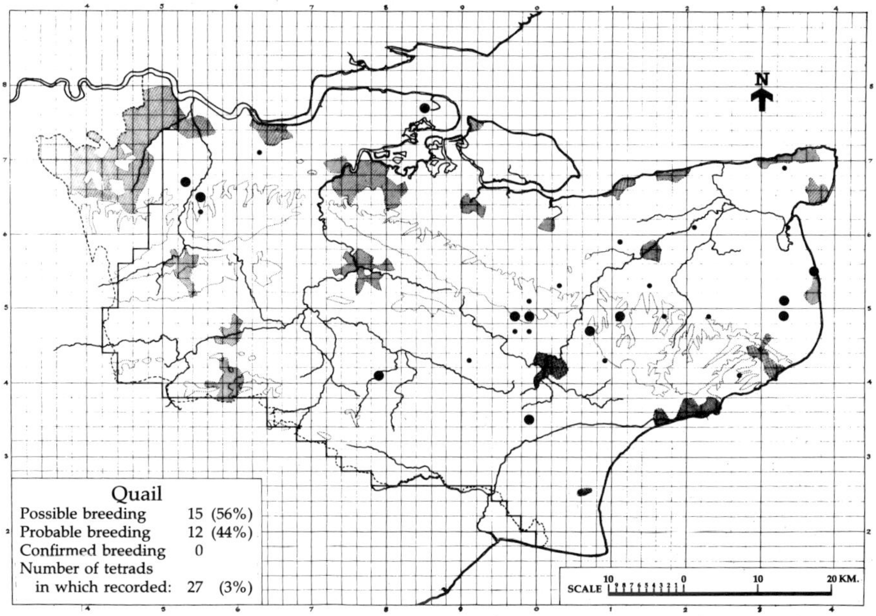

Breeding population levels are very difficult to estimate, as most recent records refer only to males calling. The map also exaggerates the annual distribution, as it includes the records for 1970, the most recent invasion year. The few records there are, however, confirm the known preference for rolling chalk downland (Sharrock, 1976) particularly between Charing and Dover.

Nesting was recorded regularly during the 1950s, even in apparently poor years when there were few records. Some localities held up to five calling males, mostly in the east of the county, and parties of four–eight were occasionally seen in autumn. The best year was 1953, when at least eight pairs probably bred in the east. Since 1959 the only definite breeding reports concern single pairs at Northward Hill in 1962 and at Stockbury in 1965, with at least five pairs nesting in the east in 1964, when autumn parties of up to six were also seen.

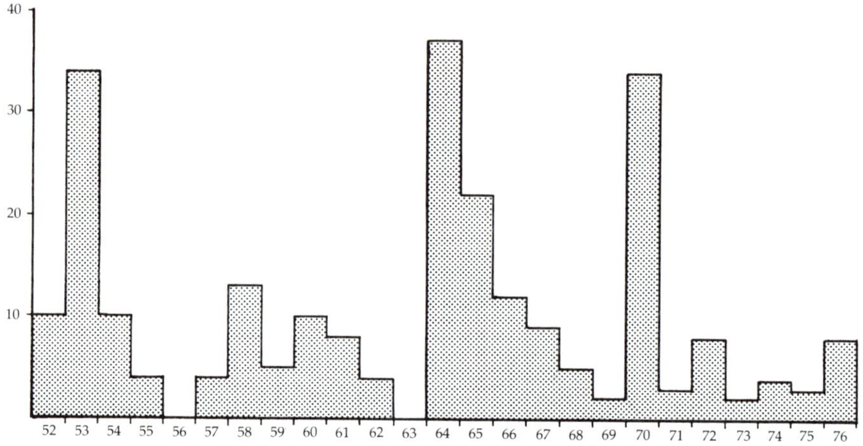

Annual totals of Quail

The histogram clearly shows the 'Quail years' and how the numbers fluctuate. The peak years involved reports from 18 different localities in 1953, 29 localities in 1964 and 17 in 1965. In 1970 there were reports from 22 localities,including three calling at both Challock and West Hougham (Dover). During a Nightingale census on the night of 23rd–24th May 1970, 18 were heard calling. Apart from three reports in the northwest, including two from the Darent Valley, the other records were again in the east of the county.

Pheasant

Phasianus colchicus

Widespread resident.

Pheasants were probably first introduced into Britain in the late eleventh century (Sharrock, 1976), though Ticehurst suggests that the Romans may have been responsible, and that the species probably became naturalised in the forests of Kent at an earlier date than in any other county. Up to the end of the eighteenth century the only race present was *P.c. colchicus* from the Caucasus, but early in the nineteenth century the Ring-necked Pheasant *P.c. torquatus* from China was introduced. Since then several other races have become acclimatised and all hybridise freely, but the white neck ring of *torquatus* is now a feature of most feral males in Kent.

Numbers are augmented annually by the large-scale release of hand reared birds, but the fairly wide distribution is much as Harrison described it.

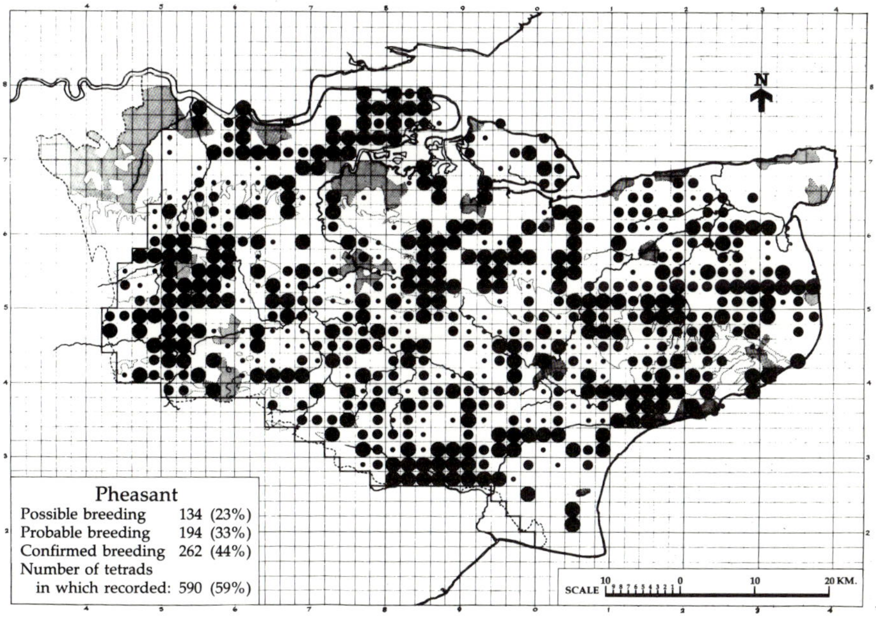

Though principally a bird of wooded agricultural land, the Pheasant occurs on wasteland with bramble or scrub cover, on marshes with small reed beds, and even neglected and overgrown gardens and allotments. It is probably genuinely absent only from Thanet, parts of the coastal marshlands, and urban areas.

Water Rail

Rallus aquaticus

Local resident, passage migrant and winter visitor.

There is little doubt that this species bred in Kent during the last century, but according to Harrison the first nest was not discovered until 1937 on the Chislet marshes. He includes several breeding records in different parts of the county since that date.

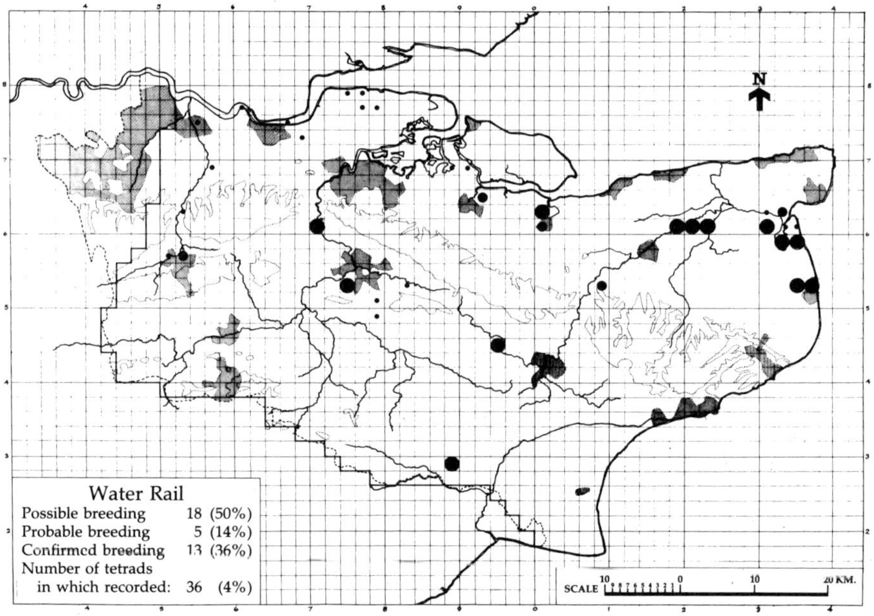

The Water Rail's preference for dense aquatic vegetation and its skulking behaviour make it a difficult species to prove breeding. However, the map shows that it is quite widespread during the summer months, finding suitably dense reed-beds on the margins of small lakes and streams, and in disused gravel workings.

The main breeding area is in the Stour Valley at Stodmarsh, where there was an estimate of 25 pairs in 1966. During the period under review there have been up to four pairs at Richborough and single pairs at Sandwich, Ham Fen and Cottington. In the south up to four pairs have bred at Sandling Park (Hythe), with occasional pairs at Dungeness and in mid-Kent at Wateringbury, Burham and the Loose Valley. On the North Kent Marshes single pairs have bred regularly at Murston and Stoke Fleet, with up to three pairs in Cliffe Quarries.

In winter the largest numbers are usually recorded in severe weather, when Water Rails are forced into the open, or adjacent to running water. Up to 30 have been seen in the Stour Valley, with up to 20 at Leybourne/New Hythe, and an unusual peak of 20 at Dungeness in January 1961.

The best evidence for spring and autumn migration comes from Dungeness, where peaks of 10–12 have been recorded in some years between 22nd March–30th April, with a maximum of 20 on 4th April 1969. Numbers there in October–November are usually much smaller, with a maximum of eight in late November 1967.

Spotted Crake

Porzana porzana

Scarce passage migrant, and winter visitor.

According to Ticehurst, the Spotted Crake was probably a more numerous summer visitor in the mid-nineteenth century than in the first half of this century, being recorded occasionally on the North Kent and Romney Marshes, and more frequently in the Stour Valley and at Cottington Marsh. Both Ticehurst and Harrison believed that the species bred, but were unable to provide the necessary evidence.

The accompanying table gives the monthy distribution of all records between 1958–76. None was reported during 1952–57 or in 1968.

J	F	M	A	M	J	J	A	S	O	N	D
	3	3	16	6	1		2	3	3	2	4

This analysis of the records suggests a change in status, to that of a passage migrant and winter visitor, rather than summer visitor. During the period under review there were no records between 2nd June–10th August, while the absence of records between 28th December–1st February is probably of no real significance.

The most frequented locality is still the Stour Valley, with 19 out of the total of 43 birds, mostly at Stodmarsh, including 12 during April–May, some of which concerned calling males. There are also seven records from both Observatories, including an unusual total of four at Dungeness during 6th–11th April 1965. Elsewhere, singles have been reported from the North Kent Marshes on five occasions, twice on Sevenoaks Reserve and in the Medway Valley near New Hythe, and once at Bough Beech.

Baillon's Crake

Porzana pusilla

Ticehurst includes details of two obtained at Cottington (Deal) in 1850, one on 19th September, the other in late October, and a third shot near Hythe in October 1870. Harrison adds that an adult male was shot, again at Cottington, on 9th May 1943.

No conclusive records of this elusive species have been reported during the period under review, but a Baillon's or Little Crake *Porzana parva* was seen at Sandwich on 12th April 1974.

Corncrake

Crex crex

Formerly bred, now a rare passage migrant.

Ticehurst records how the Corncrake bred in scattered pairs throughout the more open parts of the county during the nineteenth century, but noted a marked decline after the turn of the century. Harrison included reports of sporadic breeding up until 1947, but there has been no confirmation of nesting since. Harrison also notes an exceptionally early spring record for 12th March 1906, and six November–December records, with the latest on 30th December 1892.

	J	F	M	A	M	J	J	A	S	O	N	D	Totals
1952–66				3	6	1	1	15	29	8			63
1967–76				2				1	7		1		11

The accompanying table gives the monthly distribution of all birds seen during the period under review. Spring passage has been recorded between 15th April–23rd May, with two midsummer records involving singles near Dover on 18th June 1953 and at Shadoxhurst (Ashford) on 5th July 1961. Autumn passage has occurred between 2nd August–18th October, with an exceptionally late bird at Foreness on 7th November 1976.

The largest autumn totals involved 11 in 1959 and nine in 1964, with about half the records coming from the two Observatories. During the last decade there has been a striking further decrease, from an average of four to only one annually, and there were no reports at all for 1958, 1962, 1972, 1973 and 1975.

Moorhen

Gallinula chloropus

Resident.

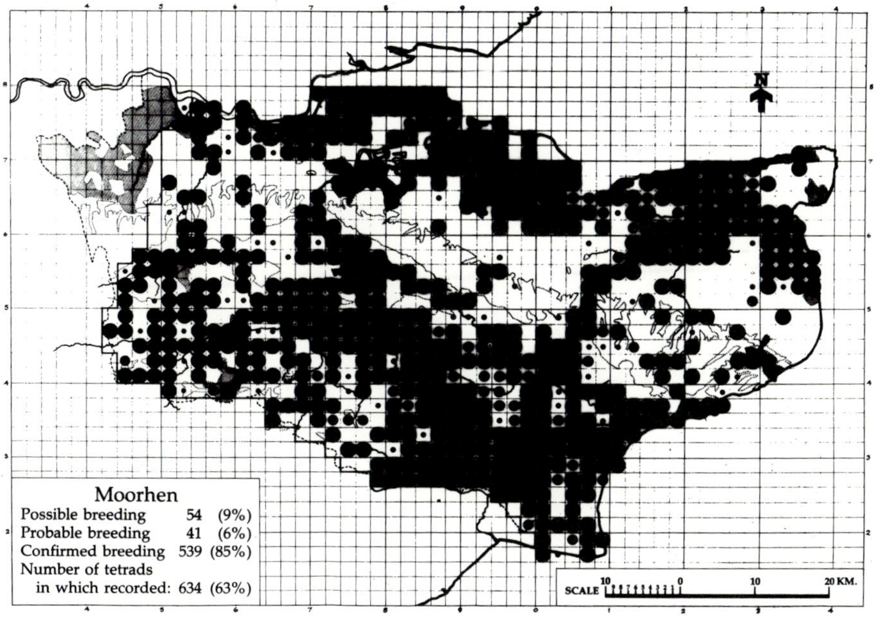

The Moorhen frequents every sort of freshwater habitat, from edges of large reservoirs, lakes and gravel pits, to the smallest pools on agricultural land. This broad habitat preference, compared with the

Coot, is clearly reflected in the differences between the distribution maps of the two species. The Moorhen nests in large numbers along all the marshland ditches, whilst nearly every village pond supports a pair or two. The Breeding Survey clearly shows its absence from the dry chalklands of the Downs, the dense urban sprawl of the Medway towns, and from parts of Thanet.

In winter flocks of 50–100 and occasionally more form at many freshwater sites, and groups are often seen feeding in the open on adjacent arable land. Moorhens are particularly vulnerable to severe weather conditions and in the winter of 1962/63 nearly 50 were found dead around the Kent coast, while many more became casualties inland.

Although our breeding birds are essentially sedentary, three ringing recoveries show that the winter population, like that of the Water Rail, is augmented by migrants from the Continent. One ringed at Sandwich Bay in September 1960 was recovered in France the following March, while two first-winter birds, both ringed at Maidstone on 3rd January 1965, were recovered respectively in Denmark in April 1966 and in Norway in April 1968.

Coot

Fulica atra

Resident and winter visitor.

Ticehurst described the Coot as a very local breeding species, abundant and generally distributed on Romney Marsh, but nesting only sparingly along the estuarine marshes in the north, where it was not found far from tidal waters, and he named only four inland breeding localities. Gillham and Homes remarked on the presence of colonies using the newly excavated pits at Cliffe and wrote of 60–100 pairs breeding in one fleet on the Cliffe peninsula. Harrison added that it was especially numerous on the Stour marshes, particularly at Stodmarsh, and mentioned several more inland breeding sites during the post-war years, often in flooded ballast pits.

The drainage of the coastal lowlands, particularly Romney Marsh, has much reduced the number of fleets suitable for nesting. However, there has been a considerable expansion of the breeding range during the period under review, and much of this is due to the creation of man-made sites, including the two new reservoirs at Bough Beech and Bewl Bridge, and the numerous gravel pits.

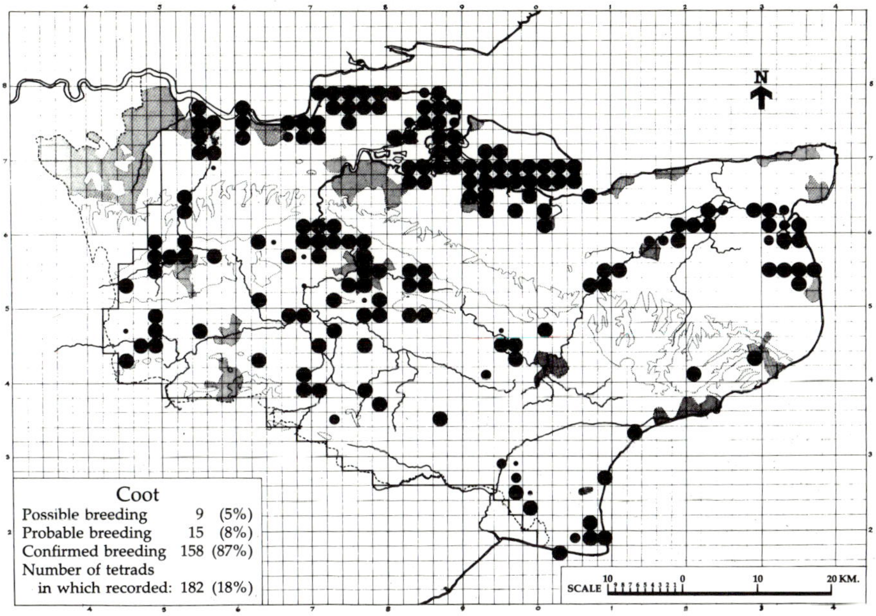

The Coot is not nearly so adaptable as the Moorhen and usually requires at least half an hectare of open water and dense vegetation for nesting. Small lakes created by damming streams often hold a few pairs and typify many of the nest sites in the Weald.

The numbers in winter are supplemented by immigrants from the Continent and flocks of 400–700 have been recorded on the North Kent Marshes at Cliffe Pools, Stoke and Capel Fleet, and elsewhere at New Hythe, Stodmarsh and Dungeness. Sytematic counts in the 1970s produced peaks of 1,500 at Bough Beech in January and November 1972, while at Cliffe Pools there were counts of 1,200–1,600 during 1971–73, with a maximum of 2,270 in January 1973.

In severe weather flocks may move onto the estuaries and on 6th January 1971 there were 250 on the sea at Reculver. Severe weather also accounted for a peak of 1,800 at Stodmarsh on 27th February 1956, and there was another high count of 1,000 there on 2nd February 1961. In January 1963 over 100 were found dead around the Kent coast.

The only foreign ringing recoveries concern two adults caught at Chetney in January and February 1963. Both were recovered in Pas de Calais, France, one was found dead there the next day, while the second survived until February 1964. Harrison includes details of one ringed at Appledore in March 1930, which was also recovered in Pas de Calais in July 1931.

Crane

Grus grus

Very rare vagrant.

Ticehurst gives details of several records up to the eighteenth century, but there were apparently none in the nineteenth nor in the first half of the twentieth centuries.

During the period under review there have been four records. Two were seen on Thanet between 9th–12th April 1956. One was present near Gravesend on 19th–20th March and two at Dungeness on 28th–29th September 1957, and an immature wintered near Dymchurch, from 30th October 1963–4th April 1964, following a widespread influx into Britain.

[In 1977 there was a remarkable series of records, involving at least two in the spring at four different localities between 3rd April–29th May and a flock of 26 on 16th October flying south over Charing and Ashford. Eds.]

Little Bustard

Tetrax tetrax

Very rare vagrant.

Ticehurst gives eight records between 1834 and 1903, and Harrison adds one for April 1940. One of the early records was ascribed to the Eastern race *T.t. orientalis*.

In recent years there have been just two records. One, a male of the Western race *T.t. tetrax*, was shot near Faversham on 5th January 1952, and a second was flushed from a field of currants near Hadlow on 10th October 1958.

Great Bustard

Otis tarda

Very rare vagrant.

Ticehurst lists eleven records between 1797 and 1883, four from Romney Marsh and the Rother Valley, two from Wye, one each from Great Chart, Whitstable and Halling and two together at St. Margaret's in 1873. Dated occurrences were 4th January and 5th–12th February.

On 11th January 1970 two were found at St. Margaret's, the same day on which one was seen on Fair Isle.

Oystercatcher

Haemotopus ostralegus

Regular breeding species, passage migrant and winter visitor.

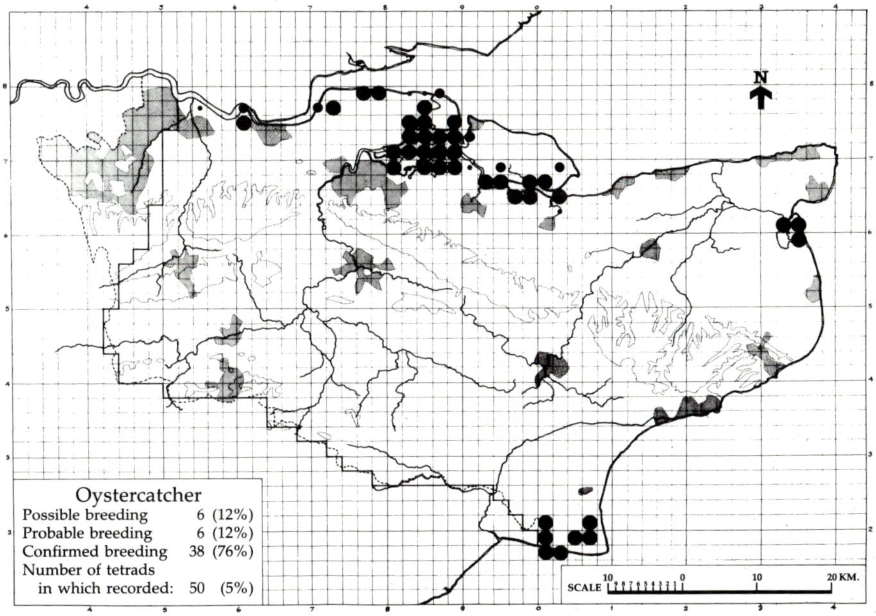

Ticehurst lamented the loss of this species as a breeding bird from the south of the county and knew of only one instance of nesting on the

North Kent Marshes. Harrison recorded breeding in the Sandwich Bay area from the late 1920s and in the north and south of the county again during the 1940s. Since then the Oystercatcher has become considerably more common, as both breeding bird and winter visitor.

The map clearly shows how the breeding populations are confined to the estuaries of the Thames, Medway and Swale, and Sandwich Bay and the Dungeness area. The largest number of breeding pairs occurs in the Medway, where regular censuses have shown an increase from 30 pairs in 1955 to 166 pairs in 1972. Elsewhere it is less numerous, with peak populations of five pairs on the Thames, 10 pairs on the Swale, three pairs at Sandwich Bay and 10 pairs at Dungeness. Although nesting is normally confined to the foreshore, or islands in saltmarsh, there is an increasing tendency for pairs to breed on arable land behind the sea walls.

	Thames	Medway	Swale	Pegwell Bay	Lade
1953/54–1960/61	16	180	2800	410	46
1961/62–1968/69	16	220	2060	850	400
1969/70–1976/77	120	640	2780	630	640

Mean winter peaks of Oystercatchers

The peak numbers each year normally occur in mid-winter, but may be recorded in any month from August–February, when the flock sizes fluctuate considerably and may match those of the normal winter populations.

At the main locality in the mouth of the Swale, the normal December–January population numbers 2,000–3,000, with peaks of 4,000 in the hard winter of January 1956, 4,500 in January 1958 and 3,500 in December 1975. At Sandwich Bay since 1962 there have been regular counts of 500–1,000, with a maximum of 1,200 in January 1966, while at Greatstone there were 1,500 in the hard winter of January 1963, with regular counts of 500–850 since 1968. At this last locality the birds usually roost at Lade Pits or on Dungeness Reserve. A parallel increase has also taken place on the Medway, where there was an unusual count of 1,000 in September 1956, but otherwise peaks as high as 500–850 have only occurred since 1971. Counts of up to 400 have recently been recorded on the Thames between Allhallows and Grain, although most birds in this area seem to be related to the Essex or Medway populations.

There is a general departure of wintering birds during March and April and the lowest counts of the year often occur in spring. The midsummer populations in June have involved peaks of 500 in the Swale, 250 in the Medway, and 200 at both Sandwich Bay and Lade, although there was an exceptional count of 700 at Sandwich Bay in June 1963.

Passage migrants occur in coastal areas in spring and autumn, though numbers involved seem quite small and diurnal movements are only recorded at regularly watched points. At Dungeness, for instance, up to 300 bird/days may be recorded in spring between late March and early May, with a peak towards the end of April, and up to 200 bird/days in autumn between August and October, with peaks in mid-September. Small numbers have also been seen departing to the northeast, or arriving from the same direction, at Shellness during the same periods.

Inland records are relatively scarce, but have become more frequent in recent years, especially at sites like the newly constructed reservoir at Bough Beech, or the gravel pit reserve at Sevenoaks. At these localities up to four birds have been recorded in all months of the year except February, April and December. The largest flocks to occur inland were 12 flying west at Stockbury on 21st January 1972 and 14 flying southwest over Gillingham on 23rd August 1970.

A few ringing recoveries give some indication of movements of Kent birds. A locally bred young bird ringed at Stoke in 1956 was recovered breeding in Lincolnshire in 1962. Recoveries during the winter in north Kent of birds ringed elsewhere include two birds breeding in Essex and one in Sussex, and three birds ringed as adults on the Wash in August.

Black-winged Stilt

Himantopus himantopus

Very rare visitor, recorded in May and September only.

According to Ticehurst, one was shot near Faversham before 1845, and Harrison records singles seen on Romney Marsh in May 1919 and May 1942. In 1945, the year that two pairs bred in Nottinghamshire, two were seen at Cooling on 9th May and at Stodmarsh on 12th May.

There have been a further five records in the period under review, with singles at Shellness on 15th September 1953, Lower Halstow on 26th September 1955, West Hythe on 23rd May 1965 and Stoke on 27th May 1967, while two were seen together at Shellness on 29th September 1957.

Avocet

Recurvirostra avosetta

Regular spring migrant, irregular in other months. Has bred.

Ticehurst records that during the first half of the nineteenth century Avocets bred on the Romney and North Kent Marshes, but by 1870 they were relatively scarce.

One pair bred successfully at Yantlet in 1958 and it is likely that this species would breed regularly in the county if suitable habitat was provided and maintained throughout the season.

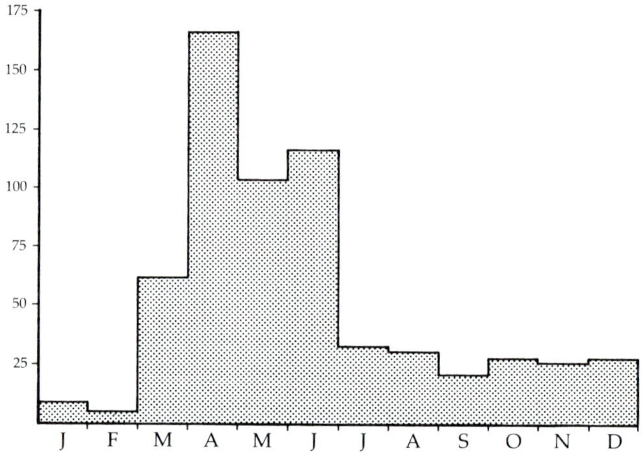

Monthly distribution of Avocets 1952–76

There has been a considerable increase in numbers during the period under review. Though spring flocks were only recorded in four years during 1952–63, they became an annual occurrence during 1968–76, and parties of four or more normally only occur during the period 16th March–4th July. An analysis of the overall numbers on spring passage shows a marked peak in the first half of April, while most of the 34 spring and early summer flocks fall into two distinct periods, with only three during the last two weeks of April and the first week of May. It is also noticeable that whereas all those at Dungeness in March–April are seen flying up-Channel, the majority in May–June refer to birds resting on various coastal lagoons. The timing and behaviour of these migrants suggests that they may have different origins, or perhaps that the later birds are simply non-breeders. Of these 34 flocks, half occurred in the Dungeness area, eight at Sandwich Bay and seven on the North Kent

Marshes, while inland there were 11 birds at Sevenoaks on 16th March 1969 and five at Fordwich on 4th July 1973. The largest numbers involved 17 flying east at Dungeness on 8th June 1963, 16 flying east there on 26th April 1968, 13 at Sandwich Bay on 11th May 1970, 13 flying east at Dungeness and 18 at Sandwich Bay on 13th April 1971, and 23 at Windmill Creek on 16th June 1973.

Flocks of four–nine have also been recorded in autumn on four occasions between 6th August–2nd September, with an exceptional record of 14 at Funton on 25th October 1976.

Two-four birds wintered regularly on the Swale, between mid-November and early March, from 1955/56 until the arctic winter of 1962/63. Similar numbers have occurred in other winters, but usually on isolated dates.

Stone Curlew

Burhinus oedicnemus

Bred regularly until 1965, now a rare migrant.

In 1823 Latham wrote of the Stone Curlew as 'not uncommon' in some parts of Kent, including the Downs and the Darent Valley. By Ticehurst's time, the numbers were obviously much lower and breeding restricted to Dungeness. Here, by the end of the nineteenth century, five pairs or fewer were breeding, threatened by egg collectors. Ticehurst considered that the protection afforded when Lydd Ranges were established pulled the Stone Curlew back from the brink of extinction, and records autumn parties of 40 in 1902 and 71 in 1905 at Dungeness.

Harrison described an increasingly flourishing breeding population at Dungeness, reaching 16 successful pairs in 1922. The next year, however, saw some unexplained calamity reduce this to a single pair, but by 1927 some 10 pairs were recorded. In the early 1950s he reported 13 out of 15 pairs to have bred successfully. He also records end-of-season flocks of 18 in 1936 and 10 in 1949 at Dungeness, with occasional records of individuals elsewhere.

In the period under review 1952–64 saw little change in the breeding strength, with between five and eight pairs on the Dungeness RSPB Reserve or nearby. The birds were usually present from late March to late October, the extreme dates being 13th March and 13th November.

Only one pair bred in 1965, and up to three birds were recorded annually in summer during 1966–72, including two females which laid infertile eggs in the same nest in 1968. In 1970 and 1972 the records involved only single birds on one date, and there have been no reports from Dungeness since.

Records elsewhere in the county have been sporadic, totalling 23 between March–October, with passage peaks in April–May and August. Most come from coastal areas, and almost all concern single birds, but three landed briefly in a field near Tonbridge, before flying off north on 6th June 1954.

One young bird ringed in 1957 was shot in Spain in October of that year.

Sharrock (1976) indicated the difficulties of locating small, scattered Stone Curlew populations because of their largely nocturnal habits, but this would not apply to the RSPB Reserve at Dungeness with its full-time warden. Although at the edge of their European breeding range, and vulnerable to afforestation programmes and agricultural cultivation, neither applying to Dungeness, Sharrock considered the English population, centred along the Chilterns, the Brecks and Salisbury Plain, to have remained more or less stable this century, so the decline of the Kent and Sussex populations appears as a sad exception. Having been at the brink of extinction before in the last 100 years, it is to be hoped that once again the Stone Curlew's fortunes will change for the better.

Cream-coloured Courser

Cursorius cursor

The first British record was an immature shot at Wingham in 1785. Ticehurst lists three more birds apparently shot in Kent: one near Margate in 1841, one at Westbrook in November 1849, and one near Sandwich prior to 1868.

The only Kent record this century concerns one watched at Dungeness on 9th September 1916.

Collared Pratincole

Glareola pratincola

Very rare vagrant.

The only pratincole satisfactorily identified as Collared was seen at Worth from 19th September–3rd October 1976.

Single pratincoles not specifically identified were seen at Reculver on 6th October 1962 and at Dungeness on 28th May 1971.

Black-winged Pratincole

Glareola nordmanni

Very rare vagrant.

One remained at Sandwich Bay from 31st August–4th September 1969.

Little Ringed Plover

Charadrius dubius

Local summer resident and passage migrant.

Harrison describes in detail the early records for the county. The first authentic record was an adult female seen on a marsh in east Kent on 2nd July 1938. From 1942 one or two were seen almost annually and the first recorded breeding involved two pairs at Cliffe in 1949, though information from the RSPB indicates that three clutches appear to have been taken in the north of the county in 1945.

Since 1952, when four pairs bred at two sites in the north of the county, the numbers of breeding pairs have slowly increased, with 10 pairs in 1962, 13 in 1967, 14–16 in 1973 and 16 in 1976.

The increase and spread in Kent has not been so spectacular as in some other counties, which is difficult to explain in the light of our proximity to the Continent. One reason for this may be Kent's long coastline. In Britain, Little Ringed Plovers are mostly inland nesters and apparently suitable sites adjoining the coast, for example on the Dungeness peninsula, have so far been ignored. Extraction of chalk has diminished and suitable quarries have overgrown, and there has been relatively little opening-up of fresh areas for sand or ballast extraction—both perhaps additional contributory factors.

The majority of the sites used are in the west of the county, with up to four further pairs in any one year breeding in the north and east. The chosen areas are usually gravel or chalk pits containing some water with flat, stony ground for nesting and a shallow edge to the water for feeding, a habitat closely similar to the river shingle banks favoured on the Continent. Other sites in the county have included flat areas of industrial waste with surface-water pools, and the shingly edge and concrete banks of a reservoir. By their very nature as newly-exposed areas, most of the chosen sites are subject to considerable disturbance. Little Ringed Plovers are fortunately not especially shy and frequently nest, or attempt to nest, at sites which are being worked. Nesting at reservoirs may be affected by changes in the water level or disturbance by anglers. Unfortunately, any disturbance, by humans or machines, is likely to leave the eggs or chicks exposed to predation by crows or mammals. At pits near Sevenoaks where predators are strictly controlled, breeding success appears to have been appreciably higher than at other pits. At Bough Beech reservoir the simpler and much more practical expedient of placing a 2″ mesh wire cage over the nest has been found to be effective in deterring predators, the adult plovers running unconcernedly through the mesh.

Spring arrival usually takes place between 19th–31st March, with only two earlier records on 23rd February 1974 and 12th March 1972. A few migrants are recorded away from the breeding localities from March until early May. Nesting sites begin to be abandoned in July and are usually deserted by mid-August. The largest numbers are usually recorded at this time, with peak counts of 14 at Bough Beech on 14th July 1974 and 13 at Dungeness on 14th August 1968. Autumn migration continues, especially near the coast, to the end of September, with the latest record on 6th October 1962.

A bird ringed as a nestling near Canterbury on 4th July 1958 was trapped in the Camargue on 23rd August of the same year.

Although Little Ringed Plovers are at present well-established in the county, their future seems to be dependent on the continuing provision, by man, of suitable nesting areas, as older ones become unsuitable by filling in, flooding or becoming overgrown. Another possible threat is the recent spread of inland breeding by Ringed Plovers, which have similar habitat preferences, take up their territory earlier and are more aggressive.

Ringed Plover

Charadrius hiaticula

Numerous passage migrant, winter visitor and regular breeding species.

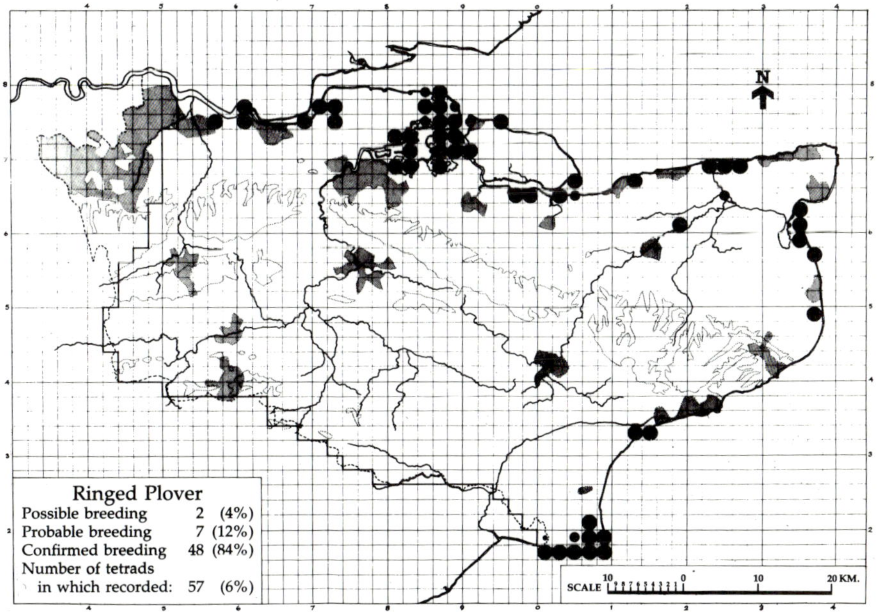

The regular breeding areas of this species are the islands, beaches and sea walls of the Medway and Swale estuaries, the beaches near Reculver and Sandwich Bay, and the shingle at Dungeness. Other temporary sites include coastal marshes which are infilled with dredgings, or otherwise made suitable by the activities of man, and Ringed Plovers frequently nest inside sea walls on areas of dry earth. On the Thames, breeding occurs inside the sea walls, and a complete census in 1973 produced 12 pairs at Cliffe Pools, 25 pairs on new pools inside the Isle of Grain refinery, with another eight pairs betweeen Swanscombe and Yantlet. Censuses of the Medway Estuary totalled up to 16 pairs between 1955–67, but the availability of artificial sites produced 14 pairs at Kingsnorth alone in 1970, and a total of 46 pairs, including 15 on Chetney, in 1972. The total numbers in the Swale have never exceeded nine pairs. Further east between Reculver and Minnis Bay there is a regular breeding population of up to 16 pairs, while a short distance inland there was a temporary occupation of the flooded fields at Grove by about eight pairs in 1961–62. Nearby, up to three pairs breed regularly between Stodmarsh and Fordwich, while there are normally up to six pairs at Sandwich Bay. In the Dungeness area the maximum population is about 20 pairs on the Reserve and surrounding shingle, and another 20 pairs, about half of them in Kent, between the Brooks and the Midrips. Two pairs also bred at Bough Beech reservoir in 1976. These figures suggest a regular breeding population of between 80–160 pairs, depending on the availability of suitable artificial sites.

	Thames	Medway	Swale	Sandwich Bay
Autumn	280	460	312	260
Winter	138	191	93	88

Mean autumn and winter peaks of Ringed Plovers 1953/54–1976/77

This species is most numerous on autumn passage during August–September, with flocks of up to 400 on the Thames, 600 on the Medway and Swale, and 500 at Sandwich Bay. The choice of the high tide roosts depends on the best available areas at the time. On the Thames the major roost was at Yantlet between 1954–63, but has been at Cliffe Pools since 1966. Although Hoo and Stoke saltings have been used on the Medway, areas of dredgings provided major roosts at Chetney between 1958–73 and at Kingsnorth since 1970, with an exceptional peak of 1,000 at this last locality on 6th September 1970. On the Swale the usual roosts are on the beach at Shellness or the saltings at Harty.

Numbers show a steady decline in October–November and unusual peaks of 500 on the Thames on 28th November 1954 and 7th December 1958 were probably late migrants rather than genuine wintering birds. In midwinter there have been up to 300 on the Thames, 400 on the Medway, 200 on the Swale, and 230 at Sandwich Bay. Elsewhere round the coast the most important locality is Reculver/Minnis Bay, where there have been up to 150 in autumn and winter.

The spring passage is very obvious in May, when flocks of up to 200 occur regularly at Sandwich Bay, and less often elsewhere, with a peak of 400 at Harty on 22nd May 1954. Most of these late migrants belong to the race *C.h. tundrae* and a record flock of 200 on the flooded fields at Grove on 13th May 1961 was considered to be of this race.

Inland records have occurred in all months of the year, but are mostly concentrated in May and August–September, when flocks of up to 22 have occurred at Bough Beech and Sevenoaks, and more commonly much nearer the coast in the Stour Valley.

Four Ringed Plovers ringed in autumn in Kent have been recovered or retrapped in subsequent autumns in France, Denmark, Finland and Iceland; four others, recovered or controlled in Kent in autumn, had been ringed in Iceland, Norway, Sweden and Germany, indicating the importance of Kentish estuaries to birds from much of northern Europe.

Kentish Plover

Charadrius alexandrinus

Uncommon passage migrant. Formerly bred.

This species was named from specimens sent to Latham by Boys of Sandwich, one in May 1787 and two in April 1791. Little is known about the Sandwich colony except that the last five pairs bred there around 1890, with single pairs again between 1932–35. At Dungeness the main colony was at Littlestone, with others between there and the point, while further west there was another colony between the Holmstone and the Midrips. In 1906 there were 44 pairs, but the last fifteen nests were found in 1928.

During the period under review there has been a marked increase in spring records, commencing in 1971. The main haunts of these birds are the beach at Sandwich Bay and the gravel pits in the Dungeness area. Elsewhere round the coast the most favoured locality is the Swale, particularly Shellness, though individuals have occurred as far up the Thames as Swanscombe.

Single birds wintered at Sandwich Bay in 1951/52 and 1952/53, while others were seen there on 15th November 1953 and at Margate on 18th February 1967. The seasonal distribution of all other recent records is shown in the histogram.

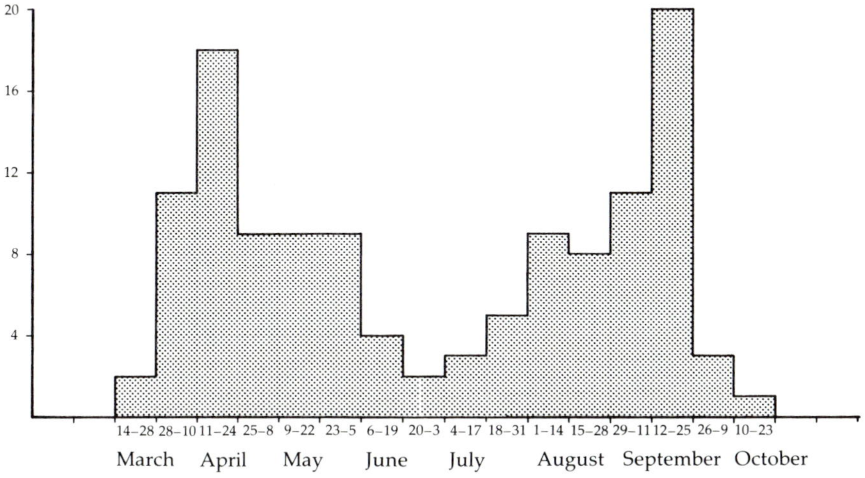

Fortnightly distribution of Kentish Plovers 1952–76

Although Kentish Plovers now occur annually in both spring and autumn, there were no spring records between 1957–62 and no records at all in 1963 and 1964. Spring records fall between 24th March–16th June, 75% since 1971. The peak year was 1971, when there were 10 at Sandwich Bay, including four on 10th April and three on 18th May, and five in the Dungeness area. Apart from three records in midsummer, the remainder refer to the period 22nd July–13th October. Autumn numbers have remained steady, apart from an influx of at least 12 in 1976. Largest numbers occur in the second half of September, highlighted in 1976, when there was one at North Foreland, two at Sandwich Bay and five on Dungeness Reserve, all on the 25th.

Away from the coast, in the Stour Valley, there was a pair at Grove on 6th July 1961 and one at Stodmarsh on 10th September 1972, while further inland, on the new reservoir at Bough Beech, there was one on 29th–30th March 1974, a pair on 22nd April and one on 24th–25th April 1976. It is interesting to note that these last records coincided with arrivals at Sandwich Bay on 28th March and at Dungeness between 23rd–25th April respectively.

Dotterel

Charadrius morinellus

Scarce passage migrant.

Ticehurst refers to a decrease in the number migrating through the county at the same time that the British population declined, a decrease which was noted throughout the country. There were no apparent changes in status in the first half of this century.

During the period under review, there have been records of about 94 birds, seen on some 31 occasions, in 16 of the 25 years. In spring records tend to be fewer, but numbers larger than in autumn. Most records relate to one–five birds, but the following larger 'trips' have been noted: 20 at Dungeness on 5th May 1956, 12 at Shellness on 20th May 1973 and 13 at Cooling from 13th–16th May 1974. Extreme dates are 9th April and 5th June. In autumn records are of five birds or less and fall between 16th August–3rd October, with a late individual at Grain on 1st November 1976.

Most records are from the coastal marshes and Dungeness, and in the light of experience in central England, migrant flocks may well be overlooked inland, especially on the Downs. As the Dotterel now breeds on the Dutch polders, a future change in status is quite possible.

Golden Plover

Pluvialis apricaria

Winter visitor and passage migrant.

There appears to have been little change in the status of this species. Numbers vary considerably from year to year and there can be large scale emigrations in hard weather. The Golden Plover is particularly numerous on the wide coastal lowlands of the Thames and Isle of Sheppey, the Wantsum, lower Stour and Sandwich marshes, and parts of Romney Marsh. In all these sites flocks of over 1,000 are recorded regularly, with peaks of over 3,000 in some years. Winter cereal fields on the Blean Plateau also hold large flocks in mid-winter. Inland the regular sites are mainly in the Weald and flocks rarely exceed 500. It is particularly scarce on the North Downs and in the west of the county.

As part of a national survey, most flocks were counted in early January 1977, producing a total of 19,345, over 10% of the English wintering population.

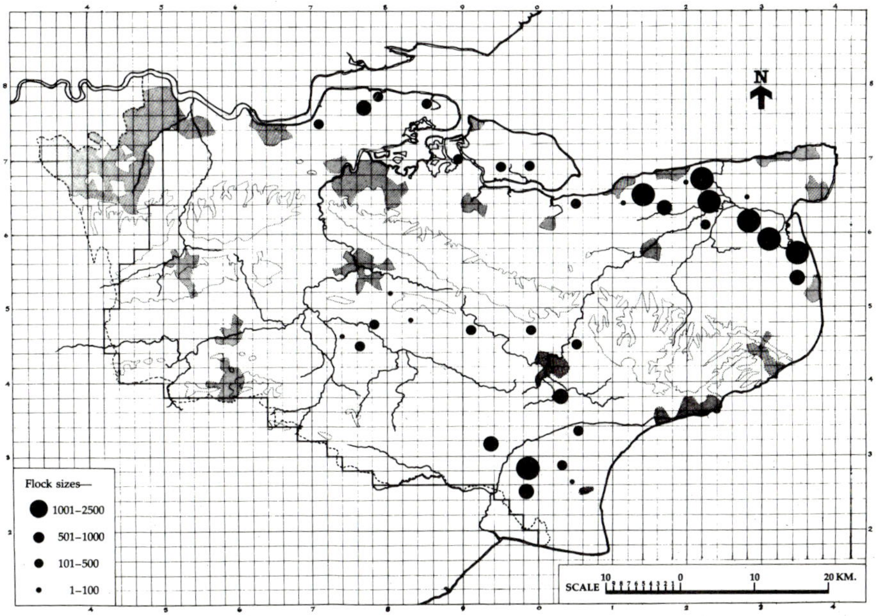

Distribution of Golden Plover flocks in January 1977

The most traditional inland site is southwest of Sutton Valence, where peak flock sizes of around 500 occur in March. It could be that some small wintering flocks are overlooked, particularly in the Weald between Staplehurst and Ashford, where several were seen in 1977. The regular wintering flocks around Ashford may well be related to the Romney Marsh population.

The first passage birds arrive in mid-July, but numbers are low and the flocks scattered in coastal areas, with a tendency to feed on tidal mudflats. Many passing through from July–September may primarily be of the northern race *P.a. altifrons*. In August 1975 a flock of over 700 was present in the Wantsum and all those still in summer plumage were of this race. The main wintering flocks arrive from late September to November, when peak counts are recorded in the east. These flocks feed mainly on lowland pasture, but often roost on plough. Although there is considerable loyalty to traditional sites, the spread of arable farming has led to some local displacements. At Sandwich, for instance, the main flocks have moved from the Point marshes, which are now largely arable, to pasture on the Worth marshes. Later in the winter, flocks move more freely onto arable, particularly winter cereals, which for a period appear to provide a satisfactory substitute for grass. The amount of interchange between wintering flocks is not known, but it undoubtedly takes place as feeding conditions change.

Numbers begin to decline in February, but increase again in March and early April. Most spring birds can be identified as *P.a. altifrons* and the spring peak is probably a result of migrants of this race passing through from more southerly wintering quarters. Most flocks have dispersed by late April, but a few stragglers can be recorded throughout May and there have been just five records in June during 1952–76.

With the onset of severe weather, they are one of the first wintering species to move out, usually southwestwards, and small parties may be seen anywhere in the county at such times. During very hard frosts, as in late December 1962, the whole population emigrates very quickly. Ringing recoveries confirm this southwest orientation. Four birds ringed on Harty in late 1962 were recovered in early 1963, with singles in Dorset and Morocco and two in southwest France. There have been other recoveries in France and also in Spain and Holland.

Grey Plover

Pluvialis squatarola

Winter visitor and passage migrant.

The Grey Plover occurs in all months of the year in the estuaries of the Thames, Medway and Swale, at Sandwich Bay and in the Dungeness area. The numbers have shown considerable fluctuations and it seems likely that, in common with some of the other small shore waders, its true population has rarely been assessed accurately. The Grey Plover is more difficult to count than other shore waders, in particular because of its habits of feeding scattered over widespread areas of mudflats and tidal creeks in the saltmarsh, and mixing with other species during high tide roosting movements, rather than forming distinct flocks.

	Thames	Medway	Swale	Pegwell Bay	Lade
1953/54–1960/61	700	530	970	81	28
1961/62–1968/69	280	540	460	180	22
1969/70–1976/77	760	760	590	180	47

Mean winter peaks of Grey Plover

The winter population becomes established during November and numbers fall in February and March, as birds begin to depart. The normal winter counts for each of the three estuaries in the north are all between 500–1,000. However, in 1954 there were 3,000 in the Swale in February and March, while a peak of 2,000 was recorded in the Thames in December 1954. Systematic wader counts, made in 1975–76 in order to get more accurate information, produced winter peaks of 1,100 in the Thames, 1,600 in the Medway and 600 in the Swale. At the other two main localities there were maxima of 400 at Sandwich Bay in January 1973 and 150 at Lade in February 1972.

Numbers in the main estuaries drop to around 200 during April and May, although there is a small but noticeable passage of adults at this time. This passage is most often observed at Dungeness, where the maximum was 80 flying east on 8th May 1954. Small flocks have also been seen heading northeast out to sea from the mouth of the Swale, the highest numbers there involving 40 on the 12th and 60 on the 18th May 1970. Midsummer flocks in June may reach a maximum of 50, but are usually considerably less.

Autumn passage occurs throughout the period July–November, although there was an early peak of 200 at Stoke on 26th June 1961. Numbers in the Medway and Swale usually approach the average winter peaks of 500–1,000, but counts in the Thames are usually smaller. Visible migration occasionally occurs on a much larger scale than that witnessed in spring, especially on the north coast, and five flocks totalling 415 were seen arriving at Shellness during a period of two hours on 18th August 1973. Three flocks totalling 155 were also seen arriving there on 9th October 1976.

There have been regular inland records of up to five birds in all months except February and June, from localities such as the Stour and Medway Valleys, Sevenoaks Reserve and Bough Beech reservoir. Spring records virtually all fall in May, while in autumn the majority are in September–October. A maximum of eight occurred at Grove Ferry on 27th January 1962.

There have been seven recoveries of birds ringed in north Kent. The only foreign recovery was of one ringed at Harty in August 1966 recovered in Denmark in August 1967. The remaining six recoveries were local.

Sociable Plover

Chettusia gregaria

Very rare vagrant.

Two singles were recorded in 1968. On 12th April one was seen near Westwell, and in the autumn one made an extended stay at Sandwich Bay from 28th September–18th November.

Lapwing

Vanellus vanellus

Widespread resident, winter visitor and passage migrant.

Harrison records considerable local fluctuations in population levels, but apart from a decrease in breeding numbers, little change in status is apparent. The decline of the breeding population has been attributed to changes in farming practice and land-use. Damp-meadow drainage and the replacement of these and the permanent pastures by arable fields and the repeated use of machinery for cultivation during the early part of the breeding season are probably significant factors.

Lapwings breed commonly throughout the coastal marshes, with smaller numbers inland, scattered through the Weald and along the Downs.

Westerly movements occur soon after breeding and are regularly noted from early June. Such movements continue throughout the summer and autumn, often reaching a peak in mid-October. Numbers in November–December tend to be lower than in a mild January, but cold weather, even a short spell of severe frosts, can result in quite spectacular southerly movements on a broad front at rates of up to 3,000 birds per hour at any one site.

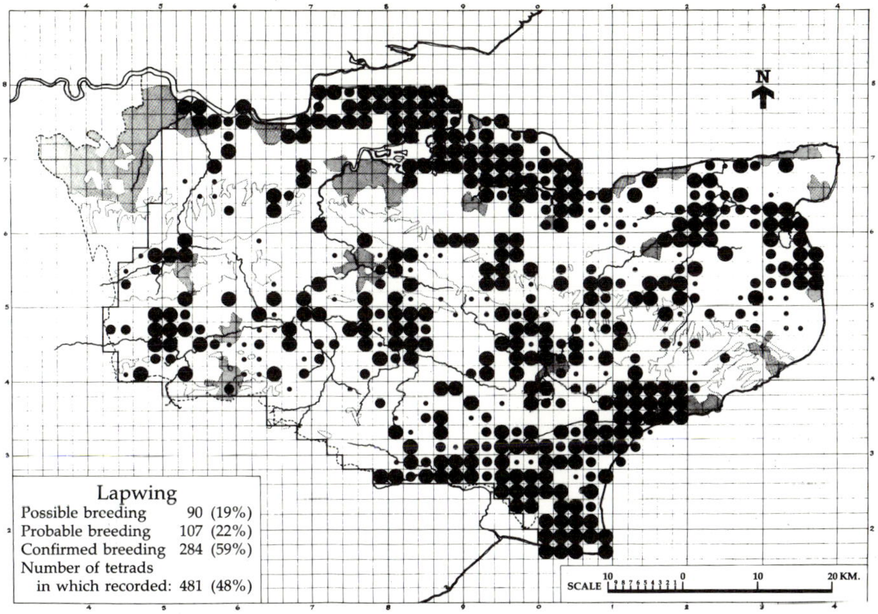

The numbers present in winter depend very much on the weather. During mild, damp winters, large numbers will remain throughout January and February. On the coastal lowlands flocks of 4–5,000 are then commonly recorded, with peaks of 8–10,000 on the Thames marshes, Sheppey, and Romney and Walland Marsh, and flocks of 1–2,000 inland. In a severe winter, such as 1962/63, very few remain in the county.

A northwesterly return movement is frequently noted between mid-February and mid-March. However, when large numbers have wintered in the county, the direction of movement is likely to be northeasterly. By March most of the local breeding birds are holding territory.

Ringing recoveries indicate the mobile nature of the Lapwing population as a whole (Mead, Flegg and Cox, 1968). Birds ringed as pulli and autumn migrants in Kent have been recovered in France, Spain and Portugal in winter, while one ringed on Chetney in December 1961 was recovered in Wexford, Eire in January 1963. Others, ringed as pulli in Holland, Germany and Norway, have been recovered in the county, but some undoubtedly come from further afield. Passage migrants have been recovered in Czechoslovakia and Poland in April, and East Germany in November, while three have been recovered in the USSR in April–May, one as far east as 69° 49′.

Knot

Calidris canutus

Winter visitor and passage migrant, occasionally present in midsummer.

The Thames, Medway and Swale estuaries hold the main wintering populations, with smaller flocks present at Pegwell Bay and Lade. As reported by Harrison, the largest flocks still occur at the mouth of the Swale, but here there has been a noticeable decline in recent years. Until 1968/69 the average winter peak was 9,500, ranging from 4,000 in 1952/53 to a maximum of 20,000 in December 1954. Subsequently an average of only 4,100 has been recorded, varying from 1,500 in 1969/70 to 6,000 in three winters since 1972/73. Numbers in the Thames and Medway estuaries also reflect this decline and the normal winter maxima are now under 1,000, though there was an exceptional flock of 4,000 present in the Medway in February 1973.

	Thames	Medway	Swale	Pegwell Bay
1953/54–1960/61	3,400	2,300	12,000	190
1961/62–1968/69	1,800	2,000	7,900	1,100
1969/70–1976/77	900	900	4,100	500

Mean winter peaks of Knot

The highest combined total of 29,000 occurred in the cold winter of early 1956, when there were 10,000 on the Thames, 5,000 on the Medway and 14,000 on the Swale, while in early 1964 the totals were 2,000, 8,000 and 10,000 respectively. In the winters of 1963/64 and 1964/65 up to 4,000 of the Swale population were feeding as far away as Herne Bay.

At Pegwell Bay there has been a similar decline and the annual winter population is now less than 500, against earlier peaks of 1,000 in three winters. At Lade, even smaller numbers winter, with 350 in 1971/72, but less than 100 since. However, in the severe weather of early 1963 there were exceptional totals of 5,000 at Pegwell Bay and 1,500 at Lade. The numbers in the northern estuaries at this time were not so unusual, and although the 4,000 on the Thames was a high count, the 5,000 on the Swale and 1,500 on the Medway were below the average peak counts, indicating a probable shift in the populations as a result of the cold weather.

Most wintering birds leave during early March, or occasionally in late February. Spring passage is often rather insignificant in April, with some adults in summer plumage during May. Flocks of up to 25 have been seen flying up-Channel off Dungeness at this time, with a peak of

285 on 6th May 1976. Comparatively few remain in June, with a complete absence of records in some years, though small flocks of up to 16 are occasionally present. However, in 1961 there were exceptional numbers, with 120 in the Medway estuary on 11th June and 200 in the Swale on 20th June.

Autumn passage commences in July, although the main wintering flocks do not normally exceed 1,000 birds until mid-October. Small arrivals and coastal movements involving up to 200 birds have been noted, with an exceptional peak of 1,630 arriving at Shellness in two hours on 7th August 1972. There is often a large build-up in numbers during November, and in the Swale the peak counts in six winters have occurred in this month, including 15,000 in November 1963.

There were 18 inland records in the period under review, spanning all months except March, April and June. They usually involved one or two birds, and half of the records were at Bough Beech. There is a surprising concentration of eight records in September, when two parties of nine have been seen, one flying southwest over Gillingham on 11th September 1963 and the other at Bough Beech on 10th September 1973.

Foreign ringing recoveries involve a Norwegian bird recovered in the Medway six years later, in the unusual month of June, and singles recovered in Greenland in July and Portugese East Africa in October. The other six recoveries all concern the east coast of England. Extensive ringing in the Swale has shown that the Kentish wintering population consists predominantly of adult birds.

Sanderling

Calidris alba

Winter visitor and passage migrant.

The favoured haunts of this species are the long stretches of sandy beaches at Minnis Bay, Sandwich Bay and Lade, with maximum winter populations of 500, 415 and 500 respectively, while in the cold winter of 1963 there were 1,000 at Westgate on 20th February. However, the Sanderling can be seen all round the northeast coast between Reculver and Sandwich Bay, with a major high-tide roost in Margate harbour, and the total population may well be larger than these figures indicate.

	Thanet	Sandwich Bay	Lade
1953/54–1960/61	94	87	117
1961/62–1968/69	345	134	250
1969/70–1976/77	225	194	323

Mean winter peaks of Sanderling

Elsewhere round the coast, the most frequent reports come from the shoreline between Shellness and Leysdown, and to a lesser extent from between Grain and Allhallows, where counts of up to 30 occur regularly during July–September, more rarely during winter and spring. In the hard winter of 1956 there were 150 at Shellness on 4th March, while later the same year there were 80 there on 7th September.

Passage migrants are most commonly seen offshore at Dungeness during April–May and July–August, while at Sandwich Bay there is evidence of migration during these same months, when numbers tend to fluctuate greatly. In all areas numbers are at their lowest in June, when only a few summering birds remain, although even in this month small flocks of 20–30 have been seen.

The first inland record occurred at Sevenoaks Reserve on 22nd May 1966, followed by others there on 27th April 1969 and 20th September 1973. However, the Sanderling has occurred at Bough Beech reservoir in six recent springs during 1969–76, with records between 27th April–6th June, including day totals of up to five, while in autumn there were singles there on 23rd July 1974 and 22nd September 1976.

Little Stint

Calidris minuta

Regular passage migrant, occasionally wintering.

The status of this species has changed considerably in the last fifty years. Ticehurst writes that Little Stints were commoner in the early part of the nineteenth century, mentions seeing flocks of only five–six in autumn and gives just one winter record. He also gives very few records for north Kent. Harrison's summary is similar, with a few spring and winter records and slightly larger autumn numbers. Gillham and Homes record a regular autumn passage in north Kent, but only give one spring record.

Winter records between December–March now occur almost annually, usually involving ones and twos. However, in early 1961 there were five on Chetney and four–six singles elsewhere on the coastal marshes in north Kent.

Spring passage is recorded annually between late March and early June, with the majority of the records in May. The numbers are variable, with only single birds in poor years. Notable peaks occurred in 1961, with counts of four–six at the Wicks, Walland Marsh and Grove Ferry between 7th–18th May, and in 1976, when there were three at Dungeness and eight at Bough Beech on 8th June.

Parties of 10–25 occur in most autumns between late July and late October. In 1961 there was an early influx involving up to 12 at Grove Ferry, 16 at Chetney and 15 at Stoke in the last week of July. However, the four major influxes during the period under review all occurred in the second half of September and continued into the first half of October, as shown below:

	1957 23/9–29/9	1960 17/9–2/10	1967 20/9–21/10	1976 25/9–10/10
Cliffe		4	31	26
Stoke	22	41	4	5
Sheppey	15	38	8	3
Sandwich Bay	11		48	32
Dungeness	55		2	7
Wicks		64	4	
Bough Beech/Sevenoaks		2		16
Totals	103	149	97	89

The Dungeness peak on 25th September 1957 involved two flocks of 35 and 20 attracted to the Lighthouse.

Inland this species is now reported regularly from Bough Beech reservoir and occasionally at Sevenoaks, more often in autumn than in spring.

Three foreign ringing recoveries have all been in France, two later the same autumn and the third in spring three years later. Another was retrapped where ringed, almost exactly two years later.

Temminck's Stint

Calidris temminckii

Occasional passage migrant.

In the past Temminck's Stints were apparently much scarcer, or perhaps overlooked. Ticehurst records few, apart from those shot in the 1860s. From the 1930s the position was much as at present, though a party of eight was seen at Yantlet on 7th August 1938. Kent is the county most visited by this species in autumn, while in spring it is second only to Norfolk (Sharrock, 1974).

During the 25 years under review 132 birds have been recorded, with reports in each year except 1970. Spring records have occurred in 13 years and autumn records in 22. Most concern one or two birds only, but there were three together at Grove on 15th May 1962 and at Dungeness on 17th May 1972, while the autumn maxima were four at both Murston on 7th September 1959 and Chetney on 9th August 1971, with five at Grove on 1st September 1961.

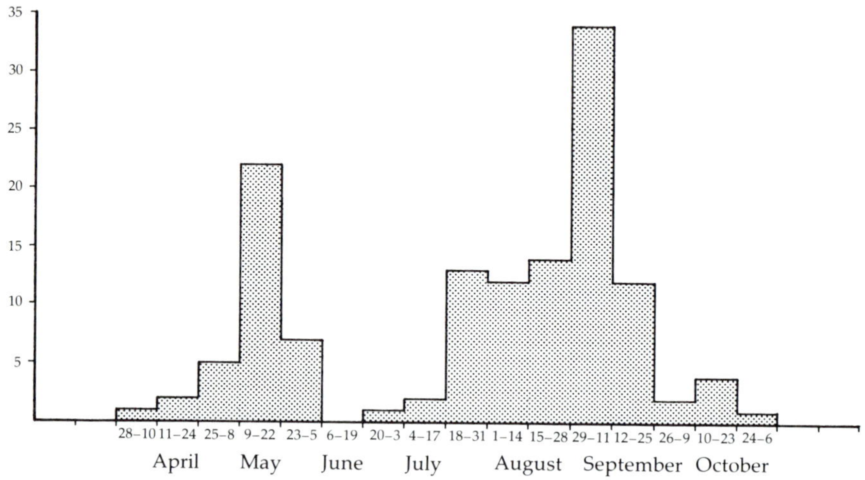

Fortnightly distribution of Temminck's Stints 1952–76

The earliest record was one at Sandwich Bay on 7th April 1974, with the majority of spring records in May and the latest on the 31st. Apart from one at Grove on 27th June 1961, autumn records occurred between 13th July–24th October, with the latest on Walland Marsh in 1953.

Most birds are seen at freshwater pools on the coastal marshes, while well inland there have been spring records in four years at Bough Beech reservoir and one autumn record on Sevenoaks Reserve.

Few Temminck's Stints have been caught in this country, so it was remarkable that one netted at Yantlet on 21st July 1962 should have been ringed at Pori, Finland on 4th August 1960.

Least Sandpiper

Calidris minutilla

Very rare vagrant.

The only record is of one seen feeding with Little Stints at Sandwich Bay on 24th October 1976.

White-rumped Sandpiper

Calidris fuscicollis

Very rare vagrant.

One was seen at Sandwich Bay on 17th August 1945.

Surprisingly, during the review period, there has only been one other record of this regular American visitor to the British Isles, again at Sandwich Bay, on 2nd October 1960. [Three more were seen during 1977. Eds.]

Baird's Sandpiper

Calidris bairdii

Very rare vagrant.

There are only two records of this American wader, the first at the Wicks from 19th–27th September 1952, and the second at Bough Beech reservoir on 22nd–23rd September 1973.

Pectoral Sandpiper

Calidris melanotos

Rare autumn migrant.

Ticehurst records one on Romney Marsh on 14th July 1908. Harrison adds three more autumn records, including two at Cottington Court on 25th August 1935 and one there on the early date of 12th July 1936, and an exceptional spring record of one at Shellness (Sheppey) on 21st May 1950.

In recent years there have been 20 records of single birds, the first in 1953 and then in 11 of the 18 years from 1959, with three in both 1962 and 1973.

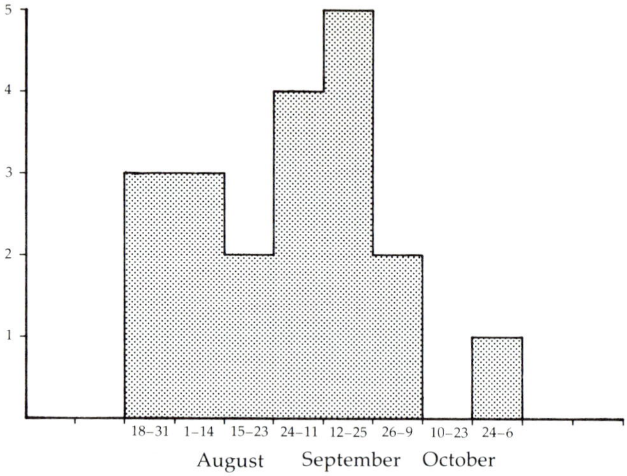

Fortnightly distribution of Pectoral Sandpipers 1952–76

Apart from a late bird at Murston on 24th–25th October 1959, the others all occurred between 23rd July–8th October, with three individuals staying for periods of 11–13 days.

The arrival of almost half of these birds before the end of August is similar to the pattern in other east coast counties, and led Sharrock (1974) to suggest that some of the earlier birds in the east may come from eastern Siberia.

Ten of the records occurred on the North Kent Marshes, three at Sandwich Bay and two at Dungeness, with a further two on Walland Marsh and one each at Westbere, Bough Beech and Sevenoaks.

Curlew Sandpiper

Calidris ferruginea

Regular passage migrant.

Harrison records parties of up to six in May–June and up to 30 in August–September.

The Curlew Sandpiper is scarce on spring passage, with records in only 13 of the 25 years under review, between 15th March–16th June and mostly involving ones or twos. However, parties of four or five have been seen in May on three occasions, while in 1971 there were 11 at Sandwich Bay on 8th–9th May and four at Chetney from 9th–16th June.

There is also an isolated record of one at Dungeness on 30th June.

	1959	1969	1971	1972		1975
	30/8–7/9	28/8–7/9	31/7–14/8	7/8–14/8	28/8–9/9	27/8–12/9
Swanscombe	30					
Cliffe	1	80	50	2	20	65
Cooling	17					4
Stoke	86		16	13	60	5
Kingsnorth	5			12	28	24
Chetney			60			
Murston	105		8	3	2	
Windmill/Capel		25			10	
Harty		135	24	175	4	20
Shellness	3	24		12		2
Sandwich Bay	11	40	15	5	20	16
Dungeness		12	1	1	1	2
Wicks		24				
Walland Marsh	20	60				1
Totals	278	400	174	223	145	139

The six largest autumn influxes of Curlew Sandpipers 1952–76

Autumn passage is generally recorded between mid-July and mid-October, the extreme dates being 10th July–20th November, but there are only seven November records, all involving single birds in different autumns. Although parties of 10–20 are fairly normal, there have been several years with no records reaching double figures. Migration tends to occur in two waves, the first in late July and early August involving adults, and the second in late August and early September involving immatures. Depending on breeding season success and the weather, either of these waves may result in a considerable passage, and the six largest influxes are shown in the table. In three autumns a marked late passage of new arrivals was recorded between 6th–19th October, with 50 at Murston and 30 at Funton in 1959, 20 at Grovehurst in 1962, and 26 at Cliffe in 1975. The maximum count of 175 was made up of 16 groups of up to 10 birds and one flock of 95 arriving at a high tide roost at Harty on 9th August 1972.

Curlew Sandpipers favour coastal sites, feeding on estuarine mudflats as well as freshwater lagoons. Inland they are very rare and the only records involve singles at Bough Beech on 19th August 1972, 19th–21st September 1973 and 16th September 1976.

An interesting ringing recovery concerns one ringed at Grovehurst on 28th August 1972, which was shot in northern France, some 250 km SSW, the next day. Another, ringed at the Wicks during the record movement on 30th August 1969, was recovered in Morocco on 7th March 1970.

Purple Sandpiper

Calidris maritima

Regular winter visitor and occasional passage migrant.

Ticehurst considered the Purple Sandpiper to be a rare winter visitor, but it is possible that it was overlooked. Harrison described it as an annual winter visitor to the rocks off Thanet.

During the period under review, there has been a marked increase in wintering numbers, with more widespread reports in spring and autumn during the 1970s.

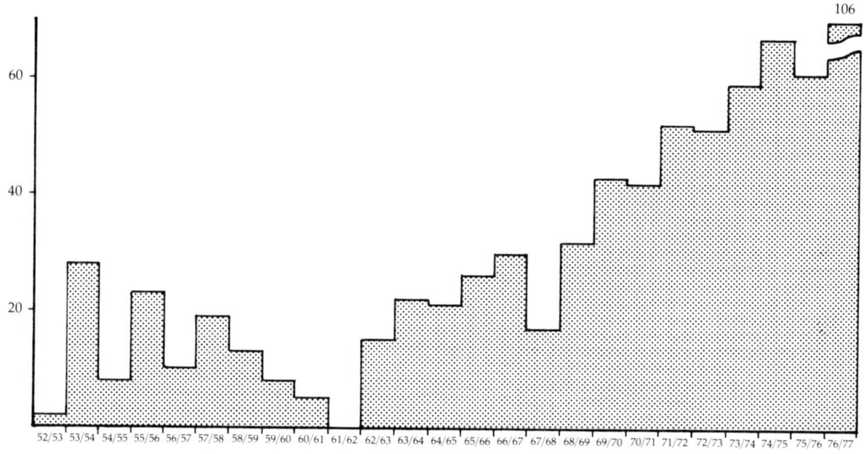

Peak winter counts of Purple Sandpipers on Thanet

In Kent the Purple Sandpiper favours the mussel-encrusted chalk rock platforms bearing patches of seaweed which exist around the northeast Thanet coast between Westgate and Dumpton Gap. Although there are two separate high-tide roosting sites, at Margate Harbour and Foreness Beach, there is a significant interchange of birds between them. On occasions the whole population may roost at one site, as in January 1977, when there was a maximum count of 106 on Foreness Beach.

Since 1969/70 a regular winter population of 5–15 birds has also been present at Dover. Elsewhere, Swalecliffe and Reculver regularly hold up to seven birds, with ones and twos less frequently wintering at Allhallows and Shellness, and once at Greatstone. Single migrants have also been recorded occasionally up the Thames as far as Dartford and in the Medway Estuary, with one–three at Dungeness and up to seven at Sandwich Bay. A flock of 22 at Sandwich Bay on 23rd February 1974 was presumably part of the Thanet population.

The earliest autumn migrant was one at Reculver on 14th August 1972, and there have been August–September records in 11 of the 25 years, but the wintering flocks do not begin to build up until late October, usually reaching a peak during December–February. However, since 1970 the flocks have remained progressively later, with small numbers now regularly present in early May. The latest record concerns three at Margate on 18th May 1956.

Dunlin

Calidris alpina

Common winter visitor and passage migrant.

The estuaries of the North Kent Marshes attract by far the largest numbers of wintering Dunlin, but an accurate assessment of the populations has always been exceptionally difficult, as the species is so widespread. Peak counts during the 1950s and 1960s were 5,500 on the Thames, 8,500 on the Medway and 9,000 on the Swale. In the 1970s special counts were organised in order to assess the size of the population more realistically. These produced the following mid-winter totals:

	Thames	Medway	Swale
1973/74	17,000	13,000	3,000
1974/75	31,000	4,500	5,500
1975/76	29,000	9,200	9,600
1976/77	20,000	18,000	10,000

Winter numbers of Dunlin on the North Kent Marshes

These figures suggest an annual winter population on the North Kent Marshes in the region of 40,000 birds. The figures for the Thames include counts of up to 6,000 in the upper reaches near Dartford.

Comparatively small numbers winter at Pegwell Bay, where regular counts throughout the period under review show an increase during the 1970s. Numbers here were at their lowest between 1963/64–1967/68, when the average winter peak was only 340.

1953/54–1960/61	1,360
1961/62–1968/69	1,240
1969/70–1976/77	2,140

Mean winter peaks of Dunlin at Pegwell Bay

Elsewhere the only substantial flock occurs at Lade, with an average winter peak of 350, though flocks of 600–800 have been recorded occasionally. In the severe weather of January 1963, however, there were exceptional flocks of 4,000 at Pegwell Bay and 3,000 at Lade, at a time when the numbers on the North Kent Marshes were considerably lower than normal.

Wintering birds generally leave in March and numbers everywhere are low in spring, reaching their lowest in June. At Pegwell Bay, for instance, the average June peak is less than 30 birds. The autumn migration quickly develops throughout July, and numbers around the coast are fairly high during the early autumn. The August–September population at Pegwell Bay averages 290 birds, approximately 20% of the winter numbers.

The wintering population builds up during the last quarter and large movements have been seen in the late autumn during cold NW winds, most frequently involving birds arriving in the mouth of the Swale at Shellness. On 18th November 1972 1,000 arrived at Shellness and 500 flew up the Thames at Allhallows, while on 29th October 1974 1,500 arrived at Shellness, 500 flew up the Thames, and 2,500 flew north at Sandwich Bay. At Dungeness the largest such movement concerned 645 flying west on 19th October 1967.

Small numbers have been recorded inland in all months of the year, but spring and autumn peaks usually remain in single figures. In winter flocks of up to 800 occur regularly on the tidal mud of the Medway in the Burham area, while the flooded fields at Grove Ferry often hold up to 200 birds, with peaks of 500 in February 1961 and February 1972. Much further inland there have been flocks of up to 30 at Sevenoaks and 40–70 at Bough Beech, with a maximum of 200 at Bough Beech on 31st January 1976.

Of nearly 200 ringing recoveries involving foreign countries, about 70% refer to the four Scandinavian countries. These and the more distant recoveries, four each in the USSR and Morocco, give some indication of the origins and destinations of Kentish wintering and passage birds.

Broad-billed Sandpiper

Limicola falcinellus

Very rare vagrant.

The only county record is of one trapped and ringed at Harty on 30th August 1970.

Buff-breasted Sandpiper

Tryngites subruficollis

Despite the regularity of occurrence of this American species in the west of Britain, there is only one Kent record up to 1976, of one near Deal on 1st August 1943. [Two more were seen in Kent in 1977. Eds.]

Ruff

Philomachus pugnax

Passage migrant and winter visitor.

Harrison recorded small numbers in spring and autumn during the first part of the century, with an increase in wintering records in the forties. Although breeding may have occurred, particularly in east Kent around the turn of the century, confirmatory evidence is lacking.

There has been a considerable increase in numbers during the last 25 years. The main flocks are attracted to the coastal lowlands, where they can be seen beside open water, on flooded fields and occasionally on plough.

In the fifties there were occasional late winter influxes, with 32 at Grove Ferry on 22nd February 1953 and 51 at Stodmarsh from 28th February 1959. Flocks of up to 40 were recorded in April and up to 20 in autumn, although 50 were attracted to the Dungeness Lighthouse lantern on 25th September 1957. Wintering parties of up to 20 also built up along the Thames marshes.

These trends continued in the sixties, with flocks of up to 27 at Grove and 40 at Cooling recorded frequently in the winter. Similarly there were many spring records of flocks of up to 40 in March–April, with exceptional peaks of 100 at Stodmarsh on 20th April 1961 and 72 at Sandwich Bay on 18th April 1967. There were more summer reports in the sixties too, with unusually large parties of 21 at Dungeness on 31st May and 15 at Capel Fleet on 22nd June in 1966, leading to the suspicion that breeding might be attempted. As in spring, the autumn passage between July–September regularly involved flocks of up to 40, with a peak of 60 at Grove on 11th August 1961.

The Thames wintering flock increased and moved to the Dartford area between 1969–73, usually involving 50–75 birds, with a maximum of 120 in March 1970, but since this period the flock has not reappeared. Numbers in spring and autumn have continued to show a gradual increase and in March 1976 there were seven flocks totalling 260 present in the county. A new development since 1974 has been the continued presence of autumn flocks of 30–50 on the Thames and Swale marshes into October–November, although numbers wintering in these two areas only involved 10–20 birds.

The early departure of males from potential breeding areas and the inconspicuous behaviour of the females combine to make proof of nesting hard to obtain, and as yet no conclusive evidence has been recorded.

Inland the Ruff is now reported regularly in spring and autumn at Sevenoaks and Bough Beech, with occasional records elsewhere. In the cold snap at the end of January 1976, two–four arrived at three widely separated localities, with up to 35 along the Medway at New Hythe.

Birds ringed on autumn passage have been recovered in France in September, Spain in December, Italy in March and Morocco in April. One, recovered at Cliffe in January, had been ringed in a previous autumn in Lincolnshire. Several have been retrapped at the place of ringing in subsequent autumns, up to three years later.

Jack Snipe

Lymnocryptes minimus

Winter visitor and passage migrant.

There has been no apparent change in status. The Jack Snipe favours boggy ground and though most frequently found on the coastal marshes, it does occur and may often be overlooked at inland localities, such as small sewage works and gravel pits, and wherever there are reedy ponds or patches of marsh. Most records tend to be of single birds, but in the most favoured haunts larger numbers occur, particularly during spring migration.

Although not normally seen in May–August, there are eight recent years with records up to 13th May, three with July records from the 5th, and eight years with August records. A few can be expected each September, but the Jack Snipe becomes far more common and widespread during October.

Prior to 1969 there were only two high counts, 15 on Walland Marsh on 24th April 1954 and 25 at Dungeness on 28th March 1960, clearly demonstrating the regular spring passage that occurs in March–April.

Consistently higher numbers since 1969 have shown the Thames marshes at Swanscombe to be the most favoured wintering locality, with January–April peaks of 25 in 1970, 19 in 1972, 21 in 1975 and 13 in 1976. The fact that the two highest counts occurred in April is further evidence of the spring migration, and in 1970 there were still five present on 2nd May. Flocks of 10–11 have also been seen nearby at Littlebrook and Dartford.

Elsewhere, the most notable peaks have been 15 at Sandwich Bay in October 1973, 20 at Allhallows in October 1974, 18 at Sevenoaks and 20 at Otford in December 1974, 26 at Allhallows and 16 at Lade in October–November 1975. More normal peaks of 5–10 birds have been seen in many winters at all the above localities, and elsewhere in the county.

Snipe

Gallinago gallinago

Local breeding species, common and widespread passage migrant and winter visitor.

According to Ticehurst the Snipe was mainly a winter visitor to Kent until the early nineteenth century, since when breeding had been recorded sporadically. Harrison included references to a few pairs breeding regularly at three or four localities in the 1940s, but Gillham and Homes concluded that the Snipe was an uncommon breeding species on the North Kent Marshes. There is no evidence to suggest any marked change in status.

The Snipe favours wet ground, such as water meadows and the marshy edges of rivers and lakes for breeding, though some will occasionally nest in drier meadows alongside river valleys. The well-drained marshes of north Kent remain unattractive, while the largest numbers breed in the Stour Valley. The highest breeding population estimate concerns 16 pairs between Grove and Westbere in 1960, with maximum numbers elsewhere only four pairs each at Cliffe and on the Rother Levels. No more than 20 pairs have been reported nesting in any one year, but no attempt has been made to census this species on a county-wide basis.

With such a small breeding population, relatively few birds are present during May–July. Spring passage is usually quite marked during March and continues through April, with peak counts of 400 both at Stodmarsh on 19th March 1960 and on the Thames marshes on 10th

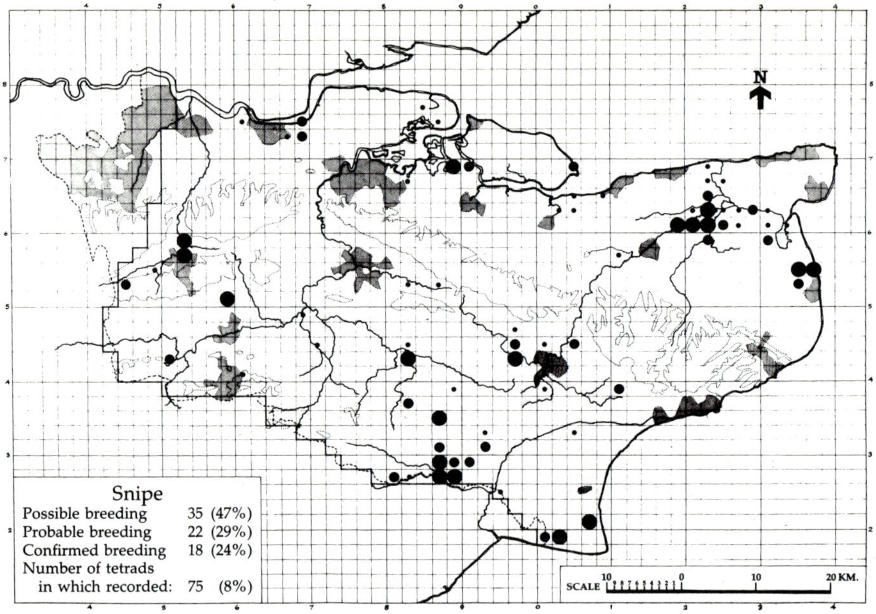

March 1975. Autumn passage may commence in late July in some years, with numbers usually reaching a peak in October–November. The highest autumn count concerns 450 on Cliffe marshes on 6th November 1975, but there was a quite exceptional influx into the Stour Valley between Grove and Stodmarsh, estimated at over 1,000, from 24th November–1st December 1968.

During the winter months flocks of 100 or more are regularly reported from suitably damp areas throughout the county, but counts of 300–500 are relatively scarce. The peak numbers occurred in January–February 1961, when there were 500 at Capel Fleet, 1,000 at Stodmarsh and 300 at Cottington.

Small numbers can be seen on migration in autumn and during cold spells in winter, with a maximum of 36 flying west at Herne Bay on 29th December 1976.

Ringing has produced some interesting overseas recoveries. One ringed at Dungeness in March 1960 was retrapped there two years later. The wintering areas of our autumn passage migrants are indicated by singles ringed at Stoke in August 1964 recovered in County Galway the following February, and one ringed at Grovehurst in September 1970 recovered in Portugal in November 1973. Of three ringed at Burham in February 1967, two were recovered six months later in the USSR, one near Leningrad and the other at Ivanova northeast of Moscow, and one 18 months later in Finland, all presumably in or near their breeding areas.

Great Snipe

Gallinago media

Very rare vagrant.

Ticehurst considered this species a rare autumn visitor and Harrison cites just four September–October records and one each for December and February.

There have been a further eight records since 1952, three between 2nd August–27th September, four between 9th December–13th January, and one on 24th April. Six birds were seen on single dates, one at Leybourne, two more in the Medway Estuary and three on Walland or Romney Marsh; one remained at Sevenoaks from 3rd–15th September 1975 and one near Rochester from 16th–25th December 1953.

Long-billed Dowitcher

Limnodromus scolopaceus

One which remained at Brookland on Romney Marsh from 9th–20th October 1946 is the only Dowitcher to have been specifically identified in the county.

Dowitcher species

Limnodromus spp.

Very rare autumn vagrant.

Early records included by Harrison, of one shot at Aldington in 1902 and a small party in east Kent on 5th November 1935, are not convincing.

Since 1961 there have been five records of Dowitchers in Kent, none of which was specifically identified. All the records referred to individuals, with the first at Grove from 29th October–26th November 1961, and others at Murston on 30th August 1966, at Sandwich Bay on 8th September 1967, at Harty Ferry on 27th September 1970 and again at Sandwich Bay on 11th October 1973.

Woodcock

Scolopax rusticola

Breeding resident, passage migrant and winter visitor.

Ticehurst considered the Woodcock to be on the increase as a breeding species, with the greatest numbers in the Weald. He also recorded the arrival of autumn migrants on Thanet in October–November. Harrison cited a number of new breeding areas, particularly in the east of the county. There is no evidence of any marked change in status in recent years.

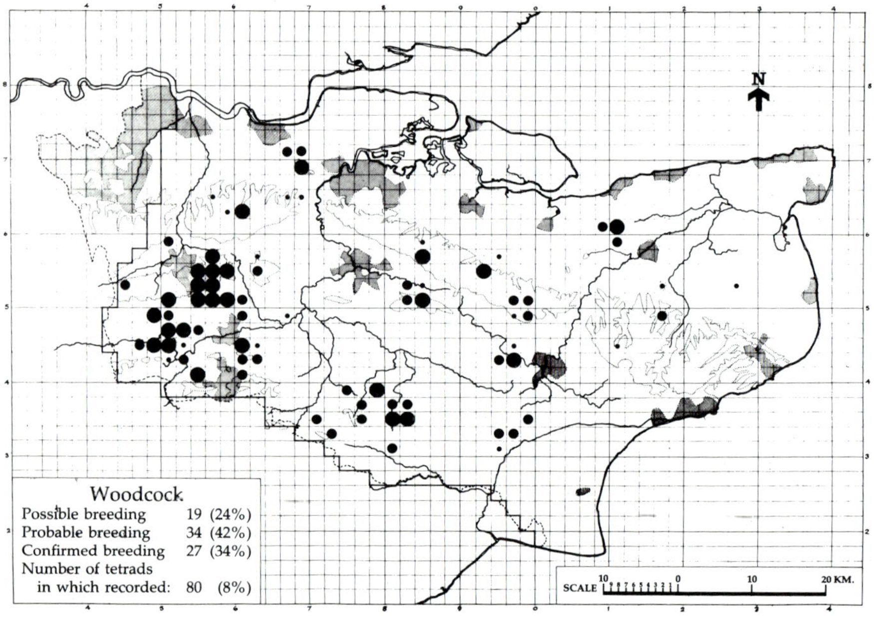

The Woodcock favours deciduous woodland, with dry ground cover for nesting and is often found in coppiced areas, but also breeds in mixed deciduous and coniferous stands and young forestry plantations. The map shows the Weald is still the stronghold of the breeding stock. Accurate estimates of the breeding populations are few, but in 1966 there were reports of seven pairs at both Mereworth and Leigh, with 15 pairs at Upper Halling. In the woodlands in the east of the county the highest estimate involved only eight pairs in 1968.

Coastal records are almost annual in spring, with records of one or two at Dungeness between 2nd March–19th April, and an exceptional peak there of 12 on 10th March 1974. There are 10 other records around the coast, with the latest on 21st April.

The autumn migration is more marked, with a few coastal reports every year. Occasionally new arrivals are seen flying in off the sea. At this season more individuals are recorded along the north and east coasts, though there are almost annual records for Dungeness too. The earliest concerns two at Dungeness on 3rd October 1974, but reports are more frequent from late October and throughout November. Later arrivals may be seen in cold weather. Most records concern single birds, but there were four at Sandwich Bay on 29th October 1966.

Estimates of winter populations have also been sporadic, but the Woodcock is most widespread and numerous at this season. Counts of 10–20 in small areas of woodland are reported in most winters, while concentrations of 30–40 occurred at Otham in 1958, Hythe in 1960, Ospringe in 1961, and at Hollingbourne and Wateringbury in January 1971.

Two ringing recoveries, indicative of the origins of some of our winter visitors, concern one ringed at Sevenoaks in January 1973 recovered three months later in Estonia, and another ringed at Margate in February 1976 recovered in Latvia in October 1977. One ringed at Dungeness in October 1953 was recovered in Ushant, France three months later.

Black-tailed Godwit

Limosa limosa

Locally numerous passage migrant, winter visitor in small numbers. Has bred.

Ticehurst and Harrison show that the Black-tailed Godwit was a scarce passage migrant, particularly in spring, until a general increase took place in the 1930s. Gillham and Homes reported flocks on the North Kent Marshes of up to 20 in winter and 100 in August between 1937–39, and one pair possibly bred in 1938.

	J	F	M	A	M	J	J	A	S	O	N	D
1953–60								161				
1961–68	24	23	94	144	15	25	198	280	199	139	24	36
1969–76	12	51	187	296	9	14	395	425	314	125	168	65
Maxima	60	105	450	490	52	40	650	600	555	360	500	260

Maxima and mean monthly peaks of Black-tailed Godwits in north Kent

The accompanying table documents the continuing increase in numbers on the North Kent Marshes. In the 1950s the only consistently high numbers occurred in August, but the Black-tailed Godwit is now a numerous passage migrant in March–April and again between July–November.

The main flock is usually present in the Swale during February–August and in the Medway between September–January, although during the 1970s there was a general shift towards the Medway in July–August. The peak counts for spring and autumn are 490 in April 1974 and 650 in July 1971. The tendency for the autumn flocks to stay later was highlighted in 1971, when 260 stayed till 19th December, and in 1972 when there were 500 present on 5th November. Flocks of up to 60 have occurred in midwinter, and there was an exceptional record of 60 wintering on the Thames in 1960/61. Another exceptional count for the Thames concerns 100 at Stoke on 15th July 1972.

In 1968 two females laid eggs in the same nest on the Thames marshes, while in 1972 a pair reared one young on the Medway. A few birds usually summer on Sheppey and breeding has long been suspected there, but never proved. In the south of the county, one pair bred in three years between 1973–76. It is noticeable that these breeding birds belong to the paler breasted European race *L.l. limosa,* whereas all the passage migrants apparently belong to the darker plumaged Icelandic race *L.l. islandica.*

Elsewhere in the county, peaks of 10–25 occur only rarely at such localities as Sandwich Bay, the Stour Valley and Walland Marsh, mostly in April and between July–September. There are also exceptional records of 50 at Greatstone on 5th September 1954, 40 at Sandwich Bay on 30th December 1959 and 100 on Walland Marsh on 13th July 1970. Well inland, at Bough Beech, the peak numbers have been 11 on 8th–9th July 1973 and 14 on 21st April 1976.

Bar-tailed Godwit

Limosa lapponica

Numerous passage migrant and winter visitor.

According to Harrison the Bar-tailed Godwit was not very numerous in spring, but was common in autumn, and he records a peak of 600 in the Swale in February 1940, an exceptionally severe winter. The impressive spring passage at Dungeness was first noted in 1937, when 2,000 flew northeast there between 30th April–2nd May.

This spring passage at Dungeness has proved to be highly concentrated and occasionally spectacular, with day totals over 1,000 being recorded between 19th April–3rd May almost annually in the 1970s. In 1972 there were 3,850 on 26th April, while the following year there was a record spring total of 8,060, including a peak of 4,190, again on 26th April. Small flocks stop off at the Wicks and on Lade Sands at this time, while rather larger counts at Sandwich Bay include up to 485 in the last week of April. Flocks of up to 24 have occurred inland at Bough Beech and rarely elsewhere during the same period, with a maximum of 85 flying northeast at Bough Beech on 22nd April 1976.

The numbers of Bar-tailed Godwits are at their lowest in June, when flocks of up to 40 have occurred at Sandwich Bay and on the North Kent Marshes.

Autumn passage starts in July, and in 1973 there were already 400 in the Swale by the 28th of that month. Up to 100 have been noted arriving at Shellness in August–September, with an exceptional total of 960 flying up the Swale on 18th August 1973. There was also an unusual peak of 500 in the Medway on 16th August 1975. These early movements all involve passage migrants, whereas the wintering birds apparently arrive during October–December.

The following table documents a steady decrease in the numbers of wintering birds during the period under review:

	Thames	Medway	Swale	Sandwich Bay
1953/54–1960/61	369	126	869	156
1961/62–1968/69		111	563	125
1969/70–1976/77		67	499	78

Mean winter peaks of Bar-tailed Godwits

Maximum counts of 1,200 occurred in the Swale in February 1957 and December 1959, while there have been up to 350 at Sandwich Bay and 200 in the Medway. Up to 500 also wintered in the Thames in the 1950s, and the highest combined totals occurred in March 1955, when there were 500 in the Thames and 1,000 in the Swale; and in the severe weather of February 1956, when there were 1,000 in the Thames and 800 in the Swale. However, the Thames is no longer used as a regular wintering area and in several years since 1964 numbers have not reached double figures, though there were 200 in December 1973. Small numbers also winter occasionally at Lade, with a maximum of 70 there in January 1963.

The Bar-tailed Godwit is relatively rare inland and the only records, apart from those already mentioned on spring passage, concern one over Westbere on 30th December 1962, two over Stodmarsh on 10th December 1967 and 30th July 1968, and 17 flying southwest at East Peckham on 14th December 1968.

Whimbrel

Numenius phaeopus

Annual passage migrant, occurring commonly round the coast and less frequently overland.

March records have occurred in only nine of the 25 years under review, with the earliest in the Medway estuary on 4th March 1961. The first migrants are usually seen in early April, with the peak spring passage occurring during late April and the first half of May, when flocks of 40–60 are recorded fairly regularly. The most favoured localities are the North Kent Marshes, Sandwich Bay and the Wicks, and by far the largest flocks were 150 at Stoke on 4th May 1958 and the same number at the Wicks on 5th May 1970. Visible migration may be observed each year offshore at Dungeness, where there was a record up-Channel movement of 230 and 71 on 19th and 20th April 1976, but where day-totals usually only involve 15–30 birds. Elsewhere the largest movements concern flocks of 70 leaving to the northeast at Shellness on 12th May 1970 and 66 inland over Bough Beech on 3rd May 1974.

There are relatively few observations for June and counts of 12 at Sandwich Bay on 11th June 1974 and 20 at Grain on 24th June 1973 are exceptional.

The autumn migration develops rapidly during July and the highest numbers are recorded during the last week of July and the first three weeks of August, when coastal flocks of up to 80 occur more frequently than in spring. There is a widespread southwestward movement which is often witnessed inland, where usually only small numbers are involved, although flocks of 20–60 have been recorded on nine occasions. Coastal peak numbers have involved flocks arriving from the northeast at Shellness, with 113 on 11th August 1972, 224 on 18th August 1973, and 100 on 27th July 1975. Numbers drop off abruptly in late August and early September and very few are seen in October. November records of singles, and on one occasion two birds, have occurred in only seven years, the latest on 30th November 1976 and 18th December 1956.

Several birds ringed in Kent in autumn have been recovered abroad, most notably during May in Nigeria and twice in presumed breeding areas in Russia, in the White Sea basin near Archangel.

Curlew

Numenius arquata

Winter visitor and passage migrant.

Harrison recorded flocks of up to 3,000 on the North Kent Marshes and a quite exceptional total of 8,000 at Pegwell Bay in February 1940, following a partial thaw in that arctic winter.

The Curlew is most numerous on the North Kent Marshes, where it feeds on the mud flats and roosts on the saltings and fresh marsh. Elsewhere round the coast it may be found in bays and estuaries, on sands and mud-flats, and on the seaweed covered rocks round Thanet.

Each of the three main estuaries in the north regularly holds flocks of over 1,000 between July–March. However, most of the really high counts have occurred in autumn, between July and September, and in mid-winter during January and February. There are several records of 2,000–3,500 for these months, and higher counts include 5,000 on Sheppey in February 1955 and March 1961, and on the Medway in August 1961, with 6,000 on the Thames in February 1966, when there were also 2,500 on the Swale. Systematic winter counts made in 1975 and 1976 produced January/February peaks of 1,950 on the Thames, 1,250 on the Medway and 1,240 on the Swale. It is interesting to note that extensive ringing has shown little interchange between the Swale and Thames populations.

The only other significant flocks occur at Pegwell Bay, where 3–500 may be seen between July–March, with peaks of 1,000 in February 1963 and October 1972. Smaller numbers also occur at Lade, where there was a maximum of 500 in February 1972.

Spring passage occurs during March–April and visible movements at

Dungeness consistently reach a peak in the third week of April. In 1969 totals of 135 and 100 flew up-Channel on 19th and 20th April, while 310 were counted on 17th April 1972. Flocks have also been seen leaving Shellness to the northeast, and in 1972 there were peaks of 125 on 16th April and 120 on 25th April.

Numbers are always at their lowest in May, but some non-breeding birds summer. The autumn passage starts early, and flocks of up to 1,500 have been recorded by the end of June. There is a widespread passage to the southwest during July–August and overland migrants are most frequently recorded at this time, with peaks of 30 over Bedgebury on 4th August 1956 and 31 over Stockbury on 20th August 1963.

The fifteen foreign ringing recoveries relating to Kent all come from the European seaboard between Finland and France, indicating that a high proportion of those wintering or on passage through north Kent are of Baltic origin. The three most southerly recoveries, two of them close to the Spanish border, all occurred following cold weather movements in January/February 1963.

Spotted Redshank

Tringa erythropus

Passage migrant, more numerous in autumn than in spring, wintering in small numbers.

Ticehurst describes this species as a rare straggler in spring, with parties of up to a dozen in autumn, and refers to one winter record. Harrison considered it to be more regular on passage, and makes several references to overwintering, particularly since the early 1940s.

The Spotted Redshank has continued to increase considerably during the period under review, and is now only absent for an extremely brief period in midsummer, generally between 20th May–10th June. Odd singles have occurred later in May in seven years, while in 1963 the first returning birds arrived very early, with eight at Murston and ten at Elmley on 6th and 9th June respectively.

Autumn passage lasts from mid-June to mid-November, the main haunts being the estuaries of the North Kent Marshes. Roosts of 20–50 have occurred regularly at Stoke Lagoon since 1963, and Windmill Creek since 1964. However, there are several other sites by the Medway Estuary which have held regular flocks of 50 or more since 1962, with 100–150 in nine years, and a maximum of 220 at Grovehurst on 8th October 1972. There is usually only one major roost in use at any one time and for most of the period under review it has been based on the south side of the Medway estuary at Grovehurst, Barksore or Chetney. However, new sites which became available on the north side of the estuary at Kingsnorth in 1973 and Grain Refinery in 1975 have since superseded them.

The first returning birds in autumn are all adults, and flocks of 20–40 now occur annually in late June. By far the largest roosts at this time were 75 at Grovehurst on 26th June 1973 and 140 at Kingsnorth on 2nd July 1975. Although numbers remain consistently high in July and August, most of the really large counts have been made in September–October. Flocks of up to 40 have occurred in early November, while at Grovehurst there were exceptionally late roosts of 97 on 26th November 1966 and 100 on 1st November 1970.

Ones and twos, and occasionally up to six together, now winter regularly on the Medway and Swale estuaries, with a few records from elsewhere. Larger parties have only occurred in four winters, with 15 at Chetney in January 1967, 21 at Grovehurst in January 1972, 20 at Capel Fleet in early March 1974 and 21 at Grain in January 1976.

Spring passage usually lasts from mid-March to mid-May, and the only two regular sites, at Capel/Windmill Creek and Stoke Lagoon, normally hold a maximum of 10–20 birds at some time during the period 9th April–9th May. The only larger numbers occurred at Stoke Lagoon in 1974, when there were 34 on 13th April and 30 on 27th April.

Elsewhere this species is not very numerous. At Sandwich Bay, for instance, there have usually been up to nine in April and again in August–September, while nearby in the Stour Valley the equivalent figures are seven and ten, with a peak of 22 at Grove on 1st September 1962. In the south, reports from Walland Marsh, the Wicks and Dungeness Reserve involve up to six in spring and ten in autumn, while inland there have been up to six at Sevenoaks and seven at Bough Beech in autumn.

The only foreign ringing recovery concerns one ringed at Grovehurst in July 1966 which was recovered in Malta in April 1968.

Redshank

Tringa totanus

Regular breeding species, winter visitor and passage migrant.

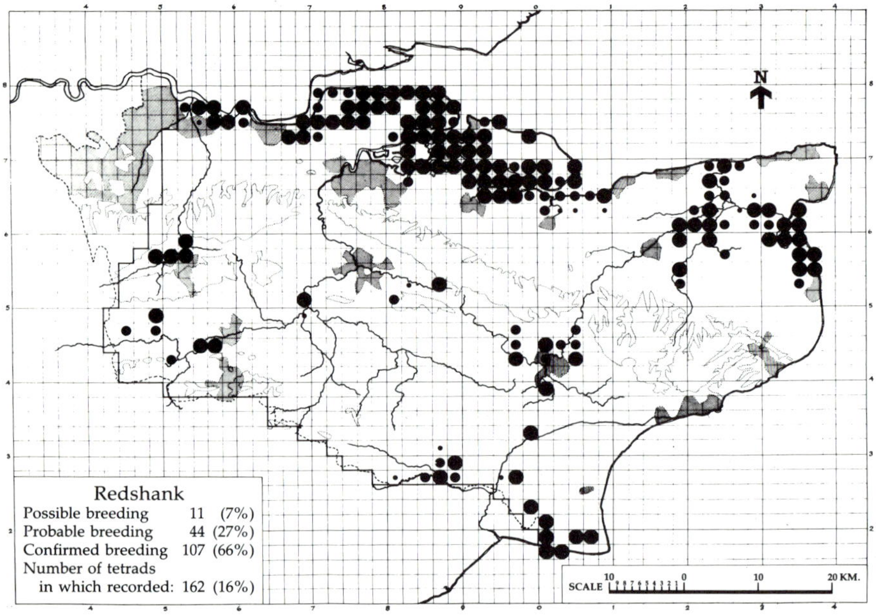

The main breeding area is the North Kent Marshes, where censuses of the Medway Islands showed a drop from 237 pairs in 1955 to 118 pairs in 1961 and only 40 pairs in 1966, recovering to 84 pairs in 1972. In addition 60 pairs bred on Chetney in 1968. Such detailed information is not available for the Thames and Sheppey marshes, where this species is also numerous. Elsewhere near the coast, there have been estimates of 32 pairs in the Stour Valley in 1966, 22 pairs near the Brooks in 1972 and 18 pairs on the Rother Levels in 1966. Much further inland, odd pairs may breed along the various river valleys and there were eight pairs in the Darent Valley near Sevenoaks in 1967. At the new reservoir at Bough Beech four pairs bred in 1976.

On the coast large flocks build up in July–August and the highest numbers for the year often occur in autumn. This is especially true of the Medway, where the autumn totals usually exceed those in winter, and

	Thames	Medway	Swale	Pegwell Bay
Autumn	460	1,530	710	200
Winter	1,320	1,070	1,010	270

Mean autumn and winter peaks of Redshank 1961/62–1976/77

where there were peaks of 3,000 in September 1962 and 3,750 in October 1975. There is then often a short-lived decrease before the mid-winter flocks build up. In winter the largest numbers are usually reported from Cliffe Pools, where there were 3,000 in February 1965, while on the Medway there was a peak of 2,500 in December 1963. At Pegwell Bay the maximum of 800 occurred in January 1963. The wintering birds disperse during March–April, but there may be temporary increases as returning migrants pass through.

Up to 200 occur in winter on the tidal mud of the Medway as far inland as Burham, while in the Stour Valley up to 100 have occurred on the fields at Grove. Further inland numbers are very small indeed and there have been no reports of more than seven.

In the hard winter of 1962/63 over 300 were found dead along the tideline, half of them at Sandwich Bay. Redshank shared with Shelduck the distinction of the highest shorebird mortality in Kent during that winter.

Ringing recoveries include singles to Norway, Finland, Morocco and Senegal, indicating the origins or destinations of Kentish birds, and measurements of trapped birds suggest that a number of the Icelandic race *T.t. robusta* occur.

Marsh Sandpiper

Tringa stagnatilis

Very rare vagrant.

Two were seen at Dungeness on 26th September 1937.

The only recent record is of one seen at Swanscombe from 28th August–2nd September 1963.

Greenshank

Tringa nebularia

Passage migrant. Most plentiful in autumn and increasingly noted in winter.

There would seem to have been a considerable change in the status of this species. Ticehurst refers to parties of three–four birds in autumn and only one or two in spring, while Harrison writes of autumn parties of 25 by 1935, and includes references to several winter records in the 1940s.

Greenshanks are most often to be found on tidal creeks or, when congregating at high-tide roosts, at nearby fresh water fleets and lagoons. The Medway, Swale and Stour estuaries regularly attract the largest numbers. As with Curlew and Whimbrel, migrating birds call frequently, and are often heard over inland localities.

In most years during the 1950s and 1960s there were one or two records in January and February in north Kent, with four at Chetney on 29th January 1964. March records were few, with a maximum of six at Shellness on 4th March 1956. In recent years the Greenshank has become less scarce in winter, with up to 20 in the Medway Estuary in January 1974, six at Yantlet and five at Windmill Creek in January 1975.

Spring migrants are seen in April and May in all areas with suitable habitat. Parties of four–eight birds are reported in most years, sometimes 10–14 or more during the first two weeks of May, with a maximum of 20 at Stodmarsh on 10th May 1970. As the Scottish breeding birds are on territory by mid-April, most spring migrants in Kent presumably belong to the Scandinavian and eastern breeding populations.

Although Greenshank have been recorded in June in six of the last 25 years, there are normally none between the 6th–25th. Sizeable parties can occur in early July, with 30 at Yantlet on 7th July 1957, but autumn migration is more obvious from the middle of the month. The first really large autumn roosts involved 50 at Stoke and 35 at Windmill Creek in September 1956, with 51 at Stoke in July and 70 at Windmill Creek in September 1960. These two localities have since held roosts of 20–40 birds, with 65 at Windmill Creek in September 1976. A new site at Kingsnorth has provided a regular roost for 40–85 birds during July–October since 1969, with maxima of 100 on 3rd October 1971 and 130 on 25th August 1976.

Elsewhere the largest autumn numbers occur at Sandwich Bay, where peaks of 15–35 are normal, while nearby in the Stour Valley there were 25 at Grove on 17th August 1962. However, in 1971 there were exceptional records of 120 at Sandwich Bay on 2nd August and 150 flying south over Elmstone on 24th August. In the south of the county up to 14 have been seen on Romney and Walland Marshes.

Numbers fall rapidly during October and before 1970 there were December records in only six of the eighteen years. Recently, November–December numbers have increased and are similar to those seen in January–February.

Inland, Greenshank are seen in most years at localities such as the Sevenoaks Reserve and Bough Beech reservoir, but unlike coastal areas, there are as many reports of small parties in spring as in autumn. The maximum counts are 13 at Bough Beech on 3rd May 1974 and 15 at Bewl Bridge reservoir on 7th May 1976.

The only ringing recovery is of one retrapped at Stoke on 10th September 1966, which had been ringed at Ledskar, Sweden on 14th August that year.

Greater Yellowlegs

Tringa melanoleuca

Very rare vagrant.

One was present in the Medway estuary between 7th September–1st October 1943.

The only record during the review period concerned one, again in the Medway estuary, on 22nd November 1972.

Lesser Yellowlegs

Tringa flavipes

Very rare vagrant.

One was identified in the Stour estuary on 19th September 1943.

Two were seen together on Walland Marsh on 19th April 1953. In 1970 one was seen on Chetney on 4th and 9th September and another, again on Walland Marsh, from 11th–18th October.

Green Sandpiper

Tringa ochropus

Recorded in all months, but most plentiful on autumn passage.

There has been little change in status during the last hundred years, though there has been a tendency for larger numbers to remain throughout recent winters, probably the result of the long series of mild winters. Both Ticehurst and Harrison considered the species to be scarcest in February and March, and indeed winter records were so few that Harrison lists most of those known to him.

This species is most frequently seen on the coastal fresh marshes, beside any fleet, ditch or pond with a muddy margin. It also visits steep sided channels in the saltmarshes at low tide. Inland it is a regular visitor to gravel pits, reservoirs and flooded streams. Green Sandpipers normally avoid exposed areas if sheltered sites are available.

There have been winter records of one or two birds regularly at several localities, both inland and on the coast, but increasingly during the last decade small parties of five–seven have been reported between December and February. March records involve similar numbers, but the appearance of birds in new localities suggests that spring passage may start early. In 1976 a total of about 57 birds was recorded during the first quarter.

Spring migration takes place mainly during April, but numbers are small, reports of one or two birds being much more frequent than those of small parties. There are few records in May after the first week, indeed in some years there have been no reports during that month and nowadays this species is at its scarcest during May.

On the North Kent Marshes migrants start to reappear in mid-June, with occasional records in the second week of the month. By the last week of June numbers are higher than at any time since the previous autumn, with widespread gatherings of six–nine birds, reaching 12 at Murston on 29th June 1965. Elsewhere, the first autumn migrants are usually seen in the last week of June, but are most obvious between early July and early September. Small parties are seen in many areas, but in most years the largest gatherings do not exceed 20 birds. Groups of 30–35 do sometimes occur in the North Kent Marshes and at Sandwich Bay, with a maximum count of about 50 in the Yantlet Creek area on 18th August 1957.

Numbers seem to drop steadily from mid-September, but small parties continue to pass through in October and November. By December only the small wintering population remains, staying in the county until early March, unless really severe weather drives them on.

The only ringing recovery is of a migrant killed in Pas de Calais, France in August, two years after it had been ringed at Herne.

Wood Sandpiper

Tringa glareola

Passage migrant. Annual in small numbers in spring, but more plentiful in autumn.

There has been little apparent change in status since the mid-thirties, but Wood Sandpipers were apparently much scarcer in the early part of this century. Despite this, there are no recent records to compare with the flock of 80–100 in the Rainham Marshes on 26th July 1867.

Wood Sandpipers frequent the muddy margins of fleets, lagoons on the coastal marshes, pools in sandpits, and reservoirs inland. Marshland flooded for long periods, such as Grove Ferry and Walland Marsh, is particularly favoured. They are not normally seen on coastal mudflats. Appearances are equally regular on the marshes of north, east and south Kent and inland at Sevenoaks, Bough Beech reservoir and in the Medway Valley.

The small spring passage occurs between mid-April and the first week of June, with the main movement in May. The earliest records are 4th April 1954 and 7th April 1957 at Dungeness. It is unusual to see more than two birds together in spring, but eight were seen at Grove Ferry between 18th–22nd May 1961 and at Sandwich Bay on 7th May 1963.

Several records in mid-June, including four at Hersden on 12th June 1972, could refer to either late spring or early return movements. However, small influxes late in the month, including seven at Stodmarsh on 26th June 1967 and five at Sandwich Bay on 30th June 1972, presumably refer to early autumn migrants.

Autumn migration gets into full swing in mid-July, with the largest numbers any time between late July and early September. Small parties may remain in one locality for several days, even a few weeks. In most years the maximum is between 8–12, but sometimes larger groups have been seen, including 18 at the Wicks on 22nd August 1952, 24 at Harty on 4th September 1958, 17 at Dungeness on 3rd August and 25 at Sandwich Bay on 6th September 1966. There are very few records for October, with the latest individuals at Harty on 30th October 1960, Grove Ferry on 29th October 1961, Stodmarsh from 23rd October–1st November 1971 and Egypt Bay on 21st November 1976.

Terek Sandpiper

Xenus cinereus

Very rare vagrant.

The only record is of one on 20th May 1973, which flew on to the beach at Sandwich Bay, joining a mixed flock of waders as the tide receded.

Common Sandpiper

Actitis hypoleucos

Passage migrant, commonest in autumn. A few winter.

Ticehurst did not know of any winter reports, but Harrison gives details of ten records between 1925–51.

The Common Sandpiper occurs regularly in small numbers on passage at favoured inland sites such as reservoirs, gravel pits, lakes and rivers, but forms sizeable flocks along coastal estuaries and beside the larger fleets and ditches on the fresh marshes. The Stour estuary apparently suits its requirements admirably and attracts the largest numbers each autumn.

Since 1952 the numbers of birds wintering has shown a slow increase, with up to 12 present in 1975/76. Most records concern one or two birds, most regularly along the Thames and at Sandwich Bay, but four were present at Dartford in January 1971 and at Sandwich Bay in January 1976. Others are occasionally recorded elsewhere on the North Kent Marshes, and at several inland sites.

Migrants start appearing from mid-March, but few arrive before late April and spring passage normally reaches a peak during the second half of May, with a few remaining until early June. The numbers are generally small, with peak counts of 10–20 at coastal localities in most years and a maximum of 25 at Sandwich Bay on 14th May 1971.

There are only occasional records after the first week of June until the return passage gets under way in early July. The main passage takes place from late July to early September, with the highest counts invariably occurring in August. Peaks of 100–150 have been recorded at

Sandwich Bay in seven autumns, with an exceptional total of 300 there on 14th August 1964. Elsewhere round the coast the peak counts rarely exceed 30, though there were 48 at Reculver on 4th September 1965. There are also widespread reports from inland localities at this time, with a maximum of 21 at Bough Beech on 10th August 1975. The numbers drop steadily from mid-September, but passage continues through October. Relatively few are seen in November, but some of these remain to winter.

The only ringing recovery is of a migrant caught at Dungeness on 20th August 1967, which was found dead in Norway on 31st May 1975, giving an indication of the origins of passage birds.

Spotted Sandpiper

Actitis macularia

Very rare vagrant.

An early record, which came to light in the 1970s (Harrison, 1975), concerning an adult male shot at Sheerness in July 1863, precedes the earliest British record quoted by the BOU.

In recent years, one in summer plumage was observed at the ARC pits at Dungeness on 28th May 1971.

Turnstone

Arenaria interpres

Winter visitor and passage migrant.

Much of the Kentish coast does not provide suitable Turnstone habitat, but the most frequented haunts are the shingle beaches at the mouth of the Swale and at Reculver, and the rocky foreshore on Thanet. Although other suitable localities exist in the Thames and Medway estuaries, at Sandwich Bay and Lade, flocks there are rather smaller and often of a more temporary nature.

	Thames	Medway	Swale	Reculver	Sandwich Bay
1953–60	109	46	650	113	
1961–68	49	57	135	133	16
1969–76	63	93	171	156	20

Mean autumn peaks of Turnstone

Autumn passage begins in July and reaches a marked peak in August–September, when flocks of up to 250 have occurred in the Thames and Medway estuaries and at Reculver, with up to 500 in the Swale. The only higher counts involve the roost at Shellness, where there were 1,000 on 14th August 1953, while in 1958 there were again 1,000 on 14th August, increasing to 1,645 on 14th September. Numbers usually fluctuate considerably during October–November, before increasing again towards the mid-winter peak.

	Thames	Medway	Swale	Reculver	Thanet	S. Bay
1953/54–1960/61	95	72	375	133	33	
1961/62–1968/69	40	47	241	187	113	33
1969/70–1976/77	63	93	286	146	300	50

Mean winter peaks of Turnstone

Winter flocks have reached 200 in the Thames, 250 on the Medway and 300 at Reculver, with an unusual count of 500 at Yantlet on 28th November 1954. As in the autumn counts, there has been a relative decrease in numbers in the Swale over the survey period. Counts of up to 500 used to occur more frequently in the 1950s than at present, with a maximum of 1,000 at Shellness on 11th January 1958. In the east and south of the county the maximum counts for many years occurred in the severe weather of February 1963, with 300 on Thanet, 110 at Sandwich Bay and 50 at Lade. In the winter of 1971/72 there were new peaks, with 400 on Thanet and 120 at Sandwich Bay. Numbers on Thanet have since tended to increase, reaching a peak of 620 at Margate harbour in December 1976. It seems that this a genuine increase, and not one due to more intensive coverage of high-tide roosts.

Wintering birds usually leave during March and there is a record of 240 seen leaving Shellness to the northeast on 20th February 1976. The largest flocks in spring are seen at Shellness and Reculver, where separate peaks of 200–300 birds may occur in both April and May as different waves of migrants pass through. Spring passage is most concentrated during the first three weeks of May, when flocks have again been seen leaving Shellness to the northeast at high tide, with peaks of 70 on 13th May and 80 on 17th May 1970. Much smaller numbers have been seen flying up-Channel at Dungeness and there was a peak of 50 at Lade on 13th May 1968.

Midsummer records in June usually only involve single figures, although at Shellness there were exceptional peaks of 40 on 17th June 1954 and 45 on 15th June 1958.

Inland records, in the Stour and Medway Valleys, at Bough Beech and

Sevenoaks, reflect in miniature the spring and autumn passage on the coast, with parties of up to six between 22nd April–2nd June and a maximum of 14 at Grove on 11th May 1961. In autumn, singles and on one occasion four together, have occurred between 14th July–2nd September, while parties of 38 and 13 flew southwest over Gillingham on 15th August 1971. Parties of two–six have also occurred at Sevenoaks on three occasions during January–February.

The only foreign ringing recovery concerns one ringed at Amager, Denmark in June 1961, which was retrapped at Harty in July 1966.

Wilson's Phalarope

Phalaropus tricolor

Very rare vagrant.

The only records of this North American wader concern singles at Walland Marsh from 21st–25th September 1970 and at Egypt Bay on 11th May 1971.

Red-necked Phalarope

Phalaropus lobatus

Rare autumn and very rare spring visitor.

To judge from comments in Ticehurst and Harrison, Red-necked Phalaropes were no commoner in the past, although the British and Irish breeding population was appreciably larger.

The only spring or summer records are of one at Sandwich Bay from 26th–30th May 1975 and two at Grove on 26th June 1962. In autumn there have been 11 records, all of single birds, between 3rd August–8th November. Seven of these occurred during August, with one in late September, two in October and the latest at Pegwell Bay on 6th–8th November 1976. All have been seen at coastal localities, especially in the Dungeness and Sandwich Bay areas.

Grey Phalarope

Phalaropus fulicarius

Rare autumn migrant, very rare in winter.

In the past the Grey Phalarope's status was apparently similar, but small parties were recorded in the invasion years at the turn of the century.

During the period under review there are records for 17 of the 25 years. All records concern single birds and are tabulated below. The majority occurred between 14th September–2nd December, and where an individual stayed for several days the record is included for the month in which it was first seen.

J	F	M	A	M	J	J	A	S	O	N	D
2		1					1	8	7	7	3

Monthly distribution of Grey Phalaropes 1952–76

The only spring record was at Shellness on 9th March 1952, and the earliest autumn record at Sandwich Bay on 28th August 1962.

A detailed analysis of the records shows that 15 occurred around the east Kent coast from Reculver to Dungeness; a further 11 on the North Kent Marshes, particularly off Shellness and Allhallows; one on Walland Marsh; and two inland at Bough Beech on 12th–13th October 1975 and from 26th December 1971–2nd January 1972.

In 1969 and 1974 four singles were seen, but in most years only one or two birds are recorded.

Among several records of unidentified phalaropes are one off Allhallows on 16th January 1955, three off the same locality on 9th November 1957, one at Reculver on 20th–21st January 1973, one at Oare from 22nd March–3rd April and one off Dungeness on 12th September 1976, all of which are most likely to refer to this species.

Pomarine Skua

Stercorarius pomarinus

Passage migrant.

Although early reports suggested that the Pomarine Skua was irregular in occurrence, Harrison found records for every month of the year and concluded that migration was probably regular off Dungeness.

During the period under review there are no records for January–March, and the most interesting development is the discovery of an almost annual spring passage at Dungeness, involving small flocks of adults. This seems to confirm earlier opinions and is probably more indicative of an increase in sea-watching than a change in status. Spring passage was first observed there on 11th May 1959, when two parties of six and 16 flew up-Channel. Since 1967 it has been observed annually. The extreme dates are 16th April–9th June, but most are recorded between 28th April–17th May, and it is during this period that small flocks of up to a maximum of 28 occur. Totals exceeding 40 have been recorded in five years, including the maximum of 162 in 1976, when there were 48 and 63 on 6th and 8th May respectively. [Another 75 flew east off Beachy Head (Sussex) on 7th May. Eds.]

The largest numbers generally occur in south or east winds, and whereas Arctic Skuas migrate in ones and twos in spring, Pomarine Skuas usually migrate in small flocks. With the co-operation of observers at Dungeness and Beachy Head it has been possible to monitor this spring passage closely. Timing these flocks has shown that they take from 55–95 minutes to cover the distance between the two headlands.

Other spring records include a party of seven seen off Folkestone on 9th May 1960, and an adult in the Swale on 26th May 1975. Recent midsummer records include two off Dungeness on 14th July 1962 and one there on five dates between 17th July–27th August 1966.

Autumn passage has been recorded between 12th August–8th December and is most obvious on the north coast from Reculver westwards into the Swale and Thames estuaries. From 1969–76 this area was given more or less continuous coverage during suitable weather conditions of strong winds from a northerly quarter, producing annual totals between four and 35, with an exceptional movement of 60 at Shellness on 11th

October 1973. Otherwise the largest numbers occurred on 29th September 1957, when there were five in the Thames and 12 in the Swale. The main passage is generally between 23rd September–21st October, although small parties have occasionally occurred later. In particular there were seven in the Thames on 10th November 1957 and eight in the Swale on 13th November 1976. Outside this period one was seen in the Medway on 24th December 1954.

Elsewhere Pomarine Skuas are uncommon in autumn. Since 1960 there have been just four records from Thanet/Sandwich, three from Folkestone/Hythe, and thirteen at Dungeness, where there was a maximum of five on 27th September 1971.

Arctic Skua

Stercorarius parasiticus

Passage migrant.

Harrison describes this species as most numerous between August and November. He also gives four winter records between 1st January–15th Februrary, a few in spring between 23rd March–9th June and a few in July.

Spring passage is most obvious off Dungeness, with the earliest recent record on 26th March. It is most concentrated between 28th April–15th May, when 10 or more often occur in a day. In spring 1976 a total of 166 flew east, with a maximum of 35 on 2nd May. Elsewhere in the county this species is rare in spring, with only seventeen other coastal records between 1952–76.

Spring passage may continue into early June and there is a midsummer lull from 11th June–12th July when the Arctic Skua is scarce. There are two unusual records around this time of singles over coastal marshes, at Windmill Creek on 2nd July 1960 and the Wicks on 7th June 1961.

Autumn passage commences in July and numbers gradually increase in early August, building up rapidly in the third week. As with other skuas, the largest movements occur along the north coast, in the Swale and Thames estuaries, where totals of 50 or more in a day have been recorded between 15th August–3rd November. The highest numbers occur in northerly winds, and are most often seen in the mouth of the Swale. The four largest movements involved 103 in a northwesterly gale on 23rd August 1969, 112 in a light northerly wind on 15th August 1971,

135 again in a northwesterly gale on 24th September 1974, and 242 in a northerly gale on 14th September 1975.

With the discovery of these large autumn movements, much interest has been shown in the possibility of overland migration. The skuas generally arrive in the mouth of the Swale in small parties, but sometimes wait offshore for several hours, when accumulated flocks of up to 35 have been recorded. Most birds then fly upriver in a southwesterly direction past Shellness and few are seen to return to the open sea, while on clear days flocks have been seen circling to such a height that they are lost to sight. In these circumstances detection of overland passage would be exceedingly difficult. However, there are two inland records of two flying west over Sevenoaks on 29th August 1971, and one plus another three flying southeast there on 14th September 1976.

The Arctic Skua is also seen annually off Thanet and Sandwich Bay in autumn, although only in small numbers. Rather more occur off Dungeness, where there are fairly regular day totals of up to 20 between mid-August and mid-October, and occasionally larger movements, with a maximum of 65 on 11th September 1976.

Numbers all round the coast decrease rapidly in November, although movements of 10–20 have been seen in the Swale or Thames until the 17th. A few stragglers occur until 23rd December in some years, and there have been four winter records between 13th January–4th March, involving singles at Reculver, Herne Bay, Cliffe and Swanscombe.

Long-tailed Skua

Stercorarius longicaudus

Rare passage migrant.

Ticehurst knew of two immature specimens in Dover Museum that were obtained in the Dungeness area between 1844–47, and Harrison gives a sight record of one over the Dungeness ternery on 9th September 1936.

There have been seven recent autumn records between 8th August–28th September, five of them of single adults, with three on the Thames at Cliffe in 1954, 1956 and 1960, another at Dungeness in 1960, and one off Thanet in 1974. Single immatures were found dying, inland at Hollingbourne, on 28th September 1966, and dead on the beach at Sandwich Bay on 24th September 1976.

There are also four spring records, again of single adults, flying east at Dungeness on 13th May 1974, and on 2nd, 10th and 15th May 1976.

Great Skua

Stercorarius skua

Passage migrant.

Ticehurst listed very few records, but Harrison documents a slight increase, with some indication of autumn passage between August–October.

The occurrences of this species have increased considerably since the early sixties, perhaps more closely linked to the expansion of the breeding population than to the increase in sea-watching. Reference to the autumn passage illustrates this well. There were no records of more than six in a day until 1963, when 24 were seen at Shellness on 13th October. Counts of 18–40 at Shellness and Herne Bay followed in October 1966 and 1967, while on 3rd November 1968 at least 70 were seen in the estuaries of the Swale and Thames. The next large numbers occurred in 1970, when there were two northwesterly gales in the space of three weeks, producing counts at Shellness of 180 on 3rd October, 82 on 20th October and 161 there the next day. These are the largest movements recorded in Kent. The behaviour of this species in the Swale is like that of the Arctic Skua, suggesting that it too migrates overland.

The autumn passage usually gains momentum from the third week of August, though there are a few earlier records in July and one at Dungeness on 22nd June 1966, which is the only record for that month. The largest numbers occur along the north coast, where there is a general increase in the second week of September, with annual peaks since 1973 of 30–80 between 23rd September–17th November. Numbers decrease rapidly in late November and there are no autumn records later than 11th December. Elsewhere round the coast this species is relatively scarce in autumn and there is only one inland record, concerning one flying northwest over Willesborough (Ashford) on 14th October 1971.

There are 13 winter records, three concerning dead birds, between 3rd January–11th March, nine of them in January, three in February and only one in early March.

A small spring passage can usually be observed at Dungeness, with up to seven in a day during the last three weeks of April. The extreme dates are 5th April–31st May. Elsewhere on the Kent coast the Great Skua is very rare in spring, with just three records off Dover, two in the Thames and one in the Medway.

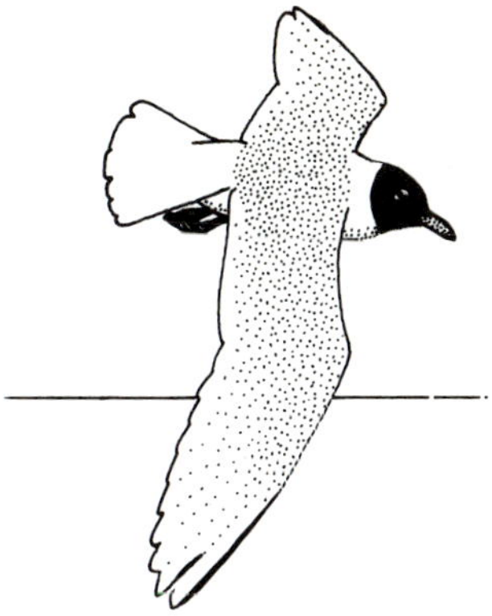

Mediterranean Gull

Larus melanocephalus

Scarce visitor, but now annual and increasing in numbers.

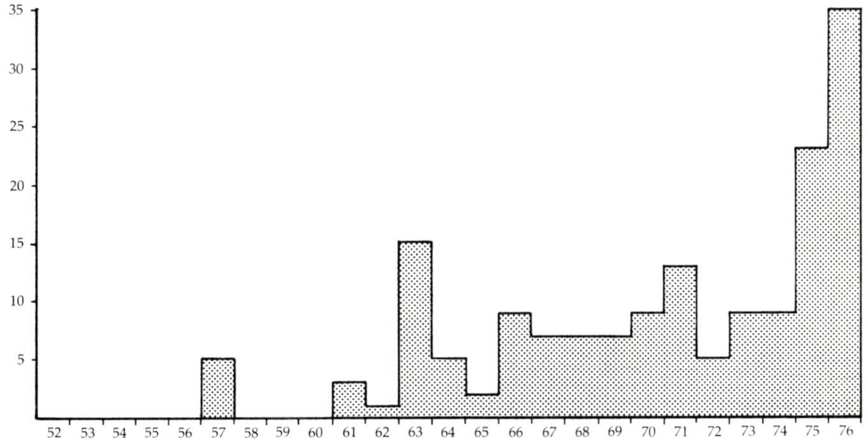

Annual totals of Mediterranean Gulls

The first county record was at Rochester on 8th March 1957. This was the first of seven records for the Medway estuary between March and July of that year, involving at least three individuals, while during the same months one was seen in the Swale and two more in the Dungeness area. In retrospect these records were the more remarkable because even now, when this species has become relatively numerous, there have never been so many records in north Kent as there were in that first year. The next reports concerned one at Dungeness in February 1961, with singles on the Thames and Medway in August and September. Since then, as the histogram shows, Mediterranean Gulls have occurred annually, with a minimum total of 171 birds during the period under review. The totals of 23 in 1975 and 35 in 1976 are again minimum figures, as allowances must be made for duplication of migrants at Dungeness.

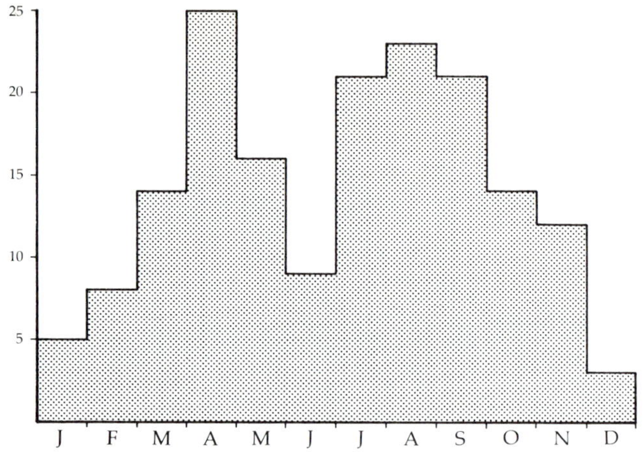

Monthly distribution of Mediterranean Gulls 1957–76

The monthly distribution of records indicates that the Mediterranean Gull is most numerous on spring and autumn passage. They are least common in the winter months, but the most lengthy stays are made by those that overwinter. Singles have twice wintered at Dungeness and there were three at Folkestone in January 1976.

Most records come from Dungeness, although Sandwich Bay and Thanet are now contributing an increasingly higher proportion of the total. The expected increase in north Kent, an area heavily populated by Black-headed Gulls, has not yet materialised. Perhaps the largest single influx occurred in 1975, when there was a steady spring passage of first-year birds at Dungeness between 22nd March–10th May, with up to four on most days and at least ten different individuals identified during this period. There have been six inland records, either at New Hythe or Sevenoaks during 1969–76, three of them in 1976.

[After showing signs that breeding might occur in 1974 and 1976, a pair laid three eggs in a Black-headed Gull colony in 1977, but the whole colony deserted as a result of human interference and the attempt was unsuccessful. Eds.]

Laughing Gull

Larus atricilla

Very rare vagrant.

The only county record is of an adult seen at Lade Pits, Dungeness on 11th May 1966.

Little Gull

Larus minutus

Passage migrant, most numerous in autumn. Occasional summer and winter visitor.

The status of the Little Gull has changed considerably in recent times. Previously it was rare in winter, spring and summer, but a fairly numerous autumn migrant. It is still rare in winter, but has now become a regular spring migrant, while small numbers summer annually and it is even more numerous in autumn than in the past.

Up to 1972 spring records were few, there being none in some years. Dungeness was always the most favoured locality, although counts of up to seven there in April and May were the exception rather than the rule. From 1973 onwards there has been a huge increase in the numbers flying up-Channel past Dungeness, with counts of up to 28 during the first half of May, and larger movements of 355 on 4th May 1974 and 100 on 1st May 1976. Other records for 4th May 1974 included 20 feeding on Dungeness Reserve and 14 flying down the Thames at Swanscombe, the latter presumably overland migrants.

Historically this species was a rarity in midsummer, but small numbers have summered since 1972. Groups of four–ten have spent May–July at Dungeness, Cliffe Pools, Stoke Lagoon and even inland at Westbere, while in 1974 there were 28 at Dungeness. These parties consist of first-year birds which arrive at the end of May, and this behaviour may be a prelude to eventual breeding in the county.

There has also been a recent change in status as an autumn passage migrant at Dungeness. Although as many as 40 occurred there on 25th October 1952, there were no other records of double figures until 1967. A pattern emerged of birds resting off-passage during August and September, with September peaks of 33 in 1969 and 55 in 1971. These birds either fed offshore on the power station outflow 'patch', or to a lesser extent on the pits just inland. This pattern still occurs, but has been gradually complemented and subsequently overhadowed by a down-channel movement of larger numbers during September and October, with peaks of 109 on 9th September 1972, 180 on 13th September and 130 on 26th September 1975, and 100–200 on four dates in October 1976, with 530 on 18th October.

In the Swale Estuary there is also a regular autumn passage between August and November, with double figures up to 57 recorded on various dates between 27th September–23rd November at Shellness in most years since 1953. This autumn passage is reflected in less frequent records of smaller numbers in the Thames and at Reculver, Thanet and Sandwich Bay. There are also records of 12–15 birds at Shellness on 12th

December 1959, 19th December 1976, and 1st and 4th January 1954. These almost certainly represent an extension of the autumn migration, for in most winters Little Gulls may either be entirely absent, or represented only by a few singles between December and March. Eight off Herne Bay on 15th March 1964 is by far the highest count for that month.

Little Gulls have occurred inland each year since 1971, usually between April–May and July–October, mostly at Bough Beech reservoir and Stodmarsh/Westbere, occasionally at Sevenoaks, but rarely elsewhere. Numbers may reach seven in spring and four in autumn, including parties of up to five. In addition, four summered at Westbere during May–July 1975, while there are single inland records for the months of February, March and December.

It should be noted that at Cap Griz Nez, on the nearest part of the French coast, there is a large up-Channel migration in spring between late March and early May, and a much larger down-Channel migration in autumn between late September and late November. The numbers involved are vastly in excess of those so far witnessed at Dungeness. The Little Gull is increasing in numbers in northwest Europe at a tremendous rate, and it will be interesting indeed to observe the impact of this increase both in the breeding season and during migration.

Sabine's Gull

Larus sabini

Rare passage migrant.

Ticehurst gives two autumn records for 1896, one of which was shot inland, at Edenbridge on 7th October. Harrison adds four more for November–December, with one in Dover harbour for most of December 1929.

Between 1956–76 there were four spring records, with singles at Cliffe on 29th March 1959 and off Dungeness annually from 1968–70, between 12th–21st April. In autumn at least 11 have been seen between 12th September–24th October, with a further single at Cliffe on 11th November 1956, and singles off North Foreland on four dates between 9th November 1975–3rd January 1976, which may refer to the same bird. Seven occurred along the north coast and six at Dungeness, where three stayed for periods of six–sixteen days.

Black-headed Gull

Larus ridibundus

Resident. Numerous winter visitor and passage migrant.

Ticehurst writes of thousands of pairs nesting in the Dungeness area in 1847, but the colony at the Oppen Pits declined to 150 pairs by 1896 and 60 in 1903, only to increase again to over 300 pairs in 1905. At that time there were two other small colonies on Walland Marsh. Harrison gives details of the fluctuating numbers in south Kent, with around 300 pairs in the Dungeness area again in the thirties and forties, while in 1948 about 400 pairs nested on Walland Marsh, with 300 at Cheyne Court fleet and 50 each at Finn's fleet and the Woolpack fleet. All these colonies were apparently then deserted. Gillham and Homes give 1947 as the year in which breeding was first proved in north Kent, though they believed that it had taken place for several years previously. By 1949 they estimated 400 pairs to be nesting.

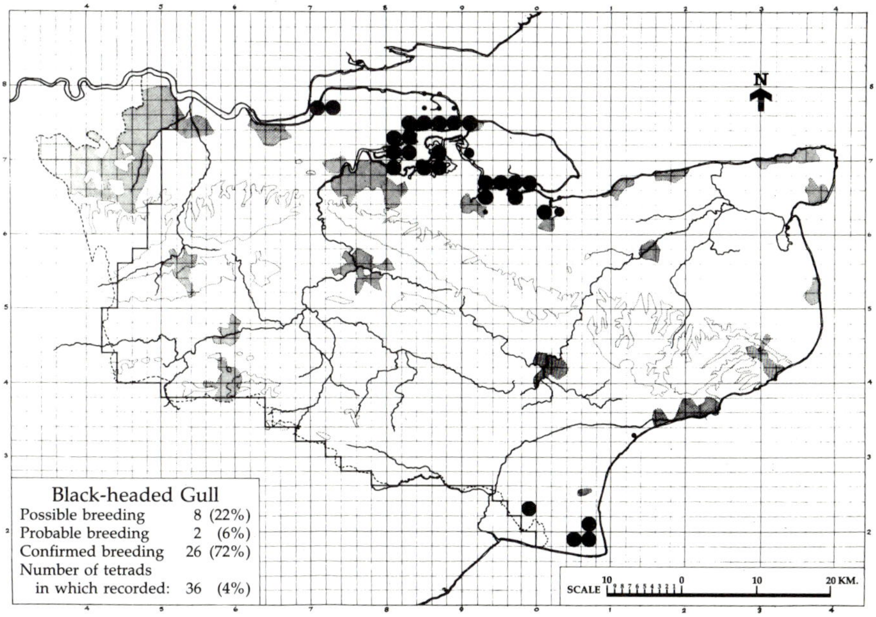

The Black-headed Gull breeds mainly on saltmarshes and on coastal clay and gravel diggings, preferably where small islands remain. In south Kent between 1952–56, up to five pairs attempted to breed on the Dungeness Reserve, up to 16 pairs on Walland Marsh and 12 pairs at the Wicks. However, there was no further breeding on the Reserve until 1964, when 15 pairs nested on the Water Tower pits, followed by 80 the next year. By 1976 over 1,000 pairs were breeding on the Reserve, with a small colony of 30 pairs on Walland Marsh. The threat to the breeding birds, particularly terns, has led to measures to limit breeding success being applied in recent years.

The numbers breeding in north Kent have also increased considerably, although erratically. The Medway and Swale Censuses give some indication of the size of the expansion. In 1955 there were 1,545 pairs on the Medway and 350 in the Swale, while in 1972 the totals were 4,964 and 1,654 respectively. On the Swale, the population has stabilised in the region of 1,600–2,000 pairs since 1965, when they were almost entirely in a single colony on Fowley Island. Since 1972 they have been equally concentrated on two islands in the mouth of Windmill Creek, and Fowley Island has been deserted. Other small colonies exist on the islands off Elmley and Sharfleet Creek and on the clay pits at Murston. In the Medway, although most islands have been occupied at varying times and in varying degrees, the colony on Stoke saltings has always been the largest, consisting of about 1,300 pairs in 1961 and 4,476 in 1972. In 1958 breeding occurred on the Thames for the first time, with 11 pairs on the clay pits at Cliffe. By 1965 there were 260 pairs, but infilling and disturbance have caused the numbers to fluctuate since and there were only 140 pairs in 1976.

The Black-headed Gull is the most widespread and numerous of Kentish gulls occurring, in varying numbers, throughout the year and regularly feeding well inland except during April–June. It is particularly numerous around the coast during autumn and winter. The two highest counts concern 60,000 in the Swale on 11th November 1972 and 50,000 there on 25th January 1975. Normally counts do not exceed 5,000 here, although 15,000 flew west past Seasalter in one hour on 12th November 1961 and 6,000 were found roosting at Shellness the same evening. There were also 20,000 at Shellness in September 1968 and again in August and October 1969. On the Thames, there have been consistently high counts from the rubbish dump at Dartford since 1967, with up to 10,000 regularly each winter and peaks of 20,000 in 1970/71 and 1973/74. In the mouth of the Thames at Allhallows there are also frequent counts of up to 8,000, with a maximum of 24,000 in December 1968.

Roosting flights to and from the estuaries in north Kent are a feature of the winter months, with counts of up to 5,000 regularly recorded over localities along the Downs. The new reservoirs in west Kent now provide additional roosts and up to 5,000 regularly visit Bough Beech, while 15,000 were counted there in January 1973.

In east Kent counts of up to 5,000 are regularly recorded at Sandwich Bay between August–January, with a maximum of 8,000 there in December 1966. There is some evidence of a northward passage there in spring, with a maximum of 1,100 on 6th March 1971, and a southward passage in autumn, with a peak of 3,000 in one hour on 1st September 1954. There is also evidence of migration at Dungeness, although generally the numbers involved are relatively small. Large numbers feed and roost in the vicinity of Dungeness and the highest concentrations can normally be seen on Lade sands, where there was a maximum count of 19,000 in October 1965.

A detailed study of the north Kent colonies between 1956–65, involving ringing several thousand nestlings, showed that early dispersal after fledging was inland, to the north and west. The mean recovery distance increased, until by mid-winter it was about 500 km, when reports of ringed birds came from much of Britain, Ireland, and occasionally France and the Iberian peninsula. Although during the second year of life mean recovery distances tended to be less, at about 300 km, it was not until, aged two, birds bred. The tendency to return to natal areas in the Thames Estuary to breed was very marked, with only a handful of the many breeding-season reports elsewhere. Most breeding adults seem to leave the county in winter, when the mean recovery distance was about 200 km, and overseas recoveries were far fewer than for first-winter birds. The average life-span was about four years, although some birds lived at least 16 years. With the fecundity of the Black-headed Gull, it is hardly surprising that the county population is increasing, despite floods, rats and disturbance by man.

There have also been many recoveries of foreign-ringed Black-headed Gulls indicating the cosmopolitan origins of our passage migrants and winter visitors. Belgium, Denmark, Estonia, Finland, France, Germany, Holland and Russia are each represented by several ringed as nestlings and later recovered in Kent, with single birds recovered from Ireland, Poland, Portugal, Spain and Sweden, and perhaps most unusual, from Czechoslovakia. Adults ringed in Kent during the winter months have been recovered in the breeding season in Estonia and Sweden.

Slender-billed Gull

Larus genei

Very rare vagrant.

The only county record is of an adult, first identified at the 'patch' at Dungeness on 21st July 1971, and seen frequently until 1st August and again from 31st August–12th September.

Common Gull

Larus canus

Scarce resident, much more numerous as passage migrant and winter visitor.

Harrison gives details of the extraordinary breeding colony on the shingle west of the point at Dungeness, far to the south of the Common Gull's Scottish breeding strongholds. Four pairs first bred in 1919, and the colony increased to a peak of 34 pairs in 1939.

During the period under review between 7–15 pairs have nested annually, up to three of them on the Dungeness Reserve.

Spring migration is noted on the coast between March and May, while increased numbers may be recorded at inland localities, particularly on close-cropped grassland, from late February to early April. At Dungeness up-Channel movements are concurrent with those of other seabirds and include daily totals of up to 1,000 in April and 500 in May. Here the proportion of adults decreases during the migration period, such that those in May are almost all immatures. Northerly movements of up to 500 in a day have also been seen at Sandwich Bay in March and April. Winter flocks on coastal pastures are joined by migrants at this time, and in March 1970 there were 3,050 at Sandwich Bay and 3,500 between Lydd and Tenterden on Walland Marsh, while 1,000 immatures were seen at Cliffe in late May 1961.

Non-breeding birds remain around the coast during the summer, but inland the Common Gull is relatively scarce between May and early July, a flock of 42 at Sevenoaks on 26th June 1974 being exceptional. Numbers increase again from late July, with as many as 3,200 at Dungeness in August and 3,000 at Allhallows in September. However, the largest numbers consistently occur around the coast between November and January, with flocks of 5–6,000 in the Dungeness area, at Pegwell Bay, in the mouth of the Swale and in the Thames. On 15th November 1969 there was an exceptional count of 20,000 going to roost at Leysdown. The pastures and playing fields along the dip slope of the North Downs attract flocks of several hundreds of Common Gulls, but in the Weald the Black-headed Gull is far commoner during the winter months.

Ringing recoveries give an indication of the wide area of origin of Kentish wintering birds, and include several nestlings ringed in each of Germany, Holland, Denmark, Norway, Sweden and Russia. Adults ringed in Kent in winter have been recovered in the breeding season in Estonia and twice in Sweden.

Lesser Black-backed Gull

Larus fuscus

Passage migrant, less numerous in winter and summer; a few pairs breed.

Ticehurst recorded the first breeding in Kent, when one pair attempted to nest at Dungeness in 1908 and again in 1909. Harrison gives details of subsequent breeding on Denge Marsh at Dungeness, with two pairs in 1931, increasing to 26 pairs in 1938, but decreasing again to only two pairs in 1947. Two pairs also nested on the cliffs near Dover in 1950.

During the period under review breeding has been recorded intermittently on the Dover cliffs, with four pairs in 1952 and up to three pairs in other years. Since 1973 one pair has also bred on the Dungeness Reserve.

Numbers are lowest during February, May and June, and there are no counts over 300 for these months. The spring passage takes place during March and April, when counts of up to 500 are frequent, particularly at Dungeness and Pegwell Bay.

The autumn migration commences in July, with coastal counts up to 500 again quite frequent, with a maximum of 1,600 along the Thames on 19th July 1970. There are August peaks of 1,000 at Dungeness and in the Thames, while in September these numbers usually apply, though there have been as many as 2,500 at Pegwell Bay and 3,500 at Allhallows.

Numbers slowly dwindle during the last three months of the year, but counts of up to 1,000 are recorded frequently, with up to 2,000 occasionally at Dungeness, Pegwell Bay and in the Swale and Thames. This decrease is further accentuated in January, when by far the largest count is 1,250 flying up the Thames on 19th January 1975.

At inland localities the pattern is similar with small numbers regularly flying over on passage in spring and autumn, but infrequently at other times. Rubbish tips attract a few migrants and occasional winter visitors. A long series of records inland at Sevenoaks has shown that the highest numbers on autumn passage consistently occur between 21st August–7th September, with monthly maxima of 111, 231 and 272 respectively for July–September.

Where separation of the two races has been recorded, it is apparent that the large coastal flocks consist of 80–100% *L.f. fuscus*, the Scandinavian race, throughout the year.

Herring Gull

Larus argentatus

Numerous resident and winter visitor.

Ticehurst and Harrison give details of the increase in breeding numbers. On the Dover cliffs, the first reference to breeding was a few pairs in 1842, increasing to 400 pairs by 1887 and 700 pairs in 1947. On the shingle at Dungeness one pair first bred in 1908, with up to four pairs until 1924. A rapid increase then took place, with 30 pairs in 1926, 200 in 1933 and many more between 1937–40. Disturbance then caused a decline to 100 pairs in 1950. Cliff-nesting on Thanet was first recorded in 1946, with three pairs in 1947, in which year a pair first bred in the Medway. One interesting change has been the spread to buildings for nest sites and the largest roof nesting colony in Britain developed in Dover (Cramp, 1971). It was first noted in 1936, increasing to 200 pairs by 1946.

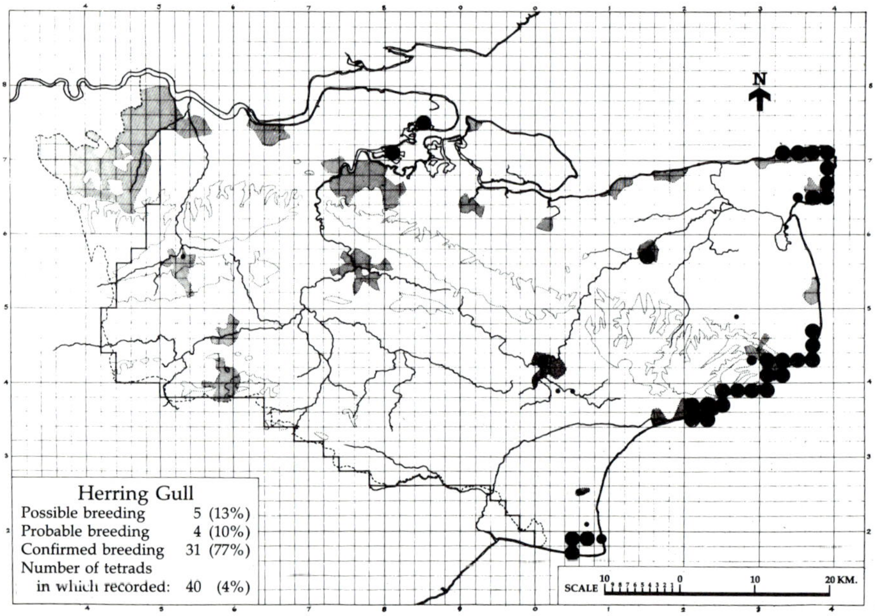

The breeding range of the Herring Gull has continued to spread during the period under review, though control measures have contained, and in some cases reduced, the sizes of the various populations.

One or two pairs continued to breed on the saltings in the Medway until 1967, but there has been no further spread into the north of the county. At Dungeness the decrease continued to a low of 5–12 pairs between 1965–67, followed by a recovery to 76 pairs in 1972, with the open shingle being deserted for island sites on the new gravel pits. Here Herring Gulls represent a hazard to the nesting terns and the success rate of nesting pairs is being controlled. The only recent estimate of the breeding population on the Dover Cliffs is 600 pairs in 1970. Cliff-nesting on Thanet increased to 20 pairs by 1965, but there has probably been no subsequent expansion. By contrast, nesting on buildings in the area, first recorded in 1961, steadily increased to 110 pairs by 1976. In Dover the roof-nesting population has stabilised at around 225 pairs, as the nests are regularly destroyed by both the Local Authority and private individuals. At nearby Folkestone two pairs bred on houses in 1956, with 20 pairs there in 1976. Breeding has also been recorded on roof-tops in towns well inland, with single pairs nesting regularly in Canterbury since 1964 and at Ashford since 1973.

The Herring Gull is numerous around the coast throughout the year, non-breeding birds forming large flocks during the summer months, but the numbers are greatly increased during the winter, particularly when storm-driven birds seek shelter. In the Swale there were flocks of 7,000–15,000 in three successive winters between 1958/59–60/61 and again in 1972/73, while in the Thames there were peak counts of 7,000 in November 1954 and 10,000 in December 1972. Elsewhere the maximum count was 3,000 at Dungeness in January 1974.

Good numbers flight well inland in winter, frequently attracted by rubbish tips. The maximum counts usually occur in December and January, with 600 at the tip in Tunbridge Wells in January 1967. At Longfield rubbish tip, near Gravesend, an estimated 3,000 were feeding daily in late 1953, flighting to Cliffe at dusk.

Birds of one or more of the yellow-legged races are now being seen regularly between July and November, with several records of up to four birds each year since 1973. The recovery of a Murmansk-ringed nestling at Elmley in February supports the view that some passage or wintering Herring Gulls may come from very far afield, although the British population is relatively sedentary.

Iceland Gull

Larus glaucoides

A rare and sporadic visitor.

Harrison lists only seven authenticated records between 1914 and 1944, and regarded the Iceland Gull as an irregular visitor from autumn to spring.

In recent years there have been 16 further records, all on single dates concerning single birds, apart from a most exceptional record of a party of five, which flew up the Thames at Cliffe on 8th April 1956.

J	F	M	A	M	J	J	A	S	O	N	D
2	2	2	9		1	1				1	2

Monthly distribution of Iceland Gulls 1952–76

There were five records between 1954–58, and the other eleven annually between 1966–71. The extreme dates for the winter period are 8th November–26th February, with a spring passage between 27th March–25th April. The two midsummer records occurred on 6th June and 11th July. To judge from plumage descriptions, 15 were first-year or immature birds, four were sub-adults and only one an adult.

The only two inland records were at Sevenoaks on 12th January 1968 and at Tonbridge rubbish tip on 6th April 1970. Of the coastal records, six were in the Dungeness area, four at Sandwich Bay, one at Reculver and three in the Thames.

Glaucous Gull

Larus hyperboreus

Occasional visitor, mostly in winter.

Harrison reports that in the winter of 1941/42 there were records from the Thames and Medway estuaries between October and February, with at least three present in January. The following winter, in the same area, there were further reports between November and February, with at least five present in December 1942. Otherwise he records only sporadic records of singles.

During the period under review Glaucous Gulls have appeared with increasing frequency, but there have been few records of more than two birds together.

Glaucous Gulls normally only occur on passage and in winter between October and May, with 33 of the 70 individuals recorded appearing during January–March. The only new arrivals in midsummer concern a total of five during July–August.

Overall, 31 have been on the south coast, almost entirely at Dungeness; 10 between Sandwich Bay and Thanet; 21 in the three estuaries of the Swale, Medway and Thames; and eight inland, variously seen at Sevenoaks, Tonbridge, Snodland and Stodmarsh during

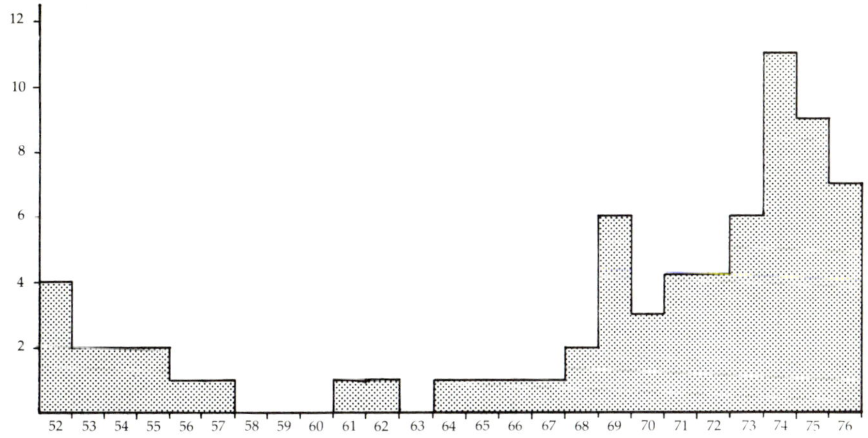

Annual totals of Glaucous Gulls

November–March. The vast majority of reports refer to first-year birds, but there have been 13 adults and only four in the intermediate, all-white plumage.

The longest resident in the county, one present at Dungeness from May 1973, was joined by four others in February 1974, but they had all

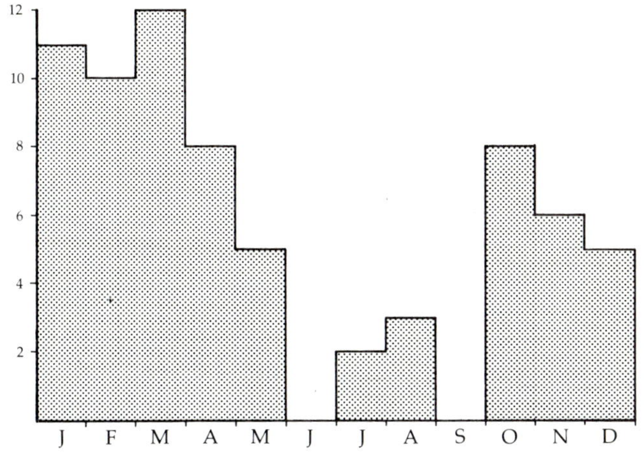

Monthly distribution of Glaucous Gulls 1952–76

left by the end of March 1974. In the following autumn, the northwesterly gales of 28th–29th October, which caused a record movement of Little Auks in Kent, resulted in an influx of five birds, with three at Sandwich Bay and singles at North Foreland and Allhallows on 30th–31st October. Similar gales in other autumns have occasionally produced single birds.

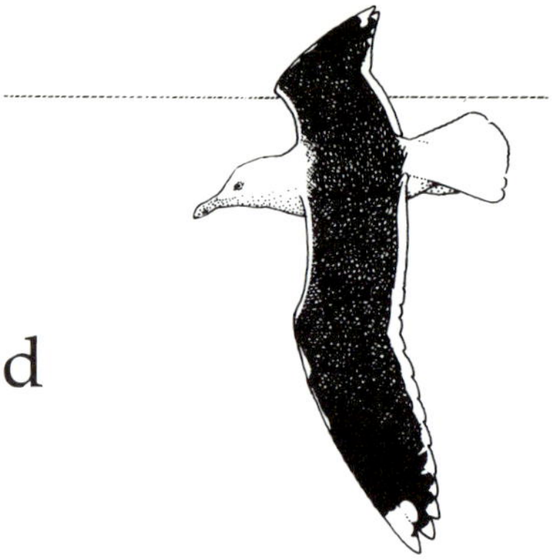

Great Black-backed Gull

Larus marinus

Winter visitor, with non-breeding birds summering.

Ticehurst, quoting Yarrell, states that until 1843 this species bred on the Thames marshes. Harrison noted a marked increase, with flocks of 300 in the 1940s compared with only 20 in Ticehurst's time.

The Great Black-backed Gull is predominantly a coastal and marine species, least numerous during the summer months, when only non-breeding birds are present. Numbers begin to increase in July and at Pegwell Bay, which is perhaps the best documented locality, and where there is also a large rubbish tip, there is usually a build-up throughout the autumn culminating in a peak around November and then a tendency for numbers to decrease again. For instance, in 1966 there were 900 on 8th July, 5,000 in August, 8,000 on 29th October and 3,200 on 31st December, decreasing further to 600 by 4th February 1967. The annual October–December population there is of the order of 2–4,000, while there have been as many as 500 in June and 1,500 in July in some years.

Autumn and winter counts in the Dungeness area are generally rather less than 1,000, but include a maximum of 2,000 in October 1971. On the North Kent Marshes there are four-figure counts between August and January, with up to 1,000 regularly and 2,000 occasionally on the Thames and Swale, plus peaks of 3,000 at Shellness in November 1966 and again at Allhallows in September 1975. The maximum count for the Medway is 630.

The shelter of the estuaries is used as a base for birds flighting inland to forage on rubbish dumps. Counts of up to 100 have been recorded at Tovil, Fawkham and Tonbridge, while at Sevenoaks there is a regular winter peak of 200 and occasionally as many as 300. Much nearer the coast, the tip at Preston attracts wintering flocks, which return to Pegwell Bay to roost, and there were 350 there in November 1971.

Two ringing recoveries, of nestlings ringed at Stavanger, Norway in

June 1963 and Shetland in July 1968, recovered at Iwade in December 1965 and at Minster in Thanet in February 1969 respectively, give an indication of a broad northern origin of wintering birds.

Kittiwake

Rissa tridactyla

Passage migrant, recently established and increasing as a breeding species.

Ticehurst classed the Kittiwake purely as a winter visitor, but a marked change in status was recorded by Harrison, with particular mention of small summering flocks of 30–100 at Dungeness in the late 1930s and 1940s. Gillham and Homes, however, recorded very few for north Kent. In recent years numbers have increased considerably and its status in the county has changed dramatically.

The colony at Dover cliffs has increased from 17 pairs in 1967, to over 500 by 1974 and nearly 1,000 in 1976. Although occasional summering flocks had been recorded previously, this was first noted as regular behaviour in 1966, slightly preceding the colonisation, when there were 45 at Sandwich Bay in May and 200 at Dungeness between June and August. Small numbers continued to summer at Sandwich Bay until 1971, whereas numbers at Dungeness increased and have regularly involved up to 600 between June and September since 1968. From Thanet round to the Thames the Kittiwake is at its rarest during the breeding season months of June and July.

In autumn major movements in the North Sea are reflected by occasional influxes in the Thames Estuary from Reculver westwards to Lower Hope Point. These may start in mid-August, but the largest movements are confined to the period between 11th October–4th December, when counts of 300–3,000 occur annually. These movements are most concentrated in the mouth of the Swale, in north or north-westerly winds. In a northerly gale on 3rd November 1968, it was estimated that there were 20,000 Kittiwakes in the Swale. Smaller movements of up to 600 may be seen in northeasterly winds. [There is considerable interest, but little positive evidence, as to whether any or all of these movements in the Swale and Thames concern birds intending to migrate overland, but on 16th November 1977 a flock of 12 flew southwest over Detling, at a time of considerable seabird movement in the North Sea. Eds.]

A down-Channel movement is noted at Dungeness in October and November, with daily totals of up to 600 and a maximum of 2,000 on 3rd October 1976, while movements of up to 200 are also noted off Thanet during the same two months.

In mid-winter Kittiwakes are apparently less numerous than at any other time of year, although this may simply be a reflection of the lack of winter seawatching. Counts of up to 200 at Dungeness, Thanet and in the Thames Estuary are infrequent from December to March. Occasionally larger numbers are seen at Dungeness, with a maximum of 800 on 11th January 1974. In addition there was an exceptional movement in the Thames Estuary on 22nd February 1959, which included 640 flying up the Thames at Cliffe and a flock of 100 at Allhallows. This was part of a widespread movement, when flocks were reported inland in south and central England. Breeding birds return early to the colony at Dover, for instance there were 450 on 20th February 1976, and the up-Channel spring migration at Dungeness lasts from February–May, thus overlapping the winter period. The normal peak counts of up to 200 at Dungeness not only apply to mid-winter, but also to these spring movements. Up to 60 have also been seen in the Thames Estuary during April–May.

Inland records are not numerous, with only 15 during 1952–76. These referred to individuals, apart from three at Bough Beech on 24th November 1973, with none between May–July.

Ivory Gull

Pagophila eburnea

Harrison includes details of two acceptable records. An adult was seen on Walland Marsh on 27th April 1947 and a bird in first-winter plumage was present at Pegwell Bay on 21st January and 17th February 1951.

Gull-billed Tern

Gelochelidon nilotica

Scarce passage migrant.

Ticehurst gives details of six specimens obtained between 1820 and 1890, while the only additional record Harrison cites is one for east Kent on 25th April 1940.

During the period under review there have been twenty-eight records in 16 of the 25 years, involving 40 birds. The monthly totals are shown, with eleven spring records between 17th April–9th July and seventeen in autumn between 4th August–4th October.

J	F	M	A	M	J	J	A	S	O	N	D
			2	5	10	2	12	7	2		

Thirteen of the records emanate from Dungeness, with nine in the Sandwich Bay area, including one at Stodmarsh, and six along the north coast between Margate and Allhallows. There were 17 records between 1956–64, when parties of two–four were seen in the Dungeness area on three occasions in both spring and autumn. All but two of the other records concern singles.

Caspian Tern

Sterna caspia

Very rare vagrant.

Harrison cites two records for 1935, one found dead at Dungeness lighthouse on 9th October and the second seen at Deal on 15th November.

There have been seven recent records, six in spring between 19th April–12th June and one on 27th July. Surprisingly, the first occurred at Mote Park (Maidstone) on 3rd–4th May 1954 and the second at Stodmarsh on 12th June 1966. The other five, between 1969–76, were seen round the coast between Dungeness and Reculver.

Royal Tern

Sterna maxima

Very rare vagrant.

The first British record of this species was of one seen at Sandwich Bay on 28th–29th July 1965.

Sandwich Tern

Sterna sandvicensis

Passage migrant and non-breeding summer visitor. Has bred in the recent past.

The Sandwich Tern has particular historical significance for Kentish ornithology, for the breeding colony at Sandwich gave this species its name. Boys obtained the first specimen, in 1784, from which Latham wrote his description (Latham, 1785).

Ticehurst seemed to be in no doubt that in Latham's time Sandwich Terns bred in large numbers at Sandwich Bay and, in all probability, equally numerously at Dungeness, where it had ceased to breed by 1847. There is no information, however, as to when it ceased to nest at Sandwich. Harrison's account shows that small numbers summered regularly at Dungeness and single pairs were known to breed again in 1896, 1935 and 1939. He also gave extreme dates of 22nd March and 19th October, with maximum counts of 50 in spring and 200 in autumn.

The first spring records occur at Dungeness or Sandwich Bay in March, with the mean arrival date around the 24th and the earliest on 11th March 1954. The main spring passage occurs at Dungeness between 1st April–16th May, during which period counts in excess of 200 and occasionally up to 570 in a day occur on several dates each spring, mostly in April. This up-Channel passage is also observed off Sandwich Bay, with a peak there of 420 on 26th April 1969.

On the north-facing coast Sandwich Terns only occur in single figures between April and June. Small numbers have summered regularly and groups of up to 20 may be seen in June off Thanet and Sandwich Bay, with up to 30 at Dungeness. [Sandwich Terns are notoriously fickle in their choice of colony, deserting one site and selecting another for no apparent reason, occasionally even in mid-season. Breeding was established in Sussex in 1975, and in 1978 a successful recolonisation took place at Dungeness. Eds.]

Autumn passage commences in July and is more widespread. At Sandwich Bay there are records of 100–160 on various dates between 12th July–15th September, while the heaviest westerly movement at Dungeness was 360 on 11th September 1976. In the Thames and Swale there have been counts of over 200 between the last week of August and the last week of September, with peaks of 400 at Shellness on 28th August 1960 and 1st September 1963, and 400 flying upriver at Cliffe in two hours on 24th August 1963. In early October there have also been counts of up to 160, both at Dungeness and in the Swale, as late as the 8th. The mean departure date is 22nd October, with the latest at Dungeness on 10th November 1968. There is also a winter record of one at Hythe on 27th December 1955.

Inland, Sandwich Terns are now recorded in most years, with small parties of up to 11 at both Bough Beech and Sevenoaks in spring and autumn. Records from the handful of other localities involve even fewer birds.

Roseate Tern

Sterna dougallii

Regular passage migrant and summer visitor in very small numbers.

Harrison gives summer records of one or two at Dungeness between May and July for the years 1924, 1928, annually between 1935–38, and again in 1948. Single pairs apparently summered in the ternery between 1935–37, although no proof of breeding was established.

Most observations during the current period occurred between May and August, with the extreme dates 20th April 1960 and 16th September 1969. The vast majority of records refer to Dungeness, where Roseate Terns have been recorded almost every year since 1953, with one pair first breeding in the Common Tern colony there in 1976.

Records are most frequent at Dungeness on spring migration in May, although almost as regular in June–August. The power station outflow is now the main attraction for this species and it is not unusual for ones and twos to spend up to three weeks feeding there. The most seen in a day is only three and the number of records varies, with up to twelve in a year. [In the light of current knowledge the much larger numbers claimed at Dungeness and published in the Kent Bird Reports between 1962–68 have since been withdrawn by the observers concerned. Eds.]

Elsewhere there are 22 records fairly evenly distributed around the coast from Folkestone into the Thames, with the majority between 8th May–16th June and 12th July–11th August. Inland there have been singles at Stodmarsh, New Hythe and Bough Beech, with six records from Sevenoaks since 1964, including an exceptional party of six there on 20th May 1971.

Common Tern

Sterna hirundo

Summer visitor and passage migrant.

The historical record of breeding in the county is incomplete. Ticehurst could only conclude that very large numbers once bred on the shingle at Dungeness, declining to about 200 pairs by 1907, and that it had nested in north Kent and also between Margate and Reculver. By the 1930s, according to Harrison, the numbers at Dungeness had not only increased considerably, but had become concentrated in a single colony on the west beach, some 200 metres wide and 1,500 metres long. The ternery then contained an estimated 1,500 pairs, but military disturbance during 1939–45 caused a serious decline, and in 1946 there were only about 50 pairs, widely scattered, with none on the west beach ternery. Many apparently moved west to breed at Rye Harbour and Pett Level in Sussex. In north Kent breeding was first reported in the Swale in 1937 and in the Medway in 1944, where there were 400 pairs in 1949.

The main breeding colonies are still on the Medway and Swale Islands, and at Dungeness, and the populations have continued to fluctuate considerably. At Dungeness the decline continued, with none breeding between 1956–60. However, since 1964 the numbers have been fairly stable, in the region of 100–200 pairs, with an increase to 245 pairs in 1976, using the islands on the new gravel pits on the Reserve.

In the Swale a number of sites have been used, including Fowley Island, Murston, Sharfleet and the islands in the mouth of Windmill Creek. The number of pairs increased to 213 in 1955, with 250 pairs on

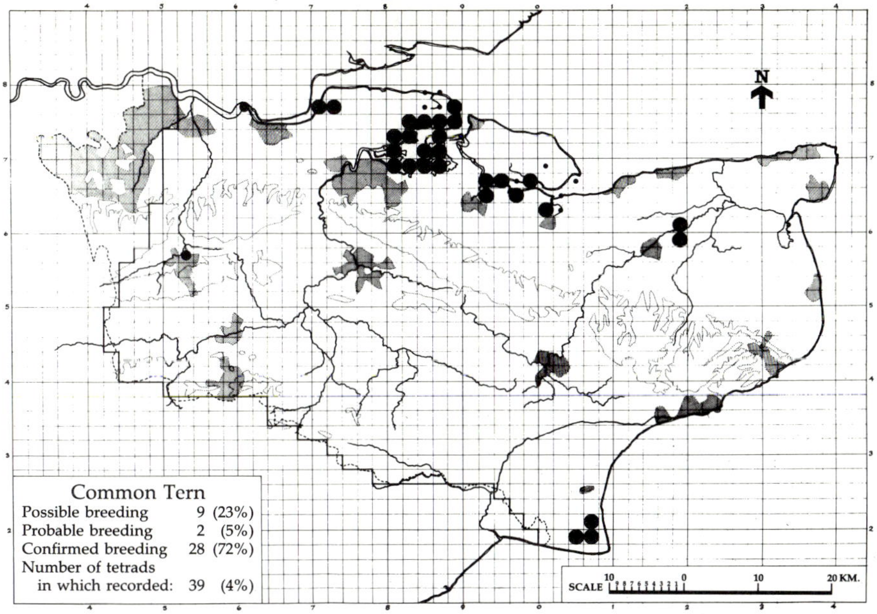

Fowley Island alone in 1965. The Murston colony has always been the smallest, with the first breeding there not until 1967 and a maximum of only 25 pairs. Since the sixties the Swale population has declined and the colony on Fowley has been deserted. Between 40–70 pairs have nested annually at Windmill Creek since 1972.

On the Medway Islands there were 683 pairs in 1955, with colonies of 147, 182 and 191 on Nor, Bee and Stoke respectively, but here too there has been a marked decline. There were 331 pairs in 1961 and only 87 in 1972, with 73 of these on the Stoke saltings.

On the Thames breeding first took place in 1958, with 27 pairs at Cliffe Pools. During the sixties the colony regularly consisted of 100–200 pairs, but has declined since 1972, with 15 pairs in 1975 and 60 in 1976. A small number of pairs now also breed on Grain, while inland one or two pairs have bred regularly in the Stour Valley since 1962, and others have summered in the Medway Valley.

For the purposes of discussing the numbers on passage, all records of unidentified Common/Arctic Terns are included under this species.

Apart from one on 26th March 1960, the earliest spring migrants are recorded between 1st–14th April. In the 1960s it was not unusual for the first three-figure counts at Dungeness to occur between 4th–11th April, but a series of cold springs has been the probable cause of delaying the main arrival by at least a fortnight in many recent years. In 1972 and 1975 the first such numbers did not occur until 1st May and 26th April respectively. As a result of day-long sea-watching at Dungeness in the seventies, four-figure totals have now been recorded on several dates each spring during the period 18th April–17th May. In 1974 there was an exceptionally heavy passage, with counts of 4,000, 2,700 and 1,200 respectively between 3rd–5th May.

Elsewhere round the coast spring numbers are comparatively low. Inland, small flocks now occur quite frequently, with a peak count of 64 at Bough Beech on 3rd May 1974 coinciding with the record movement at Dungeness, while on 18th May 1975 there were 52 there and 33 at Sevenoaks.

The autumn migration commences at the end of July and counts of 500–800 can be expected in the Thames and Swale, at Sandwich Bay and Dungeness until mid-September, with the highest numbers usually on the north coast. The largest single movement was seen on 28th August 1960, when 1,800 flew upriver at Cliffe in four hours, while 4–5,000 flew up the Swale during the day. Other high counts in these areas involve 1,500 west in one hour at Cliffe on 24th August 1963, a similar number feeding and roosting at Shellness on several dates in August 1970, with 2,000 roosting there on 6th August 1971. The highest down-Channel movements at Dungeness concern 1,500 on 9th August 1960 and 2,800 on 29th August 1967. In 1958 there were exceptionally high numbers in the Thames in October, with 1,500 flying west, then back down-river on the 4th, and 350 west on the 17th, although normally there are no counts over 100 after the first week of October.

Overland migration is more obvious and widespread in the autumn and it is apparent that large numbers use the estuaries in the north for this purpose, as witnessed in the numbers which fly up the Thames. During a period of four hours on 23rd August 1970 nineteen flocks of 5–40 birds totalling 262 flew southwest over Gillingham. The largest numbers well inland occurred at Bough Beech on 27th August 1973, when 60 flew south.

The latest autumn records usually occur in the last week of October or the first two weeks of November. The only later record attributable to this species concerns one which remained at Cliffe until 29th November 1958. There are four winter records which refer to either Common or Arctic Terns, with singles at Dungeness on 3rd December 1972, Ramsgate between 19th–21st December 1954, Sandgate on 28th December 1974, and Cliffe on 10th January 1960.

During the 1950s and 1960s, large numbers of nestling terns were ringed in the north Kent colonies. When mature, there was a marked tendency to return to the area of the natal colony to breed. The recoveries indicate a post-fledging dispersal in the Channel and southern North Sea, and coastal migration routes to winter quarters in equatorial West Africa. In addition, a juvenile trapped at Dungeness in September 1969 was recovered in Finland early in August 1975, giving an indication of the breeding grounds of some of our passage birds.

Arctic Tern

Sterna paradisaea

Passage migrant.

The problem of separating Common and Arctic Terns with any certainty has confused the historical picture, particularly with regard to breeding. Ticehurst felt quite unable to accept any breeding records brought to his notice, while Harrison refers to nesting in the ternery at Dungeness between 1923–28 and again in 1937, but with doubt being expressed at the time, these claims are not wholly acceptable.

The building of the nuclear power station at Dungeness has unwittingly provided an excellent opportunity to study terns in a variety of plumages at close range for long periods. The cooling water outflow there is a great attraction for feeding terns and much has been learned about their identification (Scott & Grant, 1969; Grant & Scott, 1969; Hume & Grant, 1974).

The Arctic Tern has been recorded between 11th April–12th November, and is apparently most numerous on passage at Dungeness, where ease of observation and observer density give an obvious bias. Counts of 20–80 may occur there in any month between April and October, although numbers are generally much smaller in June and July. The large spring movements of Common/Arctic Terns often contain a high proportion of this species. During the record movement of 4,000 and 2,700 birds on 3rd and 4th May 1974, a total of 200 Arctic Terns was counted on the 3rd and it was estimated that perhaps a quarter of those on the 4th were this species. On 9th May 1975, out of a total of 2,200 Common/Arctic Terns, 200 were considered to be Arctic.

The highest autumn count at Dungeness is 120 on 16th September 1976, while up to 100 have been recorded off Sandwich Bay and Thanet, with up to 65 in the north Kent estuaries.

Nowadays there are also a number of inland records each year involving one–three birds, most often from Bough Beech, Sevenoaks and the Stour Valley.

Bridled Tern

Sterna anaethetus

One was found dead at Dungeness on 19th November 1931.

Little Tern

Sterna albifrons

Summer visitor and passage migrant.

Ticehurst mentions several colonies on the north coast, at Sandwich, Hythe and Dungeness, while Harrison details the population changes. The colony at the mouth of Yantlet Creek and along Grain beach held a maximum of 50 pairs in 1903, with only 12 pairs in 1948. At Shellness, the colony usually contained 8–20 pairs between 1933–49, with a peak of 34 pairs in 1946, while on the south side of the Swale there are intermittent records of a colony since 1919, with up to 30 pairs between 1928–34. At Sandwich Bay, another site with a long tradition, the numbers have fluctuated considerably, with a peak of 60–80 pairs in 1934 and only 12 in 1950. The Dungeness area was the stronghold of the species, where it bred regularly on at least six sites along the west beach, with 45 pairs in 1939, increasing to 100 pairs in a single colony in 1943 and 1950. Pairs bred regularly to the north of the point in former times, but a colony of 30 pairs there in 1943 was an isolated record. Harrison also makes reference to a solitary winter record, one shot at Gravesend on 23rd December 1822.

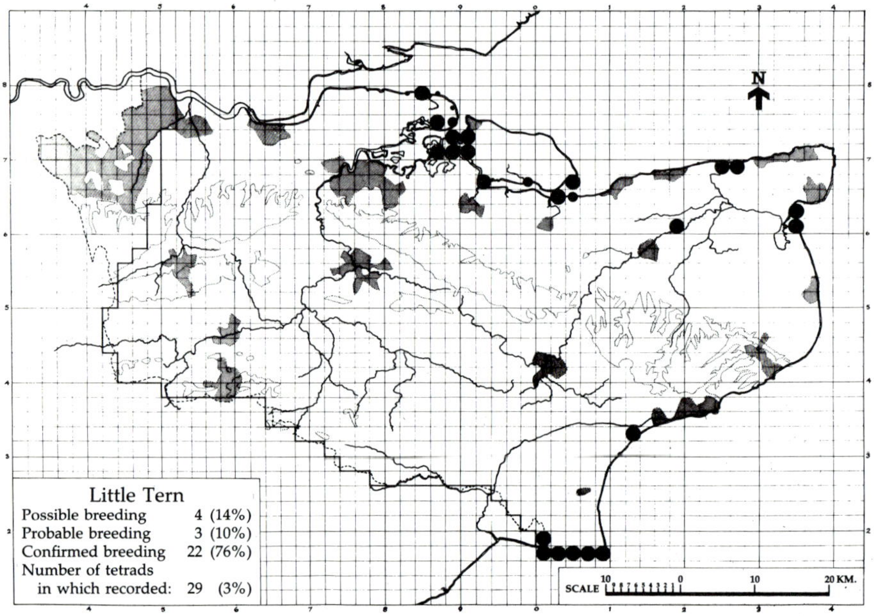

The breeding population has currently reached an all-time low, with a total of 34 pairs at five colonies in 1976, a decline from about 120 pairs at thirteen colonies in the 1950s.

The Little Tern has only bred on the Medway in recent times, with up to nine pairs on the Stoke saltings between 1952–57, while on the south Medway there was a colony of up to 36 pairs, variously based on Deadman's Island, Chetney and Queenborough between 1952–73, with no double figure counts after 1969. On Grain, up to 12 pairs bred until 1968, with only isolated pairs again in 1971 and 1974, while the colony at Shellness, which continued to hold up to 20 pairs until 1962, was also deserted between 1963–73, with one pair again in 1974 and four in 1976. Meanwhile, on the south side of the Swale, up to seven pairs bred intermittently until 1964, with one pair again in 1970.

At Reculver, up to 20 pairs have bred since 1952, with 10 pairs present in 1976. At Sandwich Bay the population has also fluctuated dramatically, with none in several years, peaks of 14 in 1954 and 20 in 1964, and four pairs in 1974 and 1976. Nearby, there was an isolated record of three pairs near Walmer in 1974, while inland at Westbere a few birds have summered and pairs attempted to breed between 1959–63 and again between 1970–74.

In south Kent the colony at West Hythe held over 20 pairs in 1952, but then declined, with the last two pairs breeding in 1961. At Dungeness the shingle colonies to the west of the point totalled 110 pairs in 1962, declining to 68 in 1971, of which only 32 were in Kent. In 1976 there were only nine pairs on the Reserve and seven more at a second colony, and in many recent years no young have been reared.

The first arrivals occur between 8th–22nd April and spring passage is most obvious at Dungeness, where up-Channel movements continue to the end of May. Counts of 60–80 have occurred as early as 21st April, but the only three-figure numbers have been seen in the first half of May, with a peak of 210 on 6th May 1976.

Autumn migration is most evident in the Thames and Swale estuaries, where flocks gather in the second half of July. There are two separate flocks which collect at high tide roosts at the Yantlet and Shellness, the largest counts being 350 and 400 respectively. Numbers decrease again in August and there are no three-figure counts here outside the period 12th July–22nd August. In 1967 a similar roost was present at Reculver, with 200 on 12th August. A late movement was noted in the Medway and Swale on 30th August 1961, when 116 flew southwest at Nor Marsh and 60 flew west at Conyer. Movements have also been noted at Dungeness, where 150 flew west on 1st August 1963. Numbers decrease rapidly in September and the last records usually occur in the last week of September or the first half of October, with the latest at Dungeness on 24th and 27th October 1975.

Inland records used to be scarce, but one–seven now occur almost every year in spring or autumn at Bough Beech and Sevenoaks, but rarely elsewhere. At Westbere and Stodmarsh, which are only 8 km inland, there has recently been an upsurge in numbers, with peaks of nine on 29th May, 20 on 30th July and up to 15 in August 1973, though these probably involve the breeding birds from Reculver, which now bring their young to feed in the Stour Valley.

Whiskered Tern

Chlidonias hybridus

Very rare vagrant.

Singles were seen inland at Bough Beech on 17th June 1973, and on Dungeness Reserve between 28th May–7th June 1976.

Black Tern

Chlidonias niger

Passage migrant.

Ticehurst makes reference to the Black Tern as a breeding species on Romney Marsh until around 1840, with five or six pairs at the Woolpack Fleet in 1883. Since then it has been recorded only on passage. Harrison gives extreme dates of 8th April and 18th October, with a spring peak of 40 in Pegwell Bay on 11th May 1946 and in autumn 123 at Leysdown on 25th August 1946. Gillham and Homes also include a winter record of two at Cliffe in January 1933.

The earliest spring record in recent years is 12th April 1953, with the first arrivals usually in the last ten days of that month. The main spring migration takes place in the first three weeks of May and the largest numbers are generally seen flying up-Channel at Dungeness, usually with day-totals of up to 68, but with occasional larger movements, e.g. 98 in four hours on 9th May 1954 and 130 in two hours on 15th May 1960. Normally these sea movements only involve 10–40 birds, while simultaneous influxes of similar numbers often occur elsewhere on the same days, feeding on the gravel pits at Dungeness, and on inland waters, particularly at Bough Beech and in the Stour Valley. Elsewhere large numbers are exceptional in spring, although there were 35 at Grain on 10th May 1960.

The spring migration continues into June in some years and influxes of 10–20 birds may occur as late as the third week. However, such numbers are infrequent and almost exclusive to Dungeness, with a maximum there of 45 at sea on 5th June 1971, and 18 on the gravel pits the same day. On 1st July 1957 there was a quite exceptional record of four flocks totalling 180 flying northwest over the Medway.

In autumn the north Kent estuaries, as well as Dungeness, attract large migrant flocks. Passage starts in early July and by the end of the month flocks of up to 70 have occurred in some years. Three-figure counts occur in most autumns on various dates between 6th August–25th September. Occasionally large flocks may be present for up to three weeks. For instance, in 1969 there were about 200 in the Swale between 17th–28th August, with 600 on the 20th, while at Dungeness there were 100–300 between 19th–31st August, with peaks of 400, 550 and 700 on the 21st, 22nd and 23rd. However, it is unusual for autumn peaks on the north and south coasts to coincide. Other large autumn totals at Dungeness concern a flock present between 26th August–12th September 1967, with 640 on the 2nd, and another flock there between 11th–26th August 1975, with 550 on the 23rd. These large numbers mostly feed over the sea, especially on the power station outflow, and to a lesser extent on the gravel pits.

The influxes on the north coast more frequently take the form of one-day movements, using the estuaries as take off points for overland migration to the southwest. The largest single movement took place on 28th August 1960: about 2,000 flew up the Swale between dawn and dusk, the majority by 1100 hours; 630 flew up the Thames between 1215–1615 hours; and a flock of 250 occurred in the Medway. Other large influxes have been noted at Shellness: with 450 on 3rd September 1962; flocks of 1,200 and 600, which came to roost between sunset and dusk on 6th and 7th August 1971 respectively; and 400 on 12th August 1972. On 23rd August 1970 flocks of 12, 16 and 26 flew southwest over Gillingham, the same day as that autumn's peak of 30 was recorded at Bough Beech. As in spring this locality supplies the majority of the inland records, with occasional flocks of 10–40 and a maximum of 103 on 15th September 1974. Elsewhere large numbers are exceptional, although there were 100 at Reculver on 12th–13th August 1967 and 110 at Foreness on 30th August 1971.

In some years the latest records occur in late September, and numbers in October are very variable. Counts of up to 20 have occurred in the first ten days, while a record of 56 flying west at Dungeness on 19th October 1967 is quite exceptional. There have been just four November records, with the latest at Shellness on 8th November 1975. There is also a mid-winter record of one feeding over a ploughed field at New Romney on 5th January 1975.

White-winged Black Tern

Chlidonias leucopterus

Scarce passage migrant.

Ticehurst includes a record of two at the Wicks on 30th May 1891. Harrison adds two more spring records, one at Dungeness on 17th May 1937 and another at Hythe on 15th May 1951.

In recent years there have been 41 records, with two in 1956, one in 1959, and then annually between 1962–76, once observers learnt to identify this species in autumn plumage.

There are eight spring records, between 9th May–1st July, and the 33 in autumn fall between 29th July–30th October.

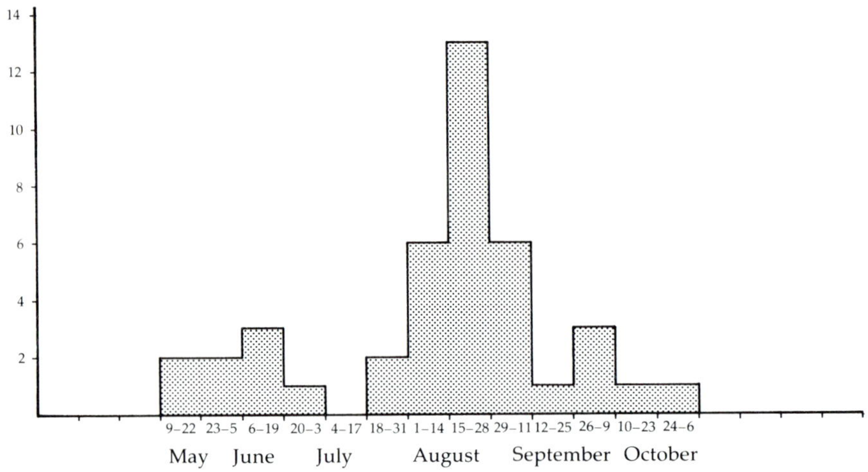

Fortnightly distribution of White-winged Black Terns 1952–76

Apart from two together at the Wicks on 19th May 1956 and two at Dungeness on 22nd August 1966, the records concern singles, with the majority at the power station outflow at Dungeness, or on the gravel pits there, with six in the Thames and Swale estuaries and two at Sandwich Bay. There are also three inland records, at Stodmarsh on 31st May 1973, at Leybourne on 29th September 1965 and the latest, which stayed at Bough Beech between 26th–30th October 1976.

A total of five was seen at Dungeness in autumn 1972, including one which stayed for a month and whose presence overlapped the stays of two others, such that there were three together for a period of three days. Others present for long periods have produced several similar records of two together at this locality.

Guillemot and Razorbill

Uria aalge and *Alca torda*

Passage migrants.

Such a high proportion of the larger auks remain unidentified that it is practical to discuss the two species together. They may be seen in ones and twos anywhere round the coast throughout the year, but larger numbers are normally only recorded at Dungeness and in the Thames estuary.

The Guillemot once bred quite numerously on the Dover cliffs, particularly at South Foreland, but successive cliff falls reduced the number of suitable nesting ledges. The only counts that Ticehurst and Harrison recorded were 60 pairs in 1895, 30 pairs in 1908 and 1912, with no evidence of nesting after 1926.

Ticehurst relates how several Razorbills were seen flying to and from the South Foreland cliff amongst the Guillemots in 1901, but nesting was not substantiated. Recently a Razorbill was seen on the cliffs there on 27th June 1971.

At Dungeness peak day-totals rarely exceed 40, but numbers vary considerably from year to year. Two peak periods are apparent: in April–May the majority of auks fly down-Channel, with a peak of 71 on 10th May 1975, while an up-Channel movement occurs in October–November, with a maximum of 113 between 22nd–24th October 1970. An isolated count of 65 was recorded on 27th January 1975. An interesting long-term trend is shown by the lack of recent April sightings, despite extensive sea-watching in the seventies, when compared with the relatively high numbers in April during the fifties and sixties. The main spring passage is now recorded in May. Similarly the autumn passage is occurring later, which is also supported by the November peaks in north Kent. An analysis of the national auk ringing recoveries (Mead, 1974) has shown how complex are movements in the Channel, but these changes in timing are probably reflections of changes in breeding numbers and productivity in colonies far to the west and north.

In the Thames estuary counts of 10–35 have been recorded regularly between the first week of November and the third week of December since 1968. These birds can be seen flying west along the north coast, past Warden Point on Sheppey and into the estuary as far as Allhallows. The largest numbers have occurred during northerly gales, with 83 at Allhallows on 3rd November 1968, and 315 and 98 at Warden Point on 17th November and 4th December 1969 respectively. Earlier peaks on

15th October 1955 and 6th October 1956, of 35 and 65 respectively, were also recorded in the Thames.

Elsewhere round the coast the only large counts concern 40, identified as Guillemots, off Dover on 25th July 1959 and 60, including 30 Razorbills, off Sandwich Bay on 19th January 1970.

As to the relative abundance of Guillemots and Razorbills, an analysis of the figures for Dungeness between 1966–72 shows that of a total of nearly 2,100 large auks seen during that period 35% were identified as Guillemots and 10% as Razorbills. The numbers picked up as a result of oiling incidents give additional accurate information: the combined totals from the five largest oil spills amount to 609 Guillemots and 238 Razorbills, a ratio of 2·6:1. This compares favourably with the counts at Dungeness, but not so well with an estimate of the total populations breeding in Britain and Ireland in 1969–70, which produced a ratio of 4:1 (Cramp et al, 1974).

Black Guillemot

Cepphus grylle

Very rare vagrant.

Ticehurst includes four examples obtained since 1844, including one in the Thames in August 1885. Harrison adds just two more, both at Dungeness, in May 1911 and February 1951.

The three recent records concern one found dying at Dungeness on 2nd August 1956, one seen alive there on 12th August 1961 and one off Deal on 15th March 1972.

Little Auk

Alle alle

Occasional late autumn visitor, scarce in winter.

The records listed by Ticehurst and Harrison include counts of up to 12 and are spread throughout the period 19th October–28th January, whereas the recent records are nearly all concentrated between late October and late November. Ten inland records were also detailed.

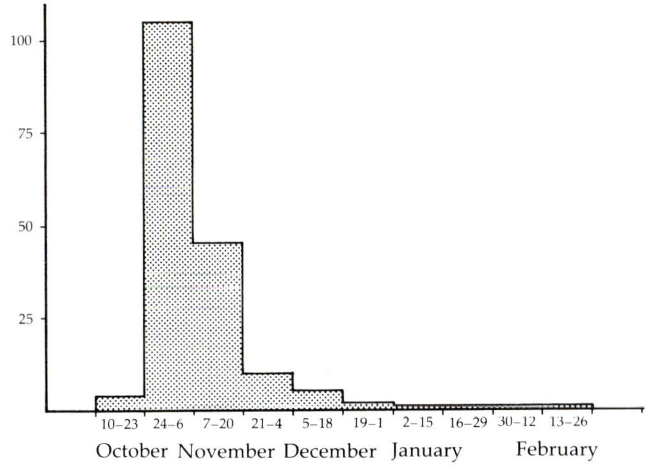

Fortnightly distribution of Little Auks 1952–76

During 1952–76 there were 70 records, involving 175 birds, between 15th October–17th February. The only records outside this period concern singles found dead at Shellness on 18th March 1956 and dying at Hoo on 25th June 1967.

Most Little Auks are seen as a result of northerly or northwesterly gales occurring in Kent or further north. Forty of the records refer to the north coast between Reculver and Cliffe, with one as far up-river as Gravesend, 17 between Thanet and Folkestone, and nine at Dungeness. The four inland records all occurred between 3rd–16th November.

This species usually occurs in ones and twos, and rarely up to seven are seen in a day. The one exception to this took place as a result of northwesterly gales on 28th–29th October 1974, which caused a large influx in the last three days of the month. On the 29th a total of 31 flew north at Sandwich Bay, eight flew west at Reculver and there were six at both Shellness and Allhallows. On the 30th there were seven at Sandwich Bay, six at North Foreland, with three at both Shellness and Allhallows. There was a large movement of Dunlin on 29th October and most of the Little Auks seen on that date were with these migrant flocks.

Puffin

Fratercula arctica

Autumn passage migrant, scarce at other times.

Harrison includes several early references to the Puffin breeding on the Dover Cliffs, but it had apparently diminished to an occasional species by 1884. During the first half of this century, it was considered an irregular autumn and winter visitor, and there were four inland records of storm-driven birds.

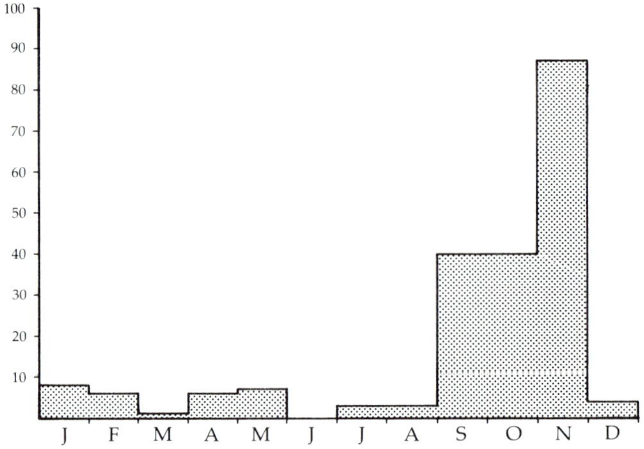

Monthly distribution of Puffins 1952–76

Excluded from the histogram to avoid bias is an additional and quite exceptional movement totalling 105 flying up the Thames off Allhallows in a northerly gale on 3rd November 1968. Otherwise the peak count is only 10 and the vast majority of sightings concern ones and twos.

Between 1952–76 there were 115 records, 45 and 25 in the Thames and Swale estuaries respectively, 35 at Dungeness and only ten elsewhere, including exhausted birds found inland at Knockholt on 21st September 1954 and at Sevenoaks on 8th October 1957.

The annual totals have fluctuated considerably, with peaks of 30 in 1954 and 1957 and 20 in 1969. At Dungeness in 1954 there were eight autumn records of one–nine birds, otherwise there are relatively few autumn reports for south Kent, though the majority of spring records occur there. It is pertinent to note too, that despite the extensive sea-watching at Dungeness in recent years, there have been no records there since 1971.

In north Kent there were good numbers in the Thames each autumn between 1955–59, with seven records of one–ten birds in 1957, but there have been relatively few since that period. On Sheppey, however, there were few records until 1969, when one–five birds were seen on six dates; since then regular sea-watching there has produced one–three records annually.

Pallas's Sandgrouse

Syrrhaptes paradoxus

Very rare vagrant.

Ticehurst includes details of records relating to three invasions of this species into Britain that were such a feature of the latter part of the nineteenth century. The first concerns one on Romney Marsh in November 1859. In 1863 a flock of six was seen on Sheppey in June, with eight at Dungeness in July. In 1888 the first of four on Thanet was seen in May, in which month a flock of 30 was also seen at Dungeness, while four occurred near Rochester in November. The last of the invasions occurred in 1908, when three were seen at Littlestone on 4th July.

The only other record concerns one at Stodmarsh on 28th December 1964, which was probably the same bird that had been present in Holland from 26th October–25th December of that year, the first in Western Europe since 1909.

Fulmar—a recent addition to the list of breeding species.

page 230

Spoonbill—an occasional visitor in small numbers.

Whooper Swans (above) and Goosander (below)—winter visitors attracted to the Sevenoaks Reserve during the severe winter of 1962/63.

page 231

Shelduck—breeding successfully at Bough Beech reservoir.

page 232

Brent Geese—regular winter visitors in increasing numbers, particularly to the Medway and Swale.

Kentish Plover—now only seen on migration, but increasingly recorded in spring.

page 233

Bar-tailed Godwits—often seen in spectacular numbers flying up-Channel past Dungeness in spring, when inland flocks – like these birds at Bough Beech – also occur.

Black-tailed Godwits—increasingly numerous on migration and now wintering regularly.

page 234

Oystercatchers—flighting in to roost at Harty, Sheppey.

Common Sandpiper—widespread in autumn and particularly numerous on the Stour estuary.

page 235

Little Stint—most numerous on autumn passage, and increasingly recorded through the winter.

Dotterel—an attractive but irregular visitor.

page 236

Little Ringed Plover—has become a more widespread breeding species.

Terns—some of the many birds attracted to the 'patch' created by the discharge of cooling water from Dungeness power station.

page 237

Little Terns—a most sensitive species, generally on the decline.

Sparrowhawks—signs of a recovery are at long last being seen after the dramatic post-war decline.

page 238

Woodcock—a well-camouflaged and secretive woodland breeding bird, more widespread and numerous in winter.

Yellow Wagtail (above) and Redshank (below)—both successful breeding species on the coastal lowlands.

page 239

Nutcracker—one of the long-staying Maidstone birds during the 1968 irruption.

page 240

Wryneck—formerly a breeding bird, now reduced to the status of passage migrant.

Hawfinch—a secretive and elusive bird, but probably widespread.
Brambling—a regular winter visitor, but in varying numbers.

page 241

Stock Dove

Columba oenas

Widespread resident and occasional migrant.

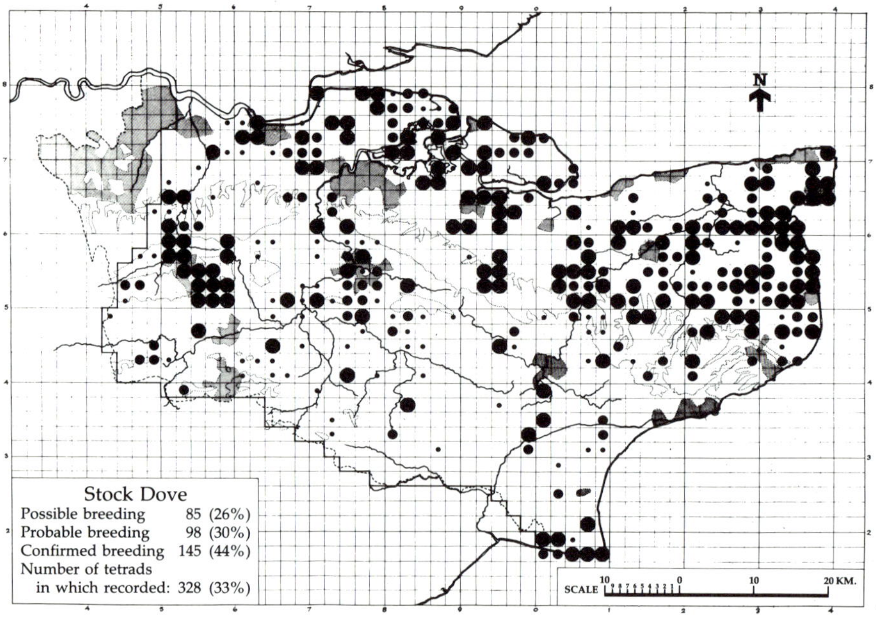

The Stock Dove is generally distributed throughout the county. Favoured habitats include open woodland, parkland and farmland with mature trees, but its marked adaptability in choice of nest sites enables it to breed successfully on the coastal marshes and shingle landscapes, where mature trees are often absent. The thin distribution along the Downs is in part due to poor coverage, but the lack of breeding evidence in parts of the Weald is not so easy to explain.

Small flocks begin to form in the autumn and during the winter months flocks of several hundred birds are recorded, particularly on the coastal marshes. The highest counts concern 500 on Chislet Marsh in January 1976, 700 on the Thames marshes in December 1970 and 800 on Sheppey in January 1975. There were several counts of 300 in the 1950s and 1960s, but these recent higher figures endorse the Common Birds Census indications that the population is increasing. Inland, flocks are generally smaller, but counts of 50–100 are not unusual, with a maximum of 450 at Stockbury in December 1971. Like other doves the Stock Dove forms large roosts in the winter months, the biggest of these involving 500 at Adisham in November 1952 and 800 at Northward Hill in December 1975.

While this species is largely sedentary, there is some evidence of migration. In spring very little passage has been recorded at the two Observatories, but in 1976 totals of 56 and 14 flew southeast at Dungeness on 22nd and 23rd April respectively. In autumn rather more migratory movements have been recorded, particularly at Dungeness from mid-October to mid-November. The numbers involved are usually small, but there was an unprecedented southeasterly passage of 620 birds at Dungeness between 16th October–1st November 1976, with peaks of 225 and 200 on the 25th and 31st respectively. At Sandwich Bay, at the same time, a northerly passage was noted, with totals of 108, 312 and 100 between 30th October–1st November.

Woodpigeon

Columba palumbus

Abundant resident and passage migrant.

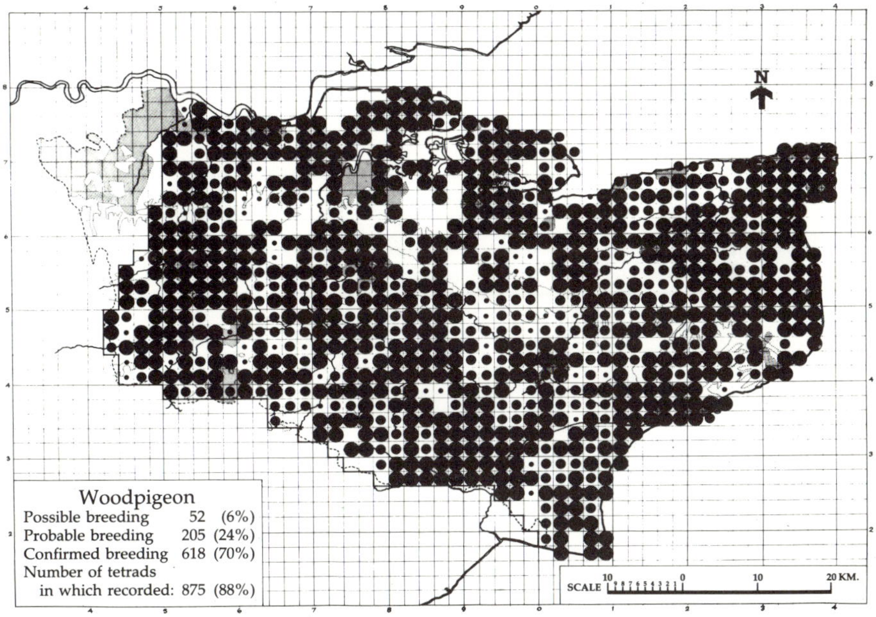

The results of the Breeding Survey show the Woodpigeon to be the fifth most widespread nesting species. Although traditionally a woodland species, it has become particularly abundant over farmland, nesting in small copses and isolated trees and bushes.

The post-breeding population gathers into large flocks, which increase in size during the autumn. From November–February flocks of 1,000 or more are present in widespread localities, with reports of 2–3,000 not unusual. Exceptionally, there was an estimated 10,000 at Stockbury between 16th–24th December 1963. Woodland roosts also increase from early November, with a maximum count of 4,000 at Northward Hill in December 1965.

Although Woodpigeons breeding in Kent are essentially sedentary, migrants from elsewhere occur regularly. Peak movements are usually in late October and November, but numbers fluctuate markedly from year to year. Counts of several hundred and occasionally 1–2,000 are recorded, usually involving birds flying southwest. In 1957 there were 10,000 feeding on cliff top stubble at St. Margaret's between 18th–21st November, with 20,000 there in early November 1959, in which year 20,000 passed southeast over Thanet on 20th–21st November. On 18th November 1969 10,000 flew south over Pembury, while at Dungeness in 1975 there was a quite unprecedented southeasterly movement involving over 55,000 birds between 4th October–21st November, with peaks of 22,000 and 20,000 on 2nd and 5th November respectively, including one flock of 6,000. This movement was widespread, with reports from several other localities, including 8,800 southwest in just over an hour at Allhallows on 4th November.

Spring passage is far less regular and marked, but has been recorded occasionally at the two Observatories. In 1962 for example, following a good autumn passage, with nearly 8,000 between 29th October–17th November 1961, 760 passed over Dungeness in March–April, with a maximum of 110 on 22nd April. Passage sometimes continues through May, but in other years there is no evidence of movement.

One of the earliest indications of the onset of a period of hard weather is the westward or southward movement of Woodpigeon flocks, both coastally and inland. During January 1963, in the severe weather, there were flocks of 3–4,000 at several localities, and considerable movements involving up to 1,000 birds. Many moved southwest and by the end of February the numbers remaining were very low.

Collared Dove

Streptopelia decaocto

Now a widespread resident.

The colonisation of Britain by this predominantly Asian species since the first-ever record in 1955 has been a most remarkable event, and the spread in Kent no less so. The first Collared Dove in this county was seen at Broomfield (Herne Bay) on 16th May 1957, with a pair at Staple (Sandwich) from 30th May, which reared two broods successfully. Another was seen at Strood on 1st August, while three fed with chickens at Tilmanstone during December.

In 1958 three pairs bred, at Staple, Tilmanstone and Margate, with another pair at Wouldham and the first record for Dungeness on 15th May. There were also reports of singles from Cliffe and as far west as Otford. The next year at least four pairs bred at Margate and another pair at Hoo, with additional reports from Staple, Broomfield, St. Margaret's and Deal, Cliffe and Wainscott.

Numbers increased greatly in 1960. On Thanet at least 31 pairs bred, with a further three pairs at Deal and one at Hoo. One or two were seen at Etchinghill (Folkestone), East Sutton and Sevenoaks in June–July. In December a number of small flocks were present, totalling 150 on Thanet, 20 at Deal and 15 at Whitstable.

In 1961 breeding was more widespread around the coast, with autumn flocks of 40–50 at Littlestone, Margate and Whitstable, while two years later there were an increasing number of reports from the Weald and the northwest of the county, with one pair breeding successfully in Maidstone.

By 1964 Kent held by far the largest number of Collared Doves in Britain, and although the main concentration was still on Thanet, with an estimated 1,500 breeding pairs, the spread westward continued.

The Collared Dove is usually closely associated with human habitation or activity, especially where grain is available. The distribution map

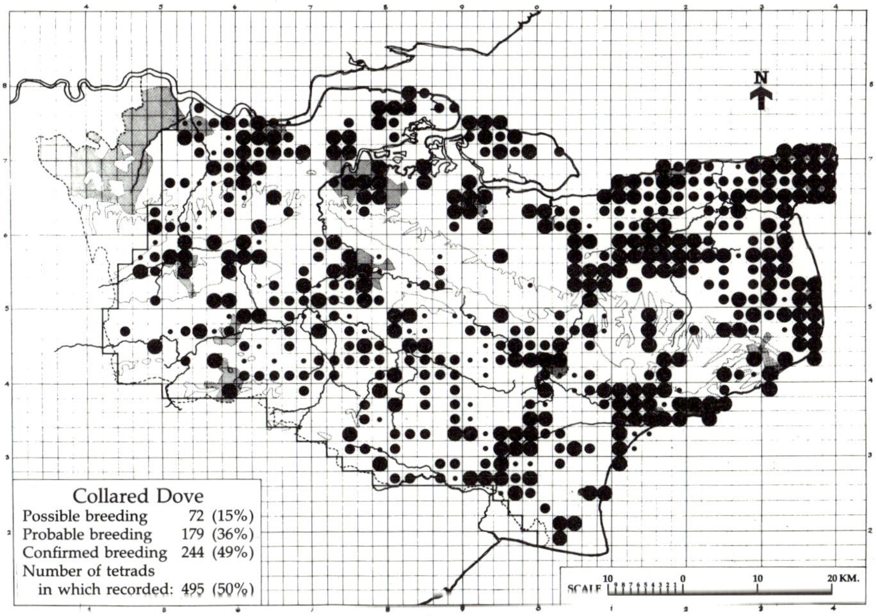

shows a concentration of breeding records around the major urban developments, which was more obvious during the initial years of the Breeding Survey. The spread into more rural areas was noticeable as the Survey progressed.

The increase in the number and size of the wintering flocks gathering near suitable food supplies, such as grain stores or poultry farms, is an indication of how the population continues to expand. By 1966 flocks of 200–300 were present at Faversham and Lydd, with 300–400 the next year at Cheriton and Dymchurch and in 1970 at Broomfield. In 1975–76 flocks of 400 were reported from Minster, Hoo and Dartford, by which time smaller flocks were occasionally present at a number of inland localities.

Regular observations at Dungeness and Sandwich Bay reveal that Collared Doves continue to reach Britain from the Continent, with small numbers arriving in spring and autumn. In 1975, however, there was a more marked passage at Dungeness, with 59 bird days during April–May, while at Sandwich Bay there was a peak of 34 on 31st May. At Allhallows 13 and 12 flew west with migrant Turtle Doves on two dates in May, while the autumn passage was more marked, with a total of 266 flying west on six dates between 28th September–19th October, including 142 on 12th October. At Dungeness too there was a good autumn passage in 1975, with 210 between 4th October–14th November, including a peak of 24 on 29th October.

Ringing shows that some of the population continues to move north and west, with recoveries from Yorkshire, Hampshire and Galway, while others become resident, with singles retrapped after seven years in Broadstairs and six years in Staplehurst.

Turtle Dove

Streptopelia turtur

Widespread summer visitor and passage migrant.

The Turtle Dove is well distributed as a breeding species, finding open woodland and arable farmland well suited to its needs.

The earliest spring migrant was one at Sevenoaks on 5th April 1960, but the mean arrival date is 19th April. Migration continues throughout May and into June in some years. Small flocks are occasionally seen during May–June, with peaks of 100–200 in six years between 26th April–16th June. Visible migration is regularly observed, particularly around the coast and in the Stour Valley, with peaks at Sandwich Bay of

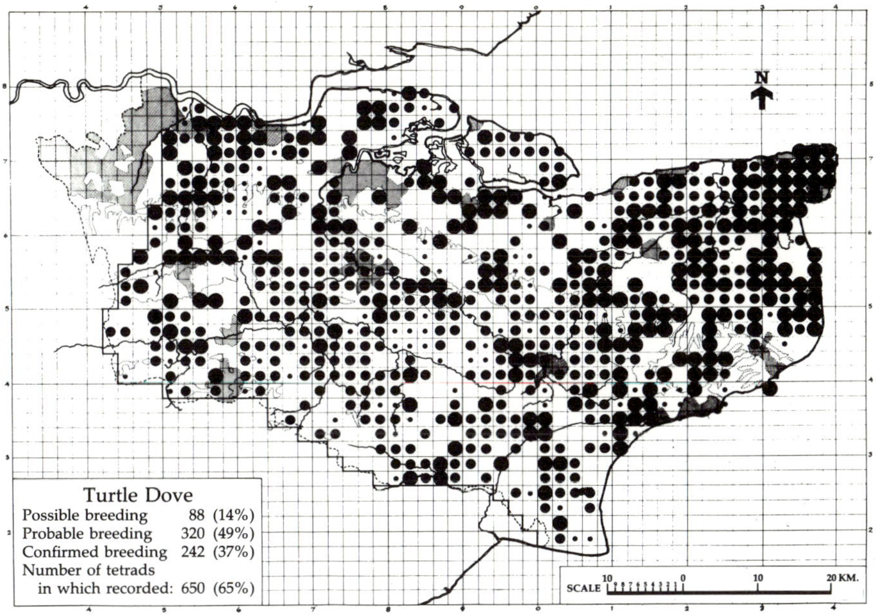

over 600 between 20th–31st May 1967 and 150 flying north on 11th May 1975. At Allhallows, also in 1975, there was a marked westerly passage in May, with 852 on the 11th, followed by 192 on the 18th, 118 on the 24th and a further 122 on 14th June.

Autumn flocks build up from early July, with reports of 100–240 in 13 years from 7th July–8th September and an exceptional count of 450 between Hoo and High Halstow on 11th September 1965. Visible migration occasionally involves day-totals of up to 100, with 200 moving west in the Stour Valley on 15th August 1962 and a similar movement at Sandwich Bay on 28th August 1965. Passage continues throughout September, with stragglers occurring annually into October. Normally last dates are in mid-October, but the latest recorded was at Swanscombe on 2nd November 1974.

There are three winter records, of one at Hythe on 29th–31st December 1960, and singles, feeding with flocks of Collared Doves, at Broadstairs from late December 1967 until the end of January 1968, and at Lydd between 13th January–3rd February 1969.

The several foreign ringing recoveries concerning Kent-ringed birds include two each from Portugal and Spain.

Great Spotted Cuckoo

Clamator glandarius

Very rare vagrant.

The only record for the county is of an immature bird seen at Dungeness on 22nd August 1970.

Cuckoo

Cuculus canorus

Common summer visitor and passage migrant.

Cuckoo numbers are subject to considerable annual variation. Parslow (1973) produced evidence of a widespread decrease over the country as a whole, particularly during the fifties, but this trend was not apparent in Kent, although poor seasons and low numbers were reported in 1966 and 1967.

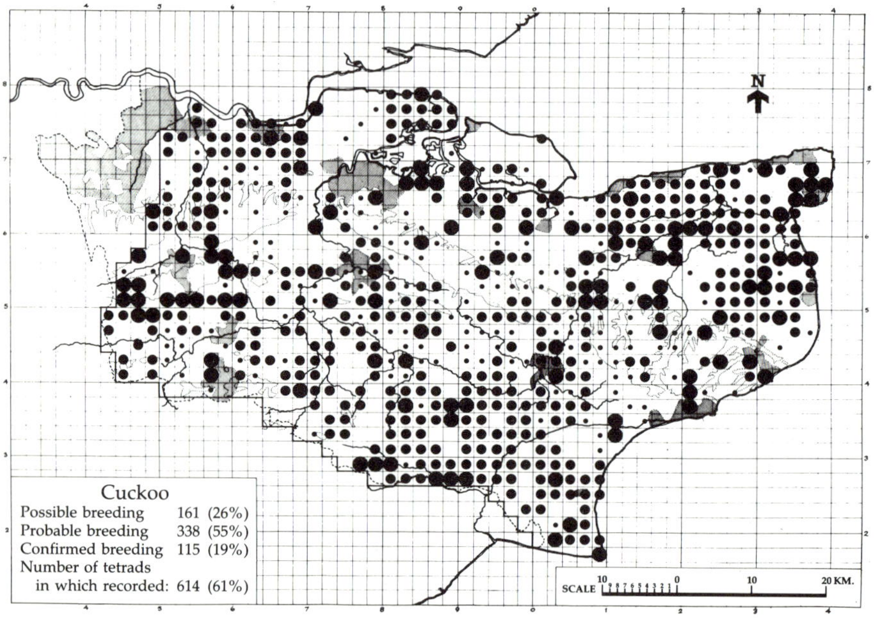

The Cuckoo is generally distributed in most habitats throughout the county, except in closely built-up areas. The lack of records from parts of north Kent and from stretches of the North Downs probably reflects, at least in part, the combined effects of lower densities and poorer coverage.

First reports usually come from the south of the county around 8th–10th April. The earliest dates are 25th March 1959, 30th March 1960 and 31st March 1958. In contrast, in 1973 there was no record before 14th April, the main influx not occurring until the last few days of the month.

Adult Cuckoos begin to leave early in July, and passage continues until late September, the great majority of the later birds being juveniles. October records are rare, but since 1970 there have been at least five and the latest dates are 6th October 1963 at Herne Bay, 8th October 1973 and 9th October 1971, both at Sandwich Bay.

At the Observatories peak autumn numbers have included 15 at Dungeness on 20th July 1963 and 11 at Sandwich Bay on 12th July 1966. Earlier peaks of 18 at Dungeness on 19th June 1967 and 15 at Sandwich Bay on 25th June 1972 may well have included local birds as well as some early migrants. A nestling ringed at Sutton Valence on 15th June 1962 was killed in Bergamo, Italy, on 2nd September of that year, indicating the relatively unusual southeast orientation of migrating Cuckoos in autumn.

Fosterers vary with the habitat, the Reed Warbler being frequently victimised in marshy areas and Dunnocks elsewhere. In 1959 a young Cuckoo was found in a Hawfinch's nest, possibly the only record of this species as a fosterer in Kent.

Barn Owl

Tyto alba

Resident.

Ticehurst considered the Barn Owl to be tolerably common throughout the county and more numerous in the wooded areas, whilst Harrison had the impression that the species had decreased throughout Kent, with a particular scarcity on Romney Marsh.

A national survey in 1963 (Prestt, 1965) indicated that the recent decline in the Barn Owl population, most widespread in eastern England, was apparently due to a combination of loss of habitat, changes in agriculture leading to a decrease in food and breeding sites, disturbance, and the effects of agricultural chemicals. The first two are obviously long-term, but the last seems the most likely reason for the sudden decrease in the late fifties and early sixties. This theory is given credence as a result of pesticide residue levels determined during laboratory examination of eight birds found dead in Kent in March and April 1962.

In Kent the Barn Owl reached an all-time low in the early sixties, with only two pairs reported breeding in 1962, when the severe winter of 1962/63 probably aggravated the already hazardous situation further. Since then, however, there has been a slow recovery, to the extent that during the first quarter of 1972 up to 12 could be seen on Romney Marsh.

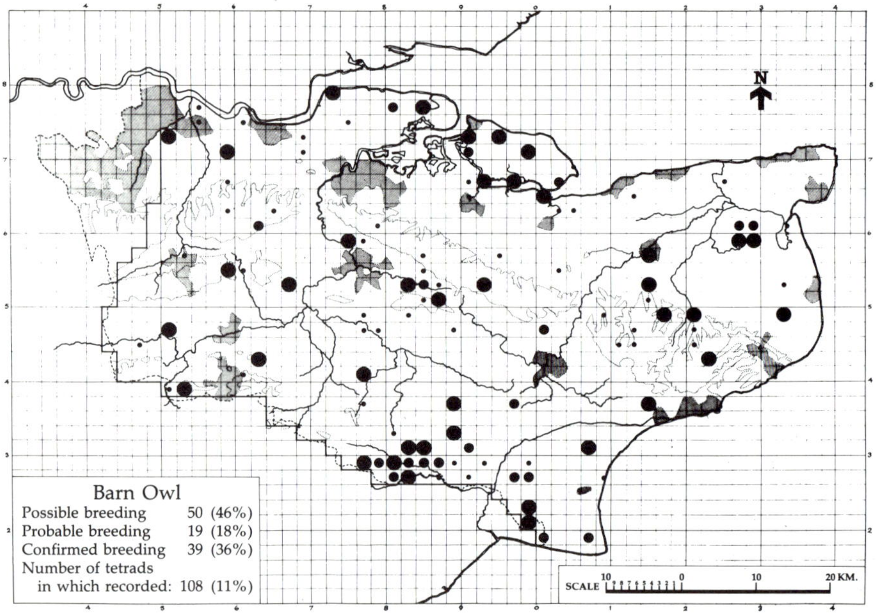

There is some dispersal in autumn and winter, particularly of young birds. One was found on the South Goodwin lightship on 29th December 1971. Another, ringed as a nestling on the Isle of Wight in July 1975, was recovered at Sandling in December 1976, and another, also ringed as a nestling at Eastchurch (Sheppey) in 1967, was found dead at Eastry (Sandwich) in September 1968. On 10th September 1976 one, which was flushed out of the hamlet at Shellness, first landed on the mud at the tideline and later circled high as it flew southeast across the Swale.

During 1971–76 a total of 34 was reported dead, mainly found on roads, indicative that motor traffic is a major hazard for the Barn Owl.

Fourteen individuals showing the characteristics of the Continental dark-breasted race *T.a. guttata* have been observed in the county during the last 25 years, all between October–April, with eight in January.

Scops Owl

Otus scops

Very rare vagrant.

There are four or five early records, but Harrison considered that only one, at Broadstairs in March 1898, was fully substantiated.

In recent years the only record concerns a badly injured bird, which later died, found on Crundale Downs (Wye) on 22nd October 1971.

Snowy Owl

Nyctea scandiaca

Possible vagrant.

Harrison mentions three unsubstantiated nineteenth century records and includes three for this century, singles on 4th March 1927, 13th January 1948 and 30th March 1950.

A female observed on Romney Marsh between 24th–31st January 1965, may have been an escape. Apparently large numbers were imported for sale in the early sixties.

Little Owl

Athene noctua

An introduced species, now a widespread resident.

Ticehurst was able to list only six records prior to 1874, when a pair was introduced to Stonewall Park, Edenbridge. About 40 birds were released between 1874–80 and the species soon spread and became established throughout the county by the beginning of the twentieth century. During the next fifty years only minor fluctuations in numbers were recorded.

A widespread, marked decline in Little Owl numbers was noted in southeast England in the late fifties and early sixties, perhaps due to the effects of certain persistent organochlorine pesticides in use in agriculture at that time.

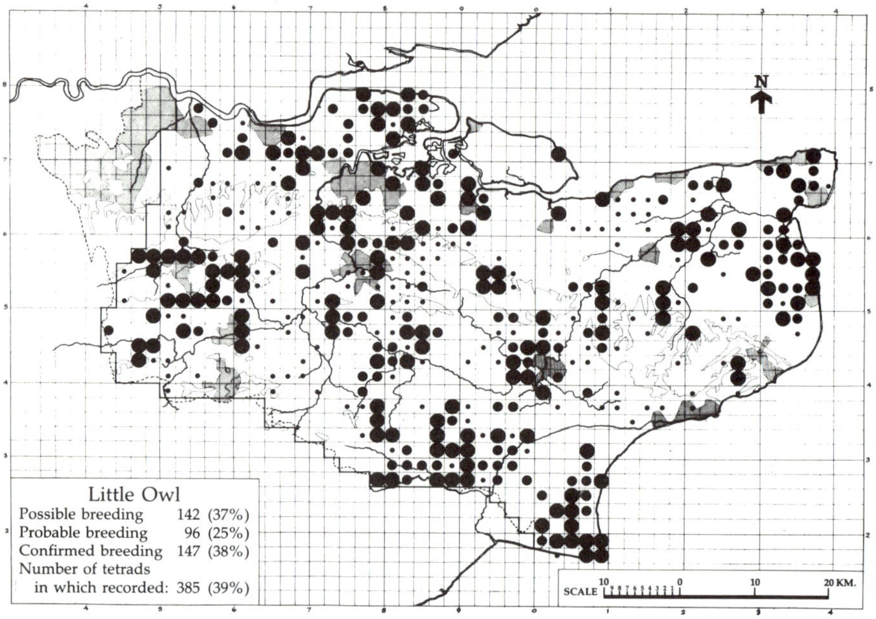

The breeding distribution map shows that the Little Owl is now widely scattered throughout the county as a nesting species. Although typically a species of the agricultural countryside, it may also be found in old orchards and parkland, on industrial waste ground, in old quarries and on sea cliffs, and it has even been recorded nesting in the shingle areas at Dungeness.

The feeding habits of the Little Owl have been well documented, but a number of interesting observations have been recorded over the years in Kent. In 1955 and 1956 earthworms were found impaled on wire outside a nest at Cliffe, while in 1956, at a site on Northward Hill, a dead Bank Vole and a Slow-worm were similarly found. At Kingston on 31st May 1960 a Little Owl was seen carrying a young Pheasant as large as itself, and at Chislet on 26th May 1962 another was observed carrying a Blackbird.

Tawny Owl

Strix aluco

A widely distributed and in some places common resident.

Harrison gained the impression that the Tawny Owl was taken for granted, particularly in the northwest and centre of the county, and was therefore under-recorded. Gillham and Homes considered it to be virtually absent from the North Kent Marshes.

This picture has changed little in the last 25 years and, probably due to its strictly nocturnal habits, it is in most years grossly under-recorded. The Breeding Bird Survey tended to redress the balance and Tawny Owls were reported from nearly one-third of all tetrads.

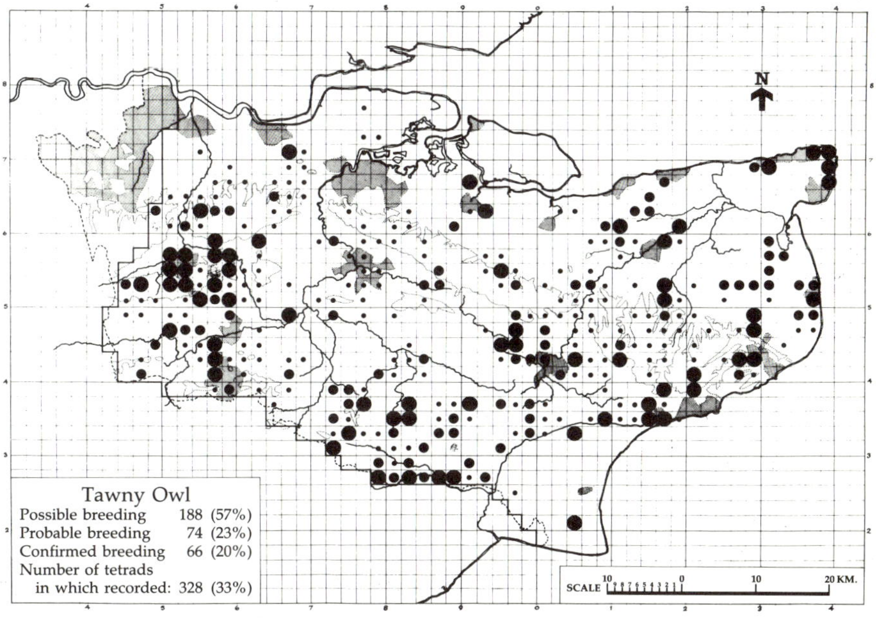

The high proportion of possible and probable breeding records show how difficult it is to establish proof of successful nesting, and often Tawny Owls are heard rather than seen. Within Kent it is recorded from all suitable mature woodland, and it is therefore not surprising that records are very scarce in the northern part of the county. It is also scarce on Romney Marsh, but at Lydd a pair has bred regularly since 1966.

Some indication of the numbers of Tawny Owls in Kent can be gained from noctural counts carried out during the Nightingale censuses in 1969–70. On 24th–25th May 1969 and 23rd–24th May 1970 the totals were

129 and 202 respectively. These counts covered most of the woodland habitats that were likely to attract Nightingales and probably represent, in consequence, a large proportion of the county's Tawny Owl population.

Long-eared Owl

Asio otus

Uncommon resident, rather more numerous in autumn and winter.

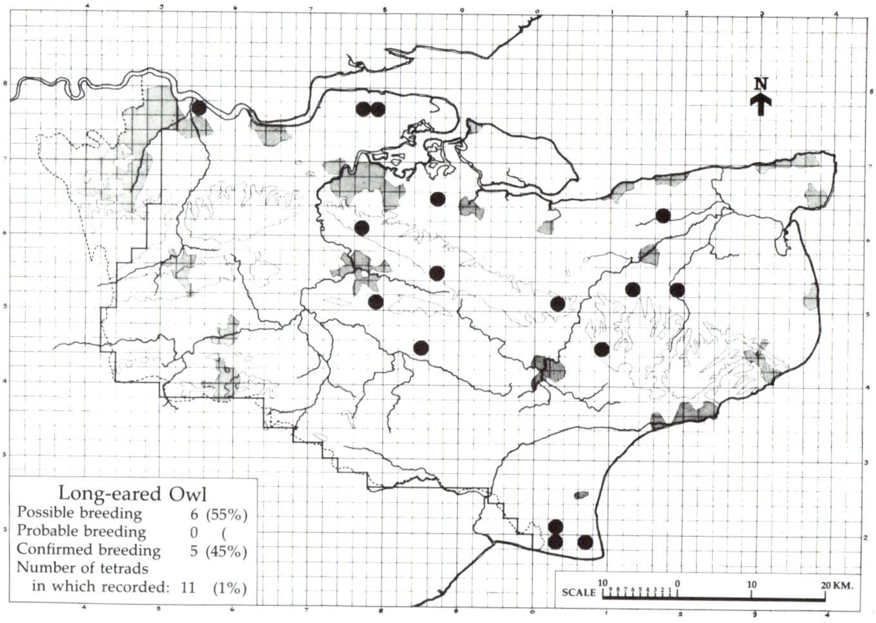

Distribution of all proven breeding records of Long-eared Owls 1952–76

The status of the Long-eared Owl appears to have changed little over the years. During 1952–76, from one–five pairs have been reported breeding annually, exept in 1960 and 1962. One–four pairs nested fairly regularly at Northward Hill between 1953–61 and one–five pairs in the Dungeness area between 1956–58 and 1963–74. Only another eleven nest sites have been reported. Old Magpie's nests are commonly used and a number have been found in small copses of hawthorns, with other nests in conifer plantations, and small isolated groups of trees, such as farm shelter-belts and copses on downland.

Autumn migrants are regularly reported from coastal localities in September–October. One ringed on Reculver marshes on 23rd September 1972 was subsequently found dead at nearby St. Nicholas-at-Wade in November, showing that some of these immigrants remain in Kent for the winter. It seems probable that these birds form the basis of the few small roosts of up to 10 birds that are regularly reported, particularly in the north of the county, during the winter months.

The autumn of 1975 saw a quite unprecedented influx of Continental birds into Kent. The first report was on 11th October, when two were seen at Dungeness, and by December there was a total of 90 Long-eared Owls in eight roosts of up to 29 birds. Further roosts were discovered in January–February, producing a total in excess of 170, with the largest of the thirteen roosts containing 40 birds. Following this exceptional winter it was surprising that only one pair was known to breed in 1976, though confirmation of nesting is not readily recorded.

A series of ringing recoveries, associated with this influx, in other parts of Great Britain show that many of these immigrants originated from the countries bordering the Baltic Sea. Earlier, in April 1954, one ringed as a nestling the previous July in Den Helder, Holland, was recovered at Gravesend, and in December 1968 another, ringed in Heligoland, Germany, was found dead at Margate. The only recovery of a Long-eared Owl ringed in Kent concerns a nestling, ringed near Dungeness in June 1974, which was found dead near Olney, Buckinghamshire in April 1976, one of the longest movements for a British-bred bird.

During January–February 1973 five roosted regularly near Elmstone and an analysis of pellets from these birds gives some indication of the winter diet of the Long-eared Owl in Kent. The contents included Bank Vole, Short-tailed Vole, Wood Mouse, probable Harvest Mouse, thrush species and Greenfinch. In contrast, analysis of about 100 pellets from High Halstow in 1965 showed that besides various rodent remains, as many as 26 House Sparrows, some Bullfinches and Dunnocks, Blue, Great, Marsh and Willow Tits, and a Starling also featured in the diet of the eight birds in the roost. There is obviously considerable flexibility, depending on the foods available.

Short-eared Owl

Asio flammeus

A regular autumn and winter visitor, breeding most years.

Breeding apparently increased greatly during the 1950s to reach peaks of nine pairs in 1954 and 14 pairs in 1957, both associated with 'plagues' of the Short-tailed Field Vole. In most years, however, less than three pairs nest.

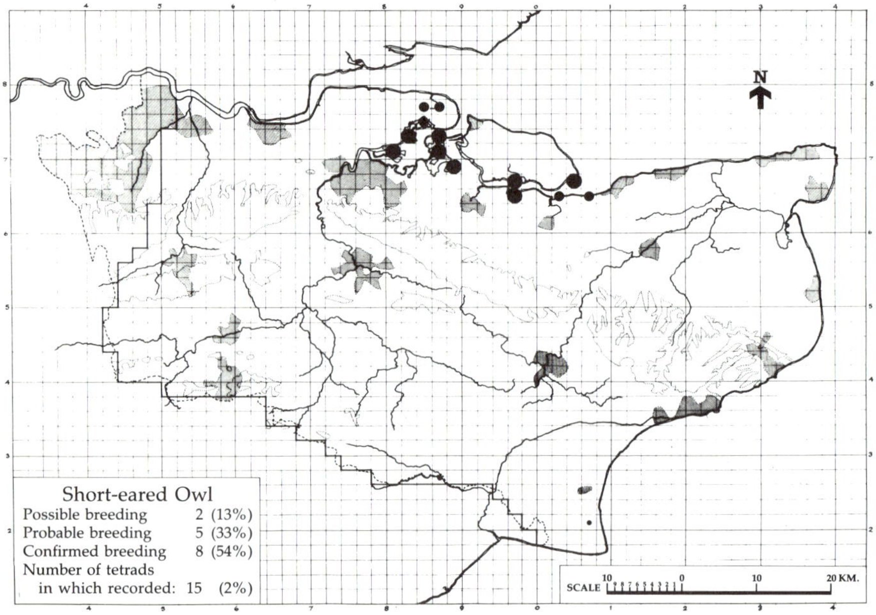

Breeding in the Medway estuary had probably taken place for several years prior to the discovery of three pairs on Nor in 1952, and indeed Harrison gives one definite breeding record for this area in 1935. One–three pairs now breed almost annually on the islands and saltings in the Medway estuary. Sheppey is the other main stronghold of this species and the first definite breeding there involved a total of five pairs in 1954. In August of that year no less than 24 birds were present at Windmill Creek, long before the normal autumn influx in October, and eight pairs bred at this locality in the peak year of 1957. In retrospect, it seems likely that breeding had also taken place in this area for some years prior to their discovery. However, since 1957 only one or two pairs have bred at Windmill Creek annually, with a notable period of absence between 1961–70. Elsewhere on Sheppey one or two pairs also bred regularly at Shellness during the 1950s and 1970s. The only other confirmation of breeding in the county was recorded at Sandwich Bay, where single pairs bred in 1955 and 1964.

As an autumn and winter visitor the Short-eared Owl reaches the Kent coast in September–October, with early migrants occasionally arriving in August. They are regularly observed flying in off the sea on the north and east coasts, more usually in October, and often arrive in a very tired state.

The main wintering areas are the coastal marshes of north and east Kent, in particular the Thames, Medway and Sheppey marshes. In east Kent they occur on the marshes between Reculver, Grove and Sandwich Bay, with the main concentration at this last locality, while in the south they occur on Walland and Romney Marshes. Inland records are comparatively few, although in recent years up to four have wintered regularly on the Stour marshes between Wye and Ashford.

Wintering populations generally reached a peak in the years between 1954–67 and then slumped to a very low level, with only a partial recovery during the 1970s. In the winter of 1954/55, there were roosts on Sheppey of 20 at both Elmley and Windmill Creek and 10 at Rushenden, with 19 on Burntwick and 17 on Chetney in the Medway Estuary. Even allowing for a certain amount of duplication, these numbers are particularly high and constitute the best winter by far, coinciding with a vole plague. At other localities the peak numbers were 22 at Stoke in the winter of 1958/59 and 16 at Sandwich Bay in 1963/64, while the last records of such high numbers occurred in 1966/67, with 20 at Windmill Creek, 12 at Elmley and 10 at Sandwich Bay. There have been far fewer reports of such roosts in recent years and they have generally been smaller, consisting of a maximum of 8–12 birds.

Some indication of the origin of our winter visitors is given by two ringing recoveries. One ringed as a nestling at Gisburn, Yorkshire on 2nd June 1957 was found dead at Ramsgate on 8th February 1958 and one, also ringed as a nestling, this time at Bytrask, Sideby (Vaasa), Finland on 14th June 1966 was found dead at High Halstow on 22nd April 1969.

Two studies of the diet of Short-eared Owls in Kent have been conducted. In 1956 the contents of a series of pellets revealed, as would be expected, mostly Short-tailed Field Voles, but also a Brown Rat and a Water Shrew, and in the same year one was seen eating a Song Thrush at Stodmarsh. Sixty-six pellets examined from birds breeding in north Kent in 1957 revealed the remains of 75 Short-tailed Field Voles, one Wood Mouse, one Common Shrew, and two beetles.

Tengmalm's Owl

Aegolius funereus

Ticehurst details two records of singles obtained in 1836 and 1881.

Nightjar

Caprimulgus europaeus

Summer visitor.

Ticehurst includes an exceptionally early record of one at Borough Green on 15th April 1902. Harrison describes the Nightjar as well distributed, particularly in the west of the county, and refers to successful breeding on the shingle at Dungeness in 1920 and 1924, and at the Lydd ranges between 1934–1940.

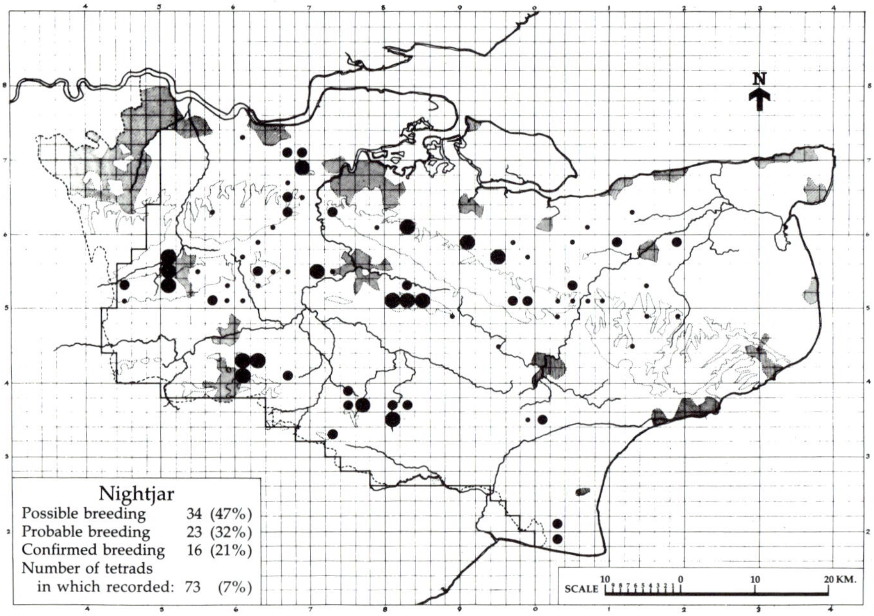

The majority of the nesting areas located in the Breeding Survey are associated with chestnut coppice or conifer plantations. Nightjars favour the more open areas with isolated, mature trees, and are often associated with bracken and newly planted conifers. The map shows concentrations along the North Downs at Cobham and Luddesdown, and in Challock Forest. Further south, on the greensand ridge, they are well distributed around Sevenoaks, Mereworth and in the King's Wood between Langley and Ulcombe. In the Weald the principal sites are in the vicinity of Pembury, and Angley Wood and Hemsted Forest near Cranbrook. In the Dungeness area pairs were seen displaying in 1968.

Numbers were probably maintained during the fifties and sixties, when the Nightjar was still to be found in north Kent, in Shorne Woods, Chattenden and Northward Hill, and in the woods north of Canterbury. Accurate estimates of the total population are lacking, but there were concentrations of five pairs in the Goathurst/Sevenoaks Commons area, east of Ide Hill, in 1959, eight pairs at Mereworth woods in 1964 and five pairs at Luddesdown the following year. However, the Nightingale census in May 1970 did produce a total of 45 birds, with rather fewer the following year. Since then there has apparently been a marked decline. The strongholds are now the Pembury, Mereworth and Luddesdown areas in the west of the county, the Cranbrook area, and Challock Forest, where five pairs were heard churring in June 1975.

The first migrants normally arrive in mid-May, the earliest record in recent years being one at Eccles on 28th April 1971. Departure is in August and September. Few migrants are seen, though there were singles at Dungeness on five dates between 4th–26th September 1965, with the latest there on 6th October 1968.

Swift

Apus apus

Abundant summer visitor.

Swifts may arrive towards the end of April, but more often and more generally appear in the first half of May. As Harrison pointed out, they must originally have been cliff nesters, but now usually breed on buildings. The map thus shows the concentrations expected in towns and villages.

The earliest date on which the Swift has been recorded in Kent is 14th April 1963 at Dungeness. Incoming birds are sometimes seen in vast numbers, often over water. There were 2,120 at Bough Beech on 13th May 1972 and on 18th May 1975 4,148 flew west at Allhallows during an 11 hour watch.

Emigration begins in early July and numbers are always small by the end of August. October Swifts are relatively scarce, but the latest dates have occurred during November, with three between the 2nd–4th and

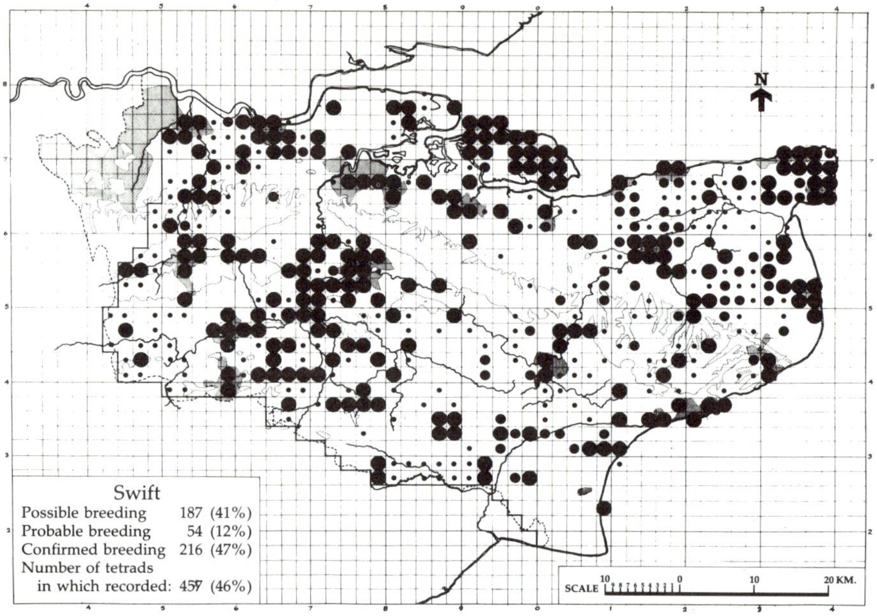

the latest on 28th November 1960 at Gillingham. Harrison records an even later one at Kingsdown (Deal) on 13th December 1913.

Weather movements in summer are usually associated with advancing fronts or thunderstorms. For example, in the last week of June 1962 large scale weather movements were noted at St. Margaret's at Cliffe, Sandwich Bay and in the Stour Valley, with at least 6,000 moving northwest at Dungeness on the 26th. Similarly on 1st and 2nd July 1970 movements were noted at Allhallows and Sandwich Bay, with 12–14,000 flying west near Herne Bay. One of the most spectacular movements was noted on 18th June 1971, when 5,000 Swifts were seen at Littlestone and 2,000 an hour flew west at Allhallows. In Folkestone, in the evening of that day, up to 2,000 screamed up and down a confined flight line in the centre of the town. Coming up into a force 8 wind, they are described as having hung in clusters of up to 100 on the walls of the Public Library. Two days later 3,000 passed north at Sandwich Bay. Ticehurst described a similar phenomenon in 1835.

Ringing recoveries are few in number, but make up fully in quality what they lack in quantity. A freshly-fledged juvenile ringed at East Malling was recovered four days later in Holland, not an expected direction of dispersal. An adult from the East Malling colony, ringed in June 1962, was retrapped almost exactly a year later at Sleaford, Lincs, 200 km to the north. Swifts are normally faithful to their colonies, and this record probably gives some idea of the very considerable distances they will forage 'away from home', especially in poor weather. Another recovery gives an idea of the unusually long life-span for a small bird, an adult ringed at Murston in June 1966 was retrapped there in June 1974.

Alpine Swift

Apus melba

Very rare vagrant.

Ticehurst gives only three dated records, between 6th July and 21st October, while Harrison describes two exceptional occurrences. On 15th July 1915 about 100 flew northwest over Kingsdown (Deal) and groups of five were seen there on 22nd July and 3rd August. On 16th May 1916 three and six were found alive in rooms of a house in Hythe. One was also seen near Birchington on 26th April 1947.

The nine records in recent years have all occurred since 1961. Apart from an exceptionally early bird at Dover on 15th March 1969 and a late one at Cliffe on 7th October 1961, all fell between 27th May–13th September, with three in June. Seven were seen along the east coast between Kingsgate and Dover, with another at Dungeness.

Kingfisher

Alcedo atthis

Resident.

No long-term change in status is apparent since Harrison described the Kingfisher as fairly generally distributed but in only moderate numbers. However, it is very greatly affected by severe winters and suffered badly in 1962/63. Only two breeding pairs were reported in 1963 and 1964, but there were many more records by 1967 and the succession of mild winters that followed enabled the population to re-establish itself.

The Kingfisher is widely distributed in the Weald and along the major river valleys, but virtually absent from the more or less waterless chalk downland and the dip slope to the north.

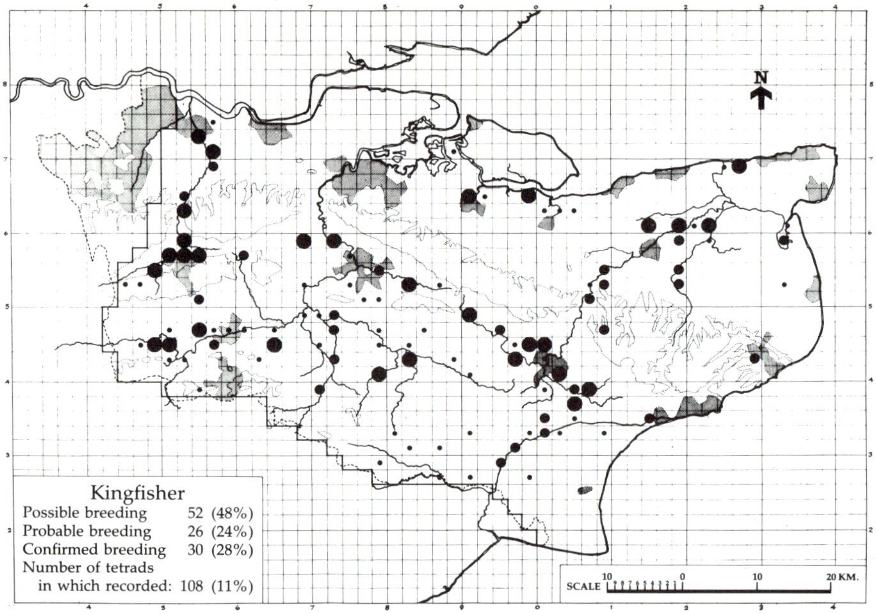

In the autumn there is a tendency for young birds to disperse, when they occasionally occur around the coast at the Observatories and increasingly on the North Kent Marshes.

The most distant ringing recovery concerns a juvenile ringed at High Halstow in July 1970, recovered near Aylesbury, Buckinghamshire a month later, some 112 kilometres WNW. Another, ringed as a juvenile at Rye Meads, Hertfordshire in June 1973, was recovered at Littlebrook six weeks later, 35 kilometres SSE.

Bee-eater

Merops apiaster

Very rare vagrant.

Ticehurst includes only three records between 1827–1882, the two dated ones referring to May and June.

In recent years there have been eight records, four for 1953–58 and a further four during 1969–74, all between 15th May–26th September. A party of about a dozen at St. Mary's Bay, Romney Marsh on 25th September 1955 was considered to have come from Plumpton in Sussex, where two pairs had earlier bred successfully. They were also heard calling the next day. Earlier the same year one was seen at Sandwich Bay. The other records all concern singles, with three at Dungeness, another at Sandwich Bay, and inland at Betteshanger and Sevenoaks.

Roller

Coracias garrulus

Very rare vagrant.

Ticehurst gives six records between 1832–94, including an exceptionally late bird at Rainham Marsh on 8th November 1888. In 1906 one was seen at Edenbridge between 20th July–22nd September.

One at Canterbury from 27th June–2nd July 1962 was probably the same bird seen later at Wye between 8th–15th July. The only other recent occurrence concerns one in Trenley Park Woods on 8th–9th June 1969.

Hoopoe

Upupa epops

Annual passage migrant in small numbers. Has bred.

The Hoopoe has been proved to breed in Kent on at least one occasion. Ticehurst gave several instances of probable breeding, but considered that conclusive proof was lacking. Harrison, however, recorded successful breeding at Hythe in 1948. Ticehurst also pointed out that for every autumn occurrence there were three in spring, and this holds true for the review period.

The extreme dates are 23rd March 1959 and 12th November 1955. A succession of late, cold springs may be partially responsible for the poor numbers in recent years. Sharrock (1974) pointed out that in the past hundred years there had been a decrease in Europe, and that the Hoopoe was largely absent as a breeding species in the Low Countries and Scandinavia. This contraction of range, probably due to climatic

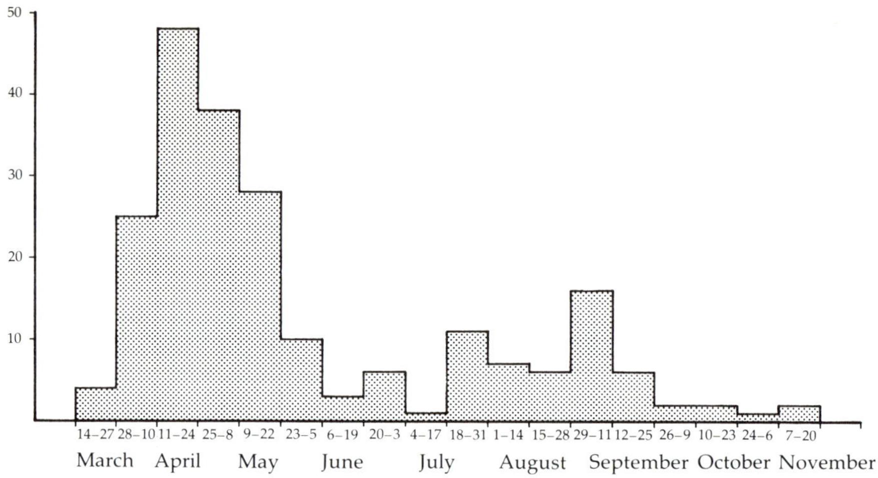

Fortnightly distribution of Hoopoes 1952–76

changes, is doubtless the main cause for the decrease in Kentish records. This decline was commented upon by Harrison, and following a short-lived peak in the late fifties it has continued.

Hoopoes have been reported from all parts of the county, but eastern and southeastern coastal areas have been most favoured. It is possible that breeding took place during the period under review, as Hoopoes can be secretive and belie their apparently conspicuous plumage when breeding.

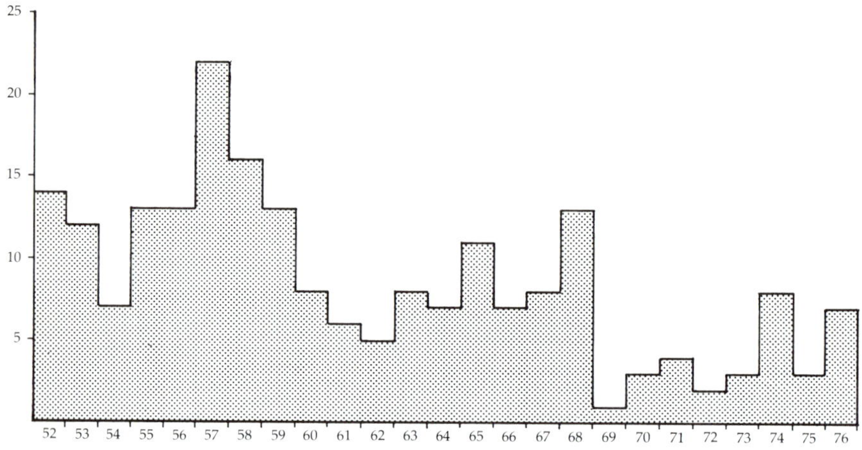

Annual totals of Hoopoes

Wryneck

Jynx torquilla

Passage migrant, possibly an occasional pair may still breed.

Ticehurst described the Wryneck as plentiful and generally distributed throughout the county, particularly in gardens, coppices and old orchards. Harrison suggests some decline, particularly in the east and southeast of the county between 1919–47, but cites evidence that points to a slight increase in the numbers of breeding pairs in some localities between 1948–52.

The decline of the Wryneck as a breeding species in England is well documented, with the majority of the breeding records during the later years of the decline occurring in Kent.

During the period under review the vast majority of breeding records have been north of a line linking Sevenoaks with Hythe, an area predominantly of chalk and greensand. Breeding was quite widespread

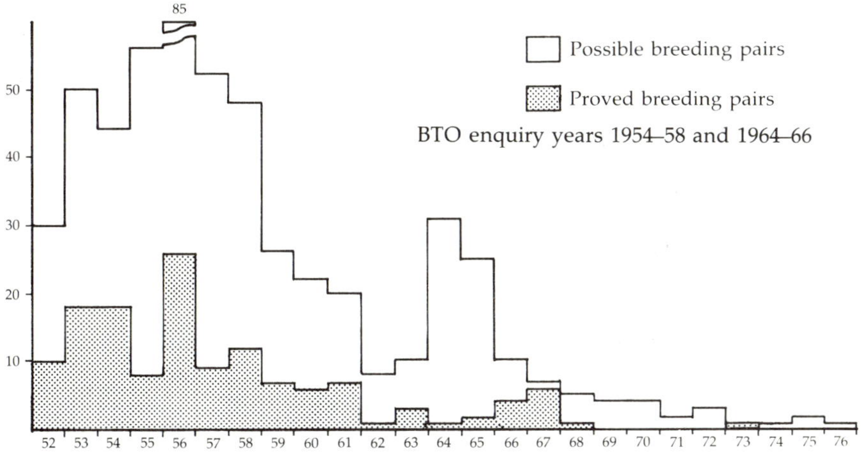

Wryneck breeding population 1952–76

within this area, particularly around Canterbury, Maidstone, the Medway towns and Dartford, with the most recent breeding recorded in the western parts of the county. The favoured sites have been old orchards and parkland, but nest boxes in mature gardens have frequently been used.

The histogram, with the data from the two BTO enquiries providing the most accurate figures, shows that the decline accelerated markedly from 1958. Apart from a single pair, at one of the traditional sites in 1973, there is no conclusive evidence of proven breeding since 1968. However, the renowned difficulty in proving breeding is confirmed by the comparative data shown on the histogram.

Spring passage has always been light, with the first arrivals in late March and only occasional records at Dungeness and Sandwich Bay Observatories. The earliest record is one at Folkestone on 23rd March 1961. Since 1969 the arrival dates have been later, usually from mid-April, and the poorest spring occurred in 1975, when only three late singles were recorded on 10th May, 16th–18th May and 1st June.

The earliest dates for 1952–76 are summarised by fortnightly periods:

March	April		May	
14–27	28–10	11–24	25–8	9–22
5	13	6		1

Autumn passage is more marked, but varies considerably from year to year, usually occurring from late August into early October, with one at Sevenoaks on 4th November 1968 the latest recorded. Since 1969 it has been heavier and more widespread, with records of singles from all parts of the county, and it is interesting to note that four of the six latest dates are since 1972. In that year Dungeness recorded its heaviest passage with 66 bird/days between 27th August–23rd September and a peak of eight on 5th September.

Green Woodpecker

Picus viridis

Widespread resident.

The commonest of the three resident woodpeckers, the Green Woodpecker frequents deciduous woodland, but prefers wooded areas with open ground. Parkland and farmland with hedgerows containing mature trees are ideal. The preference for these habitats is largely influenced by its habit of feeding on the ground, especially on ants, in areas of short grass.

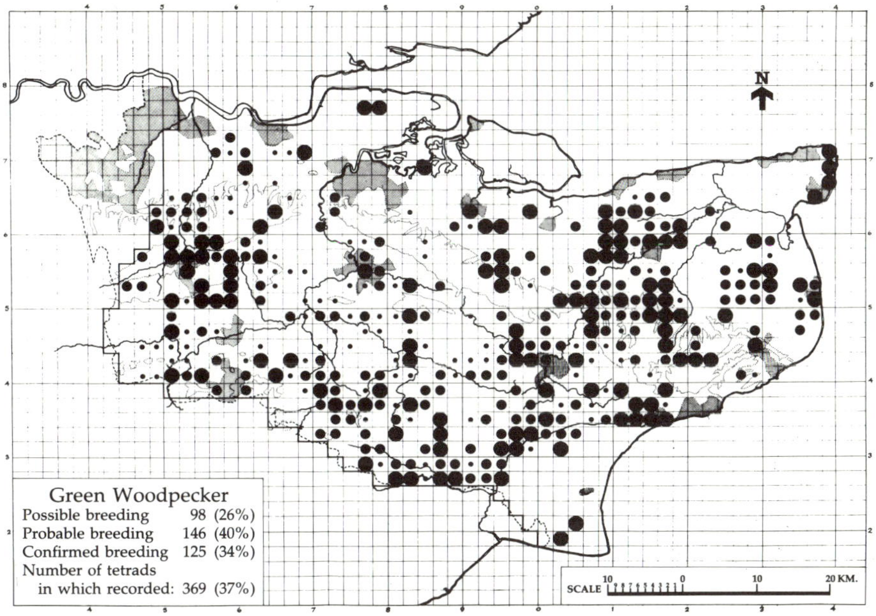

Harrison produces evidence of a general increase during the first half of this century and of a spread towards the east and southeast. It is interesting to note, too, that Gillham and Homes described it as 'surprisingly numerous' on Sheppey, where the breeding distribution map now shows a complete absence of breeding records. As a breeding species it is also fairly scarce on Thanet, Romney Marsh and the Thames marshes, where there are relatively few large, mature trees.

Green Woodpecker numbers have been influenced by changes in the area of grazing grassland. These can come about due to agricultural improvement, fertilising and mowing, or when a myxomatosis outbreak reduces rabbit numbers, in each case causing a decline in the meadow ant population.

Severe winters can also cause a marked change in status, as in 1962/63, when the numbers were considerably reduced. The recovery since then has been fairly slow, but recent reports indicate that it may just have regained its former status in some parts of the county. On Sheppey, however, it is still virtually absent and at Dungeness there has been little evidence of recovery. Between 1952–62 there were peak annual bird/day totals of 149 in 1953 and 90 in 1962. Though there were 19 bird/days in 1963, none was recorded in 1968–70 and the peak bird/day total since has only reached ten, in 1973. Most observations there occurred during March and November, suggesting passage, but there are no ringing recoveries to support this. At Sandwich Bay one trapped in September 1961 was controlled there in March 1965.

Great Spotted Woodpecker

Dendrocopos major

Widespread resident, partial migrant.

Harrison states that numbers increased and the range extended east and southeast during the first half of this century, but it is difficult to assess any change in its status accurately. Nationally there has been a general increase this century (Parslow, 1973), and more recently the Common Bird Census index has shown some marked changes, with increases of 47% in 1973 and a further 20% in 1976. It is possible that there is a short-term link here with the epidemic of Dutch elm disease, making available a greater supply of larval and adult invertebrates in the dead and dying elms.

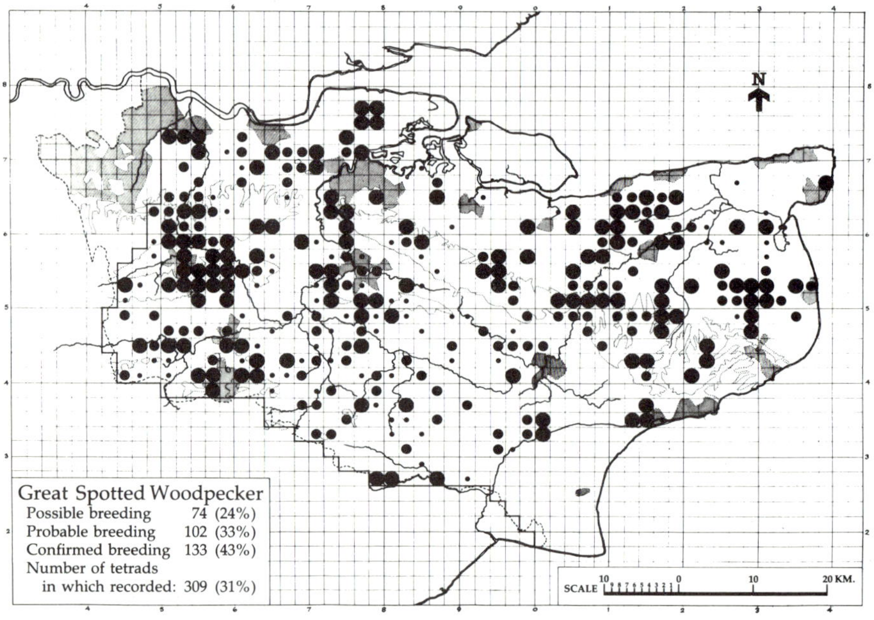

The Great Spotted Woodpecker is commonly associated with both coniferous and deciduous woodland areas, and suburban parks and gardens. It is probably more plentiful along the Downs than the map shows, but in the breeding season it is scarce on Thanet and virtually absent from the woodland-free landscapes of Romney Marsh, and the Isles of Grain and Sheppey.

In autumn there have been a number of records around the coast, a few of which do refer to Continental immigrants, although the majority appear to be Kentish birds dispersing. Two individuals of the northern race *D.m.major* in December 1929 and January 1944 are cited by Harrison. On 3rd and 14th September 1962 two were trapped at Dungeness, while in 1969 at Northward Hill one was trapped on 18th January and two on 9th March. Harrison also records one instance of the central European race *D.m. pinetorum* on 14th December 1929. The great majority of those trapped at Dungeness and Sandwich Bay are of the British race *D.m. anglicus*. One of indeterminate race, ringed at Dungeness on 1st September 1962, was recovered in Belgium in late November of that year.

An analysis of the records for Dungeness and the Isle of Sheppey gives further insight into the amount of movement that occurs. At Dungeness, Great Spotted Woodpeckers are not an annual occurrence, and there have only been two spring records, on 28th April 1971 and 29th April 1963. Apart from an irruption in 1957 involving 20 bird/days from 30th July–21st November, there have been only 22 autumn records, all between 18th July–22nd November. At Warden Point and Shellness, on the Isle of Sheppey, from 1970–76 there were 15 records, all between 20th September–13th November.

Lesser Spotted Woodpecker

Dendrocopos minor

Widely, but apparently thinly distributed.

Though Harrison suggests that the Lesser Spotted Woodpecker too, extended its range during the first half of this century, there is little evidence to indicate any marked change in status in recent years.

Reports indicate that it is the least common of the three resident woodpeckers, but there is little doubt that it is under-recorded, as it is such an elusive species. It is quite widespread away from the coast and found in similar habitats to those frequented by the Great Spotted Woodpecker. Parkland, wooded gardens, old orchards and mature alders are favoured.

It is probably more common and widespread as a breeding species than the map shows, but the only regular reports in the north of the county are from Northward Hill and Shorne woods. It is extremely scarce on Thanet, thinly distributed in the east and absent from Romney

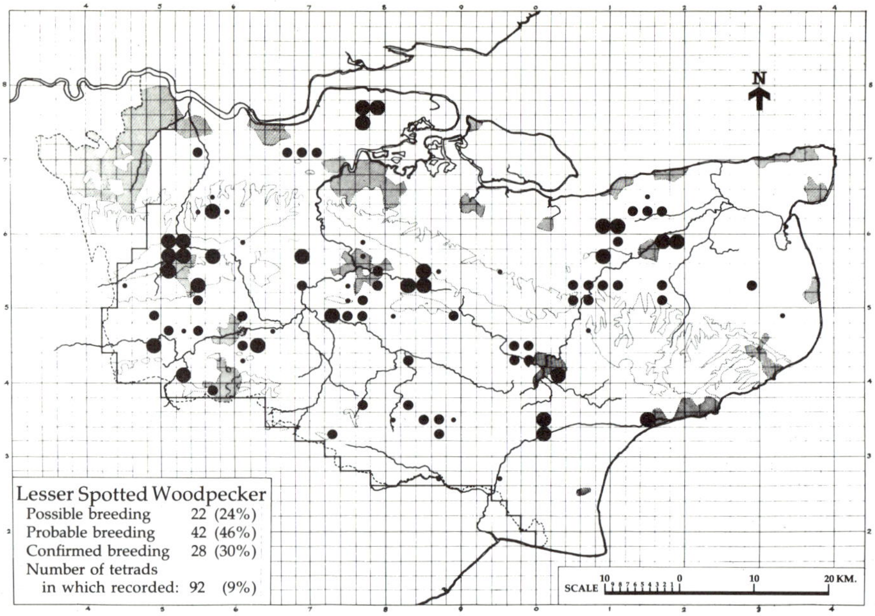

Marsh, although it does breed regularly in the woods bordering the Royal Military Canal.

Local fluctuations in the population levels may well be due to the grubbing of old orchards, and more recently there have been increases, probably due to Dutch elm disease. The population at Northward Hill, for example, increased considerably as the elms died.

One at Sandwich Bay Bird Observatory on 8th December 1976 was exceptional, and there were no reports from Dungeness during the review period.

The only ringing recovery concerns a juvenile male, ringed at Willesborough (Ashford) in July 1967 and found dead at Marden in August 1969, about 30 kilometres west, suggesting that there is probably a small autumn dispersal of young birds.

Crested Lark

Galerida cristata

Very rare vagrant.

One historical record concerns a single specimen caught on Dover Cliff on 22nd April 1879.

The only recent acceptable record is of one that was present at Dungeness between 28th September–1st October 1975.

Woodlark

Lullula arborea

Rare passage migrant and occasional winter visitor. Until recently bred in small numbers.

Harrison describes the Woodlark as a very local breeding species in small numbers, showing little change since Ticehurst's account. North-west and west Kent were the principal breeding haunts, with Tenterden and Benenden also mentioned. He also states there was no positive evidence of migration, but cites a number of autumn reports, including a party of 21 at Seal on 21st September 1943. It is not possible to estimate the number of breeding pairs involved, though it does appear that the population reached a peak in the late 1940s and early 1950s, which is in line with the national trend.

Breeding is usually associated with dry sites in sand or chalk country, with areas of short grass for feeding and scattered trees or bushes for song posts. In Kent the preferred habitat was in the chart country between Westerham and Sevenoaks.

During the 1950s breeding season records were quite widespread, though reports of confirmed breeding were few. There were records along the Downs between Cobham and Chilham, from High Halstow, Blean and Thornden Woods, Ruckinge, and Sevenoaks and Westerham. In the 1960s breeding season records were confined to the west, around Sevenoaks and Westerham, where the last breeding pair was recorded in 1969. Since 1970 there have been virtually no records during May–July.

A summary of this declining status can be compiled from the available records, but there is no explanation for the 1957 peak.

	52	53	54	55	56	57	58	59	60	61	62	63	64	65	66	67	68	69	70
Breeding pairs	1	4	3	1		8	1	1	1	1			2	1	1	1	1	1	
Additional pairs or singing males	3	2	2		2	4				1				1		2	2		1
Total	4	6	5	1	2	12	1	1	1	2			2	2	1	3	3	1	1
Localities occupied	4	4	5	1	2	9	1	1	1	2			2	2	1	3	3	1	1

Minimum numbers of Woodlarks present during breeding seasons 1952–70

In spring there is a small but significant passage from mid-March to mid-April, usually involving one or two birds, with peaks of seven at Dungeness on 10th April 1971 and eight at Sandwich Bay on 2nd April 1960. Autumn passage is more marked and almost annual, occurring between late August and early November. The majority of records fall in

October, usually involving one–seven individuals, with a peak of 11 at Dungeness on 27th October 1968.

There are relatively few winter records and they are usually associated with cold spells. Overwintering has been recorded at Dungeness, where in 1969/70 there were 15 on 6th December, four–six remaining throughout, with the last on 11th April. In 1976 one was present from 28th January–14th March.

Skylark

Alauda arvensis

Abundant resident, passage migrant and winter visitor.

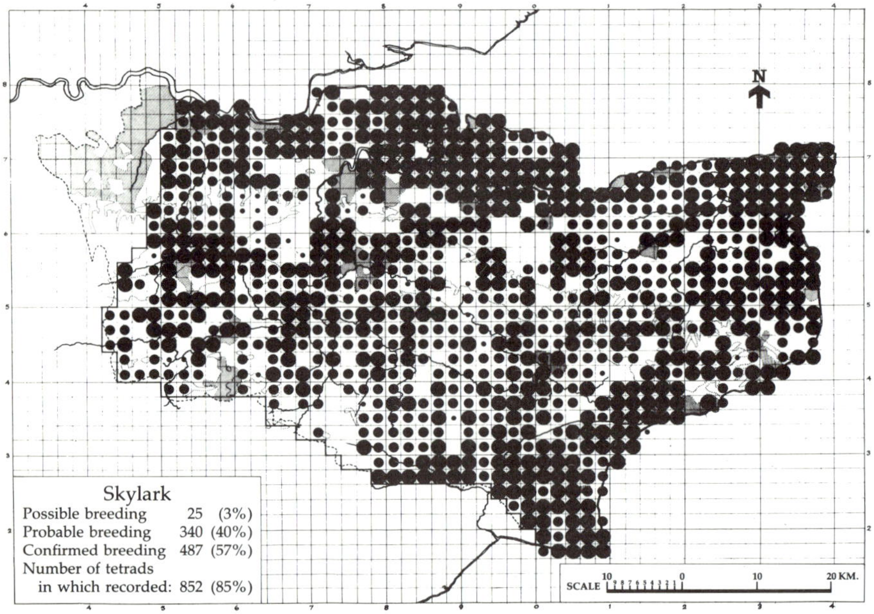

The Skylark is a widespread breeding species, at home in a great variety of habitats, provided that there are areas of short vegetation in which to nest and feed. The gaps on the map generally represent areas of poor coverage rather than absence, apart from those where there are large tracts of woodland, or areas of urban development with no wasteland. The densest breeding populations occur on the marshland meadows, and a census of part of Cliffe Marsh in 1976 produced 203 pairs in 121 hectares.

Autumn passage is recorded annually from mid-September well into November, when small parties totalling several hundred in a day may be seen flying in a westerly direction. Around the coast, the movements are more concentrated and may involve several thousands in a day, with passage at Dungeness usually northwesterly, between west and north at Sandwich Bay and west along the north coast into the Thames estuary. The largest movements usually occur during October. In 1960, for example, there were peak counts of 10,000 flying west at Allhallows on both the 15th and 16th, while on 30th and 31st October 1974 there was a more widespread movement involving peaks of 12,000 at Shellness and 4,000 in half-an-hour at Seasalter. Some continue to migrate west along the Swale, while others fly northwest across Sheppey and into the Thames.

Wintering flocks of several hundreds are normally widespread, with larger concentrations of up to 1,000 occurring during cold weather. Skylarks are influenced considerably by severe winter weather, particularly when heavy snowfalls make feeding difficult. In these conditions spectacular cold weather movements may be witnessed: on 1st January 1962, for example, 20,000 were estimated flying south over Stockbury, while 15,000 flew south-southeast at Dungeness. One ringed at Dungeness during a cold weather movement in January 1955 was recovered in May of that year in Norway.

Spring passage during March and April is less marked, with occasional peaks of 100–200 at the Observatories, and an exceptional 800 southeast at Dungeness on 4th April 1962.

Shore Lark

Eremophila alpestris

An almost annual winter visitor in varying numbers.

Ticehurst records the Shore Lark as a regular winter visitor and autumn migrant, and suggested that numbers were increasing. In contrast, Harrison suggests a decrease during the first half of this century, considering it irregular in its occurrences.

Apart from a brief period of exceptional wintering numbers, the status of the Shore Lark appears to have changed comparatively little. The histogram shows clearly how much numbers can fluctuate, and the indication is that the winter population will remain low for some years before another large influx can be expected.

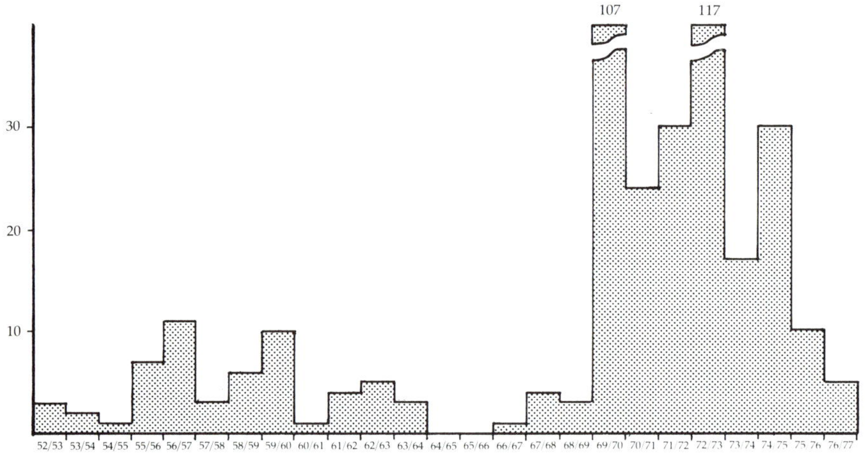

Winter totals of Shore Larks

The earliest autumn record concerns one at St. Mary's Bay, on the Thames, on 23rd September 1962. The arrival dates in 22 autumns have ranged between 6th October–16th November, with a mean about 25th October. Some of the earlier observations may refer to migrants, but many remain at, or close to the arrival localities into November and December. Numbers drop off slightly in January, but may increase again in February.

Records during March and April have only occurred in nine years, and there is very little evidence of spring migration. The majority of the latest dates refer to wintering birds. However, two isolated records, both of six birds, at Dungeness on 10th March 1972 and Pegwell Bay on 22nd April 1973 were evidently migrants. It is interesting to note that the two latest spring dates, 24th April 1973 and 27th April 1970, both follow the peak winters.

Shore Larks usually appear around the coastal fringes of north and northeast Kent, often on shingle beaches with a plentiful supply of blown or drifted seeds. They are most frequently recorded around the mouth of the Swale, eastwards to Reculver and Minnis Bay, and at Sandwich Bay, with occasional reports round Thanet and in the Medway and Thames estuaries, up river to Cliffe. Reports from the southeast coast, and at the Wicks and Brooks, are infrequent.

During the peak winters flocks of 15–40 were recorded, with a maximum count of 52 at Reculver on 1st January 1973, but in other years groups of one–five birds are more usual.

	1969/70	1972/73
Shellness	14	15
Harty	20	2
Seasalter	41	4
Reculver	4	52
Sandwich Bay	4	27
Dover	17	

Maximum flock sizes of Shore Larks in the two peak winters

Many of today's favoured localities were mentioned by Harrison, but it is interesting to note that a number of early records from the time when bird netting was commonplace occurred on the Dover cliffs. It is quite possible that Shore Larks may occur more frequently than records suggest on dry, arable land close to the coast. Records of four on Deal Golf Course on 4th November 1967 and two in a field at Fenn Street, High Halstow on 17th October 1975 tend to support this and the Shore Larks at Reculver in 1972/73 showed a preference for ploughed fields when disturbed. In such habitat they could easily be overlooked.

At Sittingbourne in January 1956, of several birds roosting between railway lines one, which was dazzled with a light, was identified as a Shore Lark, but the only true inland records both occurred at Bough Beech reservoir, with one on 19th November 1972 and two on 5th November 1973.

Sand Martin

Riparia riparia

A common summer visitor and passage migrant, breeding where suitable sites exist.

Breeding colonies are primarily restricted to sand and gravel pits, where suitable vertical banks are exploited, with colonies varying in size from a few to 800 pairs, the largest being at Sevenoaks and Trenley Park in 1968 and 1970 respectively. The breeding distribution clearly follows the greensand layer stretching across the county from Westerham to Folkestone, with other important colonies in the Stour Valley and Thanet, where they also breed in natural cliff-faces, at Sandwich, Gravesend/Dartford and the Tonbridge area, with none along the Downs or in the rest of the Weald. The Sand Martin is also an opportunist breeder, with odd pairs nesting in concrete pipes, drains, temporary 'cliffs' of dry sludge at paper mills, temporary piles of sand for motorway constructions, and at a purpose built bank on the RSPB Reserve at Dungeness.

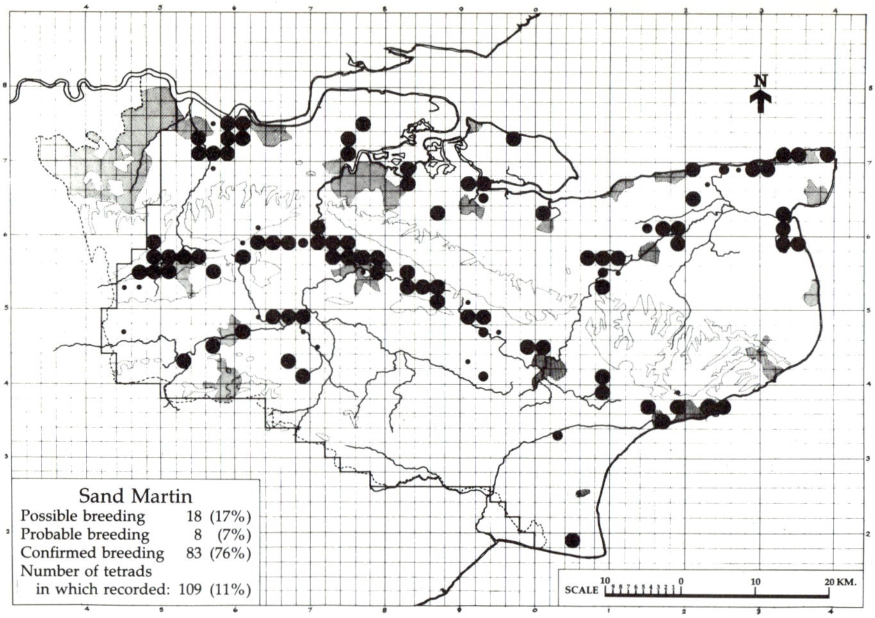

The European population declined markedly in the years 1969–73 and has not yet recovered to previous levels. Kent did not escape this drop in numbers, which has been attributed to drought in the Sahel region of Western Africa.

The first arrivals generally occur between 18th–31st March, the earliest being on 4th March 1952, but sometimes not until early April. The main arrival is in the second half of April and migration continues until late May. Observatory records in particular show that in recent years the spring migration has tended to be later and less numerous. The concentrations of spring birds are always found near fresh water, primarily along the Stour and Medway valleys, at Sevenoaks and Bough Beech. Spring reed-bed roosts last only until sufficient depth of nesting hole has been excavated, the birds then roosting in the nest holes.

The random nature of the early autumn movements in July suggests juveniles dispersing from breeding colonies, rather than true migration, and this is confirmed by ringing results.

The main passage occurs in August and September, with birds moving in large numbers west along the Thames, west and south at Sandwich Bay, and south at Dungeness, where the largest passage is regularly recorded, with peaks of up to 6,000 in a day. Migration continues until mid-October annually, with odd individuals often being seen well into November, the latest on 27th November 1966.

Communal autumn roosts of thousands in reed beds at Burham, Murston and Stodmarsh have become a feature of Sand Martin behaviour in the county since 1963. It is not until dusk that the existence of a roost becomes apparent, and it is possible (though unlikely) that some may not have been detected in previous years, despite the mass aerial pre-roost display. Roosts start building up in mid-July and continue without change of site until mid-September, usually with a peak in early August and another in early September. Up to 13,000 were roosting at Murston in August 1967. Mass communal roosting is an important feature of migration, the roosts acting as collecting or staging posts for onward migration.

Ringing at roosts has shown that the majority of the birds come from local colonies between Sandwich and Guildford in Surrey. The remainder may come from colonies anywhere in the British Isles except Ireland and the southwest. Foreign recoveries of birds ringed throughout the county at colonies, roosts, feeding areas and on migration have come from Sweden, Germany, Holland, Belgium, France, Spain, Algeria, Morocco and Senegal. Long-term ringing at the large Sevenoaks Reserve colony showed that considerable movement takes place between colonies, with the majority of the birds involved originating from the greensand colonies south of the North Downs. The importance of the Burham roost to this colony was also shown (Crick *et al*, 1978).

Swallow

Hirundo rustica

Widespread summer visitor and passage migrant.

Swallows breed throughout the county in a wide variety of sites, including wells, derelict boats and any small buildings. This enables them to occupy even the remote marsh and estuarine areas.

The earliest migrants usually arrive in March, with the earliest between Lydd and Hythe on 10th March 1952, and the mean around 25th March. However, the main spring arrival does not begin until the third week of April, with the peak movements during May. Numbers seen on spring migration are generally much lower than in autumn, but some arrivals can be quite marked. On 9th May 1967 there were 2,000 at Dungeness, while on 11th May 1975 1,000 flew north at Sandwich Bay, with 3,600 west at Allhallows, where nearly 8,000 were counted flying west on the 18th. The only recovery of a spring-ringed migrant was in Cheshire in July, two months after ringing.

Autumn migration commences in late July, but is most obvious in September, when large numbers also gather to roost in reed beds. The peak roost counts involved 50,000 at Cottington on 20th September

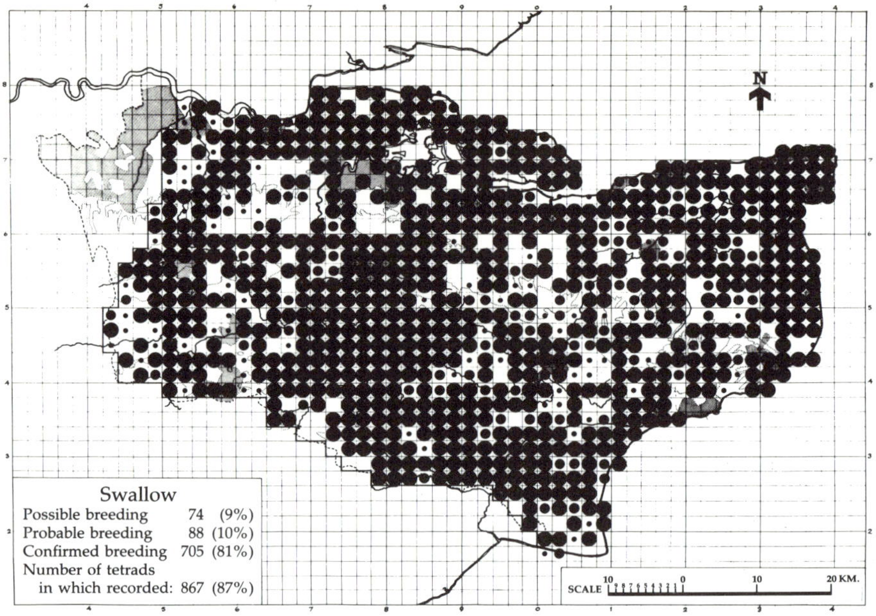

1954, and 10,000 at Burham/Snodland on 27th–28th August 1964 and 12th September 1973. Diurnal passage is more widespread than in spring. Some migrants coast north at Sandwich Bay and west into the Thames Estuary, but most passage inland and at Dungeness is southerly, though low-flying Swallows prefer to fly into the wind. Counts of 5–10,000 daily are not unusual, with peaks of 25,000 at Sandwich Bay on 7th September 1963 and 75,000 at Dungeness on 13th September 1965. Large numbers are not infrequently reported during early October, with 5,000 still moving south at Dungeness on 13th October 1967. Some birds are seen during November each year, and in seven years there have been December records, with the latest concerning six flying west at Dymchurch on 13th December 1960.

Ringing, mainly undertaken at the autumn roosts, has shown that migrants come from many parts of England and southern Scotland. After leaving Kent several birds have been recovered in France and no less than five in North Africa, between Morocco and Tunisia. Recoveries during November–March have all been in South Africa, though one bird reached Cape Province by 22nd October.

Red-rumped Swallow

Hirundo daurica

Very rare vagrant.

The first Kent record was one at Murston on 28th August 1959. Since then there have been seven more, but only one of them in autumn, again on 28th August, at Bough Beech in 1972.

The six spring records, including two in 1968, have all occurred between 20th April–21st May, with three in the Stour Valley and singles at Yalding, Dungeness and on Walland Marsh.

Of the eight records six have occurred since 1968, perhaps not surprising as there has been a recent northward extension of the breeding range into France.

House Martin

Delichon urbica

Widespread summer visitor and passage migrant.

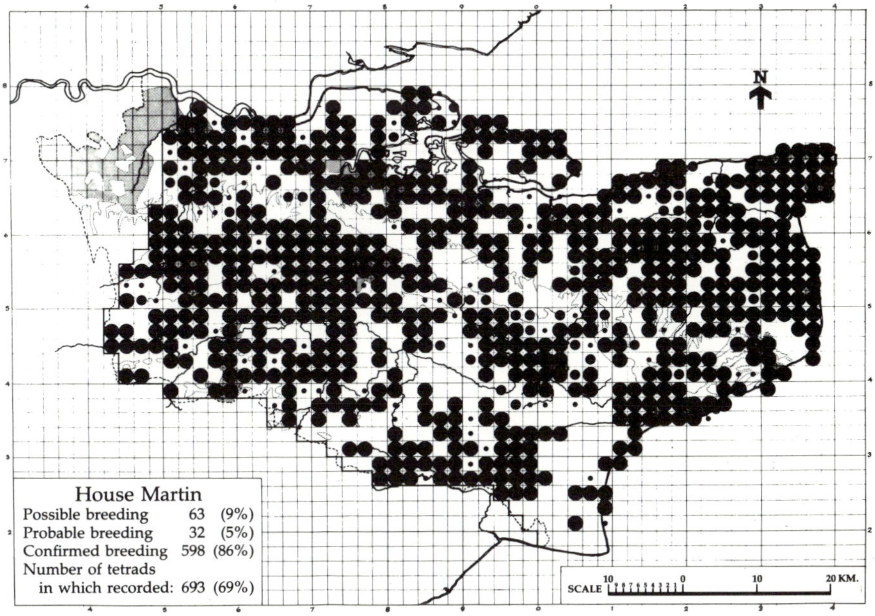

This species' present-day virtual dependence on man-made structures for its nest sites means that it is largely absent from the marshland areas. A few pairs occasionally revert to ancestral habits by breeding on the chalk cliffs between Folkestone and Dover.

In spring the House Martin arrives later than the Swallow, with only small numbers in April. The first dates range between 19th March 1957 and 20th April 1962, with the mean around 5th April. March records have occurred in just six years. The main passage occurs in May, but some breeding birds do not arrive at their nesting colonies until well into June. The numbers seen on spring migration tend to be small, although there was a widespread heavy passage on 11th May 1975, involving 1,000 per hour flying north at Sandwich Bay, 900 moving west at Allhallows and 600 north at Dungeness. At Bough Beech reservoir 1,800 were seen on 13th May 1972.

Autumn passage is also later than that of the Swallow, mainly between 21st September–8th October. Counts of up to 5,000 are quite regularly reported in this period, while on 21st September 1969 a particularly heavy movement involved 13,000 moving west in three hours at Reculver, 5,000 northwest at Shellness in half an hour, and 9,200 north at Sandwich Bay. On 3rd October 1976, in an hour and a quarter, 7,500 flew southwest at Lower Hope Point. That autumn, heavy passage continued well into October, with 4,000 at Dungeness as late as the 20th. November records occur almost annually, with December sightings in five years. The latest of these concerned three at Kingsgate on 17th December 1953, apart from two that remained at Surrenden Dering (Pluckley) until 16th January 1975. The only other winter record relates to one at Foreness Point between 11th–18th January and again on 22nd February 1970.

Away from its breeding colonies the House Martin tends to be a mystery bird. It is not found at communal roosts, either on passage or in its African winter quarters. It seems that it may be more aerial in its habits than the other hirundines, rather like the Swift. As a result, ringing recoveries throw little light on its movements. Two September migrants have been recovered at their breeding areas in Norfolk and Yorkshire.

Richard's Pipit

Anthus novaeseelandiae

Rare visitor.

Harrison records four acceptable autumn records listed by Ticehurst between 1868 and 1903, and cites two more recent records, one at Sandwich on 27th September 1946 and a second at Shellness (Sheppey) on 23rd April 1950.

In recent years there have been 13 records, all of single birds, with three in 1968, two in 1970 and singles in eight other years between 1960–76.

One on Halstow Marshes on 3rd January 1961 might better be considered as a late autumn 1960 record, as it is the only British record for January–March. The extreme dates for the three spring records are 15th April–8th May. The other autumn records fall into two distinct periods, with five between 15th September–6th October and four between 30th October–16th November.

All the records have been around the coast, with five in north Kent, five at Sandwich Bay, two at Dungeness and one on Thanet.

Tawny Pipit

Anthus campestris

Scarce migrant, recently an almost annual visitor.

Singles obtained near Lydd on 2nd August 1896 and seen at the same locality on 28th May 1919 are the only early records cited by Harrison.

Formerly this species was a very rare vagrant, but since 1960 it has become virtually an annual visitor. In the period under review 50 have been recorded, only ten of which have occurred in spring. The peak migration dates are shown clearly in the histogram.

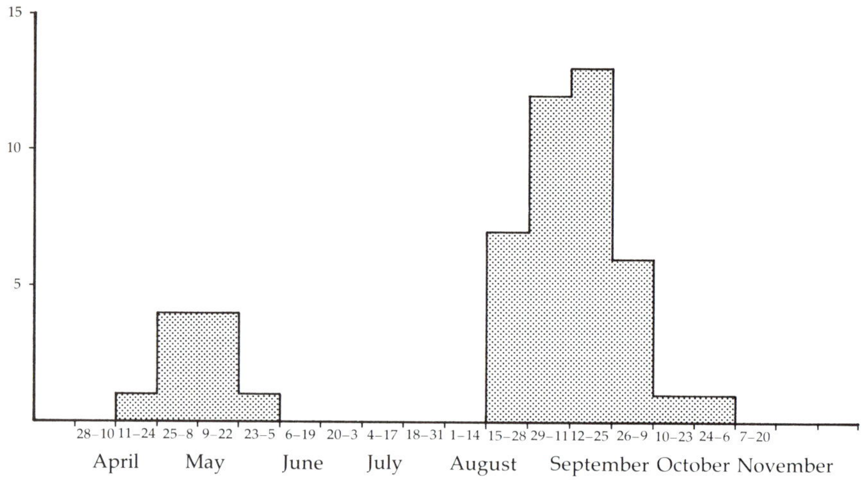

Fortnightly distribution of Tawny Pipits 1952–76

The extreme dates for spring are 17th April–30th May, and for autumn 22nd August–6th November.

The first record since 1919 was of one at Dungeness on 9th September 1956, followed by singles at Egypt Bay and Warden (Sheppey) the same autumn. There were no further records until 1960, since when at least one has been seen in each year except 1975. Between 1967–72 exceptional numbers were recorded. The peak year was 1971, when there were four spring records followed by seven in autumn. There were also seven in autumn 1967 and five in autumn 1972, with one that spring.

As would be expected, the vast majority of these are recorded in coastal localities, with over 30 at Dungeness, seven in north Kent, six at Sandwich Bay, three between Reculver and Birchington, and only two at inland sites. One was present at Stodmarsh from 6th–7th May 1973 and the latest record concerns one at Bough Beech reservoir from 4th–6th November 1976.

Tree Pipit

Anthus trivialis

Summer visitor and passage migrant.

The Tree Pipit shows a preference for open woodland, characterised by the presence of solitary trees from which the males can make their distinctive song-flights. In Kent, areas of coppiced woodland are

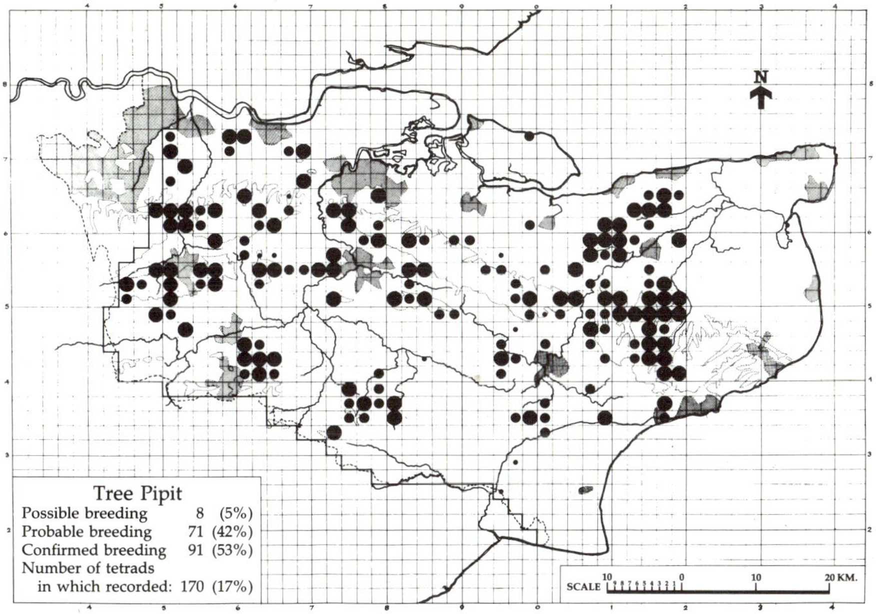

favoured and its absence from all the coastal lowlands is to be expected. It is interesting to note that the one site on Sheppey was the only breeding area in north Kent mentioned by Gillham and Homes. Areas of newly-planted conifers also provide ideal nesting conditions and there were high populations in Thornden Wood in the late 1950s, and in Clowes Wood and Mereworth in the mid-1960s, with 30 pairs at the latter site in 1965.

The earliest spring migrants were recorded on 22nd March, at Ramsgate in 1970 and Dungeness in 1975, but the mean arrival date is 6th April. The spring passage at Dungeness is usually fairly light, between the second week of April and the third week of May, with regular peaks of 10–20 in a day and a maximum of 35 on 16th April 1966.

Autumn passage is more widespread and recorded from late July, with peak numbers between late August and late September. At Dungeness there are regular autumn peaks of 20–30, with a maximum of 120 on 26th August 1971. The numbers at Sandwich Bay are relatively small, with a peak there of 37 on 21st September 1969. An exceptional fall of Scandinavian migrants around Thanet on 15th September 1968, produced a total of 52 at Reculver, and there were 70 at Dungeness the same day, but only 12 at Sandwich Bay. Relatively few birds are seen in October, and the two latest dates concern singles at Stockbury on 4th November 1961 and at Shellness on 18th November 1962.

Meadow Pipit

Anthus pratensis

Summer resident, passage migrant and winter visitor.

Ticehurst provides some evidence to suggest that the Meadow Pipit once bred more commonly, particularly along the Downs, while more recently Gillham and Homes considered that there had been a decline on the North Kent Marshes. It is likely that the loss of habitat due to more intensive farming was partly responsible.

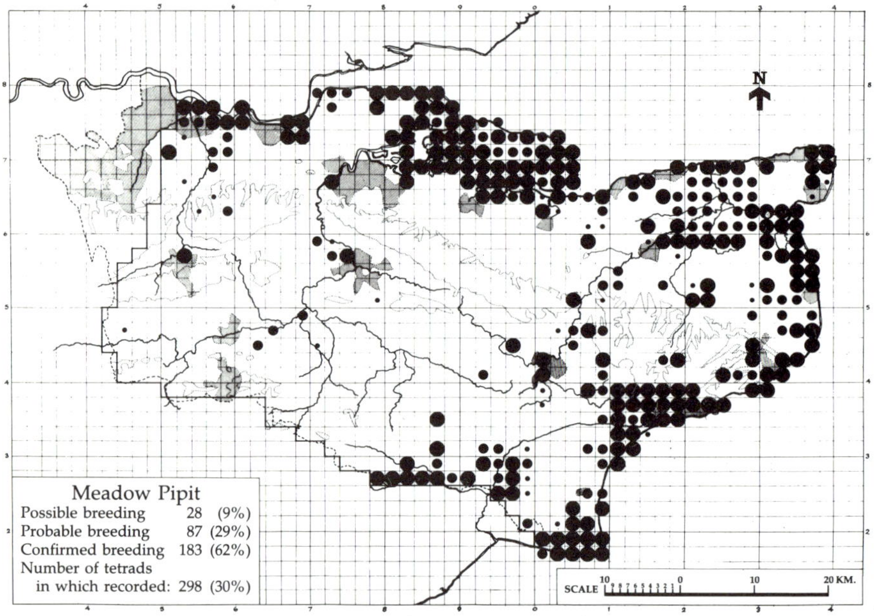

As a breeding species, the Meadow Pipit is most widespread on the coastal lowlands, and virtually absent from the Downs and the heavy, clay soils in the Weald. Some of the inland nest sites are on areas of waste ground and old gravel workings. There is little information on population densities, but a survey along the Rother Levels in 1966 produced about 50 pairs between the Royal Military Canal and Newenden, 32 pairs bred on Dungeness Reserve in 1971, while 75 pairs nested on 121 hectares of Cliffe Marsh in 1976.

Autumn passage commences in late July, reaching a peak during September. The southerly movement over inland localities is quite widespread and small flocks occur in a variety of habitats, such as damp fields and gravel pits, with autumn peaks of over 100 at Bough Beech reservoir. Around the coast the movements are more concentrated. In north Kent small flocks, regularly totalling up to 200 in a day, move west into the Thames estuary, with a peak of 400 west at Sheerness on 16th September 1966. Visible migration is generally north at Sandwich Bay and northwest at Dungeness, involving several hundreds in a day. The maximum counts were 1,100 at Sandwich Bay on 30th September 1966 and 4,000 at Dungeness on 18th September 1968. Passage may continue well into November.

During the winter months the population is at its lowest, with the small numbers widely scattered. Flocks of 30–50 occur quite regularly, with up to 100 occasionally around the coast. In severe conditions small cold weather movements occur and very few birds remain, as in January 1963.

Numbers may increase again from late February, but spring passage is most marked in late March and early April, with up to 300 in a day regularly around the coast, and peaks of 1,000 moving northwest at Dungeness on three dates between 29th March–2nd April 1960–61. As in autumn, increased numbers are also noted at inland localities, and though the northerly passage is less evident, 250 were counted over Stockbury on 9th April 1962.

There have been several winter recoveries in Spain and Portugal of birds ringed on autumn migration through Kent, while one ringed on the Calf of Man in September 1963 was retrapped at Dungeness two months later.

Red-throated Pipit

Anthus cervinus

Very rare vagrant.

Harrison records one seen at Dungeness on 5th September 1938.

The only other records concern two at Sandwich Bay on 15th September 1968, which were involved with an exceptional fall of Scandinavian migrants, and one at Dungeness three days later on 18th September.

Rock Pipit

Anthus spinoletta petrosus

Winter visitor and passage migrant. Breeds occasionally.

There has been little change in the status of the Rock Pipit in Kent since Ticehurst described it as a tolerably plentiful winter resident, most numerous along the north coast.

This species frequents the rocky coastal areas around Dover and Thanet, and the marshes, saltings and mud creeks in the tidal estuaries. In the Dungeness area it is relatively scarce, occuring most frequently on spring and autumn passage, when there have been peaks of 15–20.

In recent years there have been a number of breeding records, and presumably the birds are resident in those areas. One pair bred at Dover in 1953, with one–two pairs at Westgate in 1967–68. Between 1973–76 one–two pairs again bred at Dover and at Foreness.

Autumn passage commences in late September, with earlier records in some years, and the numbers build up during October, with a peak of 60 at Reculver on 19th October 1963. During the winter months counts of 15–30 are quite regular around the coast from Dover, into the Medway and Thames estuaries, and along the Thames as far as Dartford. Significantly higher counts have been recorded occasionally at Sandwich Bay, where there were 70 on 23rd November 1968 and 120 on 15th November 1970. The winter birds disperse during March, some remaining until the end of April, but the occurrence of returning migrants is difficult to detect around the coast.

The first inland record concerned one at Sevenoaks on 13th October 1963. Not unexpectedly others have occurred along the Medway towards Aylesford between September–March, while at Bough Beech reservoir one–five have been recorded fairly frequently since 1969, particularly on spring and autumn migration, with a maximum of eight there on 14th October 1975.

Individuals showing the characteristics of the Scandinavian race *A.s. littoralis* have been recorded occasionally in spring between 22nd February–31st March. The majority of reports concern one or two along the north coast, with an exceptional total of 12–15 daily at Sandwich Bay between 25th–31st March 1967, and singles inland at Sevenoaks on 15th March 1962 and Tonbridge on 28th March 1969.

Water Pipit

Anthus spinoletta spinoletta

Passage migrant and winter visitor.

Birds of this race have been recorded almost annually and with increased frequency since 1967. The majority occur on spring passage during March–April, with an exceptionally late bird at Sheerness on 10th May 1976.

In autumn the first arrivals normally occur during October, but singles were seen at Sandwich Bay on 14th–15th August 1964 and at Westbere on 19th September 1971. All the records in the 1950s and early 1960s referred to coastal localities, from Dungeness round to Cliffe, but since 1967 a few have wintered regularly at Stodmarsh, and there have been occasional reports elsewhere in the Stour Valley, and from Bough Beech reservoir and Sevenoaks Reserve. The maximum counts of eight were at Stodmarsh on 25th March 1975 and Littlebourne on 8th February 1976.

Yellow Wagtail

Motacilla flava flavissima

Summer visitor and passage migrant.

Ticehurst's description of the breeding distribution shows it to have been considerably more extensive than today, particularly along the valleys of the Darent and Medway. There is little doubt that the Yellow Wagtail declined as a breeding species during the first half of this century.

As the map clearly shows, this species is well distributed over the coastal lowlands, where it finds the freshwater marshes and damp water meadows that it favours. Man-made sites, such as gravel pits, sewage farms and reservoirs also provide attractive breeding areas. However, there are rather fewer records along the major river valleys than might be expected. The one record, apparently on the Downs in TQ86, actually refers to a single pair that bred during the construction of the Stockbury viaduct in 1968.

Population estimates in earlier years unfortunately neglected to define the areas involved, but a breeding census on part of the Cliffe marshes in 1976 produced 27 pairs on 121 hectares.

The first spring migrants arrive in late March or early April. The

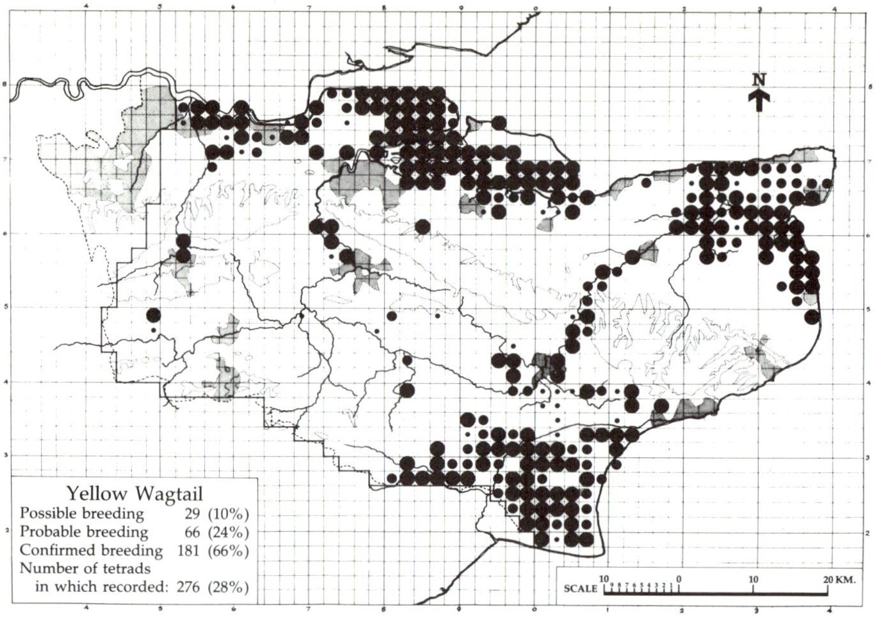

earliest concerns one on Sheppey on 9th March 1958 and the mean arrival date is 1st April. Spring passage lasts until mid-May in some years. In the early 1950s the Walland Marsh population was undoubtedly much larger than today, the spring arrivals apparently roosting in the fleets during April, with a maximum count of 280 on 30th April 1955. The only other high spring count was of 300 at Stodmarsh on 23rd April 1962, also roosting in the reed beds. Daily totals at Dungeness rarely exceed 20, but at Sandwich Bay peak counts of 30–50 are more frequent. Elsewhere there were 100 at Capel Fleet on 24th April 1966 and a similar number at Wittersham on 16th April 1967, with no such high counts since. Visible migration at Allhallows in 1975 involved 162 flying west between 2nd–19th May, with a peak of 67 on the 11th.

Autumn migration usually commences in late July and reed bed roosts at various localities are one of the major features during August. At Murston, in eight years from 1959, the roost frequently held 75–250 birds between 5th–31st August, with a later count of 125 on 21st September 1959, and maxima of 350 on 11th August 1975 and 400 between 11th–20th August 1970. At Stoke there were 350 on 28th August 1976, while along the Medway at Burham 80–100 were recorded in the mid-1960s. At Stodmarsh 100–180 were counted between 27th August–8th September in 1968–70, while nearby at Richborough the counts ranged between 150–250 during 13th July–19th September in five years from 1960–76.

Away from the roosts flocks of 50–75 occur fairly regularly in the north of the county during August, and migrants may occasionally be seen flying south from Shellness. Farther east at Reculver larger numbers occasionally occur, with a peak of 250 on 19th August 1967. At Sandwich Bay daily totals of 50–75 are not unusual, with a maximum of 120 on 22nd August 1972, while at Dungeness there are fairly frequent falls of 100–150, with a peak of 300 on 21st August 1976. Migration continues through September, but by the end of the month relatively few remain. A few are recorded annually in October and in six years there have been November records, with the latest at Sandwich Bay on 27th November 1967.

There are three records which are indicative of birds overwintering. One was seen at Sandwich Bay on 24th December 1966, one at Cliftonville the following year on 30th December, while at Dover there was one on 25th February 1970.

The Yellow Wagtails are a complex group of races breeding right across Eurasia and into extreme northwestern America. In spring the males of several races may be fairly readily distinguished, but in autumn this is rarely the case. Rarely too can females or juveniles be separated with accuracy, and the situation is further clouded by interbreeding, especially at the geographical margins of the distribution of each race.

Blue-headed Wagtail

Motacilla flava flava

According to Harrison, this race bred fairly regularly, with the last pair at Grove Ferry in 1951.

This and the British race *M.f. flavissima* sometimes hybridise and there are a number of records of this happening during the period under review. However, in 1976 a pair, both genuinely Blue-headed, again bred at Grove Ferry.

A few spring records occur annually, with at least fifteen in both 1972 and 1975, usually between mid-April and mid-May, but this race is not often identified in the autumn.

Grey-headed Wagtail

Motacilla flava thunbergi

Harrison included two early records, while there are eight acceptable records of this race in recent years, around the coast from Dungeness to Cooling. An early one was seen at Grove on 23rd April 1961, while the other seven all occurred between 5th–30th May, with three in 1971, two in 1965 and singles in 1974 and 1975.

Ashy-headed Wagtail

Motacilla flava cinereocapilla

One showing the characteristics of this race was seen at Bough Beech reservoir on 5th May 1973.

Grey Wagtail

Motacilla cinerea

Local breeding resident and passage migrant.

Ticehurst only knew the Grey Wagtail as an autumn and winter visitor to Kent during the last century, until one pair bred near Kemsley (Sittingbourne) in 1885. During 1900–10, pairs bred at Mereworth, Cranbrook, Tunbridge Wells and Penshurst. Harrison details the expansion of the breeding range, which by 1950 was quite widespread along the valleys of the Darent and Medway and their tributaries, with isolated pairs at Northfleet and Motney Hill in the north and at Dover and Sandwich in the east.

From 1952 the Stour Valley attracted several breeding pairs, the population in the Weald continued to expand, and there were occasional summering records at Cliffe.

Grey Wagtails suffer in severe winters and the hard weather of 1962/63 took its toll. However, the species recovered well, with the distribution during the Breeding Survey, from 1967–73, very similar to that in 1962.

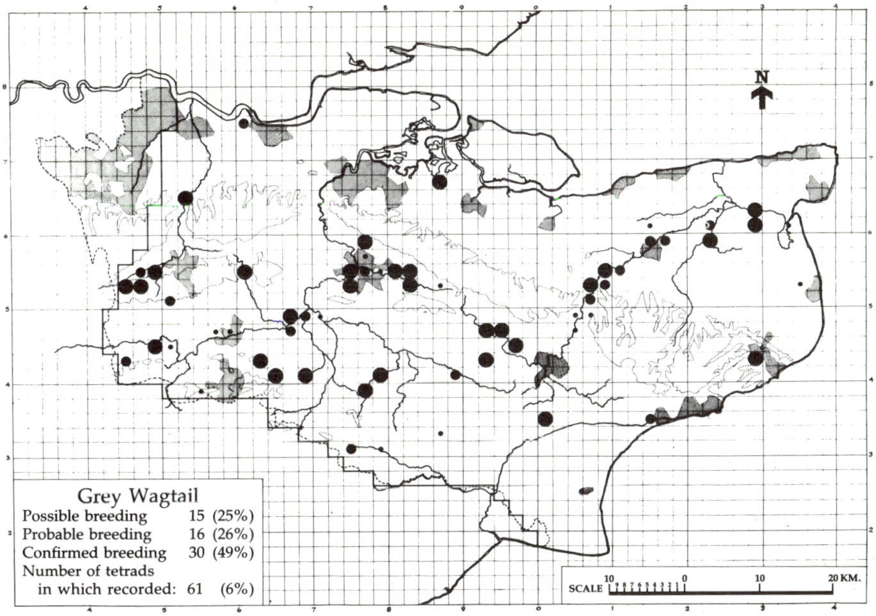

Although Kent does not offer the Grey Wagtail the fast-flowing streams of more hilly landscapes, there are enough broken water stretches, usually associated with weirs and outflows from lakes, to attract this species to nest. The largest number of these are to be found along the streams in the Weald, along the greensand between Maidstone and Ashford, and on the Stour and its tributaries.

Autumn passage is most marked during September, but a few migrants can be seen at various localities around the coast and into the Thames estuary from late August to early November. The spring passage is almost negligible by comparison, with most records in March.

1952–56	1957–61	1962–66	1967–71	1972–76
10	32	17	64	95

Mean annual bird/day totals of Grey Wagtails at Dungeness 1952–76

The table gives some indication as to how the population fluctuates, but the pattern of movement at Dungeness is fairly constant, with a complete absence of spring records in some years and the peak numbers invariably in September. Both 1971 and 1972 produced exceptional totals of 149 and 166 bird/days respectively, including peaks of 20 on 25th and 26th September 1971. There was an early peak of 53 in 1959, with 25 in 1962, but only three in 1963 following the severe winter. There were still less than 10 in 1964–65, but over 40 again in 1966.

There are no Kent ringing recoveries to show the movements of these birds, but the numbers trapped, along with more breeding records, help to confirm that the population is increasing.

In the winter months the distribution is more widespread, and Grey Wagtails may be attracted to sewage works and gravel pits, into towns or to the coast.

Pied Wagtail

Motacilla alba yarrelii

Widespread resident and passage migrant.

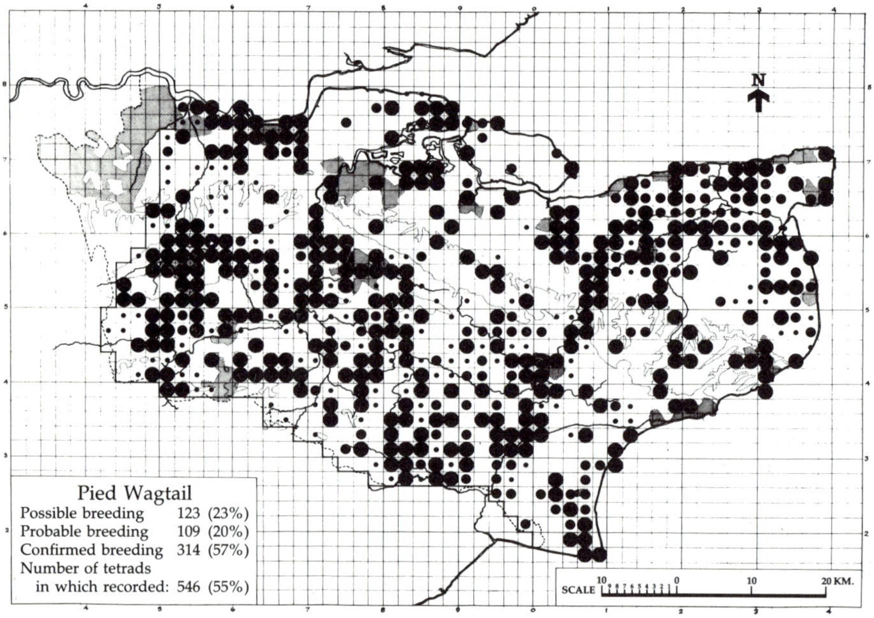

The Pied Wagtail is fairly well distributed as a breeding species, but may be absent from woodland and scarce in some areas of intensive arable farming, where there is a lack of suitable nest sites.

Some autumn and winter roosts have been reported almost annually, the majority associated with reed beds of varying sizes. At Burham, 500 were estimated present in November 1964 and again in October 1966. In October 1974 over 300 were counted flying to roost in Pfizer's factory at Sandwich, while Swanscombe sewage farm attracted a maximum of 260 in January 1973. The only other sites with counts exceeding 200 are Leybourne and Murston, but roosts of 50–150 were quite widely reported. Though the highest totals generally occur in October, the roosts may well hold small numbers into early May and build up again rapidly from late July.

Regular passage movements are noted around the coast in autumn from late August to mid-November, but the numbers involved are generally low, with day totals of 20–40 at Dungeness. A slight spring passage also occurs, usually between early March and late April, and visible movements have been quite marked at Dungeness in some years, with a quite exceptional total of 450 arriving from off the sea in about fifteen minutes on 16th March 1957.

Three birds ringed in summer in Kent, two of them juveniles, have been recovered during the winter months in Portugal, indicating that at least part of the Kent breeding population is migratory.

White Wagtail

Motacilla alba alba

Harrison includes a few references to this race breeding, but the White Wagtail is most evident on spring passage, when it is more easily identified, and when it occurs throughout the county from early March to mid-May, and into June in some years. On autumn passage it is less obvious, but there are reports from mid-August until late November. Since 1970 there have also been a few records of one or two during December–February, particularly from the Sevenoaks Reserve.

On 1st July 1975 a single adult was seen with two flying young at Littlebourne.

Waxwing

Bombycilla garrulus

Almost annual winter visitor, with occasional irruptions involving large numbers.

Ticehurst describes four irruption years between 1840–1909, while Harrison gives details of three more during the next 50 years. The largest in 1946/47 involved over 200 birds, with a maximum of 45 at Ramsgate in December.

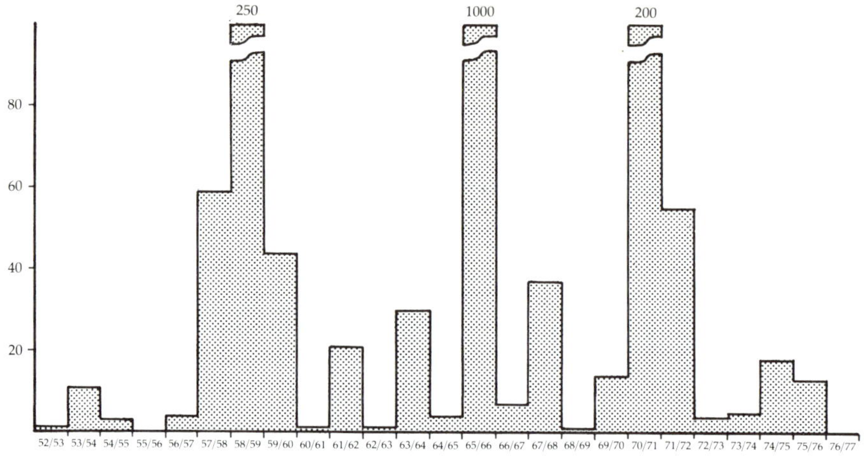

Winter totals of Waxwings

In most winters the numbers are accounted for by less than nine records, usually involving single figure flocks. Apart from the three winters with large irruptions, the only exceptions have been 10–15 records in November–December 1957 and 1959, a flock of 17 at Sandwich in January 1960, and flocks of 30 near Canterbury in January 1968 and Folkestone in December 1971.

The vast majority of records occur in November–March, but there have been earlier arrivals in five years, the earliest on 20th October 1965. Following the major irruptions, small numbers have remained into April, with the latest on 15th April 1971. The only other April record concerns two at Wrotham on 5th April 1975.

In the winter of 1958/59 there were reports from 10th December–13th April, with a maximum of only seven in December, but three flocks of 20 in the New Year and peaks of 40 at Sandwich Bay on 31st January and 100 at Boughton on 16th February.

By far the largest irruption in Kent occurred during the winter of 1965/66, when there were numerous, widespread reports between 20th October–10th April. Flocks of 20–50 were recorded at two localities in October, 11 new localities in November, and six more in December, with additional peaks of 100 at Whitstable on 27th–28th November and 85 at Gillingham from 23rd–28th December. During January–February flocks of 15–30 were seen at nine localities, the majority in the west of the county. It is difficult to assess accurately the numbers involved, but in all probability there were over 1,000 birds.

A further irruption occurred in the winter of 1970/71, between 21st October–15th April. Flocks of 20–50 were reported from eight localities, with a maximum of 60 at Westerham on 18th December. In the peak month, December, 200 birds were estimated to be present in the county, with almost as many remaining into January.

Dipper

Cinclus cinclus

Very rare winter visitor.

Ticehurst lists at least ten records between 1840–1909, and considered those specimens that he examined to be of the British form *C.c. gularis*. Harrison adds one for December 1944.

Since 1955 there have been seven records, two of which concerned birds that were trapped and ringed, and all were of the nominate race *C.c. cinclus* that occurs on the Continent. The extreme dates are 31st October 1976 and 21st March 1966. The Loose and Len streams have hosted singles for three–four month periods during three winters. Others have been seen on the Royal Military Canal near Hythe, at Sandling Park near Folkestone, and at Sandwich Bay, where one was seen to arrive from the east and alight on the beach on 31st October 1976.

Wren

Troglodytes troglodytes

Widespread and abundant resident.

The county Breeding Survey showed the Wren to be the sixth most widespread breeding species. Such gaps that exist on the distribution map are generally in areas which were poorly covered. The only suggestion of genuine absence comes from small areas of the Thames, Sheppey and Romney Marshes. Woodland, of whatever size, is probably the preferred habitat, together with waterside vegetation, but there are few areas where Wrens cannot find sufficient cover to nest and feed.

The Wren is notoriously prone to heavy losses in severe winters and in 1962/63 it suffered heavily in Kent, as elsewhere in Britain. Dramatic evidence of this is reflected in the Dungeness ringing totals, with 104 in 1962, followed by totals of 12–19 during the next three years. However, the population recovered rapidly, and in one small wood near Sandwich, for example, there were two pairs in 1964 and 27 territories in 1974. By 1976 in some areas the population had more than doubled its pre-catastrophe 1962 numbers. An example of annual fluctuations in the

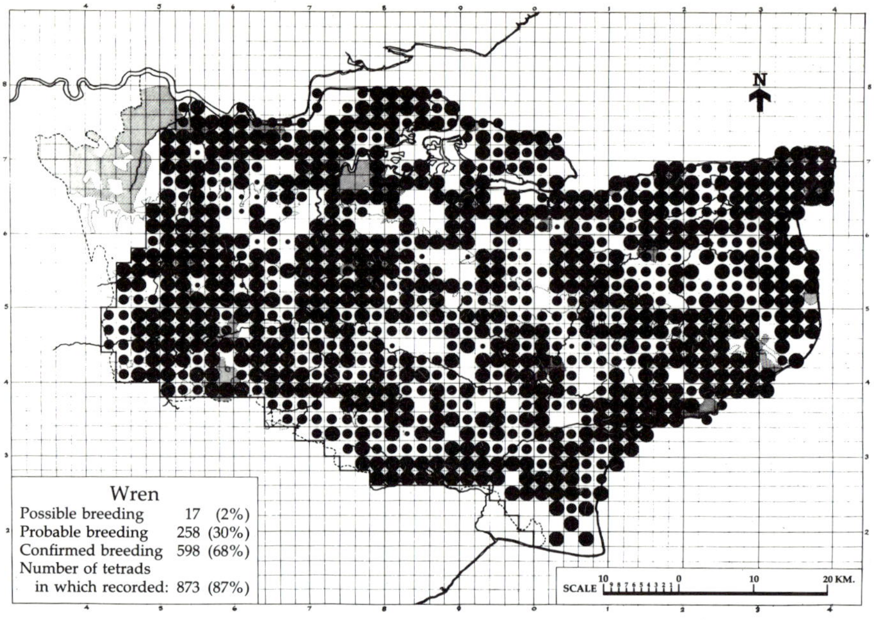

population comes from census work at Northward Hill, where there were 212 pairs in 1975, but only 100 the following year.

Earlier writers hesitated to commit themselves to the possibility of immigration, even though as early as the turn of the century Ticehurst wrote of increased numbers on the south coast in October. Ringing has now confirmed that immigration does occur. For obvious reasons it is most noticeable at the Observatories, but there are also a number of reports from the coast of Sheppey. The peak period is from the last few days of September to the end of October, and occasionally into November. The highest day-totals reported by the Observatories have been 60 at Dungeness and 43 at Sandwich Bay. The return spring migration is comparatively small.

Amongst many short-range recoveries of ringed birds are others illustrating these movements: two ringed at Dungeness in September 1961 were recovered in France later that winter, while another ringed there on 3rd October 1959, having arrived with Goldcrests and Firecrests, was recovered three months later in the Camargue. Evidence of birds with a more northerly origin comes again from a Dungeness-ringed bird, trapped on 21st October 1975, and retrapped at Ottenby, Sweden on 8th April 1976; and from two autumn-ringed Gibraltar Point birds, recovered at Dungeness two months later, showing that all arrivals may not come direct from abroad. One ringed at Reculver on 23rd October 1973 was recovered at Doncaster, Yorkshire on 21st April 1974.

Dunnock

Prunella modularis

Abundant resident. Irregular small-scale passage migrant.

The Dunnock is an enigmatic bird, inconspicuous and much taken for granted, thus its status received little attention in Ticehurst or Harrison, or more recently, in most observers notes to the Kent Bird Report. With its liking for any form of broken cover, be it woodland, gardens, scrub or hedgerows, the widespread distribution revealed by the Breeding Bird Survey is hardly surprising.

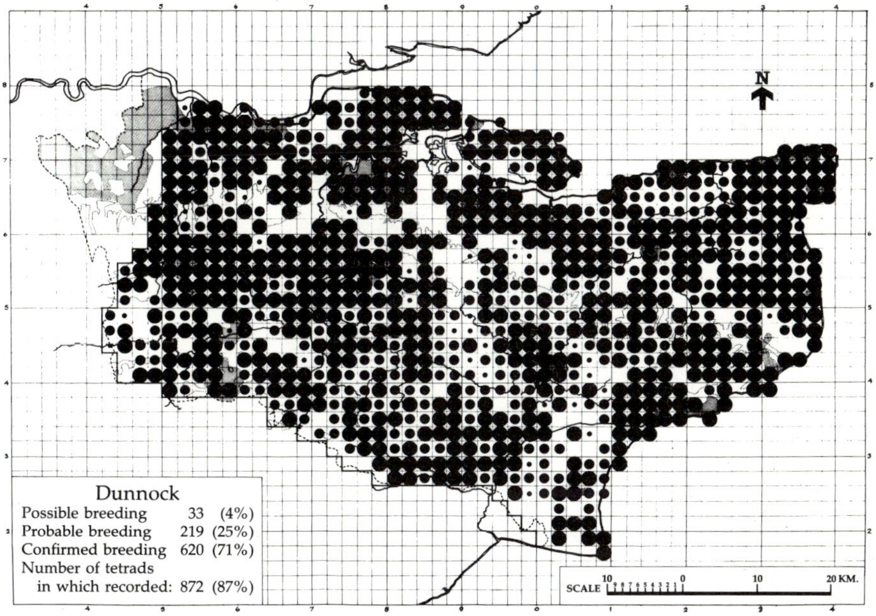

The Dunnock proved to be the seventh most widespread species in the Survey, missing only from a handful of marshland and downland tetrads, where almost certainly it fell victim to under-recording. Population densities may be higher than expected, with breeding season woodland censuses at Northward Hill indicating between one and two pairs per hectare between 1960–75.

Ticehurst could find no evidence of migration and quotes Eagle Clarke as not seeing Dunnocks whilst on the Kentish Knock light-vessel. Harrison, on the basis of 16 specimens obtained between 1921–47, concluded that immigration occurred on a small scale. He could find no suggestive observations from coastal areas, which is in interesting contrast to the present situation.

In the early 1950s, each autumn saw reports of one or two migrants trapped at Sandwich Bay or Dungeness, but from 1957 onwards there are regular reports of passage or influxes in late September, October and November, from many coastal areas, including the Thames as far up-river as Lower Hope Point, with daily maxima of 30–100 birds. The autumn of 1976 saw an unusually marked influx, with Dunnock numbers on many days in September at several coastal sites exceeding 100 birds. Numbers peaked at Dungeness when 250 were recorded on 29th October.

The first mention of a small spring passage came in 1962, and reports since 1970 suggests that this may be becoming both more regular and more pronounced, with March peaks of 50–100 birds at Sandwich Bay or Dungeness.

Despite the large numbers ringed, both on the coast and inland, there are as yet no recoveries giving any indication of the origin or destination of these migrants, most showing movements only over a very short distance.

Alpine Accentor

Prunella collaris

Very rare vagrant.

One was seen at St. Margaret's on 1st May 1932.

The noteworthy feature of the two recent records is that they too occurred in early May, with one at Ramsgate cemetery on 7th May 1975 and another at Dungeness on 8th May 1976.

Rufous Bush Robin

Cercotrichas galactotes

The only record is of one seen at the Wicks, on the Kent/Sussex border on 12th September 1951.

Robin

Erithacus rubecula

Widespread and numerous breeding resident, passage migrant and winter visitor.

There has been no marked change in status since Harrison wrote, and the Robin remains one of our most familiar birds. It favours most types of woodland, hedgerows, scrub and gardens, and in chestnut coppice it is often the most numerous breeding species. The highest densities are probably reached in well-wooded suburban areas, woodland edges and open woodland with scrub.

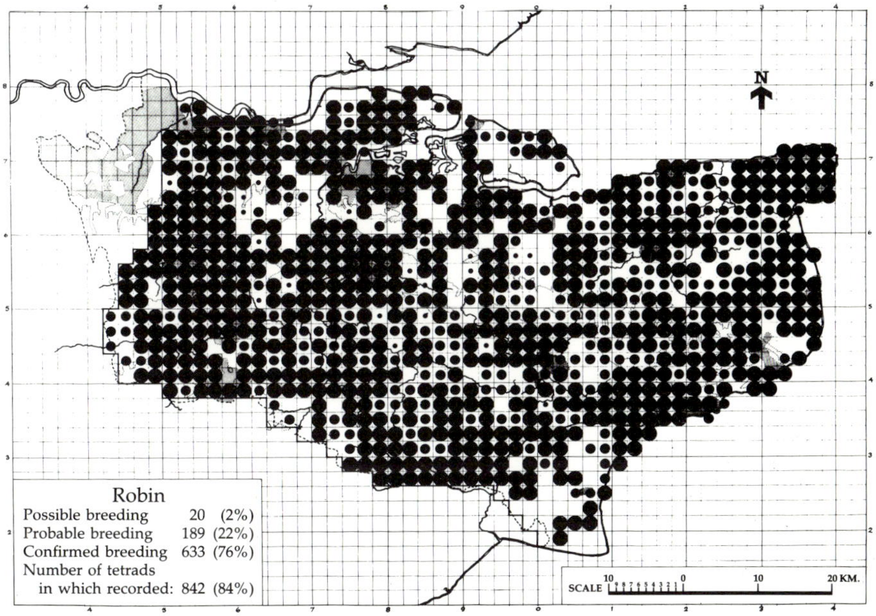

There is a marked absence from some of the open coastlands on the North Kent Marshes and Dungeness, and while most of the inland gaps probably represent poor coverage, they correspond in some places to areas of extensive 'prairie' farming, where hedges and scrub have been grubbed. Examples can be seen on the cereal-growing North Downs dipslope, the lowlands east of Ashford and much of Romney Marsh.

The population is augmented by passage migrants and winter visitors. Spring passage is noted mainly on the coast in March and April, with daily peaks at the Observatories rarely exceeding 50. An exceptional passage was recorded at Dungeness in March 1958, with 500 on the 26th and 350 the next day. In autumn, passage is usually noted from

September–November, with peaks in October. Estimates of over 100 are regularly recorded and usually associated with northeast winds and falls of Scandinavian migrants. Such falls can be very localised, as on 15th September 1968, when there were 400 at Sandwich Bay and many hundreds at Herne Bay. In other years Dungeness has recorded the largest numbers, and in 1976 there were two major falls in October, with 500 on the 19th and 600 on the 25th. Although the largest numbers are usually recorded along the coast, increases are often noticeable inland.

All ringing recoveries abroad concern birds ringed between September–April and there is no evidence of Kentish breeding birds migrating. The main direction of passage is southwest, from N.E. Europe to the Iberian peninsula, following the Continental coastline. An unknown proportion remain to winter in Kent and elsewhere in Britain. There are several, mainly autumn and winter recoveries from France, Spain and Portugal. On return passage there have been spring recoveries from Germany, Norway and Belgium. Further evidence of origins is provided by a bird ringed at Loose in November 1964 and recovered in Poland in October 1967. Another ringed in Norway in May 1973 was recovered at Deal in February 1975.

Thrush Nightingale

Luscinia luscinia

Very rare vagrant.

The only record is of one which was trapped at Sandwich Bay on 23rd August 1968.

Nightingale

Luscinia megarhynchos

Breeding summer visitor, locally common.

Harrison considered the Nightingale to be abundant and widespread, but most numerous in the woodlands of the Weald and the wooded commons around the Greater London boundary. He noted too that there were marked local changes in population, with numbers fluctuating from year to year.

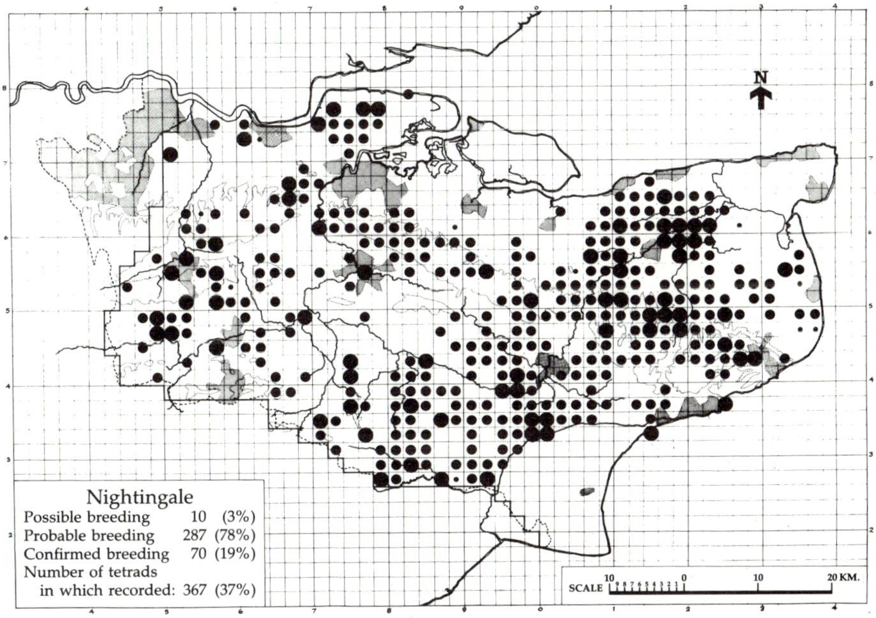

The secretive habits of Nightingales make breeding difficult to prove absolutely, hence the high proportion of 'probable' records. The largest concentrations are found in the extensive woodlands bordering the Stour Valley and Romney Marsh. The Nightingale is scarcest in parts of the western Weald and on the North Downs dipslope, and few are found above 170 m, most being below 130 m altitude. Favoured habitats are woods with dense understories of hazel, hornbeam or hawthorn, thick hedgerows and scrub, especially in disused chalk pits, and increasingly, young unbrashed conifer plantations with most growth below five metres. Although isolated shaws and copses are occupied, the general lack of suitable woodland in the intensive agricultural areas along the North Downs dipslope, Thanet and open marshes of Sheppey and Romney Marsh explains the absence there. The scarcity towards the Sussex border may in part reflect less intensive coverage, although the apparent shift eastwards of the main area of concentration since Harrison wrote may be real and reflect modern coppicing practice, with the clearing of standards. Studies in Ham Street Woods (Stuttard & Williamson, 1971) have shown that the age of coppice and the density of standards can have a significant effect on Nightingale densities, with the highest in areas of four to ten years growth and invariably with more than 50 standards per hectare.

In east Kent there have been considerable variations in woodland management practice, with the most consistently high densities in neglected coppice and scrub and in unbrashed conifer plantations. In one wood a population of 36 singing males in 1966 was reduced to eight in 1971, due to modern coppicing. In another a population of 41 in 1969 reduced to 13 in 1970 and two in 1971, due to clearfelling for conifer planting. [By 1978 the plantation had grown sufficiently to support 23 pairs. Eds.]

Year	Singing Males	Coverage (%)	Extrapolated Totals
1966	(145)	33	450
1967	(212)	50	430
1968	413	100	413
1969	410	100	410
1970	492	100	492
1971	279	100	279
1972	(61)	20	300
1976	(94)	25	400

Singing Nightingales censused in east Kent (from Hudson, 1979)

A programme of censuses covering east Kent woods from 1966–71 and the whole county in 1969–71, provided not only valuable estimates of the Nightingale population, but information on their distribution and habitat preferences. This was followed by a National Nightingale Survey in 1976. The county-wide data include totals of 694 singing males in 1969, 977 in 1970 and 502 in 1971, while an extrapolation of the limited counts made in 1976 suggest a population of 730 pairs in that year. This represents about 20% of the national population (Hudson, 1979).

Nightingales are very secretive on passage and only small numbers are recorded at the Observatories. First arrivals, usually at breeding sites, occur between 5th–20th April, with a mean around the 13th and the earliest at Dungeness on 30th March 1968. Passage continues well into May. Autumn passage is noted mainly in late July or August, with last dates between mid-August and mid-September. There have been just two October records in recent years, with the latest at Stodmarsh on 4th October 1960. However, Harrison includes two later dates, at Dungeness on 15th October 1923 and Sandwich Bay on 30th October 1947.

One ringed at Dungeness in August 1952 and recovered in Portugal in September 1953 is the only foreign recovery and indicates a south-westerly orientation in autumn.

Bluethroat

Luscinia svecica

Rare spring migrant, but almost annual on autumn passage.

Ticehurst and Harrison included over twenty records from 1842–1951, with the majority between 28th August–15th October, just two in May and singles on 2nd February and 15th March. Only two individuals of the White-spotted race *L.s. cyanecula* were definitely identified.

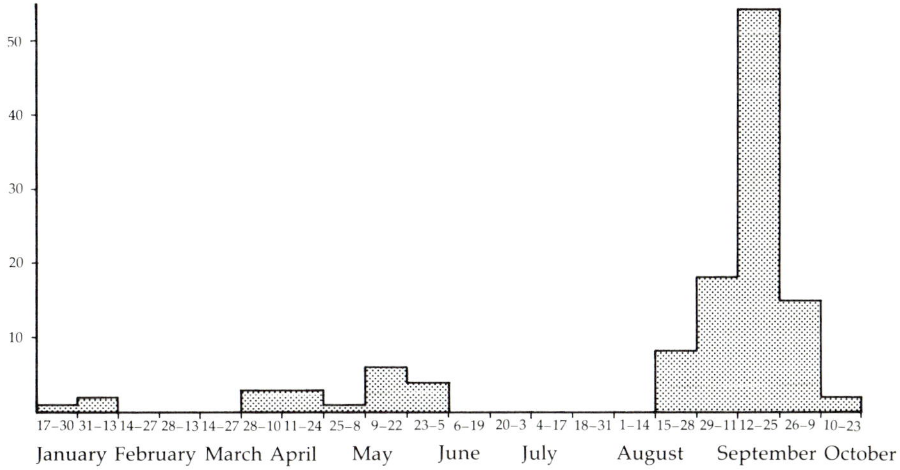

Fortnightly distribution of Bluethroats 1952–76

Spring records have occurred in nine years, with a maximum of four in 1975. The 17 records mostly fall into two distinct periods, with six between 1st–15th April and 10 between 16th–29th May. Three of the former were males of the White-spotted race, as was one on 5th May 1959, and this suggests overshooting during northward migration (Sharrock, 1974). All the males in the later period have been of the nominate, Red-spotted race *L.s. svecica* and all but two in 1959 have occurred since 1970. They are linked to the increasing occurrence of other Scandinavian drift migrants in late May, during periods of northeast winds. Sharrock found most late May records up to 1968 confined to northern Scotland, so the change is in all probability genuinely recent.

A total of 97 birds has been recorded in autumn, with one–seven in 17 years and a marked peak of 10, 26 and 13 birds between 1967–69, but only one during 1973–76. Most occurred between 21st August–6th October, with a further two on 18th October 1969, and arrivals were often associated with falls of Scandinavian migrants during east winds. Only three, all in 1960 and 1962, were identified as *L.s. cyanecula*. A tendency for peak numbers in the second and third weeks of September is emphasised by the multiple arrivals of six, including four at Sandwich Bay, on 13th–15th September 1967; 17, including eight at Sandwich Bay and five at Shellness, on 15th–16th September 1968; and eight, including five at Dungeness, on 20th–21st September 1969.

The only winter records concern singles at Dungeness on 23rd January 1960, New Hythe between 11th February–4th March 1968, and Loose on 9th February 1972.

Bluethroats favour damp scrub and reedbeds, although they occur in any cover on migration, particularly around the coast. They are particularly skulking and it is likely that some pass through unnoticed each year away from well-watched localities. The Observatories have accounted for 74% of all records, with 62 at Dungeness and 24 at Sandwich Bay. A further 22 have occurred at other coastal localities, including 10 at Shellness (Sheppey), and only nine at inland sites.

Red-flanked Bluetail

Tarsiger cyanurus

Very rare vagrant.

The only record is of a first winter male killed, probably by a weasel, in a Heligoland trap at Sandwich Bay on 28th October 1956.

Black Redstart

Phoenicurus ochruros

Local breeding species, winter visitor and passage migrant.

Harrison documents the change in status during the first three decades of this century, from a rare visitor, to a regular passage migrant and winter visitor, eventually becoming a local breeding bird. The first recorded nesting was at Ringwould (Dover) in 1930. After 1940 it was known to breed almost annually, reaching an early peak of about 15 pairs in 1948.

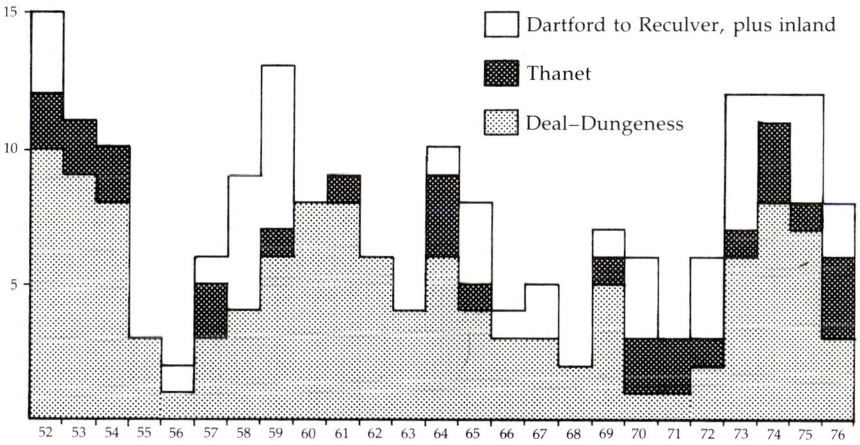

Occupied sites of Black Redstarts

The Kent breeding population has fluctuated between two and 15 pairs during 1952–76. Although the proportion of the national population dropped from about 40% in 1952 to 20% in 1973, the sites in the Dover area are among the most regularly occupied in the country.

The histogram above shows the maximum number of breeding pairs reported each year, based on proved pairs and singing males. The peak years correspond fairly closely to the national peaks (Fitter, 1965, 1971 and 1976). Not all singing males are necessarily paired, but on the other hand some pairs are almost certainly overlooked each year, particularly since the favoured habitats do not attract close attention.

Breeding success can be high. Nine pairs raised 82 young at Dover in 1952 and 24 young were reared by five pairs at Dungeness in 1974, and up to three broods have been recorded.

Although pairs have bred on the chalk cliffs, it was the bombed urban sites along the Thames and in Dover which attracted most of the early colonists. Since the mid-fifties such sites have disappeared and alternative habitats in industrial and derelict buildings, dockyards and especially large power stations have been favoured. Territories are sometimes established in well populated town centres, with males singing from shop roofs and lamp posts, but there is a preference for large, often enclosed sites, where human disturbance is minimal. It could be that the unstable nature of most of the chalk cliffs discourages the establishment of regular sites there, but the failure to colonise many apparently suitable urban sites inland is unexplained.

The most regular sites have been in towns along the Thames, on Thanet, and between Deal and Folkestone. Breeding has been regular on the Dungeness Power Station since 1962 and there have been less regular breeding attempts in most coastal towns between Rochester and Herne Bay. The predominance of coastal breeding is striking, and the only breeding attempts inland have been in Maidstone in 1959 and 1964, and Canterbury in 1959 and 1975, with a singing male at Sevenoaks in May 1973.

Reports of wintering birds were infrequent until the mid-sixties, since when a few individuals have wintered regularly at coastal sites, mainly on the chalk cliffs of Thanet and around Dover.

Spring passage reaches a peak during the last week of March and the first three weeks of April, predominantly on the east coast between Thanet and Dungeness, with only a scattering of records elsewhere. The highest day-totals have been recorded at Dungeness, with up to 25, although peaks of 10 are more usual there, with smaller numbers at Sandwich Bay and on Thanet. Although some are British breeding birds, most are probably overshoots *en route* for breeding quarters further east in Europe, as indicated by six migrants ringed at Dungeness in spring. Five were recovered in the same year in Germany, and one in France during the following breeding season (Langslow, 1976).

Autumn passage is mainly during October and November, and records are more widespread, with more inland than in spring. Daily peaks rarely exceed those in spring and Dungeness again records the highest numbers, with day-totals in October occasionally exceeding 10 and twice reaching 20.

There are two January recoveries from Spain, and one from Portugal, of birds ringed at Dungeness the previous October. These support the view that autumn passage mainly comprises drift migrants from further east, *en route* to wintering quarters in Iberia. The breeding sites in Britain are vacated much earlier in the autumn. A fledgling ringed in Sussex in 1947 was recovered as a breeding male in Dover in 1952, indicating some interchange within the English populations.

Redstart

Phoenicurus phoenicurus

Regular passage migrant and local breeding species.

Although Ticehurst indicated a decline in the breeding population in the latter half of the last century, Harrison concluded that the Redstart had re-established itself as a tolerably common summer visitor breeding mostly in the north and northwest of the county, less numerously in mid-Kent and elsewhere in very small numbers.

Unfortunately there were few accurate estimates of populations before the mid-1950s, but it is evident that there has been a decline during the period under review.

Between 1956–65 over 20 presumed breeding pairs were regularly recorded, mainly from west Kent, with some traditional sites such as Knole Park (Sevenoaks) holding substantial populations. There is also an isolated record of 32 singing males in Mereworth Woods in 1965, which suggests that some important sites may be overlooked. Since 1965 less than 15 pairs have been reported annually, with a larger proportion in woodlands around Canterbury and Ashford. This bias is undoubtedly due to the amount of census work done in east Kent in recent years.

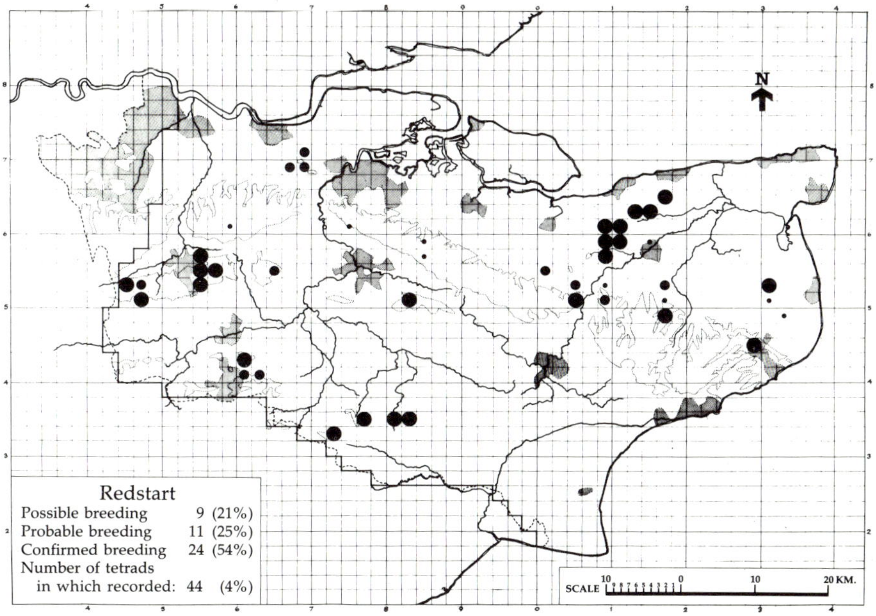

The two areas of concentration, the Blean and Sevenoaks woodlands, are shown clearly. Redstarts favour parkland and open, mixed woodland, with old timber, so that much of the coppiced woodland of Kent is unsuitable. However, small blocks of well grown and open coniferous planting are regularly occupied in some areas. There is a clear preference for woodland on higher ground, though there is a marked paucity of records from some apparently suitable woods and parks along the North Downs. The reason for this is not known, although Sharrock (1976) suggests an aversion to woodlands on chalk elsewhere in Britain.

The first birds usually arrive in early April, with migration continuing into May. March arrival dates were recorded in seven years during 1952–76, with the earliest at Hythe on 12th March 1960. Peak numbers at the Observatories occur in late April or early May, but rarely exceed 10 in a day. However, large falls of 40–50 birds occurred at Dungeness on 29th April 1963, 3rd May 1965 and 18th April 1970. They probably represent part of the northeast European population drifted off course, as evidenced by a bird retrapped at Fair Isle on 25th May 1971, after being ringed at Dungeness six days earlier. Regular spring passage has certainly declined, reaching an all-time low in 1974 and 1976, with less than 30 bird/days at Dungeness and only a single bird at Sandwich Bay in each year.

In autumn Redstarts are more widespread, with more inland records. There has been an overall decline in the numbers recorded, with greater fluctuations at the Observatories. Most move through between late August and early October, with the latest records normally in the last week of October. There are four later dates in November, including the latest at Reculver on 15th November 1963. Since 1962 day totals of between 20–40 have been usual at Dungeness, with between 10–20 at Sandwich Bay. Peaks are invariably associated with falls of Scandinavian migrants, the most spectacular of which occurred on 15th September 1968. Along the northeast coast from Sheppey to Sandwich Bay there were estimates of 350 at Sandwich Bay, 150 at Shellness (Sheppey) and 100 at Reculver.

Further evidence of the decline of this species, particularly as a passage migrant, is shown by an analysis of the annual ringing totals at the Observatories. At Dungeness there was an average of 117 for the period 1952–68, compared with 36 during 1969–76, while at Sandwich Bay the figures were 33 and 23, representing decreases of 69% and 30% respectively.

A bird ringed at Heligoland in May 1972 and retrapped at Margate in September 1972 indicates a northeasterly origin for at least some of the autumn migrants. Most continue southwestwards and there have been five autumn and winter recoveries in Portugal, three in Spain and one in Morocco.

Whinchat

Saxicola rubetra

Widespread passage migrant, but declining as a breeding species.

As a breeding species, Ticehurst considered the Whinchat to be confined to gorse-covered heathlands in the interior of the county. Harrison recorded an increase in the number of breeding records, with a much more widespread distribution. Although no estimates of numbers are available for comparison, there has clearly been a decline in recent years.

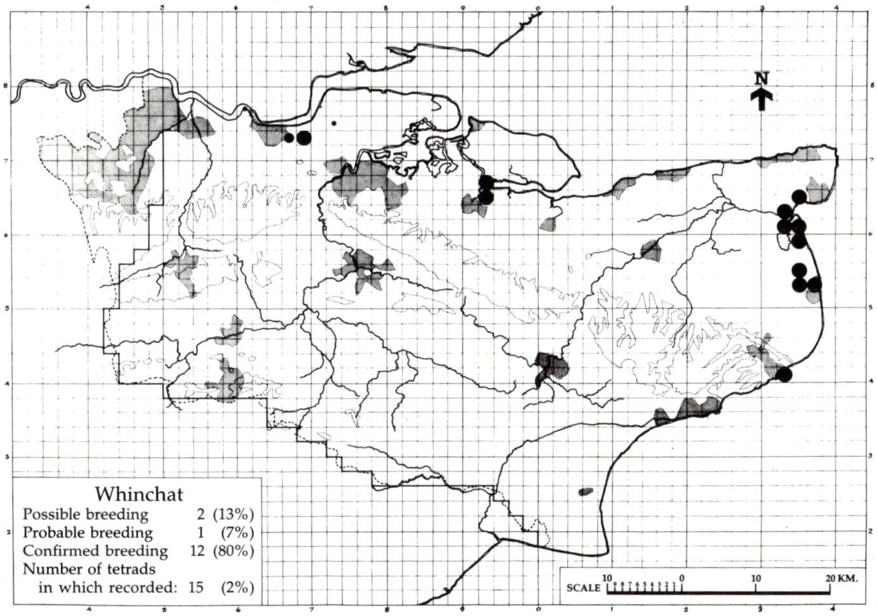

Between 1954–66 an annual average of nine pairs was reported, with peaks of 13–15 pairs in three years, but the average for 1967–76 was only two, with a maximum of five pairs in 1969 and none in 1971 or 1975. The Whinchat's position as a breeding species must now be very tenuous, and since 1952 nearly all the nesting records have come from lowland marshes close to the estuaries of the Thames, Swale and especially the Stour.

Parslow (1973) noted a decline in southeastern England and it seems likely that the increase in arable farming at the expense of grass and the reclamation of marginal land such as the heaths have been major factors. Coincident with these changes in agricultural practices was the widespread eradication of rabbits by myxomatosis after 1955, and many areas of ideal breeding habitat of tussocky grass with thinly scattered tall weeds or small bushes vanished under a dense cover of scrub. In the Stour Valley favoured haunts were grass banks and field corners with a few hawthorns. Almost all the known sites have now been ploughed and the hawthorns grubbed out. Inland the ploughing of the chalk downs and the suburban extension of London destroyed many of the traditional haunts.

The first birds usually arrive in the third week of April and passage, which is noted mainly on the coast and up river valleys, extends to late May. Peak daily counts at the Observatories have been in late April or early May, but rarely exceed 10. During 1952–76 there were only seven first arrival dates before 15th April, including one on 25th March 1974.

Autumn passage begins in late July, with peaks from mid-August to mid-September and only stragglers after mid-October. Passage is on a broad front, with inland records frequent. Regular observations at Langley Park Farm (Maidstone) since 1970 have revealed a marked passage there, with almost daily records from mid-August to late September and a peak of 15 on 12th September 1973. The largest numbers are usually recorded from the Sandwich area, autumn peaks regularly reaching 60 or more, with 135 there on 11th September 1971 and 115 on 15th September 1974, the latter coinciding with the exceptional peak of 170 at Dungeness the next day. Peaks of 30–35 are more usual at Dungeness, and at other coastal localities counts of 20 or more are quite frequent.

In 11 of the years under review the last dates occurred in November–December, with the latest at Minnis Bay on 3rd December 1967 and at Stodmarsh on 17th December 1961. Two other records, more indicative of overwintering, involve singles at Minnis Bay from 11th–31st December 1960 and at High Halstow on 16th February 1958.

Although numbers recorded on spring passage have declined in recent years, the contrary is true for the autumn, probably because Continental as well as British-breeding birds pass through Kent at that season. The autumn orientation is southwestwards and two ringed birds have been recovered in Spain and one in southwest France.

Stonechat

Saxicola torquata

Passage migrant, winter visitor and very local breeding species.

Ticehurst concluded that the summer and winter distributions were markedly different, and wrote of immigrants arriving in September. He listed a number of inland breeding localities along the Downs between Dover and Maidstone, on Dartford Heath and Tunbridge Wells Common. Harrison described little change in status until the severe winters of the 1940s, which wiped out the breeding population. One pair bred again near Dover in 1951.

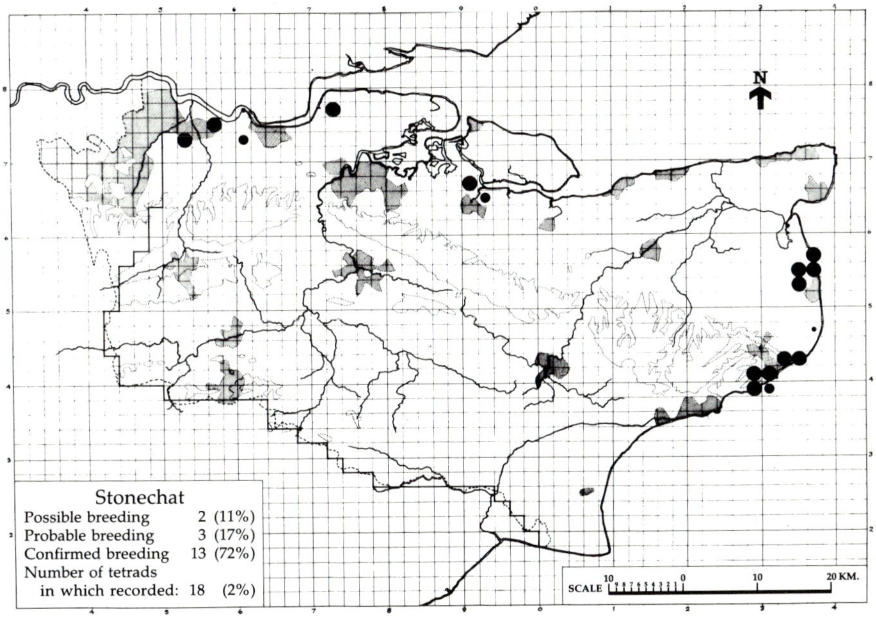

The present coastal distribution probably reflects the surviving remnants of suitable habitat as much as the ameliorating influences of the sea. More marginal habitats, such as rough pasture, are sometimes occupied, as in 1964, when an exceptional total of 16 pairs bred. Elsewhere in Britain young coniferous plantations are increasingly favoured (Parslow, 1973), but there are no such records for Kent. The most regular sites are now gorse patches along the coastal chalk Downs near Dover, although odd pairs breed fairly regularly around the coast between Herne Bay and Deal, especially at Sandwich Bay, and irregularly at Dungeness and on the Thames marshes. The annual breeding population averages less than four pairs. Although several pairs bred along the Stour Valley in 1964, there has been only one recent breeding record well inland, at Tunbridge Wells in 1966. This pair could have been associated with the nearby Ashdown Forest population, just over the border in Sussex.

There has been a marked increase in the wintering population during the mild winters of the 1970s and the Stonechat is now widespread all round the coast, with counts of up to 15 regularly at Sandwich, Dungeness and Cliffe. Inland too the increase has been widely noted, especially along the Stour Valley. Wintering individuals and pairs favour marshes and agricultural land, gravel pits, waste land, golf courses and even woodland clearings.

Spring passage occurs in March and April along the coast, but peak day-totals at the Observatories rarely exceed 10. In autumn passage begins in mid-September and extends to late November, with peaks in October. The winter of 1962/63 clearly had a substantial detrimental effect on the total British population and numbers recorded on passage were much reduced. Bird/day totals at Dungeness during September–November illustrate this well, with 195 in 1961, 184 in 1962 and only 24 in 1963. Recovery was rapid, however, after the exceptional breeding season in 1964. Peaks of up to 20 in a day are now not unusual at the Observatories. The largest numbers still occur on the coast, but inland records have become much more frequent since 1970. A southwesterly movement in autumn is evidenced by two Dungeness-ringed birds recovered in October–November in Spain and one in France.

Wheatear

Oenanthe oenanthe

Passage migrant and local breeding summer visitor.

Harrison considered the Wheatear to be numerous, breeding commonly around the coast from Dungeness to the Stour, but less commonly on Thanet and in north Kent, with few inland since the turn of the century.

Dungeness is still the most important breeding site. On the Reserve the population has declined from around 80 pairs in the early fifties. The marked fall in 1955–56 may well have been linked with the loss of rabbit burrows as breeding sites, following the large-scale eradication of rabbits through myxomatosis. However, this was followed by an increase to around 60 pairs in 1961, but since then there has been a steady decline to only 10 pairs in 1976. A remarkable range of nest sites

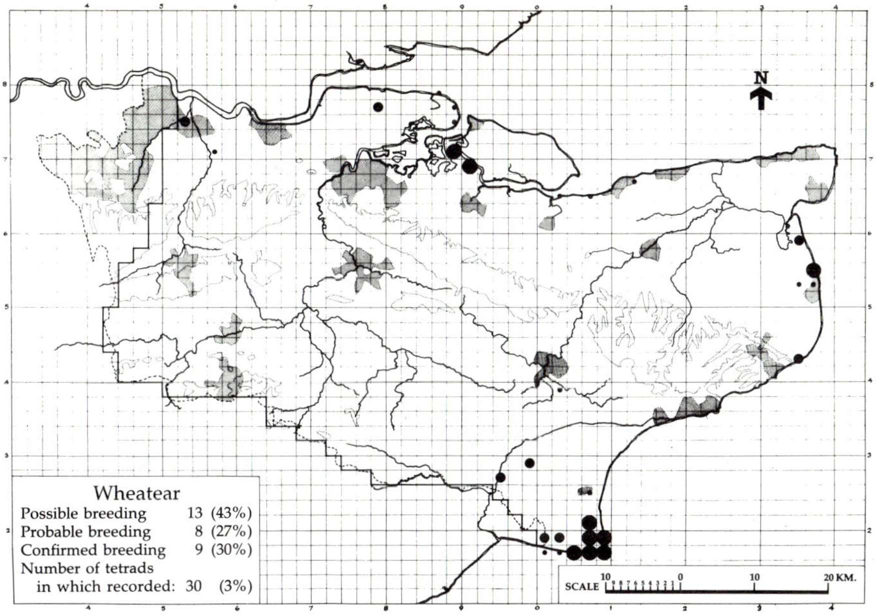

has been recorded there, including ammunition tins, drainpipes, a wellington boot and a trilby hat!

Elsewhere breeding is now very irregular, and most of the possible breeding records mapped probably refer to late migrants, which overlap with the breeding season of early arrivals. Single pairs occasionally nest on Romney Marsh, in the Sandwich Bay area and on the North Kent Marshes, occupying a diverse range of sites within a few miles of the coast. These include coal slagheaps, sandpits, golf courses, seawalls and even recently-burnt coppice. It is surprising that such an adaptable bird does not now maintain a regular breeding population away from Dungeness.

The first spring arrivals are usually seen in the second and third weeks of March, with the mean around 12th March and the earliest at Lower Rainham on 15th February 1958. Early passage is most marked on the coast between Thanet and Dungeness, with daily peaks of up to 75 at Dungeness and up to 55 at Sandwich Bay mostly occurring between mid-April and mid-May. The largest falls include 150 at Dungeness on 16th April 1970 and over 110 at Foreness on 19th April 1975. Inland reports generally involve less than five birds, but on 27th March 1967 there were 34, including a flock of 23, near Clement Street in the Darent Valley. Passage continues throughout May, when there are more reports of the larger, Greenland race *O.o. leucorrhoa.*

Return passage begins in late July or early August, with the main autumn peaks between 16th August–27th September. The largest numbers are recorded on the coast, especially at Dungeness, where daily peaks of up to 120 are not unusual. Elsewhere daily peaks rarely exceed

70, except for 150 at Foreness on 19th September 1972 and an exceptional fall of 250 at Shellness (Sheppey) on 15th September 1968, during a substantial arrival of Scandinavian migrants. Inland records are more widespread and small numbers can be seen almost anywhere on open fields of short grass or plough. Last departure dates are usually in the period 28th October–23rd November, with the latest at Littlestone on 8th December 1974 and Broadstairs on 9th December 1970. Individuals of the Greenland race are seen every autumn and are probably as regular at this season as in the spring.

Birds ringed at Dungeness have been recovered in France and Spain in both spring and autumn, suggesting a consistent orientation of migrants in both seasons.

Black-eared Wheatear

Oenanthe hispanica

Very rare vagrant.

The only record is of two males identified at Denge Marsh on 25th May 1974, with one remaining until the 29th.

Black Wheatear

Oenanthe leucura

Very rare vagrant.

The only record is of one seen at Greatstone on 17th October 1954.

Rock Thrush

Monticola saxatilis

The only county record concerns an adult male seen at Dungeness on 23rd June 1933.

Swainson's Thrush

Catharus ustulatus

Very rare vagrant.

The only record of this North American species is of one trapped at Sandwich Bay on 27th October 1976.

Ring Ouzel

Turdus torquatus

Regular passage migrant.

Ticehurst gives details of three breeding records between 1875–1887 and Harrison adds single records for June 1910 and July 1930. He also adds details of two winter records: two at Dungeness on 24th January 1924 and one near Deal on 17th January 1940. There have been no summer or January records since.

During the review period spring passage has been observed between 17th March–30th May and typically involves very small numbers. Day-totals of six–nine birds have occurred in only four years at the Observatories, all between 18th April–4th May. Although the majority of records tend to be coastal, one or two are seen at widespread inland localities.

Autumn passage has been observed between 8th August–26th November, with August records in six years. There have also been four December records, which may refer to overwintering birds, though none has been recorded later than the one at Newington on 19th December 1971.

Exceptionally, as in 1970, the number on spring passage may exceed the autumn total, but normally autumn reports are far more widespread, with the largest numbers invariably seen around the coast, particularly at Dungeness. There, day-totals of at least 10 have been recorded in 14 years, on various dates between 14th September–25th October. Comparable numbers have only occurred elsewhere in four years, at Folkestone, Dover, Sandwich Bay, Broomfield (Herne Bay) and Warden Point (Sheppey). Large falls, involving counts of 30 or more, have been recorded in just five autumns. On 11th October 1959 there were 10 at Folkestone and 30 at Dungeness, while on 2nd October 1965 there were 50 at Dover and 20 at Dungeness. In 1966 there were 100 at Dungeness on 7th October, with a later influx of 30 there on the 25th. During the exceptional fall of Scandinavian migrants on 15th September 1968, there were 210 at Dungeness and 60 in the Sandwich Bay area. Finally, there were 75 at Dungeness on 25th October 1976.

The number of birds ringed in the county has remained relatively small. Of the four recoveries notified, one ringed at Dungeness on 25th October 1966 and recovered at Heligoland, Germany on 1st May 1971, lends support to the belief that birds passing through Kent originate from northern Europe rather than Britain. The most distant recovery was of one, also ringed at Dungeness, at Taillet, France.

Blackbird

Turdus merula

Abundant resident, passage migrant and winter visitor.

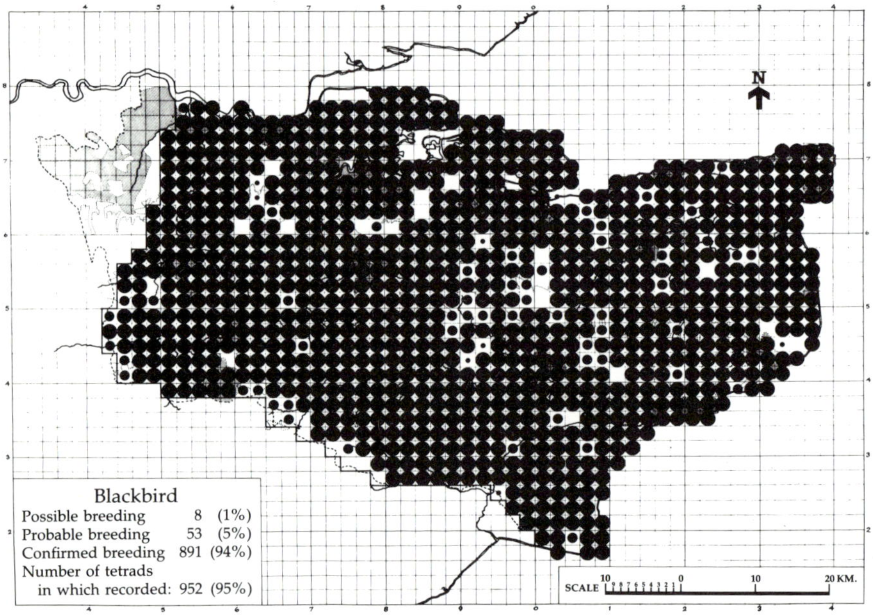

Though mainly associated with gardens, parks and woodland, the Blackbird can be found in all parts of the county in a wide variety of habitats. The results of the Breeding Survey show it to be the most widespread species, the blank tetrads on the map indicating poor coverage rather than absence. An exceptionally late nest was reported in 1953, when a nest with eggs was found at Snargate on 10th December.

The autumn passage generally occurs late, and the relatively few peaks of 500–2,000 at the Observatories have all been recorded between 13th October–13th November. In addition there was a huge arrival on 5th November 1961, when 12,000 were estimated along a half-mile stretch of coastline at Sandwich Bay. Smaller numbers were seen flying west at St. Margaret's and on Sheppey the same day. The return migration in March is regular, but far less conspicuous than in autumn.

Reports of significant numbers at inland localities usually refer either to roosts, with a maximum of 2,500 at Newington in January 1975, or to birds feeding on fallen apples, as at Allington where there were a similar number in November 1964.

Ringing recoveries, mainly from the two Observatories, have provided ample documentation of the various migratory trends that may be noted in the county. Their complexity was evident at Dungeness as early as 1955, when three birds, all ringed within 11 days of each other in October, were recovered the same winter in Aberdeenshire, Hampshire and Spain. Between 1952–66 there were 93 overseas recoveries of Dungeness-ringed birds, from an area bounded by Norway to the north, Finland to the east, and Spain to the south. Migrants were drawn from breeding areas from Germany northwards, wintering from Britain to Spain. Subsequent recoveries have tended to confirm this pattern. A Blackbird ringed at Kingsgate as an adult male in May 1959, and thus hatched in 1958 or earlier, was found dead there in late June 1971, providing a fascinating instance of longevity.

Fieldfare

Turdus pilaris

Widespread winter visitor and passage migrant.

Vast numbers are sometimes seen on autumn passage and often later in winter with the onset of hard weather. Normally, larger numbers of Fieldfares than Redwings remain through the winter.

The earliest autumn migrant was one at Sandwich Bay on 17th August 1975 and 18 there on 19th September 1953 is the highest count for such an early date. Numbers increase generally during October and in some years there are quite spectacular movements in the second half of the month and the first half of November. Such movements typically occur in cold NW winds, when birds are seen arriving at the two Observatories and heading on a broad front across the county into the wind, numbers being most concentrated along the 'leading line' of the north coast into the Thames. The largest single movement occurred on 5th November 1961, when visible migration involved 2,000 at Dungeness, 8,000 at Sandwich Bay, 5,000 at Grove, 11,000 at Allhallows and 8,000 at Cliffe. Movements of 1,000–2,000 per hour have been observed in several other years during the same period.

It is difficult to separate normal migration from hard-weather movements, but typically the latter occur in December and January. Good examples were witnessed in 1968, when 5,000 flew northwest at Dungeness on 13th January and 3,000 passed southwest in three hours over Sutton-at-Hone on 28th December.

Large winter roosts are seen regularly, notably at High Halstow, where there were up to 4,000 throughout November 1968, and at Elmstone and Newington, where counts of 6,000 are regularly reported. Large gatherings of up to 5,000 have also been seen at apple-dumps at Bredgar and Littlebourne, while 12,000 were present at Bicknor on 6th–7th January 1970, during a period of hard weather.

The timing of the return passage is obviously dependent on the weather, but typically it occurs in March, with smaller numbers in April and occasionally into May, as on 1st May 1960, when there were 200 in a field at Harrietsham.

During the period under review there have been a number of summer records, all but one since 1966, with 12 singles in June, nine of these at Sandwich Bay, and four singles in July. In addition there were up to five at Sandwich Bay between 27th–31st July 1976. Harrison wrote of the possibility of future breeding, and the increasing frequency of summer sightings, paralleled with the southerly spread on the Continent, makes this likelihood even more probable in the near future.

Ringing recoveries throw some light on the extent of the movements north, east and south, particularly those made within a year of ringing. Thus a young bird from Sweden was recovered at East Peckham the following January. A first-winter bird at Cliffe in January reached Oslo, Norway in May and an adult ringed in Dartford in February was found in Norway, nine months later. Another ringed at Burham in December was found in Finland the following August. Onward movement in winter is shown by a bird ringed at Lower Shorne in October and found in Portugal the following February. There are several other recoveries, though not in the year after ringing, from France, Spain, Italy and Norway.

Song Thrush

Turdus philomelos

Abundant, widespread resident and passage migrant.

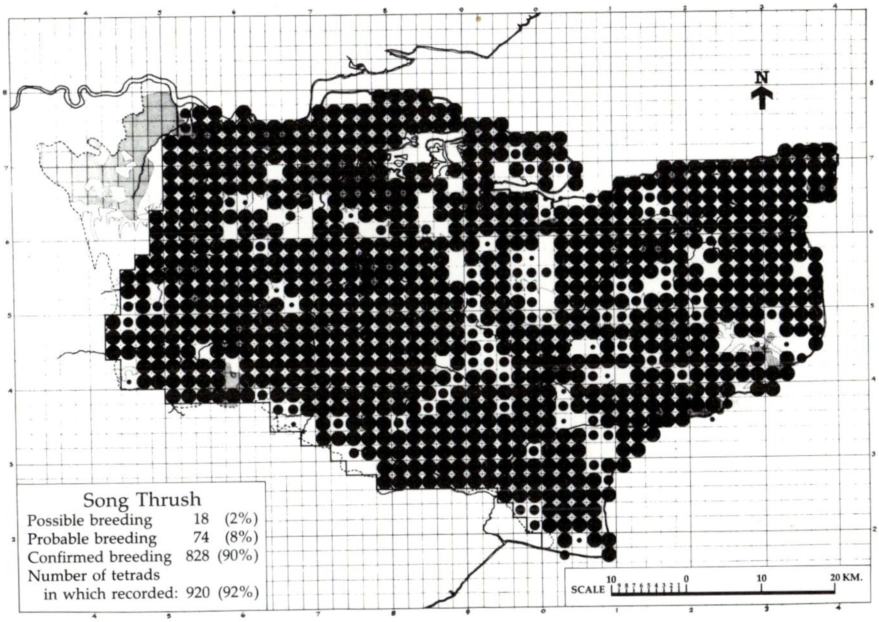

The results of the Breeding Survey show the Song Thrush to be the fourth most widespread breeding species, but it is doubtful if any of the blank tetrads represent genuine absence, except possibly from the shingle at Dungeness.

Exceptionally late nesting was reported in the autumn of 1953, when there was a particularly mild spell of weather from mid-November onwards. A pair was seen feeding young in the nest at Tenterden on 23rd December, while a fledgling and a newly laid egg were found in late November at two other localities.

Coastal areas provide evidence of autumn migration and a return movement in March and April. Small influxes are also noted occasionally at inland localities. Hard-weather movements occur and severe weather, as in 1962/63, may lead to a decrease in numbers for a short period.

The autumn passage is the earliest of the winter thrushes, usually about a week earlier than that of the Redwing, concentrated between the last week of September and the first week of November. In comparison with Redwing the day totals are very small, with coastal peaks of up to

500. However, during a large movement of Redwings between 10th–13th October 1969 there were up to 1,000 Song Thrushes at Warden Point, 2,000 at Sandwich Bay and 750 at Dungeness. The same relative scarcity applies also to winter roosts and hard-weather movements, when Song Thrushes appear in association with other thrushes, but in much smaller numbers. The largest roost involved 1,000 at Elmstone in November 1969, while day-totals of up to 250 have been recorded at the Observatories during hard weather in December and January.

Well over fifty ringing recoveries from the Continent provide confirmation of a regular southwest passage in autumn, with a number later the same winter, particularly from France, Spain and Portugal. In some cases, as in 1962/63 when there were 10 recoveries in France, they indicate hard-weather movement. That same winter four were also recovered in Cornwall, with one in Northern Ireland. One ringed at High Halstow in October 1969 was recovered surprisingly far south at El Kelaa, Morocco, the next June. Other recoveries from Denmark and Holland offer some clue as to the origin of these birds.

Continental-type Song Thrushes *T.p. philomelos* have been regularly noted in both spring and autumn at the two Observatories and occasionally inland, and the ringing evidence obviously supports this.

Redwing

Turdus iliacus

Widespread winter visitor and passage migrant. Has bred recently.

Harrison mentions a dead juvenile at Kingsdown on 27th July 1945 and a juvenile was seen at Kingsgate on 7th August 1953. Since the late sixties there have been an increasing number of summer reports. In June 1968 a pair was present for four days at Sandwich Bay and one ringed there on 24th May was controlled again on 7th September. During the 1970s there were a further eight records of singles between 2nd–26th June, five of them at Sandwich Bay.

Breeding was first proven in 1975, when three pairs were known to nest. One pair bred at the same site in 1976, in which year a juvenile was trapped at Sandwich Bay on 22nd July.

The earliest autumn record was one at Dungeness on 29th August 1973. This species is more numerous than the Fieldfare in September, and the main passage is two weeks earlier, invariably reaching a peak during October. Counts of 40 at Sandwich Bay on 15th September 1968 and 420 there on 25th September 1976 are by far the highest numbers for such early dates, while arrivals of 100–200 have been noted on 30th September in three other years. Falls, or movements involving several thousand birds in a day, may occur anywhere round the coast during October or early November, with a maximum of 6,000 flying northwest at Sandwich Bay on 10th October 1974. Huge nocturnal movements are often noted during the same period around the coast.

The numbers remaining in winter vary considerably from year to year, and hard-weather movements often occur in December and January. The largest numbers involved 7,200 northwest at Dungeness on 12th December 1967 and 9,300 northwest at Dover on the same date in 1969. More severe weather can lead to a mass emigration, as on 1st January 1962, when there was a widespread southerly movement including 5,000 over Rochester and 3,000 over Dungeness. Large roosts occur in some winters, notably at Elmstone, where the highest estimates were 6,300 on 19th December 1969 and 6,000 in November 1971, and at Newington, with 6,000 in January 1975.

Spring passage is most evident in March and is largely nocturnal, although counts of up to 1,000 have been recorded around the coast. Smaller numbers are seen during April, while the Redwing is generally much scarcer than the Fieldfare in May.

Ringing recoveries show the origin of some of our wintering birds. A young bird ringed in Finland in June 1955 was recovered at Thurnham in December of the same year, while one ringed at Cliffe in December 1964 was recovered at Perm in the USSR the following June. Evidence of onward passage is shown by several records of birds ringed in Kent and later found on the Continent, while another bird ringed at Cliffe in December 1964 was recovered in Devon in early March of the same winter.

Mistle Thrush

Turdus viscivorus

Widely distributed resident and partial migrant.

The only gaps on the breeding distribution map which are not merely reflections of observer cover are probably those in some low-lying coastal areas devoid of trees.

The Mistle Thrush is a very early breeding species which gathers in conspicuous post-breeding flocks as early as late May. On 30th May 1974, for example, at least 66 were seen at Sandwich Bay. During

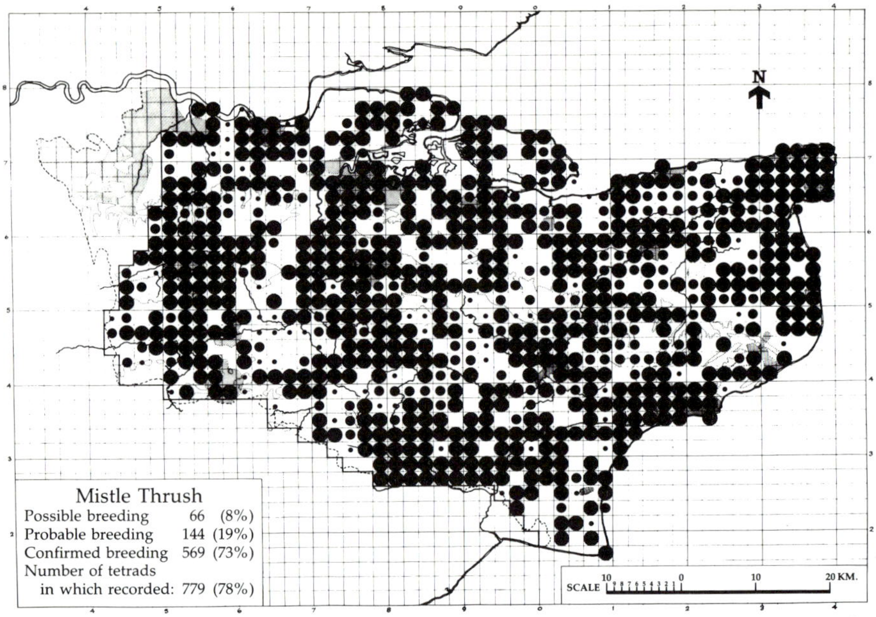

June–September flocks of up to 50–60 are widespread. Rarely, however, have gatherings of over 70 been reported, 80 at Windmill Creek on 14th July 1963, 230 feeding on yew berries at Boxley on 25th October 1964, and 200 at an apple dump at Littlebourne on 13th January 1963, are the only ones on record. The last of these reflects hard-weather concentration at a rich food source. Like all the thrushes, Mistle Thrush numbers are severely affected by unusually hard winters. Numbers ringed at Dungeness dropped from an average of 12 before 1962 to only three during 1963–67.

Although the Mistle Thrush is not so obvious an immigrant as the other thrushes, and daily totals at the two Observatories rarely exceed 30, there is plenty of evidence of a small-scale influx in autumn. In late September and October a westerly passage has been observed at Allhallows and a southerly movement at Sandwich Bay. There have also been several arrivals at Ramsgate at this time, involving up to 50 birds. Onward movement is well illustrated by a full-grown bird ringed at Stockbury on 23rd November 1965, which was recovered just five days later in Oise, France.

Two other foreign ringed recoveries concern two nestlings ringed at Dungeness and Littlestone, both recovered the following November in France.

Cetti's Warbler

Cettia cetti

A very recent colonist, which has become a locally common resident.

One trapped at Dungeness on 31st March 1968 was the first confirmed record for the county. There were no further records until November 1971, when another occurred at Dungeness and at least three were found at Stodmarsh. This was the start of a remarkably rapid colonisation, reflecting the northwest spread of the species in Europe (Bonham and Robertson, 1975).

The few colonists in the Stour Valley remained throughout 1972 and breeding was suspected. In 1973 there was a significant spread along the Stour Valley and one was heard singing in Mote Park (Maidstone) in April and May. Breeding was proved at Stodmarsh, where three recently fledged young were seen in the company of adults on 25th June. This was the first breeding record for Britain. In 1974 the spread along the Stour Valley continued and six pairs were known to breed. The only record away from the Stour was one at Langley on 15th September.

A comprehensive census in the 1975 breeding season produced a total of 61 singing males in the Stour Valley, with further singles that year at Sevenoaks in May and Burham in October. In 1976 five pairs were known to breed in the Stour Valley and there was an increase in the number of reports elsewhere, with one or two at Hothfield, Langley, Loose and Murston out of the breeding season. [This last site was colonised in 1977, the first new breeding area outside the Stour Valley. Eds.]

The Stour Valley records are mainly from areas of damp willow and hawthorn scrub in old gravel workings and flooded mining subsidence between Chilham and Grove Ferry. The census in 1975 (Harvey, 1977) revealed that although most sites were wet for at least part of the year, about 18% were dry and included scrub on wasteland, woodland scrub, and gorse on sandy commons. Bramble was found in all sites, the large clumps along railway lines being especially favoured, and willow or hawthorn and *Phragmites* in most.

Records of singles, particularly in east Kent away from the Stour Valley, may be linked with post-breeding dispersal. Some, however, like

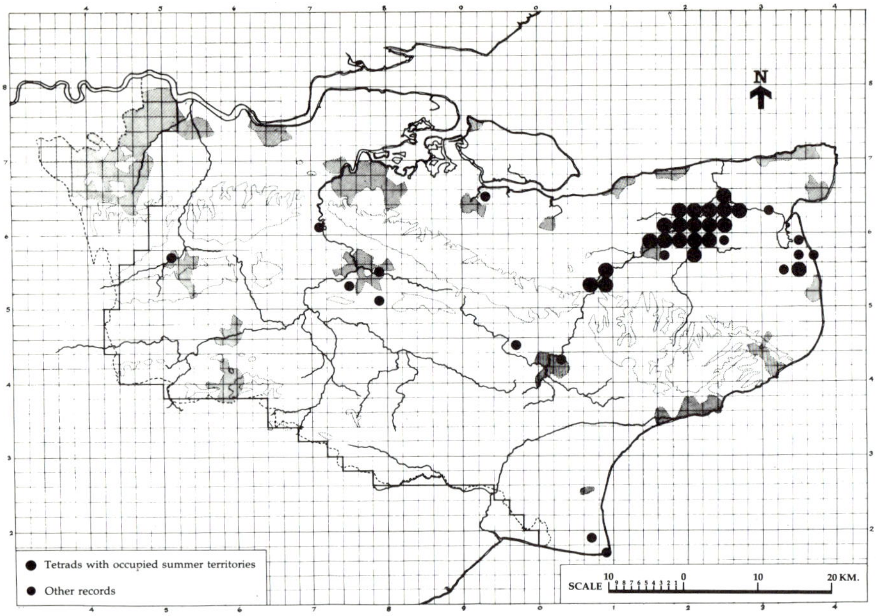

Distribution of Cetti's Warblers 1972–76

the birds trapped at Sandwich Bay on 31st March 1974 and 17th November 1976, are more likely to be new arrivals from the Continent. At Dungeness too there were four autumn records in 1975–76. Over 100 Cetti's Warblers have been ringed in Kent and retraps indicate local movements between sites, as well as providing evidence that some individuals survive for at least four years.

Grasshopper Warbler

Locustella naevia

A widespread, but local breeding summer visitor, subject to marked annual fluctuations.

This species is difficult to prove breeding and it is likely that most of the possible breeding records represent breeding pairs. However, the map shows many more pairs than are actually present in any one year, since it includes the high population count in 1970.

The Grasshopper Warbler favours dense low undergrowth and scrub,

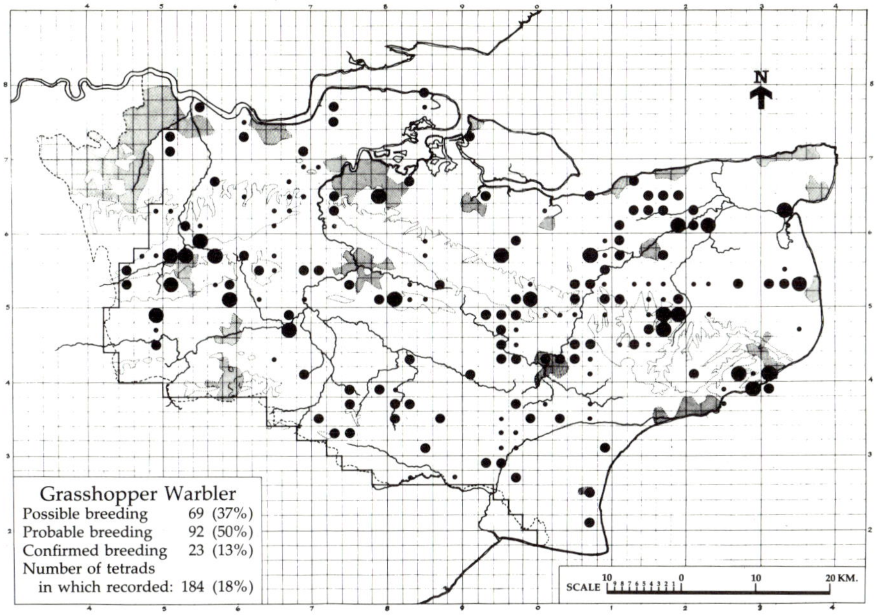

usually including brambles, long grass, sedge or reed, in both wet and dry locations. Where such habitats are relatively stable, as in parts of the Stour Valley, near Murston, and on downland sites near the Medway towns and Dover, there are regular breeding populations, albeit in fluctuating numbers. Most of the population, however, breeds in scrub in woodland, especially in young conifer plantations, where individual sites become unsuitable after a few years, when the trees grow too tall, and where felling eventually produces new sites.

The concentrations in large woodland areas near Canterbury and Ashford and in south Kent correspond to recent conifer plantings and there have been particularly high densities in the Challock, Lyminge and Hamstreet woodlands. Countywide woodland surveys revealed 46 singing males in 1969, 171 in 1970 and 78 in 1971. There was an apparent increase in the population during the 1960s, but since 1971 the Grasshopper Warbler appears to have declined. This may reflect a localised drop in conifer planting, or alternatively, adverse influences in the wintering areas. Numbers of migrants trapped at the two Observatories have also declined since 1970. At Dungeness an annual average of four–five during 1952–70, with a maximum of 13 in 1960, decreased to only one or two during 1971–76.

In spring the first arrivals occur between 7th–30th April, with the mean around the 17th. Return migration begins in mid-July and extends into early October, with the latest at Sandwich Bay on 13th October 1970.

The first British recovery overseas was a bird ringed at Dungeness on 3rd August 1960 and recovered at Tarbres, France, 18 days later.

Savi's Warbler

Locustella luscinioides

A very local summer visitor.

There was no acceptable record of this species in Kent until three were identified at Stodmarsh on 18th April 1960. Pitt (1967) described the subsequent colonisation and suggested that Savi's Warblers could have been misidentified as Grasshopper Warblers *Locustella naevia* between 1951–59. Although this is possible, Grasshopper Warblers have themselves occurred annually in the same area of Stodmarsh since at least 1952.

The first Savi's Warblers generally arrive between 6th–18th April, with extreme dates of 28th March 1968 and 18th May 1961. They can usually be heard into early August, with the latest sight record on 9th August 1975. When not singing they are very inconspicuous, so it is impossible to be certain when the last birds usually depart. There are no records from the Observatories.

60	61	62	63	64	65	66	67	68	69	70	71	72	73	74	75	76
3	2	2	3	4	12	8	4	3	6	3	5	6	3	3	3	3

Numbers of singing Savi's Warblers in the Stour Valley 1960–76

As the table shows, Savi's Warblers have occurred annually in a small area of the Stour Valley. The early peak in 1965 has not since been equalled and the population of 3–6 singing males represents about half of the British breeding population.

The most regularly occupied sites have been in Stodmarsh NNR, but in at least four years singing males were found up to three kilometres away in other parts of the valley. The habitat requirements are fairly specialised, open *Phragmites* reed beds with an understorey of sedges and often patches of marsh dock and reed meadow grass. Occasionally monospecific stands of *Phragmites* are occupied if there is an abundance of dead reeds at water level, but generally the encroachment of dense reed cover obliges the birds to change sites. A falling water level may also be necessary and certainly changes due to the influence of high spring tides, as well as cold late springs, have reduced the population in some years.

Proof of breeding has not been obtained annually. Birds were seen carrying food to two sites in 1960 and three newly fledged young were seen near one of them on 2nd July. Two pairs were proved breeding in 1964–66, with single pairs successful in 1972 and 1974–76. It is likely that more pairs have bred, and most singing males are probably paired.

Unmated males, often conspicuous by their continuous song throughout the season, occur in some years.

In north Kent two–three males summered at one site in 1969 and 1970, and in June 1974 one was heard singing at a second locality, but breeding has never been proved away from the Stour Valley. A migrant at Seasalter on 29th April 1973 is the only other record.

Moustached Warbler

Acrocephalus melanopogon

Very rare vagrant.

The only record concerns one seen at Cliffe on 14th April 1952.

Aquatic Warbler

Acrocephalus paludicola

Rare autumn migrant.

Harrison lists a number of records for the first half of this century, the most convincing being at least nine in autumn, between 19th August–25th September in the Dungeness area.

During the period under review there have been 13 records, with singles in 1955 and 1959, eight between 1961–64, including three in each of the last two of those years, and then none until 1975, when there were two, followed by one in 1976. All have been between 2nd August–27th September, a marked similarity with Harrison's dates, and with those elsewhere on the south coast of Britain.

Eight records at Dungeness reflect the south coast bias nationally. Two have been seen at Sandwich Bay, two in the north of the county at Stoke Fleet and Lower Hope Point, and one inland at Sevenoaks on 21st August 1964.

Sedge Warbler

Acrocephalus schoenobaenus

A locally numerous breeding summer visitor and passage migrant.

The Sedge Warbler favours a variety of wetland habitats, usually including scrub and other low, thick vegetation, but generally avoids uniform stands of *Phragmites*, preferring denser cover for nesting. When numbers were high in the 1960s there were frequent breeding records well away from water and some of the isolated dots on the map represent such sites.

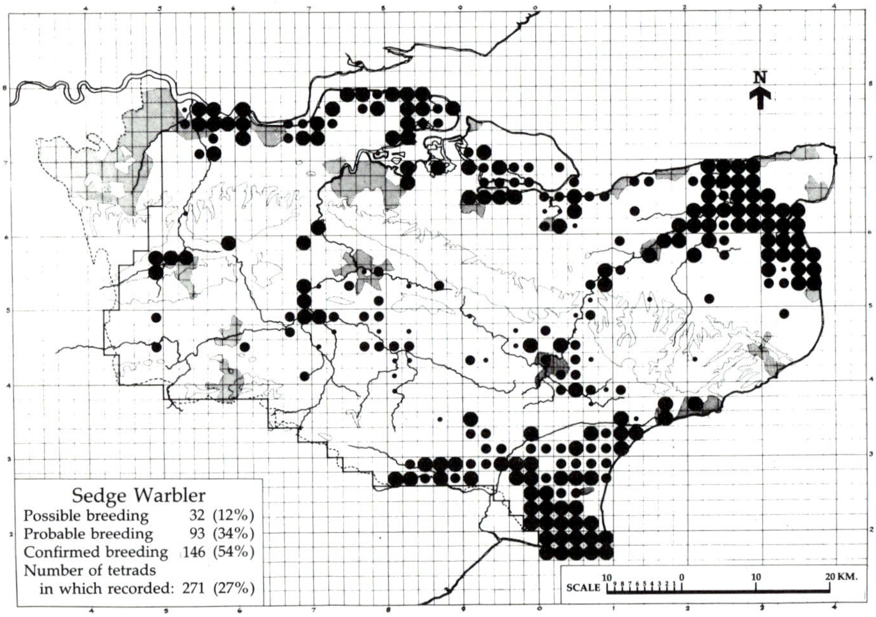

The major concentrations are in the east Kent lowlands, the Romney Marsh and Rother levels, and the North Kent Marshes. Smaller numbers breed in the other river valleys and clay vales inland, but the number of suitable sites is limited. Not surprisingly, the Sedge Warbler is absent from most of the dry chalklands. With increasingly intensive agricultural practices in the lowlands, traditional breeding sites are diminishing, but well-vegetated gravel pits have compensated for this in many areas and can hold high densities. In the middle Stour Valley, between Fordwich and Grove, there were estimates of 1,300 singing males in 1965, but only 320 pairs the next year, and 400 in 1970.

The annual ringing totals at the two Observatories clearly show a population drop in 1969, which parallels that of the Whitethroat and

Redstart. At Dungeness the average annual ringing total for 1952–68 was 180, dropping to 86 for 1969–76, a decrease of 52%, while at Sandwich Bay the average fell from 89 to 53, a drop of 40%.

Apart from one at Stodmarsh on 9th March 1963, the first arrivals occurred between 26th March–14th April, with the mean around the 7th. Peaks of up to 60 have been recorded at the Observatories between 26th April–18th May, with 100 at Dungeness on 3rd May 1962.

In autumn young birds begin moving out in July and migration continues into early October. At the Observatories the peak is reached between 23rd July–11th September, with day totals up to 70 and a maximum of 150 at Dungeness on 15th August 1964. In seven years the last departure dates have occurred after 14th October, with the latest at Stodmarsh on 1st November 1968.

It is thought that Sedge Warblers may make the journey to Africa in a single 'hop', but the only foreign recovery from Kent suggests that some movement may occur before this major stage is undertaken. One ringed at Murston in early August 1969 was recovered at Nantes, northwest France, three weeks later.

Marsh Warbler

Acrocephalus palustris

A scarce late spring and summer visitor.

The difficulties of separating Marsh and Reed Warblers both in the field and in the hand are well documented, and many Kent records can no longer be ascribed to this species with certainty. Harrison details a number of records since 1905, including satisfactory breeding records in the Medway Valley from 1926 to 1938 and at three sites in east Kent.

Since 1952 reliable records have come mainly from the Stour Valley. Reported breeding records from north Kent in 1963 and from the Stour Valley and Appledore in 1973 are inconclusive on the evidence available, and the late Dr. J. G. Harrison considered that similar doubts must be attached to the birds at Sevenoaks, and that records there since 1952, including some exceptionally early dates, might refer to mimetic Reed Warblers. Breeding has not been convincingly proved in recent years.

In the Stour Valley, where Marsh Warblers have occurred in at least five sites in recent years, some Reed Warblers and at least one Garden Warbler have picked up mimetic singing skills and continued to sing in this way in subsequent years when no Marsh Warblers have been present! Some of the reported Marsh Warblers in this area have certainly been misidentifications. After the peak years in 1974–75, when up to four males held territory in May–June, with two paired, only one or two males occurred in 1976, interestingly in quite different sites. During the same period, there were spring migrants at Dungeness, where one was trapped on 31st May 1974, three were singing and another trapped on 18th May 1975, and one was singing on 3rd June 1976. One was also singing at Sandwich Bay on 18th May 1974.

Twelve autumn migrants have been trapped between 29th July–29th September, but it is now known that most young birds in autumn cannot be identified with certainty and some of these may not have been genuine records.

Favoured breeding season habitats have a luxuriant growth of scrub willow, willowherb, meadowsweet, nettles and other vegetation. Birds arrive from the third week of May into early June and sing into July, especially if unmated. Mimicry of nearly twenty species has been reported.

Marsh Warblers are locally common in northeast France and it is to be expected that some birds may overshoot in late spring and summer and breeding atempts will continue to be made, but continuing vigilance will be necessary to avoid the doubts which have applied to past records.

Reed Warbler

Acrocephalus scirpaceus

A locally numerous breeding summer visitor and passage migrant.

The Reed Warbler is largely dependent on *Phragmites* for breeding sites, particularly favouring thick stands along dykes and rivers, or reedbeds with numerous intersecting open channels. To a lesser extent it occurs in other waterside vegetation, especially near breeding concentrations, and there have been increasingly frequent breeding records in scrub, dry hedgerows and even cereal crops. In such habitats confusion with the much rarer Marsh Warbler becomes a danger, particularly as some Reed Warblers show highly developed mimicry in their songs.

The major concentrations are in the east Kent lowlands, Romney Marsh and the Rother levels, the Medway Valley and the North Kent Marshes. Particularly large populations have been reported from Murston, Burham and Snodland, while the middle Stour Valley probably has one of the largest populations in Britain. In 1965 an estimated 705 pairs bred, with 600 in 1970.

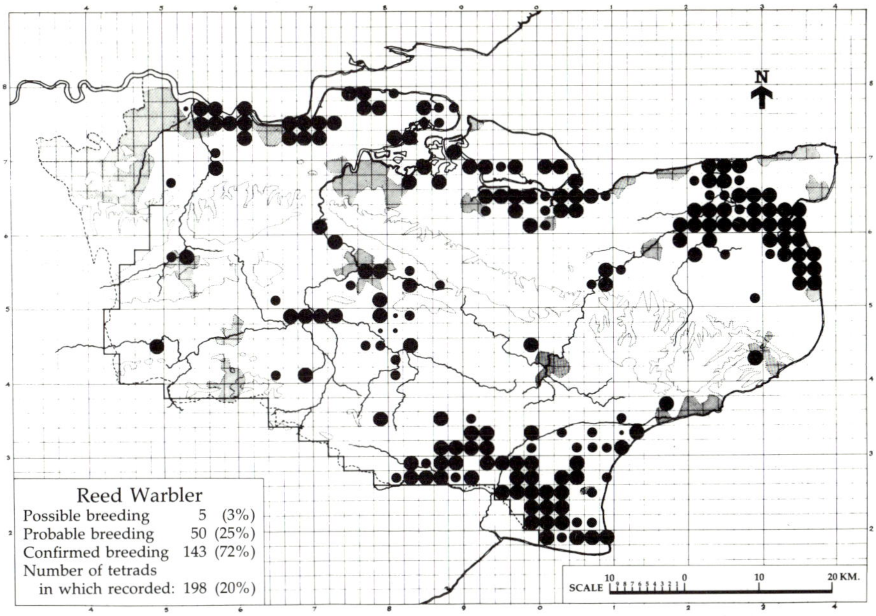

It is interesting to note that comparative ringing figures at Dungeness during the periods 1952–68 and 1969–76 show a spectacular increase, rising from an average of 19 to 99 per year, including an exceptional peak of 326 in 1975. The equivalent figures for Sedge Warbler show a 52% decrease.

The spread into a wider range of habitats might perhaps be linked with this decline in Sedge Warblers. However, the Reed Warbler is vulnerable to habitat destruction. The drying out of reedbeds, the spread of scrub, and the clearing of well-vegetated dykes in farmland, have all led to local declines. Recaptures in succeeding years of ringed birds suggest considerable loyalty to breeding sites.

The first spring arrivals occur between 5th–27th April, with the mean around the 17th. Spring migration at the Observatories is not very heavy and usually reaches a peak in May. In autumn, peaks of 20–40, although sometimes occurring as early as 23rd July, are normally recorded between 21st August–10th September. At Sandwich Bay a high day-total of 75 was recorded on 21st August 1964, while at Dungeness there was an exceptionally heavy autumn passage in 1975, with peaks of 50 on 28th August and 80 on 21st September. October records occur almost annually, and there are November records for the 6th and 8th, with the latest at Langley on 14th November 1976.

Although migrants can be seen almost anywhere in autumn, there is a clear funnelling along the Stour Valley to the coast, and the Sandwich Bay ringing totals are generally two or three times higher than those at Dungeness. Once across the Channel, Reed Warblers orientate south-west and move down the western European coastal zone to reach their

African wintering quarters *via* Mauritania. There are many recoveries of Kent ringed birds along this route, including six in Portugal and six in northwest Africa.

Great Reed Warbler

Acrocephalus arundinaceus

Rare spring visitor and autumn vagrant.

Although there were several early records, Ticehurst considered only two to be sufficiently well documented, the first at Sittingbourne on 4th May 1853 and the second at Wingham on 14th September 1881. The only acceptable record added by Harrison was at Stodmarsh between 20th May–1st June 1950.

The first record for the period under review was at Dungeness on 3rd August 1959 and between then and 1974 there were 16 birds, all singles, in ten of those years, with a maximum of three in 1971.

Of the twelve spring records between 5th May–13th June, six were at Stodmarsh, four at Sandwich Bay and two at Dungeness. None stayed more than two days. Two of the autumn records between 3rd–23rd August were at Dungeness, and one each at Wingham and Sandwich Bay.

Olivaceous Warbler

Hippolais pallida

Very rare vagrant.

The only record concerns one ringed at Sandwich Bay Bird Observatory on 27th September 1967.

Icterine Warbler

Hippolais icterina

Scarce autumn passage migrant, very rare in spring.

Harrison documents only four records. The first British example of this species was obtained at Eythorne (Dover) on 15th June 1848, another was shot at Crockham Hill on 15th May 1902, one was seen on the Kentish Knock Lightship on 22nd September 1903 and two were seen at Dungeness on 12th September 1916.

During the period under review 52 birds have been recorded, with the first at Benenden on 6th August 1952, since when there have been only seven years when the species has not been recorded. There have been only seven spring records, all between 5th–28th May, plus a singing male at Whitstable from 14th–17th June 1975. Five of these were at Dungeness, including two on 17th May 1975, one at Sandwich Bay, and one singing at Northward Hill on 21st May 1976. It is likely that these spring records represent overshooting migrants.

August		September		October
1–14	15–28	29–11	12–25	26–9
6	8	15	12	3

Fortnightly distribution of autumn Icterine Warblers 1952–76

The 44 autumn birds have all been seen between 6th August–8th October. Twenty-one of these were at Sandwich Bay and 19 at Dungeness, with the one at Benenden mentioned above and singles at Worth on 16th August 1973, Shorne on 7th September 1972 and Northward Hill on 8th October 1967.

Suitable alder groves, favoured for nesting, do occur in Kent and the fact that widespread breeding occurs in northern France and Belgium suggests the possibility that such an event could happen in Kent.

In addition there have been eleven records of unidentified *Hippolais* warblers. Apart from one on 11th May, all were seen in autumn between 11th August–22nd September and mainly at the Observatories, apart from singles at Kingsgate on 11th August 1968, Shellness (Sheppey) on 28th August 1972, and Ramsgate on 21st September 1975 and 22nd September 1970. Considering the observers' field notes most of these were probably Icterine Warblers.

Melodious Warbler

Hippolais polyglotta

Rare passage migrant.

There have been just eighteen records in Kent, with the first at Dungeness on 2nd August 1959. In ten of the years since, one or two Melodious Warblers have been recorded, with four at Dungeness between 19th–30th August 1965.

The four spring records have all been at Dungeness between 23rd–28th May, with singles in 1966 and 1968 and two in 1972. All but two of the fourteen autumn records have occurred between 30th July–9th September, with one on 26th September 1962 and an exceptionally late bird, the latest recorded in the British Isles, on 7th November 1976 at Dengemarsh. There have only been three other records away from Dungeness, two singles at Sandwich Bay and one at Warden.

Dartford Warbler

Sylvia undata

Scarce visitor.

This species has a fluctuating population, resident across a narrow stretch of southern England, but it last bred definitely in Kent in 1891 on Hayes Common, although this is outside the present-day county boundary. Its distribution in nineteenth-century Kent, according to Ticehurst, was on the heath and common land in the north and west of the county. A shy, skulking species, it is possible that it has been overlooked since, but this seems unlikely. Its main habitat, extensive gorse-clad heathland, is now rare in Kent. Harrison lists just three records during the next fifty years, with singles at Dungeness on 28th October 1914 and 4th June 1926, and two in Lyminge Forest in October 1937.

The first records during the period under review occurred in 1957, since when 26 birds have been seen, with records almost annual since 1967. The severe winter of 1962/63 almost eliminated the British population and this was reflected by an absence of Kentish records between October 1962 and February 1967.

J	F	M	A	M	J	J	A	S	O	N	D
	2	2				1			9	9	3

Monthly distribution of Dartford Warblers 1952–76

The late autumn bias, from 8th October onwards, strongly suggests that the birds may be part of a post-breeding dispersal from the British breeding sites further to the west. This was particularly noticeable in 1961, when no less than six occurred at Dungeness between 5th November–26th December, two being trapped. This was an excellent breeding year for the species in Britain and similar autumn dispersal records occurred elsewhere in southern England.

The almost unprecedented record of one at Dungeness on 30th July 1970 suggests the possibility of a more southern origin, as it occurred at a time when other southern migrants were also seen.

Only four have been seen away from Dungeness. One remained at East Sutton, feeding in a field of kale, between 16th November–29th December 1957. Singles were seen at Sandwich Bay and Bough Beech on 10th and 24th October 1974 respectively, and one was seen at Hamstreet Woods on 12th November 1975, just possibly the same bird that had been seen at Dungeness two days earlier.

Subalpine Warbler

Sylvia cantillans

Very rare vagrant.

One record only, of an adult female trapped at Dungeness Bird Observatory on 31st October 1976. Interestingly, on 9th May 1976 an adult male was observed singing in Darrick Wood, Orpington, which lies just outside the county boundary.

Sardinian Warbler

Sylvia melanocephala

Very rare vagrant.

One record only, of a female trapped at Dungeness Bird Observatory on 17th April 1973.

Barred Warbler

Sylvia nisoria

Scarce autumn passage migrant.

Harrison records only one, at Dungeness on 4th October 1951.

During the period under review 26 individuals have been identified, with one–three in all but nine of the twenty-five years. Where the age was given, all have been immatures.

August	September		October	
15–28	29–11	12–25	26–9	10–23
3	9	8	4	1

Fortnightly distribution of Barred Warblers 1952–76

Apart from one found freshly dead at Kennington (Ashford) on 13th November 1971, the extreme dates are 15th August–17th October, with an obvious peak during September.

Twenty-two of the records have been equally divided between Dungeness and Sandwich Bay Observatories, and the other three not already mentioned concern singles at Shellness (Sheppey) on 28th September 1958, at Worth on 25th September 1966, and at St. Nicholas-at-Wade on 29th August 1976.

Lesser Whitethroat

Sylvia curruca

Summer visitor and passage migrant.

The Lesser Whitethroat is widely distributed throughout Kent, but more sparsely than any of the other breeding *Sylvia* warblers. It shows a preference for lowland scrub interspersed with tall trees, and for tall farmland hedgerows. It tends to be less obvious than the Whitethroat, because of its more skulking nature and the absence of a song flight.

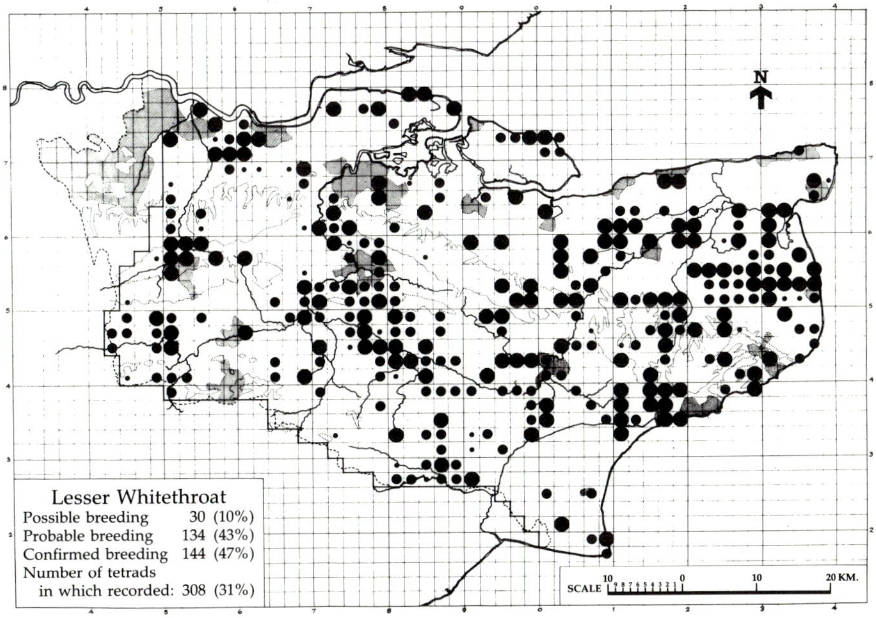

The first migrants are recorded in mid-April, the range of first dates falling between the 8th–28th, with the mean around the 18th. Spring passage at the Observatories is very light, with peaks of 20–30 in only four years at Dungeness, on various dates between 28th April–19th May.

Autumn passage is more protracted, and day-totals of 20–60 have been recorded frequently at both Observatories between 16th August–29th September, with peak counts of 150 at Sandwich Bay on 21st August 1964 and 100 at Dungeness on 6th September 1976. Late migrants have usually departed by mid-October, but singles have been seen as late as 30th October, 11th and 22nd November and 2nd December. In addition, one was seen at Lydd Woods on 9th November 1968, with presumably the same bird there again on 15th February 1969.

The only other winter record concerns one at Margate on 9th January 1974.

Unlike the majority of our summer migrants, the Lesser Whitethroat migrates southeast across the eastern Mediterranean to reach its winter quarters in northeast Africa, returning in spring even further to the east. This loop migration is reflected in recoveries of two Kentish-ringed birds from Italy in September 1964, and from the Lebanon in April 1959.

Whitethroat

Sylvia communis

Summer visitor and passage migrant.

This species is widespread throughout Kent wherever areas of scrub occur, such as woodland fringes, golf courses, marshes, hedgerows and waste ground.

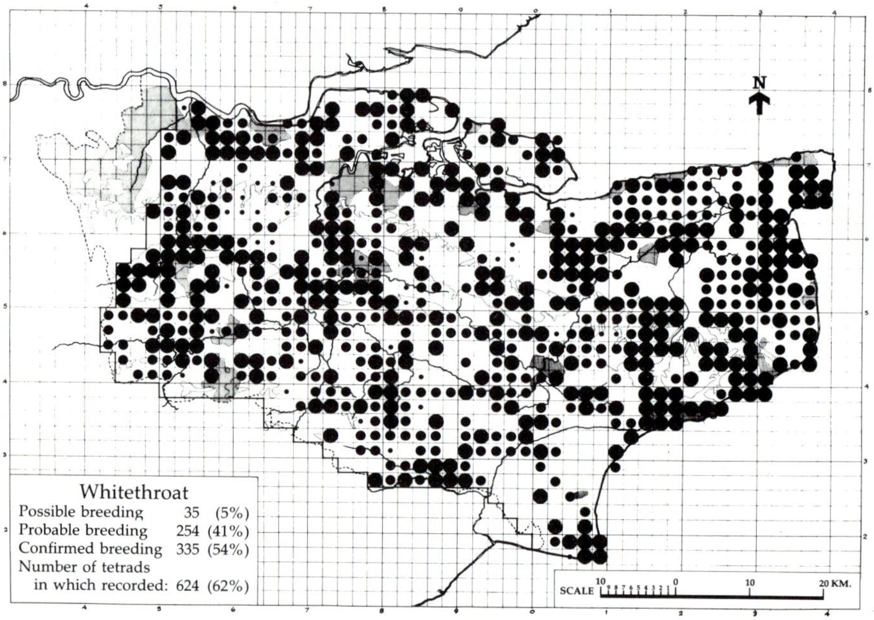

In 1969 the Whitethroat population plummeted quite dramatically throughout Britain and the numbers remained low, dropping even more in 1972 and 1973. The following year no breeding occurred at Dungeness for the first time on record. Since then however, the trend has been reversed and the numbers are on the increase.

The annual ringing totals for the two Observatories demonstrate well the extent of the population crash. At Dungeness there was an average of 678 for the 17 years 1952–68, falling to an average of only 81 for the eight years 1969–76, a reduction of 88%. At Sandwich Bay there was a similar drop from an average of 119 during 1952–68 to only 22 for 1969–76, a reduction of 82%.

It is interesting to note that Harrison records apparently marked fluctuations in population numbers, with an increase in the late nineteen-thirties from a low level around the turn of the century.

Apart from one at Barming on 5th March 1961, the first spring arrivals have all occurred between 23rd March–20th April, with the mean around 7th April. Spring peaks of up to 300 occurred commonly at Dungeness between 24th April–18th May prior to the population crash in 1969, with an exceptional fall of 1,000 there on 5th May 1957. Counts of up to 100 have also occurred at Sandwich Bay, but more rarely.

On autumn passage peaks of 50–100, and occasionally as many as 200, have occurred at Dungeness between 11th August–21st September, while day-totals of up to 100 have also occurred at Sandwich Bay. The latest departure dates usually fall between 4th October–3rd November, but in 1967 singles were seen at both Observatories on the 10th, with the latest at Sandwich Bay on 15th November 1953.

In addition there are two records of wintering birds, one at Higham on 24th December 1962 and another at Funton on 23rd January 1972.

Garden Warbler

Sylvia borin

Summer visitor and passage migrant.

Closely related to the Blackcap, this species occupies similar habitats, showing some preference for the dense scrub areas in deciduous woodland. It also adapts well to mixed scrub and will rapidly colonise new conifer plantations. The Garden Warbler is found throughout Kent, but less densely than the Blackcap, a situation reflected nationally. Both species are scarce breeding birds on Sheppey and Romney Marsh, where there is virtually no woodland.

On spring migration the earliest and main arrival dates occur significantly later than those of the Blackcap. The earliest record in recent years is one at Sevenoaks on 28th March 1972, though there was an earlier one on 25th March 1913. During the period under review all other first dates have occurred between 6th–28th April, with the mean about the 15th.

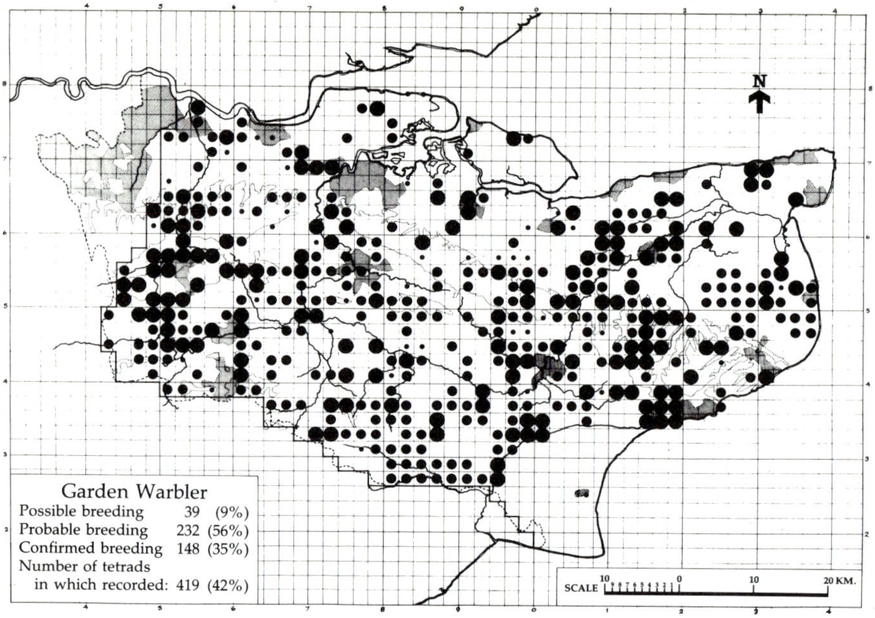

Spring passage is most evident in May and peaks of 20–50, with 100 quite exceptionally on 18th May 1966, have been recorded at Dungeness, but not at Sandwich Bay, between 2nd–23rd May.

Autumn passage is more protracted and widespread, with peaks at both Observatories of 20–30, and on one occasion 75, during the period 20th August–5th October. In the exceptional fall on 15th September 1968 there were 250 at Sandwich Bay. The latest dates usually occur during October, but there are November records for seven autumns since 1958, with the latest at Shellness on 17th November 1974.

Blackcap

Sylvia atricapilla

Summer visitor and passage migrant, wintering regularly in small numbers.

This summer migrant is widespread throughout Kent, wherever there is deciduous woodland, particularly containing mature trees with shrubby undergrowth.

Because of the presence of overwintering birds, the early and late dates of genuine migrants are difficult to ascertain and the number of

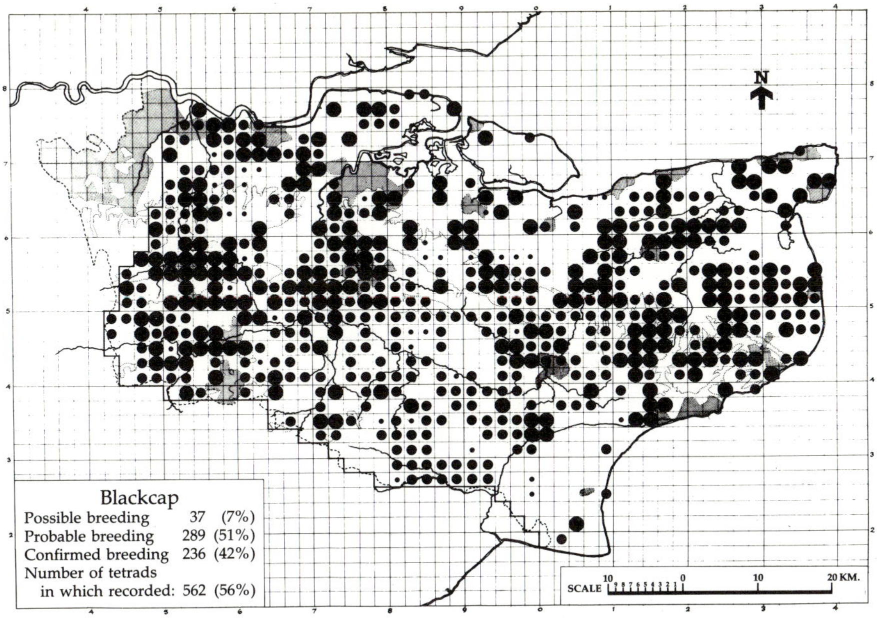

records for March and November vary considerably from year to year. In most years the earliest spring migrants start arriving in late March, although in a number of recent years the first dates have occurred later, between 2nd–14th April. In autumn passage may continue into early November.

Spring arrivals of more than 20 birds at the two Observatories are relatively rare and with one exception have occurred between 28th April–7th May. The autumn passage is much heavier, and peaks of 20–50 have been recorded at the Observatories between 12th September–9th October, while in 1975 and 1976 an interesting new development involved peaks of 20–30 at Dungeness as late as 16th–29th October.

In most winters there are a number of records between December and February, and some of these involve individuals visiting garden bird-feeders. In the winter of 1974/75 there was a peak of 14, followed two years later by an exceptional total of 35, including nine trapped and ringed in a Margate garden between 10th December–22nd January.

There have been several recoveries of Kentish-ringed birds from the western Mediterranean, in France, Spain and Tunisia, as well as recoveries elsewhere in Britain, which have been mainly on the east coast.

Greenish Warbler

Phylloscopus trochiloides

Very rare vagrant.

There have been seven records of this eastern warbler. The first was trapped and ringed at Dungeness on 17th September 1957. Since then there have been four more autumn records between 30th August–26th September, one at Sandwich Bay on the earliest date, the other three at Dungeness.

In addition there have been two summer records at Dungeness, on 9th June 1962 and 6th June 1975, the latter a male in full song.

Pallas's Warbler

Phylloscopus proregulus

Rare autumn vagrant.

The first Kent record of this attractive warbler was of one found feeding in sea buckthorn at Sandwich Bay on 23rd November 1958. The next was trapped at Dungeness on 31st October 1963.

A notable influx in 1968 involved two at Sandwich Bay on 19th October, one remaining until the 21st, with another on the 24th, and one at Dungeness on 20th October. One at Dungeness on 5th November 1971 died the following day and is preserved in the Harrison Zoological Museum at Sevenoaks.

In 1975, three arrived at Sandwich Bay on 11th–12th October, one remaining to the 15th and another to the 19th, while a fourth bird arrived there on the 24th and one was also seen at Dungeness on the 21st. Away from the Observatories, one was seen at Shellness (Sheppey) on 30th October 1976. Thus twelve of the thirteen records have occurred between 11th October–5th November.

Yellow-browed Warbler

Phylloscopus inornatus

Scarce autumn vagrant.

Harrison cites only one acceptable record, at Dungeness on 24th September 1915.

A total of 35 was recorded during the period under review, including 12 at Dungeness and 17 at Sandwich Bay, with two others at Folkestone, and singles at Sandwich, Reculver, Shellness (Sheppey) and Gillingham. The records occurred in fifteen of the twenty-five years, including nine consecutive years between 1967–75.

Apart from one at Dungeness between 21st–23rd November 1970, all the records fall in the period 17th September–1st November. Seven birds stayed for periods of two–five days, all the others being seen on single dates. The peak totals of five in 1968 and six in 1975 coincided with the two influxes of Pallas's Warblers.

Radde's Warbler

Phylloscopus schwarzi

Very rare vagrant.

The only Kent record of this Siberian species was of one trapped and ringed at Dungeness on 3rd October 1962. It was retrapped on the 7th and last seen on the 8th.

Dusky Warbler

Phylloscopus fuscatus

Very rare vagrant.

The first Kent record of this Asiatic species occurred at Dungeness between 10th–15th November 1967. It was trapped and ringed on the 11th and considered to be a first-year female. The only other record concerns one seen in Grain Moat on 30th October 1976, the same day that a Pallas's Warbler was seen at Shellness (Sheppey).

Bonelli's Warbler

Phylloscopus bonelli

Very rare vagrant.

This warbler, which breeds well to the north in France, has been recorded on only four occasions in Kent. The first was trapped at Dungeness on 2nd September 1963. The next, at Sandwich Bay between 3rd–29th June 1967, was also trapped. The other two were both at Dungeness, on 20th September 1970 and 4th September 1976.

Wood Warbler

Phylloscopus sibilatrix

Summer visitor with very local breeding distribution, and passage migrant.

Harrison considered the Wood Warbler to be an abundant summer visitor, breeding commonly in the woodlands in the west of the county, but scarce elsewhere.

The Wood Warbler is still most numerous in the west of the county, but it is very thinly distributed, even there. It favours mature woodland, particularly sessile oak, with a good canopy and sparse ground vegeta-

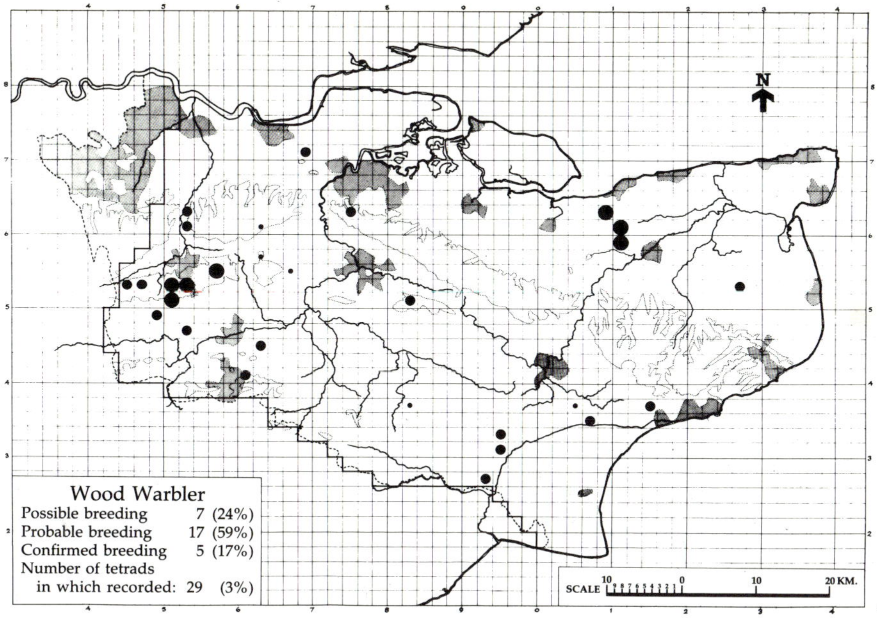

tion. It is also found in birch, chestnut coppice, and occasionally in beech along the Downs.

In addition to the localities shown on the map, there have been summering records from Lyminge Forest, on the Downs at Westwell and more widely in the Hemsted Forest area. In 1964–65 there were one–two at Northward Hill on seven dates between 8th May–7th June, but normally the Wood Warbler is a very rare visitor in north Kent.

It is possible that the Wood Warbler is overlooked, despite the distinctive and delightful song. The known breeding sites are not checked every year, but even so it is likely that the breeding population does fluctuate annually, as suggested by the accompanying histogram.

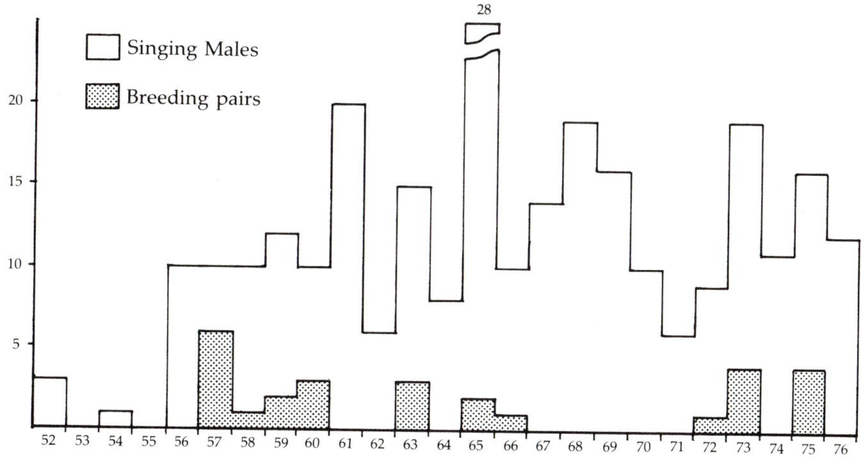

Pairs of Wood Warblers breeding and singing males

The densest populations have been recorded in the Sevenoaks area and at Tunbridge Wells, where there were nine singing males in 1975, four of which were paired and bred successfully. Apparently a number of singing males remain unpaired.

In spring the mean arrival date is 23rd April, though in some years there are no records until the second or third week of May. The earliest records are at Hythe in 1953, Luddesdown in 1959 and Ramsgate in 1961, all on 5th April. In autumn there are slightly more widespread reports from late July into September, with the latest at Hythe on 27th September 1965.

In contrast to the overall decline in breeding numbers, the numbers recorded at the two Observatories have increased quite considerably, as shown by the accompanying histogram.

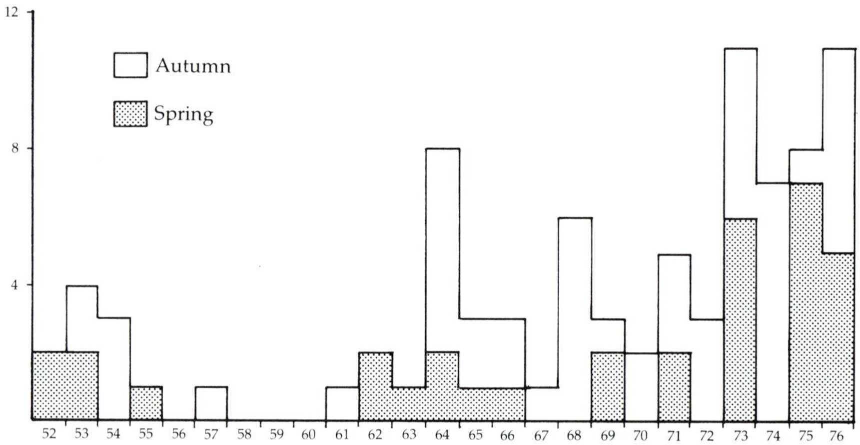

Annual totals of migrant Wood Warblers at the Observatories

At Dungeness 22 have been recorded in spring between 18th April–18th May, with 12 at Sandwich Bay, rather later, between 25th April–25th May. In autumn, however, there have been 28 at Sandwich Bay and 24 at Dungeness, between 18th July–19th September, with maximum autumn totals of seven and six at Sandwich Bay in 1974 and 1976 respectively.

Chiffchaff

Phylloscopus collybita

Summer visitor and passage migrant, wintering in small numbers.

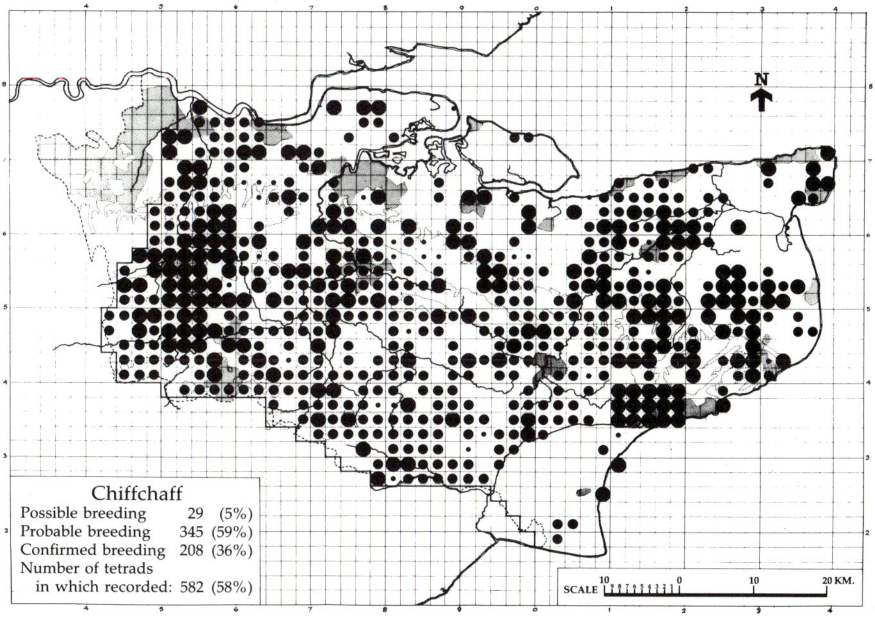

The Chiffchaff is rather more exacting in its ecological requirement than the Willow Warbler, needing tall trees as song posts, and for this reason is very local in comparatively treeless districts, especially around Thanet and Stourmouth, on Romney Marsh and Sheppey. Some of the inland gaps are probably due more to poor coverage during the survey than genuine absence. Although almost as widespread throughout the county, it is never as numerous as the Willow Warbler.

The earliest spring dates are confused by the presence of over-wintering birds, but the mean arrival date is around 11th March and by the third week of March numbers are increasing rapidly. The peak falls at Dungeness were 100 on 18th April 1975, and 75 as early as 26th March 1958, but 20–50 is more usual.

The main autumn departure occurs during September and early October. Large falls have occurred at the Observatories and elsewhere on the coast at this time. At Dungeness autumn peaks of 50–150 are quite usual between 6th September–4th October, with exceptional totals of 500 on 11th September 1956 and 600 on 21st September 1967. In 1976, after the long hot summer, there were 300 on 27th September and a further 200 as late as 19th October. At Sandwich Bay peaks of 40–80 are normal, with a maximum of 150, also on 21st September 1967. Stragglers are frequently recorded into late November and occasionally into December.

It is difficult to ascertain the numbers overwintering, but there have been fairly regular reports since 1960, frequently of birds foraging in low vegetation and reed beds. The number of records is as follows:

J	F	M	A	M	J	J	A	S	O	N	D
20	28										49

A proportion of the December records, particularly at the Observatories, refer to late migrants. There have been very few reports of individual birds remaining at one site throughout the three months, with the notable exception of singles at New Hythe/Leybourne in 1974/75, 1975/76 and 1976/77. A record of at least four nearby at Eccles on 4th February 1971 is also exceptional.

Ringing recoveries reveal a northwest/southeast orientation of migrants within the British Isles. Several recoveries in Spain confirm the southwest movement from Kent in autumn, notably singles ringed at Dungeness on 28th September 1959, recovered near Lograno in north Spain on 11th October, and at Stockbury on 29th August 1962, recovered near Cadiz on 23rd October. A Chiffchaff ringed at Dungeness on 17th October 1969 was recovered in Norway on 14th May 1970.

Birds showing the plumage characteristics of both northern races, *P.c. abietinus* and *P.c. tristis*, have been recorded, primarily at the Observatories. There were two at Dungeness on 3rd April 1965 resembling *abietinus*, but all the others occurred between 30th September–18th January. The monthly distribution is as follows:

J	F	M	A	M	J	J	A	S	O	N	D
2			2					1	7	10	7

Willow Warbler

Phylloscopus trochilus

Abundant summer visitor and passage migrant.

The Willow Warbler is widely distributed, breeding wherever there is open woodland, or in bushy areas with small trees. It is relatively scarce on Thanet, Romney Marsh and Sheppey, all localities without much bushy cover. Many of the inland gaps on the map probably indicate poor coverage rather than absence.

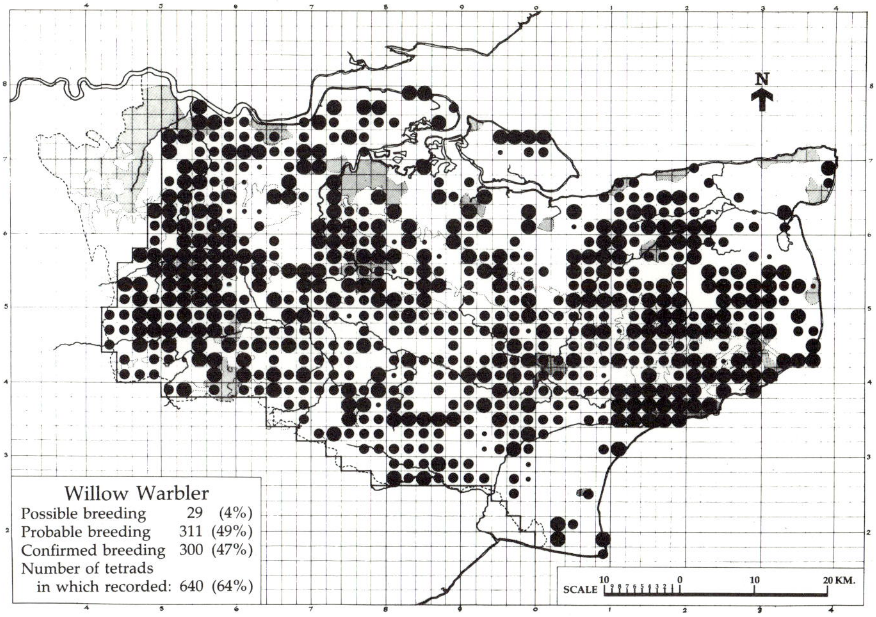

There are two exceptionally early spring dates. One at Northward Hill on 1st March 1961 was seen well and heard singing, while on 10th March 1952 seven were seen at Sandwich and one at Lydd. Otherwise the first arrival dates have occurred between 20th March–5th April, with the mean around 28th March. It is usually mid-April before the main arrival takes place, when woods and parkland become alive with Willow Warblers. Large spring falls are occasionally recorded at Dungeness, with over 1,000 in the trapping area there on 13th April 1955 and 450 on the same date in 1972. In 1975 the peak numbers were later, with 300 on 11th May and 250 on the 18th. An analysis of the ringing data shows that males appear to precede females by as much as two weeks.

Emigration begins in late July and is mainly complete by the end of September, though stragglers may be seen until late October in most years, with the latest at Sandwich Bay on 24th November 1968. Peak numbers at the Observatories include 300 at Dungeness on 11th August 1975 and 175 at Sandwich Bay on 15th September 1968.

The results of ringing show the normal southwest orientation of passage birds in autumn, with singles ringed at Sandwich Bay on 16th August 1953 recovered near Avila in Spain on 31st, and at Dungeness on 5th September 1954 found near Bordeaux a fortnight later. Other recoveries relate to birds breeding in Scotland or northern England and passing through Kent on migration. A first-year bird ringed at Arnhem in the Netherlands on 18th August 1973 was retrapped at Dungeness on 19th May 1975.

An indication of the abundance of this species is shown by the numbers ringed, as with 13,111 at Dungeness and 4,247 at Sandwich

Bay between 1952–76 it is the most frequently ringed species at both Observatories.

Birds of the Northern race *P.t. acredula* are recorded annually at the Observatories, generally towards the end of each passage, in May and September. Some nesting in Scotland show *acredula* characteristics and it is of interest to note that a pair in Chattenden Woods between 16th–22nd June 1963, and one carrying food at Northward Hill on 28th May 1968, also showed some characteristics of this race.

Goldcrest

Regulus regulus

Widespread breeding species and passage migrant.

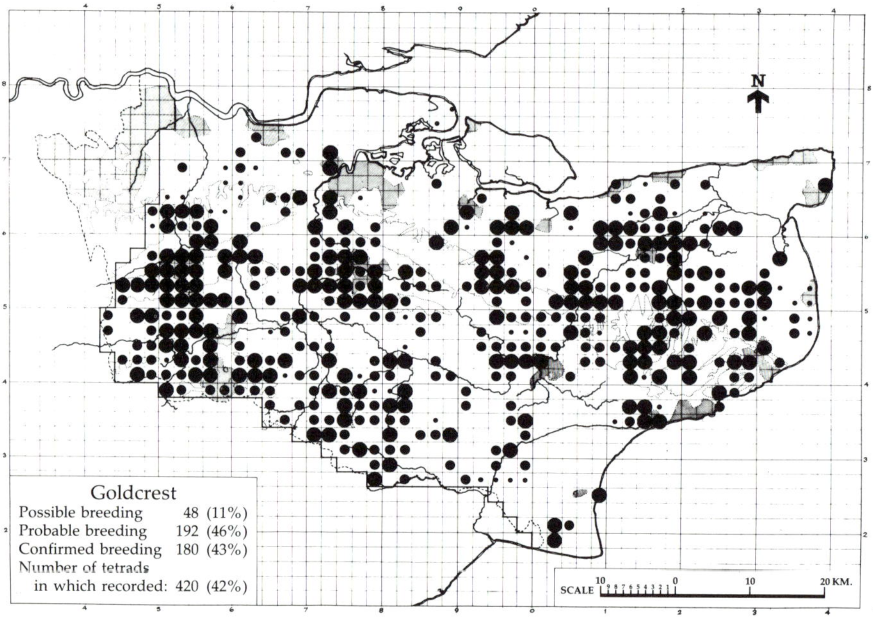

The Goldcrest is well distributed as a breeding species and can be expected wherever there are conifers. Not surprisingly it is virtually absent from North Kent Marshes, Thanet and much of Romney Marsh. There is little information on population levels, but in May 1975 there were 100 singing males in Lyminge Forest.

The numbers of this species show marked fluctuations and may be severely depleted during hard winters. A comparison of the Dungeness figures for 1962 and 1963 clearly shows the effect of the intervening savage winter.

	Spring			Autumn		
	Peak	Bird/days	Ringed	Peak	Bird/days	Ringed
1962	200	244	32	300	1067	172
1963	1	2	0	9	49	7

Kentish Common Birds Census figures reflect the national pattern of a steady increase following this severe winter. On one woodland plot there were still none in 1966, two pairs in 1969 and eight pairs by 1973.

Away from the Observatories Goldcrests are rarely systematically recorded, often occurring in only small numbers. Although overwintering regularly, there are few significant records for December–February, the highest counts being 60 in Lydd Woods in January and February 1969, and 200 on Hosey Common (Brasted) in December 1965.

This species is most widespread and common during autumn passage, particularly in October. Coastal peaks of 100 or more have been recorded between 29th September–9th November, and large falls have occurred along the north coast between Shellness and Thanet, and on the east coast at St. Margaret's, as well as at the two Observatories. At Sandwich Bay 500 were ringed between 4th–6th October 1959, while in 1962 there were peaks of 250 there and 300 at Dungeness on 22nd–23rd October. However, the largest single influx occurred in October 1975, with 600 each at Dungeness and Sandwich Bay, 250 at Shellness and 100 each at Broadstairs and Bishopstone on the 10th–11th, with a further influx of 750 at Dungeness on the 14th. Increased numbers were also noted elsewhere round the coast and at a number of inland localities.

Spring passage is recorded annually at the Observatories and is most evident during March and April, with birds present into early May in some years. Peak numbers usually involve day-totals of less than 50 birds, but include estimates of 200 at Dungeness on 11th April 1962, at Sandwich Bay on 16th April 1967, and again at Dungeness on 29th March 1976.

For such a small bird there is a surprising number of ringing recoveries. The majority show the origins of our autumn migrants, with six retrapped at the Observatories or High Halstow within two weeks of being ringed in Poland, East Germany, Norway, the Low Countries and Norfolk. One ringed at Sandwich Bay on 2nd November 1975 was recovered in the Netherlands eight days later, another ringed at Sandwich Bay in October 1966 was controlled on Bardsey the following April, while one ringed at Dungeness in October 1973 was retrapped in Poland the following September. In spring a returning migrant, ringed in France in November, was retrapped at Lydd in March, while one ringed at Sandwich Bay in April was retrapped six weeks later in Lincolnshire.

Firecrest

Regulus ignicapillus

Regular passage migrant, now wintering regularly. Has bred.

Ticehurst regarded the Firecrest as a regular autumn visitor, particularly to the east and south coasts, but rare in spring. Harrison was able to add a few winter and inland records, but Gillham and Homes found none for north Kent since the turn of the century. Clearly it was a regular autumn visitor, but infrequent at other times.

During the period under review spring passage has been recorded at the Observatories between early March and early May, with occasional records up to 1st June. The peak numbers occur in the last two weeks of March, with counts of up to 18 and a maximum of 25 at Dungeness on 23rd March 1972. Smaller numbers occur during April, while there was a late peak of 15 on 3rd May 1972. Singles have occasionally been recorded inland in spring, with a general increase during the 1970s.

The possibility of breeding first became evident in the early 1970s, when single males were occasionally heard singing in May. In 1975 there was an exceptional influx and 36 singing birds were found in mature conifer plantations in Lyminge Forest. Three singing birds were also discovered at Bedgebury, where one pair bred successfully.

Autumn passage is most evident at the Observatories between mid-September and mid-November, with occasional records elsewhere around the coast during the same period. One at Dungeness on 28th August 1959 is the earliest, with counts of up to seven in early September. Although small peaks may occur in late September and early October, the highest numbers have occurred at Dungeness in the last two weeks of October and the first week of November, with regular day-totals of 20–30 and a maximum of 70 on 1st November 1974. At Sandwich Bay the highest total was 20 on 25th October 1968. Passage continues to the end of November in many years, although this timing has recently become confused by wintering birds.

Wintering birds are most commonly recorded at Dungeness, with up to six there in most winters since 1967/68. Elsewhere they occur only singly, usually at scattered inland localities.

In contrast to the Goldcrest, ringing recoveries are few, despite the fact that over a quarter of the 1,700 Firecrests ringed in Britain up to 1976 had been trapped at Dungeness. The only Kentish recovery is of a bird ringed at Dungeness on 31st October 1967 which was retrapped in Spain exactly two months later.

Spotted Flycatcher

Muscicapa striata

Widespread summer visitor and passage migrant.

Ticehurst described the Spotted Flycatcher as evenly distributed throughout the county, being more numerous in wooded districts. Harrison considered that there had been no change in the status of this 'abundant' summer visitor, and apart from some slight query on the measure of abundance, much the same seems true of the period under review.

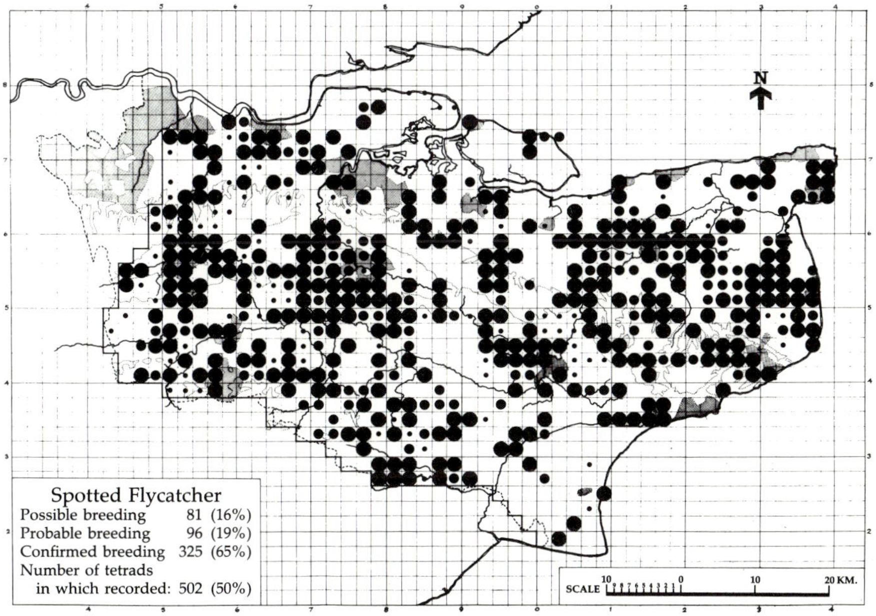

The Spotted Flycatcher is widely distributed as a breeding species through the county, especially in well-wooded areas, and is lacking or difficult to record from largely treeless expanses of marsh or farmland, from areas of climatic exposure, particularly to wind, like the crest of the North Downs, and from heavily built-up urban centres.

Ticehurst considered the Spotted Flycatcher one of the last migrants to arrive, and the same is true today. In many years the first would not be expected until early May. The earliest arrivals have been recorded between 14th April–10th May, with the mean around 29th April. Spring passage is generally light, with day-totals in excess of ten at the

Observatories unusual, but there were 50 at Dungeness on 20th May 1973 and a quite exceptional fall of 300 there on 18th May 1975.

Surprisingly, on autumn passage, which is normally heavier than in spring, the Spotted Flycatcher is rarely as numerous as the Pied. Migration usually starts in mid-August and continues into October. Peak days at the Observatories involve 10–15 birds, and a maximum of 30 at Dungeness on 27th September 1975 was unusual. Last dates usually occur in October, up to the 20th, with the latest during the period under review at Sandwich Bay on 26th October 1969. However, Hudson (1973) notes two later dates, one on 31st October 1911 and another at Littlestone on 3rd November 1951.

Migrants ringed on passage at the Observatories have been recovered during the breeding season in places as widely separate as Northern Ireland, the Outer Hebrides and Berkshire. A Dungeness-ringed migrant was recovered in Spain later in the autumn, and a breeding bird from Betteshanger was recovered in Arles, in southern France, in late September of the same year. One ringed as an adult in July 1960 at Cliffe was retrapped, alive and well, seven years later at High Halstow, an unusual life-span for so small a long-range migrant.

Red-breasted Flycatcher

Ficedula parva

Regular but scarce autumn migrant, very rare in spring.

The first for the county, in 1943, is documented by Harrison and was seen at Medhurst Row (Bough Beech) on the relatively unusual date of 8th May. Harrison also notes a single bird at Brookland and two together at Herne Bay in September 1951.

During the 25 years under review the Red-breasted Flycatcher has gradually established itself as a regular migrant of almost annual autumn occurrence, with 45 individuals between 22nd August–1st November, which are tabulated as follows:

August	September		October		November
15–28	29–11	12–25	26–9	10–23	24–6
3	6	4	15	12	5

There have also been three spring records at the Observatories between 11th–19th May, and one on the most unusual date of 18th July

1974, near Westerham. This last is one of only four inland birds, with another at East Malling in 1959 and two at Trottiscliffe in 1968. The great majority of autumn records come from the Observatories, with 16 at Sandwich Bay and 17 at Dungeness. Elsewhere round the coast singles have been seen on six occasions between Allhallows and Seasalter, twice on Thanet and once at Aycliffe. Most records refer to single dates, but individuals have occasionally remained for up to four days.

Pied Flycatcher

Ficedula hypoleuca

Passage migrant, more numerous in autumn than in spring.

Ticehurst wrote that previously the Pied Flycatcher was infrequent in occurrence, but considered that by the turn of the century there could be no doubt that it was a regular migrant in spring and autumn.

As in Ticehurst's day spring records are relatively few, with only singles in some years and a maximum total of 24 in 1975. Passage has been recorded between 6th April–4th June, with the mean first arrival date around 20th April. Most occur along the south and east coasts, with peaks of four at Kingsgate on 27th April 1953, six at Sandwich Bay on 8th May 1955, and three at Dungeness on 7th and 15th May 1965.

Midsummer records are very rare, with a male inland near Canterbury on 28th June 1967, and singles at Kingsgate on 28th June 1956 and Sandwich Bay on 17th July 1974.

Autumn migration is much more marked and although most reports are coastal, each year a few individuals are reported from widely scattered inland localities. Passage has started as early as 29th July, with the first records usually in early August. Large arrivals of 30–75 birds have been recorded at the Observatories in most years between 10th August–5th September, and occasionally as late as 30th September. Such numbers can also occur elsewhere round the coast and the most widespread and largest falls took place between 2nd–4th September 1961, when there were up to 33 at Warden, 38 at Reculver and 40 at Sandwich Bay; and on 10th August 1968, when there were 43 at Sandwich Bay, 30 at Folkestone and 60 at Dungeness. Last dates usually occur in October, up to the 25th, with a very late bird at Cooling on 6th November 1964.

One ringed at Dungeness late in August 1960 was recovered in Spain less than two weeks later, and one ringed at Margate on 3rd May 1972 was retrapped at Riding Mill, 455 km to the northwest in Northumberland, on 3rd June. Riding Mill is well to the east of the Pied Flycatcher's British breeding range, so presumably this bird was making for Scandinavia.

Bearded Tit

Panurus biarmicus

Local resident, passage migrant and winter visitor.

Bearded Tits bred on the North Kent Marshes and perhaps on Romney Marsh in the eighteenth century, but declined during the nineteenth century, with very few recorded after 1865. Although records in general remained sparse until the 1940s, up to six pairs bred again on the Halstow Marshes between 1905–12. During the winter of 1941/42 over 100 were present at Cottington Court (Deal), but they left in March. However, a small colony re-established itself in the area, only to be wiped out in the 1947 winter.

The first record for the period under review was in 1959 when a male was present at Northfleet from 13th December. There were several records in 1960, including one breeding pair, and again in 1961, with at least four pairs at three sites in north Kent, plus wintering individuals at Sevenoaks and Stodmarsh. In 1962 at least five pairs bred at Stodmarsh and two in north Kent. In spite of the hard winter in 1962/63, the minute population survived, some even feeding on kale, and seven pairs bred in 1963. The breeding population has risen steadily, with peaks of about 70 pairs in 1965 and 100 pairs in 1975. Since the early sixties, Kent has held 10–20% of the British breeding population.

The main stronghold is in the Stour Valley, in the large *Phragmites* reed beds between Stodmarsh and Westbere, but population estimates are incomplete. In 1965 and again in 1975 systematic counts produced 60 and 80 pairs respectively. In north Kent the population has fluctuated considerably as a result of habitat changes, but on the Thames marshes there was an encouraging peak of 17 pairs in 1976. The only breeding record from Romney Marsh concerns one pair in 1967. The flooding of coastal reed beds by salt water and infilling at the important Murston site, where the numbers dropped from a peak of 28 pairs in 1974 to only five in 1976, and at Cottington, where up to seven pairs have bred, have been particularly detrimental.

The population reaches a maximum in August–September and there is usually some irruptive behaviour and emigration from the breeding sites in October. Small parties get restless and rise high in the air, calling persistently, but the numbers involved vary from year to year depending on the success of the breeding season. Occasionally numbers at Stodmarsh reach 200. In October–November, and to a lesser extent in March–April, there are more widespread reports, along river valleys, in gravel pits and small, isolated reed beds throughout the county.

Small numbers are also recorded regularly from coastal sites in autumn, suggesting arrival from the Continent, and a few have actually been seen coming in off the sea. At this season and during the winter months they may be found in a variety of other marshland vegetation, including *Salix* scrub, reed mace and willowherb. Migrant parties have also occurred in winter cereals and even in woodland at some distance from water. Small numbers also winter inland in Kent, particularly in the reed beds at Burham. The winter population in the breeding areas may be as low as 10% of the peak autumn numbers.

Ringing recoveries, particularly of Murston birds, show that up to 75% move over 100 km, mainly into East Anglia or southwest, with the most distant to Plymouth, 340 km WSW. Another, ringed in its winter quarters at Burham on 21st November 1964, was retrapped on the island of Heligoland on 22nd March 1967. There is considerable loyalty to breeding sites and six birds handled at Murston during one breeding season and retrapped elsewhere during the autumn and winter have since returned to Murston in subsequent breeding seasons.

The Kent population now seems large enough to survive the natural hazards of occasional hard winters, and as long as suitable breeding habitat is maintained safe from human destruction, Bearded Tits should continue to thrive.

Long-tailed Tit

Aegithalos caudatus

Common resident. Scarce and irregular passage migrant.

Primarily a bird of scrub, Long-tailed Tits are well able to thrive in most Kentish woodlands with a dense understorey, on downland, and on farmland where adequate hedges remain. By virtue of this habitat preference, they are also able to capitalise on man-made areas with dense vegetation following derelictions, such as chalk pits and sand or ballast workings. Thus it is not surprising that they are widespread as a breeding bird.

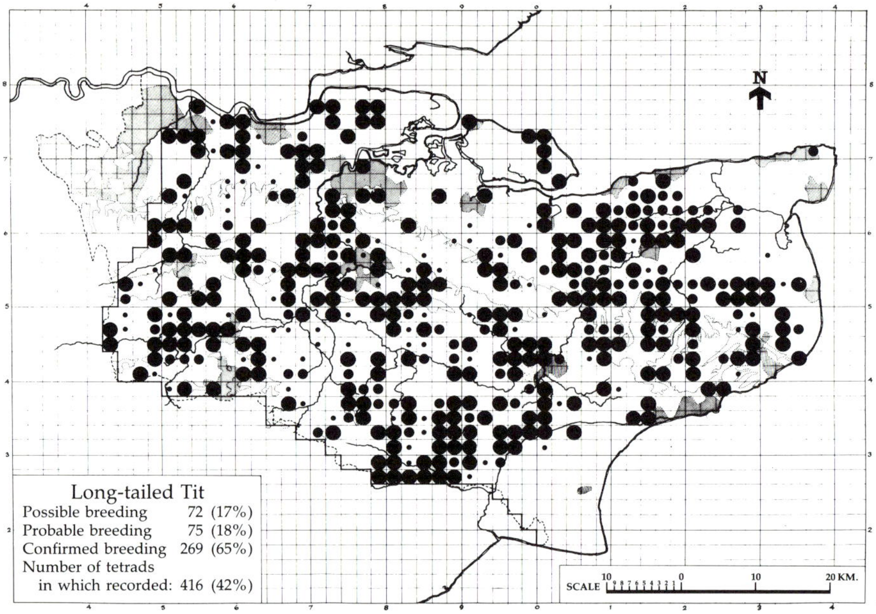

The lack of records from areas of apparently suitable downland is probably more a reflection of the difficulties of survey than an indication of absence, but the remaining sparsely populated areas of the North Kent Marshes, Thanet and Romney Marsh have long been so. Even Prentis writing in 1894 about Rainham marshes could only remark that they were 'once common' there, and Gillham and Homes traced only a single record for Sheppey.

Locally and nationally Long-tailed Tit numbers may vary greatly from year to year, the fluctuations generally caused by a susceptibility to severe winters when mortality may reach 80%, although in some cases local scarcity may be due to hedgerow removal. During the period under review 1962/63 saw such a period of severe weather. In autumn 1963 the maximum flock size of the few reported was 12 birds, against the many reports of 30–50 birds together in normal years. Signs of recovery were apparent as early as 1964, and records increased steadily to roughly present-day levels by 1970. Even in winter the Isle of Grain, Sheppey, Thanet and Romney Marsh are areas where flocks are the exception rather than the rule.

At the Observatories the situation also seems to be changeable. With the exception of some birds caught up with other species in the massive tit invasion from the Continent in autumn 1957, Long-tailed Tits were scarce vagrants at both Dungeness and Sandwich Bay in the 1950s. Autumn 1960 saw 37 at Dungeness against the 1952–59 grand total of 24, but thereafter they became so scarce again that two in September 1967 were the first recorded since 1964. More recently, autumn and winter flocks seem again to be a regular feature, and 10 were watched arriving high off the sea at Sandwich in November 1974. Further evidence of Continental immigration comes from three records of white-headed birds *A.c. caudatus*: two at Folkestone on 31st March 1960, one at Warden on 16th March 1963 and 12 at Ham Green on 24th October 1967.

Ringing recoveries show an interesting picture of a local wanderer rather than sedentary resident, with flocks commuting, close-knit, over several kilometres. Two longer-distance recoveries are from High Halstow in January 1968 to Walton, Surrey 65 km west in April 1969, and from Cliffe Woods in September 1970 to Leeds (Maidstone) 25 km south-southeast in January 1971.

Marsh Tit

Parus palustris

Widespread, but rarely numerous resident.

Ticehurst considered the Marsh Tit of rather more local distribution than either the Blue or Great Tit, but in the Weald he thought it by far the most numerous tit in the heart of woodland. He found it less common in the east, absent from Thanet, and rather less abundant north of the Downs. Harrison noted little change, but cited a few records from the Grain peninsula and one from Sheppey.

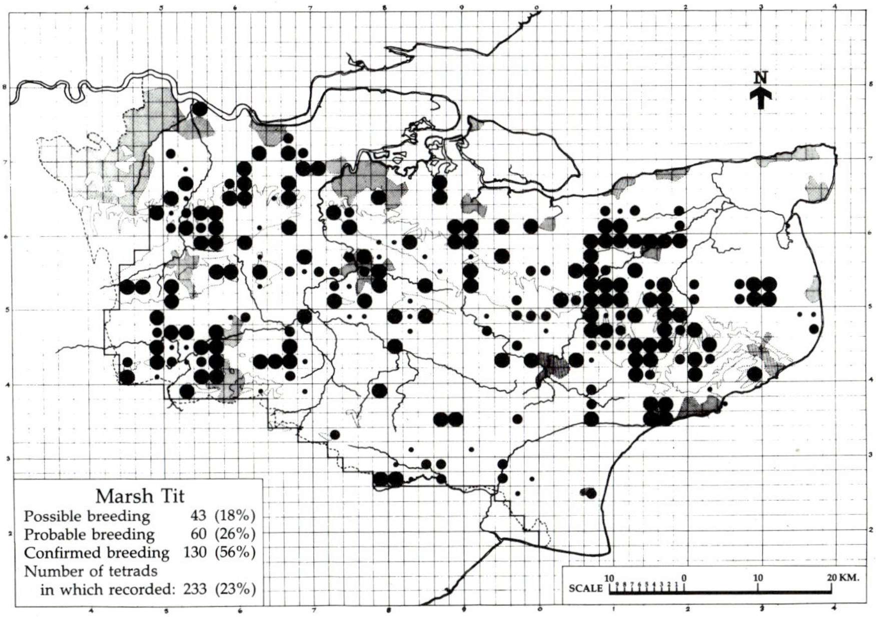

Records during the period under review were thinly scattered, but also included a few reports from Northward Hill, on the Grain peninsula, in the late fifties and mid-sixties.

The difficulties of separating Marsh and Willow Tits are emphasised in the notes on the latter species and some caution must still be applied when comparing the two maps because of the possibilities of confusion, even though calls and song are most likely to be heard during the breeding season. The Breeding Bird Survey indicates that the Marsh Tit is the more widespread, with records from 233 tetrads compared with 168 for the Willow Tit. This predominance is most noticeable in the east of the county, as the following table shows:

	Both species	Marsh Tit	Willow Tit
West Kent tetrads	22%	46%	32%
Central Kent tetrads	19%	38%	43%
East Kent tetrads	14%	72%	14%
All tetrads	19%	50%	31%

Marsh Tits seem to be most concentrated along the chalk land of the Downs, especially east of Ashford, and in the Weald west of Tunbridge Wells, with a thin distribution along the three river valleys and their tributaries. This corresponds only in part with this species' stated preference for drier habitats and deciduous woodland (Sharrock, 1976).

As might be expected of a sedentary species, reports from coastal areas are few. The only Observatory records concern singles at Sandwich Bay on 16th September 1961 and 8th September 1966, and at Dungeness on 7th October 1968.

Willow Tit

Parus montanus

Widespread, but thinly distributed resident.

Since the 'discovery' of the Willow Tit in Britain by Hartert in 1897, the separation of this species and the closely related Marsh Tit has continued to tax the abilities of birdwatchers. In the field, and even in the hand, no one character can guarantee separation, except for call or song. The most commonly used features are all subjective and vulnerable to the vagaries of weather, light and time of year.

Not surprisingly, Ticehurst thought the Willow Tit 'somewhat rare', and mentions Tunbridge Wells, Biddenden, Speldhurst and Faversham as localities where it occurred. Harrison recorded surprisingly few and suggested that the Willow Tit was much more selective than the Marsh

Tit, preferring damp, old woodland. He considered the population most abundant in west and central Kent and the bird absent from the east and southeast of the county.

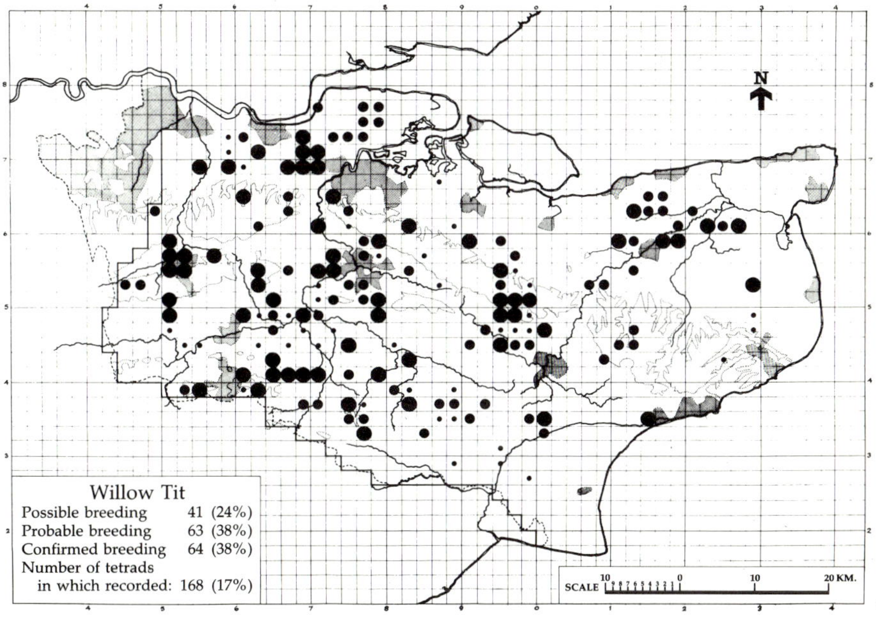

The Breeding Bird Survey suggests that the distribution is much the same as in Harrison's day, though reports are more numerous, with a concentration on the heavier soils of the Weald and to the east in the Stour Valley. The Willow Tit also occurs more regularly in the woods on the Grain peninsula, where the Marsh Tit is only rarely recorded, though in the main the distribution does bear out the stated preference for damper woods and river valleys (Sharrock, 1976).

Ringing recoveries show that the Willow Tit is sedentary in the county, and the few coastal reports include singles at the Wicks on 9th October 1966 and at Sandwich Bay on 22nd August 1968 and 11th September 1973. The August bird at Sandwich Bay was trapped and thought to be of the race *P.m. rhenanus* from west-central Europe. One at Dungeness in October–November 1968 and March–April 1969 may have wintered, while another occurred there on 29th May 1975.

Coal Tit

Parus ater

Widespread but rarely numerous resident. Irregular passage migrant.

'About as numerous as Marsh Tit' was Ticehurst's comment, adding that Coal Tits were locally plentiful in conifers and orchards. He considered them decidely more common on the Weald than north of the Downs, where they were the least numerous tit of all, a statement echoed by Gillham and Homes. Harrison considered Coal Tits to be common residents in suitable districts, particularly in the west of the county.

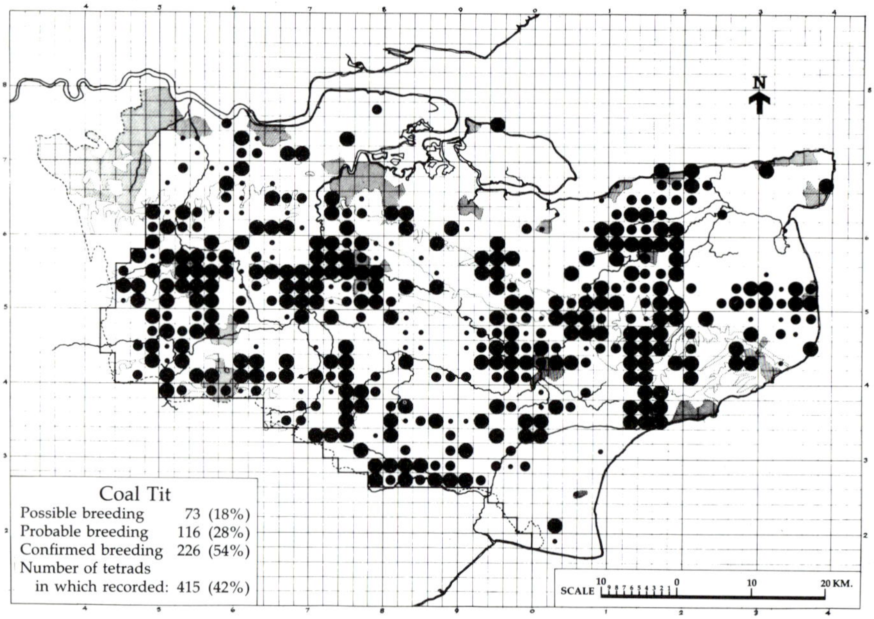

It would certainly seem that there has been little change in the Coal Tit breeding distribution with plentiful records on a broad axis east–west through the county, including the Downs. The North Kent Marshes, Thanet, the Stour Marshes and Romney Marsh are still the main areas of absence of breeding birds. It may be that since Harrison's time breeding numbers have been reduced, despite the coming towards maturity of many of the county's conifer plantations, and this suggestion is endorsed by the paucity of breeding records in 1975 and 1976.

Ticehurst could find no references to birds of the Continental race *P.a. ater*, but Harrison documents several from coastal areas in autumn. Fortunately *P.a. ater* is reasonably easy to separate from the British race, even in the field, because of its clear blue-grey back and mantle, lacking any trace of olive. In most autumns of the period under review there were at least a few records of birds with 'continental' plumage characteristics, usually on the coast at Dungeness and Sandwich Bay. Mostly these involve only individuals or small parties, but movement was greater in 1959, 1969, 1971 and 1972 when peaks of 10–20 were reported from the two Observatories on various dates between 21st September–28th October.

By far the greatest influx occurred in 1957, as was the case with Blue and Great Tits, and involved several coastal and inland localities. The immigration spanned 14th September–31st October, and was most noticeable around Thanet in late September, when a total of 28 flew northwest past Sandwich Bay between 20th–27th September. At Dungeness there was a peak of 40 on 6th October, while inland a flock of 30 flew west at Wye on 25th October. Most of the birds involved were considered to be of the Continental race, including 18 trapped at Dungeness between 6th–13th October.

The first spring passage record was of five at Dungeness, again Continental birds, on 2nd April 1960, and there have been occasional records of smaller numbers since at the Observatories.

Coal Tits suffered severely in the hard winter of 1962/63. Small parties were reported foraging in many gardens during the winter, and breeding numbers in 1963 were reduced, but not apparently, as drastically as Long-tailed Tits, as in most areas a few pairs could be found. A considerable recovery was reported in 1964.

Blue Tit

Parus caeruleus

Common resident. Passage migrant in variable numbers.

Although ancestrally forest canopy birds, Blue Tits continue to adapt to the changes wrought by man on the landscape. This includes the exploitation of farmland and gardens for feeding and the use of man-made nest sites, sometimes unintentionally provided, but often deliberately in the form of nestboxes. As breeding birds they are widely

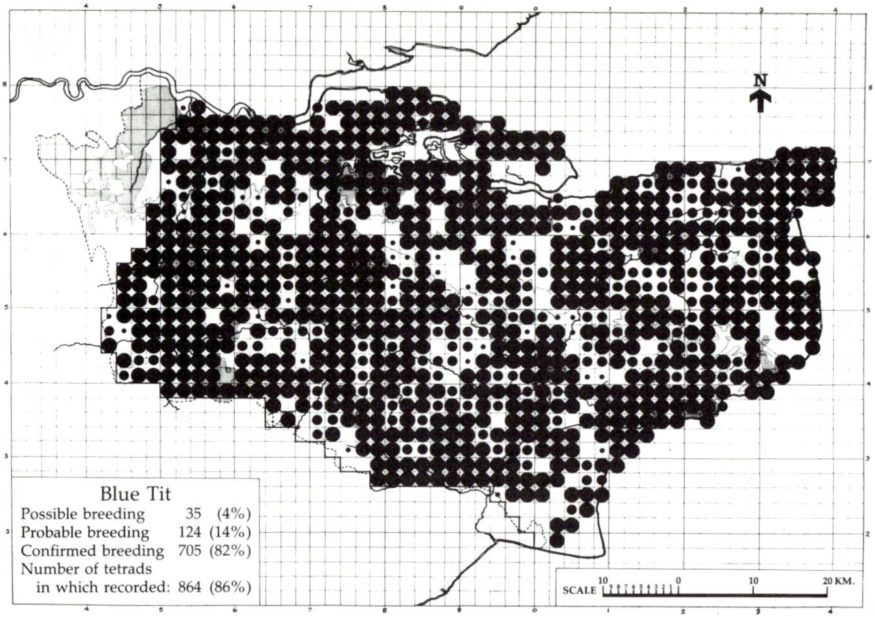

distributed and numerous in many habitats, with records not unexpectedly lacking only from the marshland adjacent to the Thames and Swale, and on Romney Marsh. This situation does not seem to have changed over the last 100 years, and only in 1963 was any real diminution of breeding numbers recorded following the severe winter, and it seems that normality was quickly restored thereafter.

In winter foraging individuals or parties penetrate even the marshland areas, seeking food in the reedbeds, e.g. 40 at Stodmarsh on 5th November 1968 and 65 there during January 1971. Ticehurst regarded a similar movement to overwinter in the marshes as a regular October feature.

The actual numbers present in any one locality may be much higher than expected, evidenced by the 250 individuals ringed, with few retraps, in the first three months of 1961 in an East Malling garden, and by the 250 ringed at Northward Hill during October 1965. Significantly, of these Northward Hill birds, 25 trapped on 3rd October were distinctly grey in plumage and very light in weight indicating recent arrival, probably from overseas.

Each spring sees small movements, rarely of more than 25 birds daily, at the Observatories in March and April. Each autumn larger movements occur, often involving 60–100 birds, at many coastal localities. The timing of the autumn movement is very variable. In 1974 there were reports of larger numbers than usual as early as 5th August, but in general influxes occur during September and October. Some evidence for the Continental origin of these birds comes from the observation of many round the light of the Royal Sovereign light-vessel on 19th October 1952, and from birds with plumage characters and measurements of the Continental race *P.c. caeruleus* at Appledore on 2nd September 1956 and Sevenoaks in December 1963, where 26 were ringed.

Blue Tits are subject also to autumn irruptive movements, when numbers far above average are recorded, usually coastally, but often also inland, where many may remain through the winter. In varying degrees 1954, 1961, 1965 and 1974 were irruption years, including peaks of 100 at Warden Point on 7th October 1961 and 100 at Sandwich Bay on 6th October 1974. An exceptionally heavy influx of Continental origin was noted nationally in 1957, being particularly marked in Kent. Large numbers of Blue Tits were seen in all coastal areas from Lower Hope Point to Dungeness between 15th September–27th October. Up to 90 were recorded on two dates at Sandwich Bay with a peak of 800 there on 27th September, while at Dungeness there were up to 50 on several dates, with the peak of 275 on 6th October, a day when 60 flew in off the Thames at Cliffe Fleet. Several hundreds were also counted inside the sea wall at Minnis Bay on 20th October. Early in 1958 high overwintering numbers were reported from many areas inland, and the outgoing spring passage at the Observatories was heavier than usual. An indication of the origins of the birds came from two ringing recoveries: birds ringed at Dungeness on 11th October and New Romney on 12th December were recovered in spring 1958 on the Le Havre light-vessel, France and in northern Germany respectively. Although large numbers of Blue Tits are ringed in the county each year, movements over 50 km are exceptional.

Great Tit

Parus major

Common resident. Passage migrant and winter visitor in variable numbers.

Ticehurst and Harrison shared the view that the Great Tit was generally distributed throughout Kent, except in eastern and northern coastal areas, and was less numerous than the Blue Tit. Eagle Carke, quoted by Harrison, found five dead Great Tits of the Continental race *P.m.major* on the deck of the Kentish Knock light-vessel on 26th November 1903, and Harrison comments that many subsequent observations give the impression that immigration was often considerable.

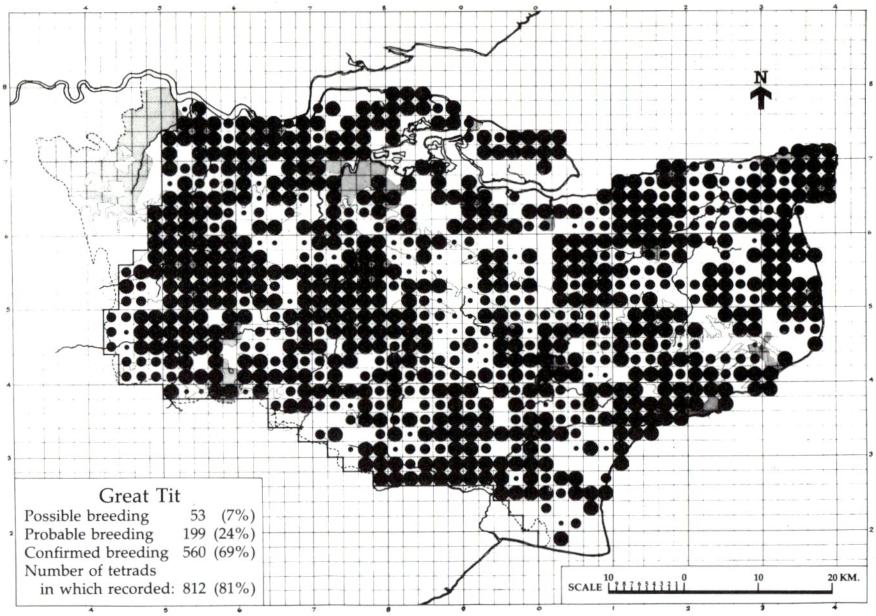

The Great Tit is obviously still well distributed and well able to exploit most natural and many man-made habitats in the county, winter and summer alike. It is a common nestbox user and a regular visitor to garden bird-tables, even in the heart of urban areas. Ticehurst refers to its habit of fruit-pecking in autumn, a harmful trait that still persists, but one that must often be offset by the good done in eating fruit pests, particularly codling moth caterpillars. The Great Tit is lacking from large, open expanses, usually of marshland, in parts of the extreme north, east and south of the county, and unlike the Blue Tit, does not often forage out into reedbed areas in search of food in winter.

In most years passage at the Observatories is very light, but includes spring peaks of 67 at Sandwich Bay on 30th March 1974 and 100 there on 27th March 1976. Similarly in autumn peaks of 30–40 have been recorded occasionally at both Observatories, mainly between 20th October–9th November, with some immigration also noted along the north coast. However, autumn 1957 and spring 1958 stand out as quite exceptional, as they do for Blue Tit and Coal Tit. The influx in 1957 was first noted at Herne Bay and Dungeness on 16th September, and continued until the end of October, with birds remaining in large numbers in some areas. Dungeness saw a peak of 50 on 6th October, and large numbers were reported with Blue Tits inside the sea wall at Minnis Bay on 20th October. Next spring heavy coastal movements of returning birds were reported between Kingsgate and Dungeness from 6th March until 19th April. Maximum counts involved 70 at Dungeness and 64 ringed at Littlestone on 29th March, 100 coasting northeast at St. Margaret's on

30th March, 30 at Sandwich Bay on 7th April, and 30 trapped at Kingsgate between 12th–19th April. Ringing recoveries from this period included one ringed at Dungeness on the peak date of 29th March, which was recovered the next day in the department of Somme, France.

There has been a total of 11 foreign ringing recoveries, involving Germany, Holland, Belgium and France. More spectacular movements concern one ringed in Kent in January 1974 recovered in Poland during 1975, and one ringed in the USSR in September 1975 recovered in Kent in March 1976.

Nuthatch

Sitta europaea

Resident, but patchily distributed. Locally common.

Ticehurst considered the Nuthatch to be fairly numerous in mature woodland, orchards and parkland, but less common in east Kent, scarce on Sheppey and unknown in Thanet. He commented that it was abundant on the Sussex borders. Harrison gave much the same impression, stressing the abundance in west and northwest Kent, and indicating that, unlike Treecreepers, Nuthatches need seeds and nuts, not insects. Thus the type and age of tree is important, mature oak, beech and hazel being favoured.

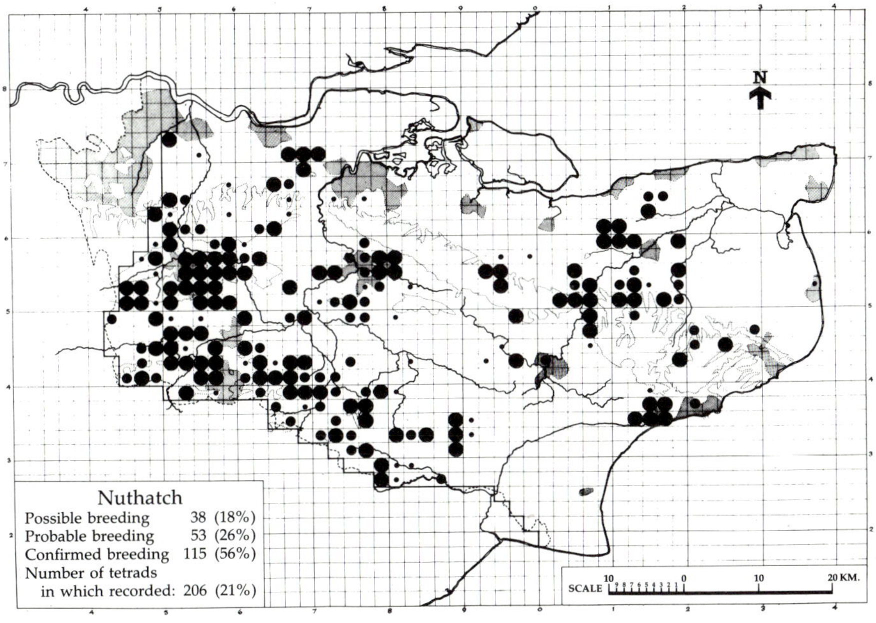

Much the same is still true of the Nuthatch breeding distribution, although no longer can it be called abundant in northwest Kent. The stronghold near the Kent/Sussex border is clearly apparent on the map. The Nuthatch is very much a bird of woods and parks with mature broad-leaved trees, versatile in that it regularly visits nearby gardens and feeding tables in winter, but apparently nowhere near so catholic in its habitat choice as it is on the Continent. In Kent it is surprisingly absent from many apparently suitable areas, and as the Nuthatch is both conspicuous and noisy during its display period in spring, this is unlikely to be the product of under-recording. Sharrock (1976) comments on the patchy distribution of the Nuthatch throughout Britain.

It is unclear what the limiting factors are. Food and nest-sites seem readily available, and nestboxes are commonly used. Nuthatches seem generally dominant if there is inter-specific competition for a nest, and once established, secure their 'home' by plastering round the entrance and any cracks with mud.

The first breeding on the North Kent Marshes was recorded when a pair nested at Murston in 1954, and one driven indoors by a storm to roost overnight on a coat-peg in Ramsgate on 22nd October 1955 was noted as one of the few records for Thanet. In 1961 it was thought that breeding had occurred in Trenley Park in east Kent, and by 1963 a considerable increase was recorded in breeding numbers there, and at Thornden and Church Woods. In 1964 a pair bred near Tenterden, and since then there have been a few breeding records from south Kent.

Nuthatches are sedentary birds, borne out by a handful of local ringing recoveries, and by several long series of retraps at particular sites. Thus the autumn and winter distribution closely resembles that of the breeding season. Interestingly, in contrast to the Treecreeper, Nuthatches survived the 1962/63 severe winter apparently undiminished, doubtless because of the continued availability of their vegetable food.

Treecreeper

Certhia familiaris

Widespread resident. Perhaps irregular migrant.

Both Ticehurst and Harrison considered Treecreepers to be generally distributed, but nowhere numerous, and less common in Thanet, north Kent and the open areas of Romney Marsh.

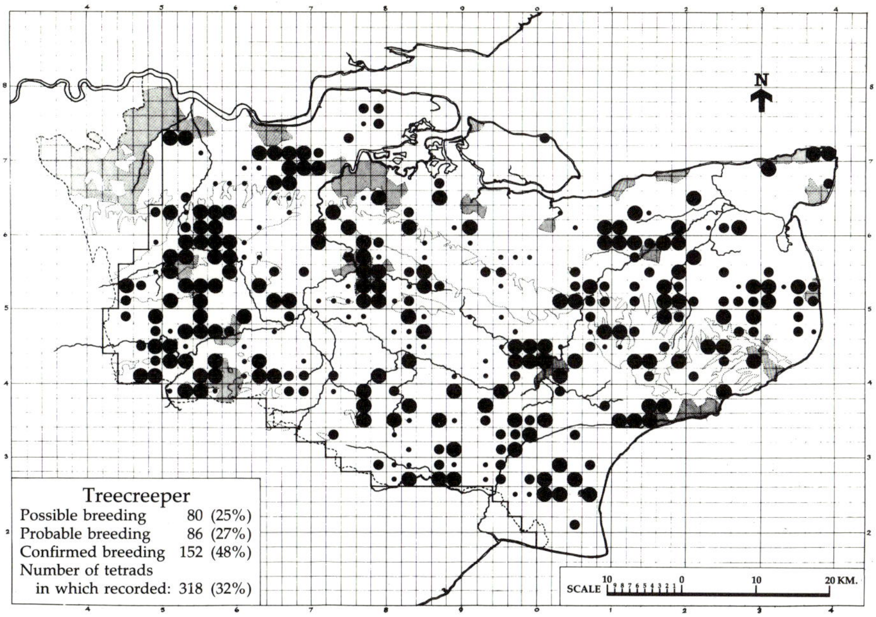

The Breeding Bird Survey clearly shows little change in this distribution, and as the county ringing results show the Treecreeper to be of a sedentary nature, much the same applies to the distribution throughout the year. The map also indicates that this species is much more versatile in its choice of habitat than the Nuthatch, even though its habit of remaining well-concealed on tree-trunks, and its briefly-uttered song, may lead to a general under-recording.

In winter they make use of shallow concavities excavated in the soft fibrous bark of *Wellingtonias* as traditional roost sites. This habit has been recorded at East Malling and in Mote Park, and doubtless occurs elsewhere.

Treecreepers apparently suffered considerable losses during the 1962/63 severe winter, and in 1963 there were widespread comments on its absence. However, in 1964 a general recovery was noted and in March 1965 there was a surprisingly high count of 16 males in song at Northward Hill, more than twice the normal population there.

Coastal records are most unusual. One was seen at Shellness, accompanying an influx of Goldcrests on 29th September 1958. The first Sandwich Bay record was on 12th August 1960, and there have been five autumn and winter records and one in spring since. At Dungeness the first on 10th October 1957 was thought to be either of the Scandinavian race *C.f. familiaris* or the Continental race *C.f. macrodactyla*. More recently, there were singles in October 1969 and August 1971.

Short-toed Treecreeper

Certhia brachydactyla

Very rare vagrant.

One trapped at Dungeness on 27th September, and retrapped there on 30th September 1969, has after much research been accepted as the first British record of this species. Further singles, trapped at Worth on 26th September 1973 and nearby Sandwich Bay on 4th April 1974, have also been accepted as belonging to this species.

Golden Oriole

Oriolus oriolus

Annual but scarce spring visitor, now breeding again in small numbers.

Ticehurst describes the Golden Oriole as a regular summer visitor between 1834–1909, with most records from east Kent or the Weald. Breeding was proved in seventeen years, most regularly at Elmstone and Dumpton Park, and probably occurred more frequently. Harrison could find only one record, in 1932, indicating an unexplained scarcity until the forties. Between 1939–51 there were about twenty records, including probable breeding at one site.

From 1952–76 there were seventy-one records, involving 80 birds, in every year except 1960. Breeding probably occurred in at least three years and was finally proved in 1976. [Subsequent detailed surveys have revealed a small breeding population of up to ten pairs. Eds.]

The extreme dates are 18th April–3rd July. The histogram shows a preponderance of coastal records up to mid-May, and since most refer to sightings on one day only, they probably concern passage migrants. Records after early June are more indicative of local breeding birds.

The only other records are three in late July–early August, probably local breeding birds, and singles in east Kent in late September 1976, at Northward Hill on 29th September and Folkestone on 2nd November 1959, an exceptionally late date.

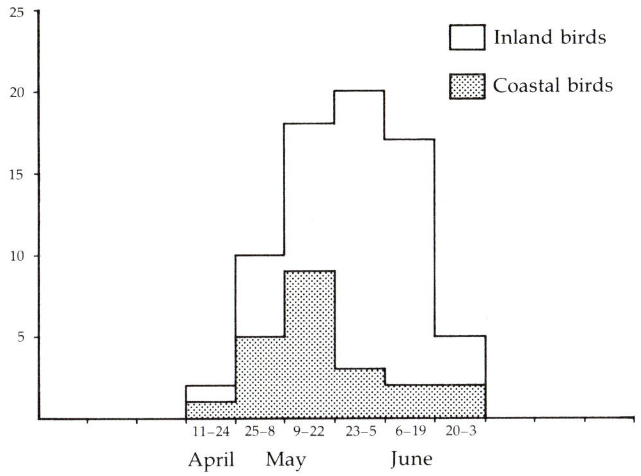

Fortnightly distribution of Golden Orioles 1952–76

Although over 80% of the records refer to single birds, usually singing males, it is possible that accompanying females have been overlooked. Over 70% are from east Kent, with most arrivals along the coast between Thanet and Dungeness. There are a few records for the Weald and the Hoo peninsula, but virtually none from the Downs, probably because of the lack of surface water.

Golden Orioles favour parkland and well wooded country, with scattered copses, shaws and open water. There are only four records from large blocks of woodland. Although the males are noisy on first arrival, they can be very quiet once breeding and this, plus the abundance of cover, probably explains the paucity of proved breeding records.

Red-backed Shrike

Lanius collurio

Annual passage migrant in small numbers and now a very rare and irregular breeding species.

Harrison gives details of the decline which first became evident in the 1930s, and describes the Red-backed Shrike at the end of the 1940s as a regular summer resident of local distribution, exhibiting marked fluctuations in numbers and showing a tendency to decline. He also includes two remarkably early records, at Sevenoaks on 26th March 1948 and at Ramsgate on 29th March 1949.

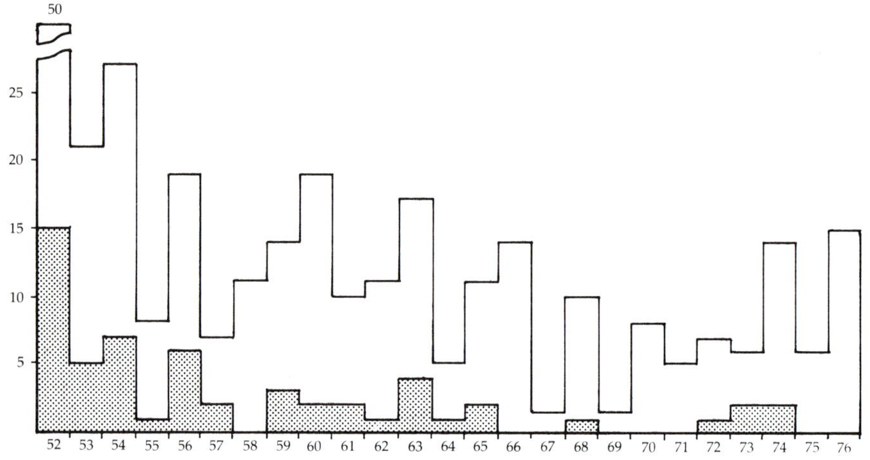

Annual totals and breeding pairs of Red-backed Shrikes

The histogram shows clearly how the decline continued through the fifties, and by the late sixties the Red-backed Shrike had ceased to breed regularly. During this period the breeding areas were widely distributed, extending over most of the traditional haunts, from Hythe in the south to Dover, north to Eastry and along the Stour Valley to Canterbury in the east; in the Medway Valley between Chatham and Maidstone, and below the scarp face of the Downs to Hollingbourne; further along the Medway to West Farleigh and Tonbridge; at Tunbridge Wells and Otford in the west, and Swanscombe in the north. It is evident, that apart from south facing bushy slopes, chalk pits and extensive young larch plantations were the most favoured breeding sites. Since 1968, breeding has only been proved at two sites, with single pairs present during 1972–74 and 1973–74 respectively.

As a migrant the Red-backed Shrike remains scarce in spring, with only one–three records in most years, normally between 30th April–15th June, and no records before 16th May in twelve years. The earliest in the period under review was one at Leybourne on 31st March 1957, with others at Burham on 9th April 1956 and Preston on 20th April 1952. The numbers of autumn migrants have fluctuated considerably, from none in 1969 to 10–12 in seven years between 1952–66 and again in 1976. The majority of the records come from the Observatories and probably do not involve British breeders. Passage normally occurs from late July to late September, though there have been October records in seven years, with the two latest both on 30th October, at Smallhythe in 1960 and Sandwich Bay in 1974.

Lesser Grey Shrike

Lanius minor

Very rare vagrant.

Ticehurst gives details of one seen on the North Downs on 15th May 1897.

The only other records concern singles near Lydd from 29th August–1st September 1956 and on Crundale Downs, near Wye on 20th September 1976.

Great Grey Shrike

Lanius excubitor

Regular passage migrant and winter visitor.

Ticehurst considered the Great Grey Shrike regular in autumn and winter, the largest numbers occurring in November, and most frequently to the north and east of the Downs. Harrison noted little change, but numbers have varied, and there has apparently been an appreciable increase during the period under review.

From 1952–64 there were, on average, about four records annually, increasing between 1965–70 to about 6–12 each year. Since then there has been a marked increase, both on autumn passage and in winter, while in 1971 there was an unusual spring passage involving 12 coastal migrants between 13th March–19th April.

Approximate numbers present in the three peak winters are shown in the following table:

	1973/74	1974/75	1975/76
Autumn	10	20	25
Winter	10	25	30

Singles at Dungeness on 24th August 1970 and Sandwich Bay on 25th August 1961 are the earliest autumn records. Otherwise there are none until 13th September, while in the three peak years above the autumn passage was heavily concentrated in the period 3rd October–6th November. Most of these autumn migrants occur along the north and east coasts, especially on Thanet, at Sandwich Bay and Dungeness, with up to three together at Sandwich Bay in October 1975.

Wintering birds may be quite widespread, though practically none have been recorded in the Weald and relatively few along the Downs, although this may possibly reflect observer coverage. The most regular site is the Stour Valley, around Stodmarsh, where one or two have occurred annually since 1959. Otherwise the most frequent reports come from the Thames marshes upriver from Cliffe, in the Darent Valley around Sevenoaks, the Medway Valley near Maidstone and along the greensand ridge between Maidstone and Ashford.

There are usually very few records indicative of spring passage, with the latest dates being 23rd April, at Chatham in 1956 and Dungeness in 1966. There is also an unusual midsummer record of one at Dover on 22nd June 1953.

Woodchat Shrike

Lanius senator

Rare passage migrant.

Ticehurst gives details of eight between 1830–1907, and Harrison adds a further four between 1934–47. Of the nine dated records six were in May, one in June and two in July.

J	F	M	A	M	J	J	A	S	O	N	D
			1	3	4	2	6	3	2		

Monthly distribution of Woodchat Shrikes 1952–76

During 1952–76 there were 21 records, 10 of them at Dungeness and three at Sandwich Bay. Of the others, six were seen around the coast from Kingsdown to Allhallows, and another at Littlebrook, while the only inland sighting was of one at Boxley on 4th July 1953.

The extreme dates of the two passage periods are 25th April–4th July and 13th August–15th October. Most of the records concern single dates, with one each in spring and autumn involving stays of three days, while there have been three exceptionally long stays in autumn for periods of 15–23 days. All but one of the autumn records refer to immatures.

Jay

Garrulus glandarius

Widespread resident and passage migrant.

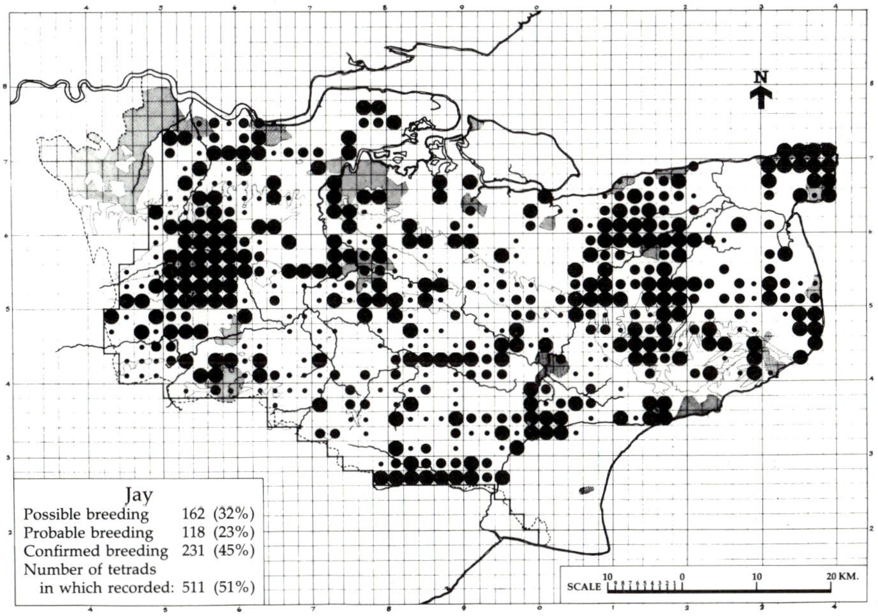

The distribution of the Jay as a breeding species is limited by the presence of woodland. It is conspicuously absent from the coastal marshes. It breeds in pines at St. Margaret's Bay and, somewhat surprisingly, in urban Thanet, where there are holm oaks, but few beech or oak trees.

One of the interesting features of this species in Kent is the irruptive nature of the autumn movements. It has long been known that many of the passage and winter birds are of the nominate Continental race *G.g. glandarius,* and small groups may be seen arriving off the sea around the coast from mid-September and throughout October. Increased numbers and some migration is also noted at inland localities. Heavy movements probably reflect the annual variation in the crop size of such trees as oak, hazel and beech, which perhaps provide about 75% of the Jay's food.

The four largest irruptive movements were noted in 1957, 1963, 1965 and 1975, but the most significant of these was in 1957. Between 14th–27th September that year, widespread reports all round the coast totalled well over 1,000 birds. A few were seen flying west along the Thames, several large flocks were seen near Herne Bay, including one of 139 on the 23rd, a number of small groups coasted south at St.

Margaret's Bay, then southwest across Romney Marsh, where flocks of 15–20 were seen daily, and a few were noted at both Observatories. In 1965 the influx was largely concentrated at Dungeness between 18th–20th October, when 113 flew northwest. In 1963 and 1975 the influxes occurred between 18th September–31st October, totalling around 200 each year, but in more widespread localities than in the other two irruptions, including several well inland.

Spring passage was first noted at Dungeness in 1956, but migrants are recorded only sporadically, usually in May. In 1964, for example, 12 flew west at Deal on 4th May, there were 23 at Sandwich Bay the next day, and eight there on the 31st, with singles at Dungeness on three dates during the month.

The density of the population is difficult to assess, but quite large numbers are indicated by a bag of 70 shot at Badger's Mount (Shoreham) in April 1971, and over 50 first-year birds caught and ringed in Farningham and Joyden's Woods in 1975.

One ringed at Dungeness on 12th October 1955 was recovered in Zeeland, Holland on 2nd June 1956.

Magpie

Pica pica

Widespread resident.

The Magpie is well distributed throughout the county, breeding successfully in a wide variety of habitats, from bramble thickets on the shingle at Dungeness to town parks and gardens.

Out of the breeding season it is sometimes gregarious, occasionally forming sizeable flocks during the winter months. Counts of 30–80, sometimes referring to roosts, have been reported from widespread localities, with a maximum of over 100 in Chattenden Woods in January 1955.

Harrison refers to influxes from the Continent in late September and October, but there has been little evidence of passage in recent years. The only suggestion of migration is one or two, seen flying out to sea at Dungeness on several dates between 21st March–18th April 1962.

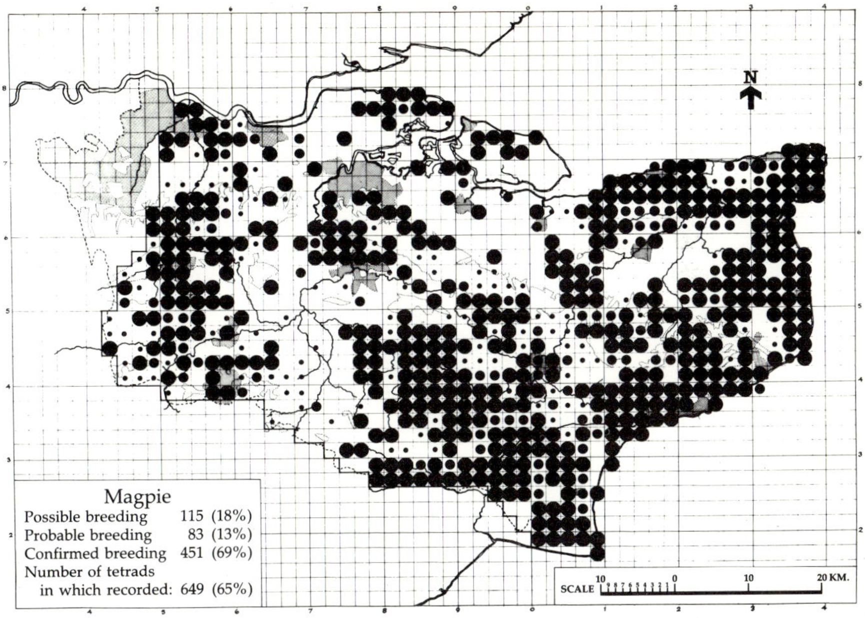

Nutcracker

Nucifraga caryocatactes

An irruptive species, generally a very rare vagrant.

Harrison lists five fully authenticated records, all between October–January. One was considered to be of the nominate race *N.c. caryocatactes*, but was not accepted as such, and the other four were all of the Siberian race *N.c. macrorhynchus*. Two in the autumn of 1911 were part of a small irruption into Britain.

Apart from the unprecedented influx of autumn 1968, when nearly 30 were recorded, and the related reports the following year, there have been only three other sightings in recent years. Singles were seen at Ashley (Dover) on 25th December 1958 and Dungeness on 5th September 1967, with two at Bedgebury on 27th December 1972.

The first of the arrivals in 1968 were on 7th August at Denton and 9th August at Quex Park, two early individuals associated with the first influx from the Continent. A larger influx, involving about 16 birds, occurred between 22nd August–11th September. Early arrivals were mainly in the east, in coastal areas, but some moved well inland beyond their points of landfall. Four were seen together near Dover on 24th August, but all the other reports were of singles. During the rest of September and October, singles were reported from five more localities, while in November–December there were reports from another five localities. Two remained resident near Maidstone into 1969, one until March, the other until at least June and probably until the end of the year. Another appeared at Thornden Wood (Canterbury) from 22nd–25th June, with the last at Dungeness from 25th–27th September 1969.

As far as can be ascertained from field descriptions, ringing data and photographs, all the 1968 birds were of the Slender-billed or Siberian race *N.c. macrorhynchus*.

Chough

Pyrrhocorax pyrrhocorax

Formerly bred.

Ticehurst and Harrison concluded that the original colony on the Dover Cliffs dwindled in the early eighteenth century. A pair, obtained in Cornwall, then escaped and re-established a small population there until about 1850.

Jackdaw

Corvus monedula

Abundant resident and regular autumn migrant.

The Jackdaw is widely distributed throughout the county, nesting socially in loose colonies and frequently feeding on open pasture.

There are very few estimates of breeding populations, but there were about 40 pairs on the cliffs between Folkestone and Dover in 1972, up to 40 pairs on the Sandwich Bay Estate up until 1974, when the demolition of the Guilford Hotel chimneys markedly reduced the thriving colony there, and 75 pairs at Northward Hill in 1976.

Post-breeding flocks in July occasionally exceed 300 and there were 1,000 at Eastchurch on 30th July 1961, but the largest concentrations

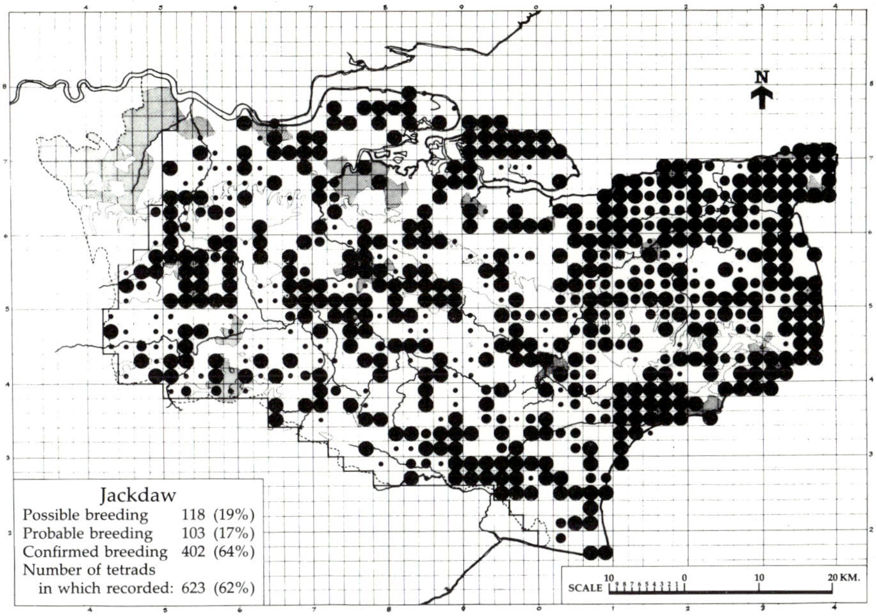

occur in winter roosts. Roosting flights are recorded annually in various parts of the county and in some winters have exceeded 1,000 birds at Adisham, Bishopsbourne, Hollingbourne, Northward Hill, St. Mary's Bay and Waldershare.

At Dungeness, where the species is scarce in some years, there is sometimes a light, but noticeable spring passage in late March and early April. The autumn passage in October–November is much more marked and visible migration was noticed as long ago as 1909 and earlier (Harrison). The movement is generally west to northwest and has been recorded at Dungeness, Sandwich Bay and along the north coast to Shellness and Allhallows, occasionally involving up to 300 birds in a day.

One ringed in West Flanders on 26th April 1958 was shot on 12th June at High Halstow, suggesting that some local birds may winter on the Continent.

A female of the Scandinavian race *C.m. monedula* was shot at Sevenoaks on 3rd April 1955. Others showing the characteristics of this race have been identified in the field, but it must be remembered that 'grey-hooded' individuals appear among our local populations (Harrison).

Rook

Corvus frugilegus

Abundant resident and partial migrant.

The Rook is a bird of agricultural land, using hedgerow trees and woodland of various kinds for nesting. Flocks feed commonly on permanent pasture and arable farmland.

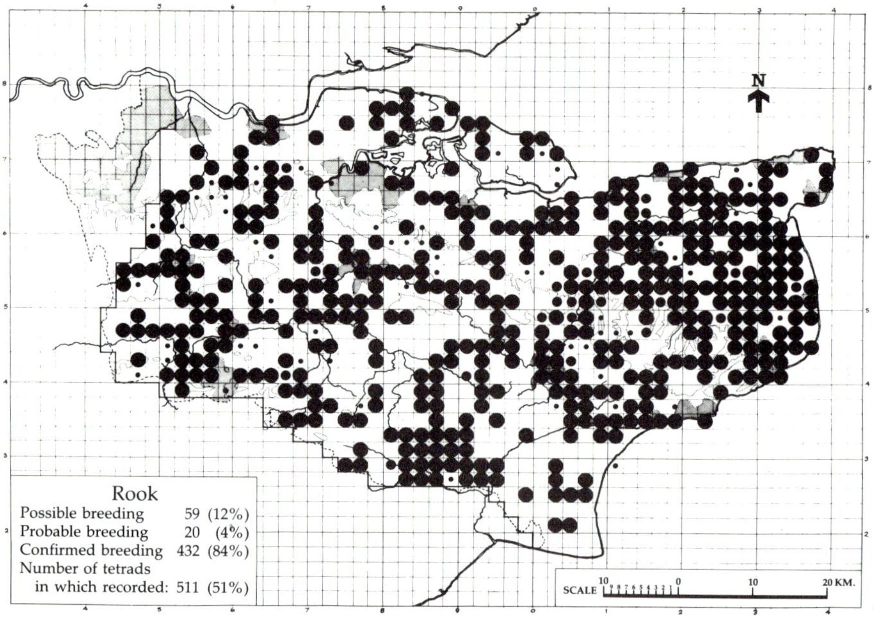

Although large traditional rookeries may be used for many years, smaller ones appear and disappear quite rapidly, for various reasons. The increasing loss of elms as a result of Dutch elm disease in the seventies has had a marked effect on the north Kent landscape and is surely responsible for the decline of rookeries there, which is shown by comparing the two maps.

There is no doubt that the Rook has declined considerably in the last 25 years. Harrison recounts in detail the results of a census by the Ministry of Agriculture in 1949. A more recent survey, organised by the BTO in 1975, provides comparative data (Munns, 1978):

	1949	1975	% decline
Number of nests	39,696	12,826	68%
Number of rookeries	509	536	

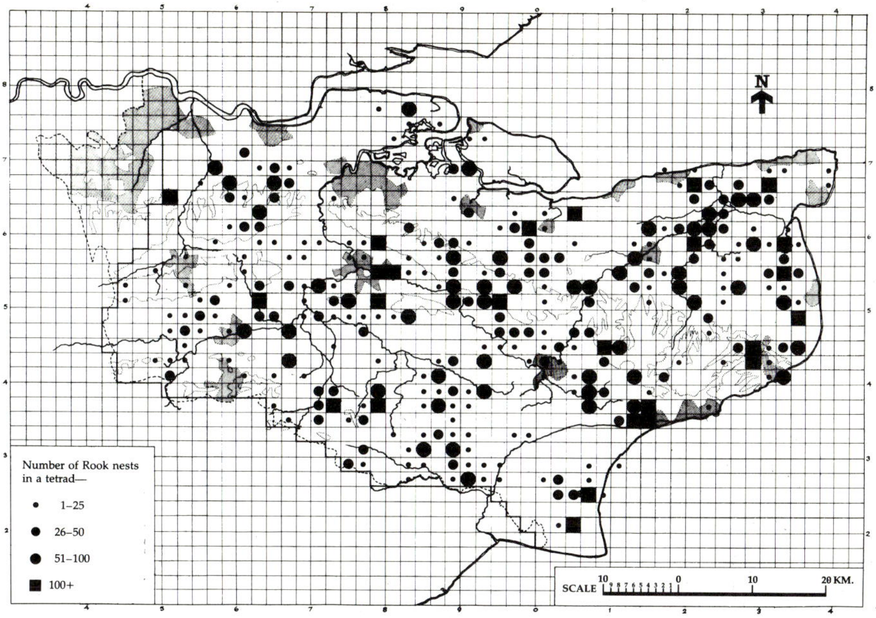

Distribution of Rookeries in 1975

The actual number of rookeries shows no great change, but reflects the trend towards smaller ones, of less than 25 nests, which represented 68% of the 1975 total. The largest rookery that year, at Elbridge House, Stodmarsh, contained 296 nests compared with 650 in 1949, in which year there were eight rookeries with over 300 nests.

Post-breeding flocks in July and August can be large, and in the winter months concentrations of 1,000–3,000 birds going to roost have been reported fairly frequently.

Some evidence of diurnal migration has been witnessed almost annually, usually during the second half of October and early November, when immigrants from the Continent can be seen arriving on the east coast or moving west along the Thames estuary. The peak counts have involved daily totals of 1,700 at Shellness on 30th October 1966 and 1969, 1,500 at Allhallows on 27th October 1956 and a similar number flying southwest in two and a half hours at Sandwich Bay on 29th October 1961. Light spring movements are also recorded at Dungeness in some years.

Carrion Crow

Corvus corone corone

Widespread resident, passage migrant in small numbers.

Since Ticehurst's time, when this species was particularly scarce in the Weald and on Romney Marsh, there has been a considerable increase in numbers, largely at the expense of the formerly common Hooded Crow. The spread onto Romney Marsh during the twenties and thirties is well documented by Harrison.

The Carrion Crow now breeds throughout the county.

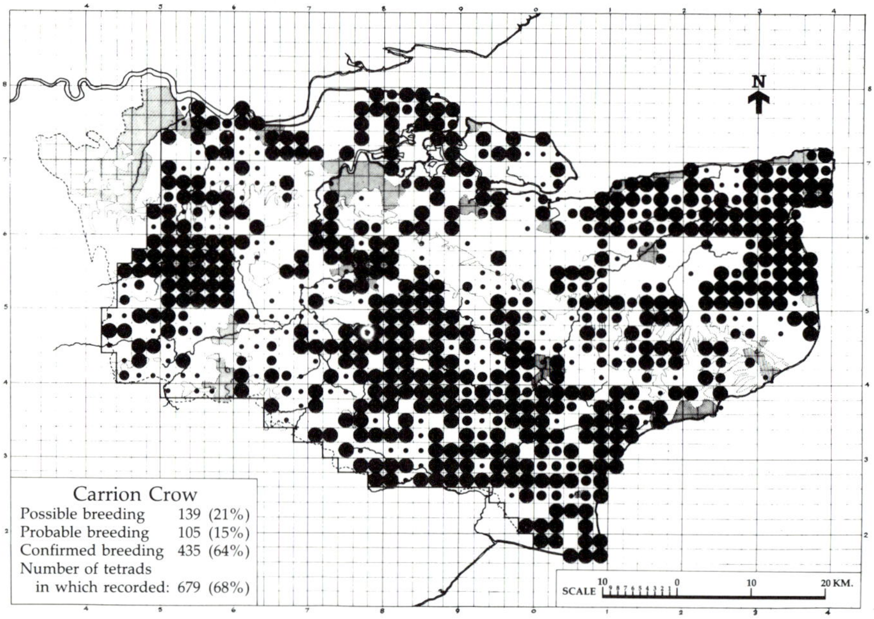

In autumn small numbers can be seen on passage from late September until early November, along the Thames estuary, and at various points round the coast. The peak movements involved 200 flying west along the Thames on 29th October 1966 and over 100 in one flock flying northwest off the sea at Folkestone on the same date in 1973.

A smaller spring passage during March–April has been witnessed regularly at Dungeness, and occasionally elsewhere round the coast, with a peak of 100 flying north at Dungeness on 9th April 1962.

Since the late sixties gatherings of over 100 have been reported with increasing frequency. Most often these occur during the winter months and some are attracted by rubbish tips. The highest count is 230 at Sandwich Bay in April 1969. In January–March, and again in July 1976, over 100 were seen going to roost at Joyden's Wood.

Hooded Crow

Corvus corone cornix

Winter visitor and passage migrant.

There has certainly been a decrease this century, since Ticehurst regarded the Hooded Crow as a common winter visitor and numerous autumn passage migrant. Harrison considered it exceedingly numerous in severe winters, but Gillham and Homes quote several hundred at Swalecliffe in January 1948 as exceptional.

Since then, the numbers wintering and on passage, although fluctuating, have diminished considerably.

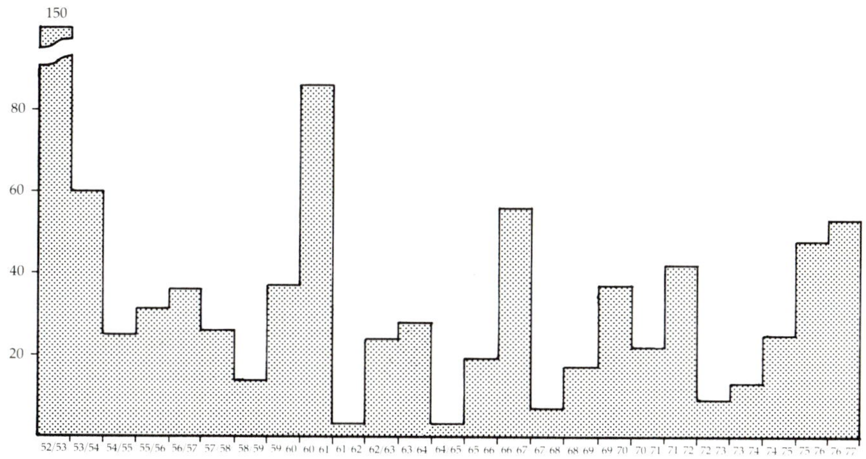

Winter totals of Hooded Crows

Apart from a quite exceptional flock of 46 on flooded fields north of Deal on 15th February 1953, the mid-winter peaks vary from just one in 1961/62 to 23 in 1953/54, which included a flock of 10, again north of Deal. Between five and 10 is more usual, with no other flocks of more than 12.

Autumn passage can be quite marked during the second half of October and early November. The high total for 1952/53 is partly accounted for by totals of 11 flying south at Sandwich Bay on 18th October, and 18 flying west at Swalecliffe and 11 west at Cliffe on 9th November. A study of diurnal migration at Allhallows in 1976 produced a total of 12 flying west between 1st–13th November. The earliest autumn record is 1st October 1970, with the mean arrival date around 20th October.

Spring passage is less obvious, but there have occasionally been noticeable increases in numbers in late March and early April. The only other large flock in recent years was 25 at Sandwich Bay on 25th March 1961. At the same locality there have been peaks of 12 on 15th April 1967 and eight on 18th April 1970, while there were seven at Dungeness on 27th March 1964. Strangely, the two worst autumns, with one record in each, followed the spring peaks of 1964 and 1967. The mean departure date is around 25th April, but there have been May sightings in seven years.

During June–August there have been 15 records, all of singles apart from two at Graveney on 10th June 1958, with nine of these in the Sandwich Bay area. The only September records concern one, again at Sandwich Bay, on 12th September 1967, and one on Walland Marsh from 25th August–29th September 1954.

The majority of the records are coastal and those wintering favour the coastal marshlands, occasionally following the river estuaries further inland. However, quite a number of reports concern individuals attracted, like other *Corvidae*, to rubbish tips, and up to four have been seen at Sevenoaks. Very occasionally there are records from along the Downs and at well-watched sites like Bough Beech reservoir.

Raven

Corvus corax

Rare visitor. Formerly bred.

Ticehurst records that breeding ceased towards the end of the last century, with the last nests at Lullingstone Park in 1844, Cobham Park some years before 1868, and the cliffs between Dover and Folkestone, where there were three in 1841, in about 1890. Around the turn of the century singles were obtained occasionally in the east or southeast of the county and more recently one was seen flying over the Medway estuary on 17th October 1948.

Since 1952 there have been 13 records, all but one in the north or west of the county. Some probably refer to the same individuals, and in some cases they may possibly refer to escapes.

Singles were seen at Cliffe on 8th March 1957 and Warden (Sheppey) on 8th November 1959. In 1960 there was one at Lydd on 3rd May and two flew west at Sevenoaks on 2nd July. In 1963 there were singles at Northward Hill on 3rd March and 29th December, the first being exceptionally tame and almost certainly an escape, while in 1965 there were two there on 3rd January and one again on 21st February. In 1967 one flew north over Hildenborough on 7th July and two were seen there on 21st August. In 1973 singles were seen at Sevenoaks on 25th September and nearby at Wrotham on 30th October, and one flew west, again at Sevenoaks, on 12th April 1975.

Starling

Sturnus vulgaris

Abundant resident, winter visitor and passage migrant.

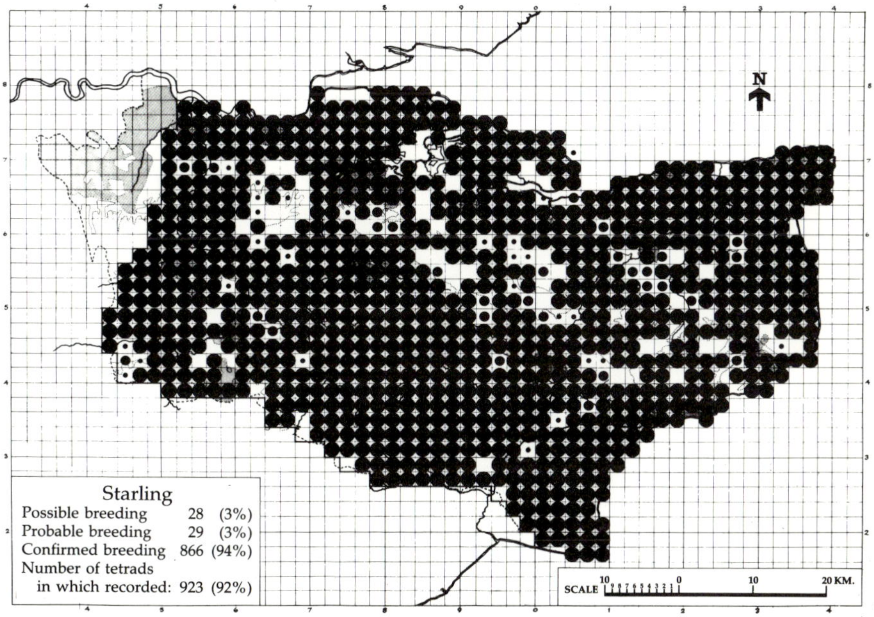

The Starling breeds at greatest densities in built-up areas and in mature woodland, where there is a plentiful supply of nesting holes, but it is highly adaptable and is scarce only in the most open habitats. The apparent scarcity along the Downs is perhaps more a reflection of poor coverage during the Breeding Survey, which showed the Starling to be the third most widespread breeding species.

Post-breeding flocks begin to form in June, and while the majority of these are probably local birds, flocks such as those on Romney Marsh draw individuals from further afield. One bird ringed as a nestling in Belgium in May 1975 was trapped at Dungeness just a month later. Some westerly movement has also been observed at this time. During

14th–30th June 1975 a total of 4,088 flew west at Allhallows, further evidence of early immigration.

The bulk of immigration takes place from late September until late November, with the heaviest passage usually recorded in the last two weeks of October and the first week of November. Although much of the passage takes place at night, it often continues throughout the day. Movement is generally west or northwest and is heaviest and most obvious at the coast. Vast numbers have sometimes been recorded, the largest visible movements occurring in October 1966, with 50,000 at Shellness on the 16th, 54,000 there on the 26th and 25,000 at Dungeness on the 29th. Other very large movements concerned 50,000 at Dungeness on 24th October 1970 and 23,000 at Allhallows on 30th October 1974.

Many of the birds which are seen arriving in autumn continue further west in Britain, but large numbers remain and during the winter enormous roosts are formed. Each year many roosts of up to 10,000 birds have been reported, with a few of up to 100,000 and some even larger. Some roosts are used year after year, but with considerable fluctuations between years and at different times during each winter. Others are used for a few years and then abandoned. One roost which has held high numbers for many years is Wenderton Wood, near Wingham, where between one and two million birds were estimated to be present in November 1958, with some coming from as far afield as Dover. This roost has also been recorded as holding over one million birds in November 1962 and November 1974. Other roosts estimated to contain 500,000 or more birds have occurred at Walland Marsh in 1958, Maidstone Cemetery during the 1960s, Gravesend between 1971–75, Great Chattenden Wood in 1974 and Langley in 1975, while in November 1974 there were an estimated 1,650,000 roosting at Stodmarsh.

During severe winters, weather movements both into and away from Kent occur, as on 1st January 1962, when 1,200 flew south over Rochester, and 1,500 south at Dungeness. Heavy snow had fallen over much of Britain the previous day. On 31st December 1968, in contrast, 740 flew northwest at Dungeness, an example of a mid-winter influx from the Continent.

Departures of Continental birds take place mainly during March, reaching a peak in the third week, but visible passage is much lighter than in autumn. Totals of 6,000 flying east at Sandwich Bay on 14th March 1963 and 3,500 southeast at Dungeness on 22nd March 1965 are examples of fairly heavy movements during spring passage.

Starlings breeding in Kent are largely sedentary, but there is a tendency, especially among juveniles, towards dispersal. A few reach the Continent, but conclusive evidence of Kent-ringed nestlings doing this is sparse. The majority remain in Kent or move elsewhere in southern England. Some birds ringed as juveniles in Kent in summer, have been recovered in subsequent breeding seasons west to Somerset and north to Nottinghamshire. It is probable that at least some of these were birds which had settled away from the natal area, although the possibility of their being birds from the recovery areas, which had joined the Kent post-breeding flocks, cannot be discounted.

The breeding areas of the autumn immigrants form a belt running east-northeast across Holland, Germany and Poland to the USSR, from which there are many ringing recoveries. A typical one, from the easternmost limits, concerns a nestling ringed at Gryozovets, USSR 58°N 40°E in May 1959 and killed in Hythe in February 1961. Some birds have also come from Scandinavia, or the southern USSR and Czechoslovakia, but perhaps only when severe weather disrupts the usual distribution patterns.

Rose-coloured Starling

Sturnus roseus

Very rare vagrant.

Ticehurst gives details of seven records between 1840–91, the three dated ones occurring in June. Harrison adds one for Dungeness in June 1937 and another at Tunbridge Wells in February 1951.

During the period under review there were singles at Tunbridge Wells on 11th January 1953 and Bredhurst on 31st December 1964. In east Kent, there were singles at Sandwich on 11th September and Canterbury from 20th November–12th December 1971, and at Sandwich again from 22nd–27th February 1972. The most recent record concerns one at Northward Hill on 22nd May 1976. All were adults, and with this species the possibility that they were escapes from captivity must inevitably be borne in mind.

House Sparrow

Passer domesticus

Abundant resident.

Ticehurst records large numbers arriving from the east and southeast during the autumn and quotes figures of 2–5,000 daily passing the Varne lightship in October 1887. Migration on this scale has not been recorded since.

During the 25 years under review records relate mostly to large roosting or feeding flocks, and perhaps more interestingly, to autumn movements.

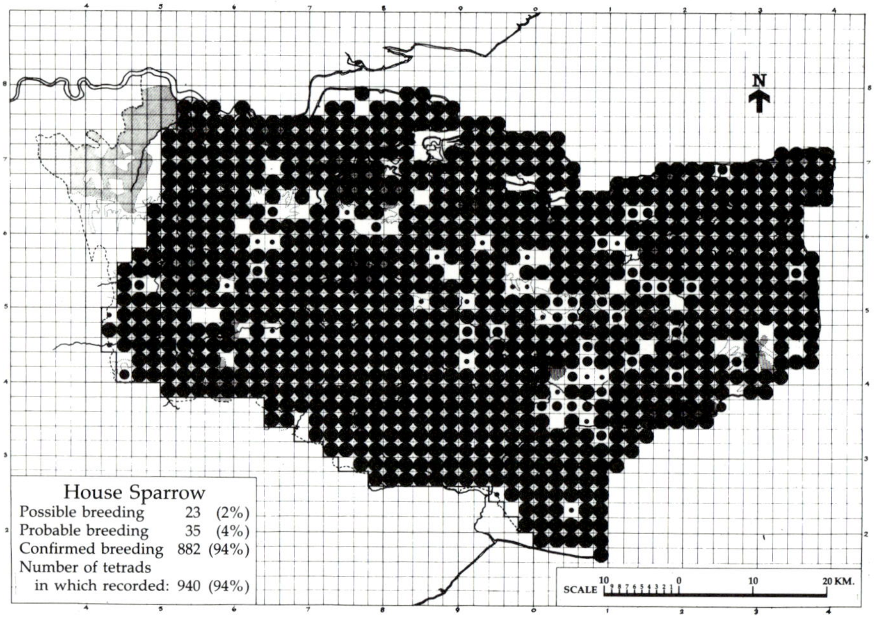

The Breeding Bird survey showed the House Sparrow to be the second most widespread species in the county, breeding practically everywhere, except where there is absolutely nothing that could serve as a nesting site. The absences are generally due to poor coverage, though they are probably genuine on the coastal stretches of the North Kent Marshes and the shingle beach at Dungeness.

The largest numbers recorded refer to roosting flocks, with maxima of 5,000 at Dartford and Littlebrook in December and January 1974/75. Here even in the summer months there have been peaks of 4,000.

Smaller roosts of 1–3,000 are widely reported, frequently using thick hedgerows.

The House Sparrow is an opportunist feeder and large numbers have always flocked to cornfields, before and after harvest, and small flocks are often encountered feeding on the shore with finches and buntings in winter. Not easily explained are the autumn movements, principally in October at Dungeness, where small flocks fly southeast, often during movements of finches, with occasional peaks of 200 in a day. Spring movements are rarely recorded.

The recovery of one ringed at Dungeness on 15th May 1960 in Belgium on 1st November the same year confirms cross-Channel movement, but remains one of very few foreign recoveries of this species. The two Observatories have provided eight more recoveries more than 50 km distant, the furthest being 102 km from Dungeness to the Suffolk coast, and 82 km from Sandwich Bay to Sussex. One ringed near Maidstone on 24th August 1961 was recovered, barely two months later, over 100 km away in Hampshire on 14th October. There are several reports also of longevity up to six years, with one almost reaching 10 at Dungeness, ringed on 30th June 1961, it was found dead on 17th March 1971.

Tree Sparrow

Passer montanus

Widespread breeding species, winter visitor and passage migrant.

Ticehurst considered the Tree Sparrow a rare breeding species, more common in winter, but Harrison documents a considerable colonisation during the first half of this century.

There is little doubt that the breeding range of the Tree Sparrow has continued to expand since 1952. It is predominantly a hole nesting species, commonly found in wooded areas and hedgerows, but it also breeds in Sand Martin nest holes and takes readily to nest boxes. A number of less usual sites have been recorded, with up to 15 pairs in the structure of occupied Grey Herons' nests at Northward Hill in 1954–55, two pairs in disused crow nests at Dungeness in 1970, and two pairs even nested in a hut on the jetty at Bee Ness in the Medway Estuary in 1961. With this adaptability, there seem few places in the county where the Tree Sparrows will not ultimately breed successfully, apart from the truly urban areas.

Diurnal movements may be observed at various points around the coast, particularly in autumn. The general direction is westerly, with

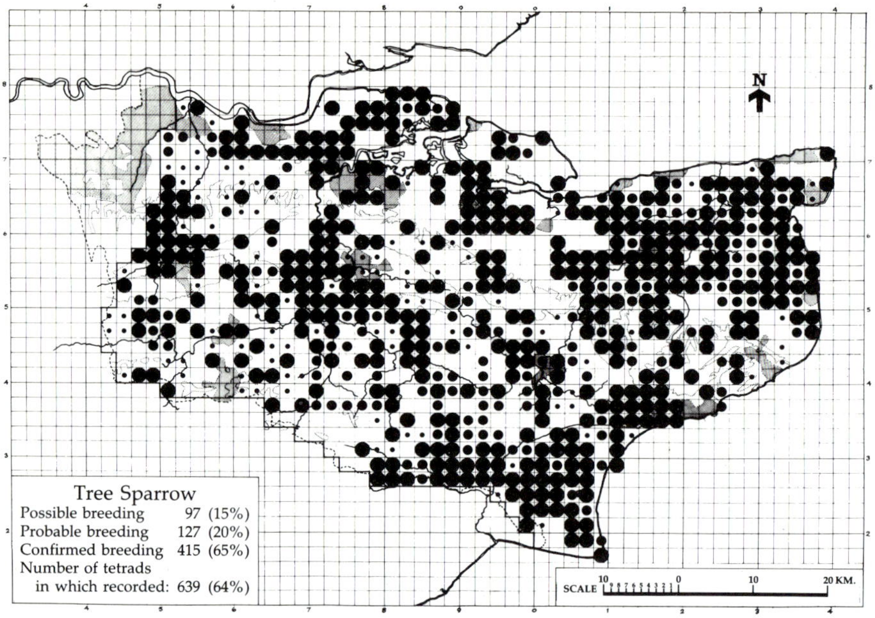

birds usually flying northwest at Dungeness, north at Sandwich Bay and then west along the north coast into the Thames Estuary. Although passage may commence in late August the peak numbers invariably occur between 5th October–5th November, in which period day totals of 1,000–1,500 have been recorded on five dates at Dungeness, with a maximum of 2,000 there on 20th October 1970. Elsewhere round the coast peak totals vary between 250–500. Inland too, numbers increase during the autumn and flocks of 200–400 are not uncommon, remaining throughout the winter in stubblefields, or wherever weed seeds are readily available. The largest flocks reported are 1,000 at Stockbury on 17th March 1966 and 1,500 at Wormshill on 10th December 1960. The wintering flocks may show a slight increase again in April during the spring passage, which is on a much smaller scale from late March to late May, when peaks of 50–75 are quite unusual, even at Dungeness, though 129 flew west at Allhallows on 27th March 1976.

Ringing recoveries confirm the Continental origin of some of our winter visitors. One ringed at Cap Gris Nez on 29th September 1959 was retrapped at Stockbury on 3rd October 1960. Another ringed at Sandwich Bay on 8th November 1959 was recovered in Holland on 28th June 1960. Several other recoveries show an east–west movement within Britain.

Chaffinch

Fringilla coelebs

Abundant resident, passage migrant and winter visitor.

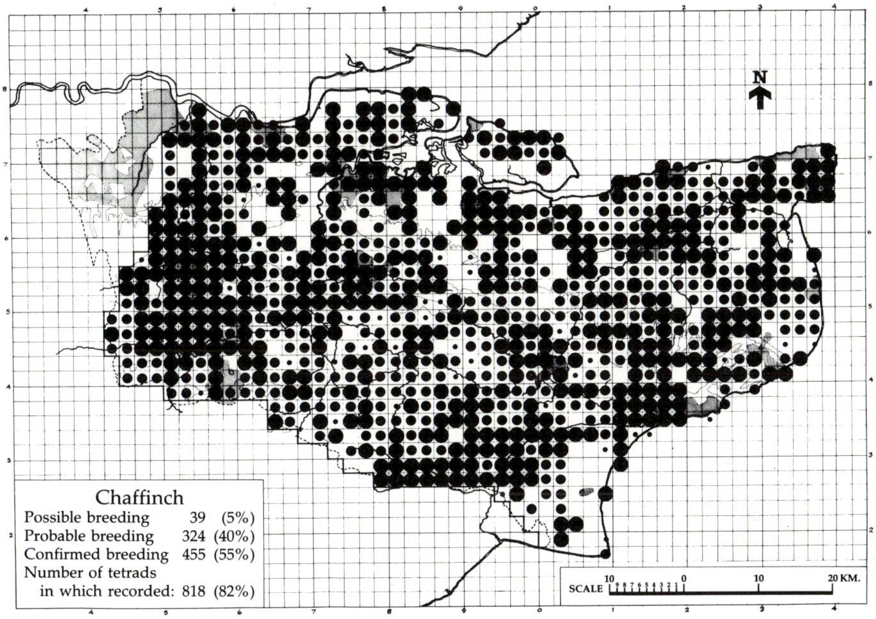

A widespread breeding species, favouring mature broad-leaved woodland, but occurring wherever there are trees or bushes. Probably genuinely absent only from the treeless marshland of the North Kent Marshes and the shingle stretches at Dungeness.

Autumn passage during October–November is highly concentrated during the last three weeks of October, when west or northwest movements of several thousand birds in a day are often recorded at the Observatories, along the north coast, and occasionally inland. In 1958, for example, there were 9,500 at Dungeness and 2,000 at Shellness on 19th October, while at Sandwich Bay there were 7,000 and 3,000 on 22nd and 23rd October. In 1967 another marked autumn passage was recorded involving 2,200 at Sandwich Bay on 14th October, 5,000 over Stockbury on the 22nd and 23rd, and 7,000 at Seasalter on the 26th, with 7,000 at Dungeness and 2,000 at Cliffe on 5th November. The largest movements tend to occur in bright, clear weather, and moderate or fresh headwinds from a westerly quarter.

In the winter months feeding flocks of several hundreds may be attracted by beech mast or weed seeds, while roosts of 1,000–2,000 are recorded occasionally, but there are no other counts recorded to compare with the roost at Newington, where there were 10,000 in December 1970 and 5,000 in December 1971.

Spring passage is commonly observed on the coast in March–April, with large visible movements at Hythe involving 2,200 flying east on 30th March 1958 and 1,300 on 24th March 1960. On 23rd March 1975 2,150 flew east at Allhallows and 2,300 flew north at Sandwich Bay.

Of 55 overseas ringing recoveries, 35 concern Holland and Belgium, while the others include six each in Germany and Finland, three from Denmark, two from France and singles in Norway, Sweden and the USSR.

Brambling

Fringilla montifringilla

Regular winter visitor and passage migrant in varying numbers.

Harrison was able to cite winters in the early forties when the numbers of Bramblings varied considerably in alternate years, and both he and Ticehurst commented on the marked variation in numbers from year to year.

This pattern has prevailed during the period under review, when the numbers on autumn passage have been recorded more systematically and probably reflect the roughly biennial pattern in the production of mast by beech trees. Apart from a very early male at Hoo on 6th September 1959, the first autumn arrivals occur between 15th September–15th October, with the mean around 3rd October. There is often a significant visible migration during October–November, when good numbers may occur during large Chaffinch movements. The peak usually occurs during the last three weeks of October, with maxima of 450 flying west at Allhallows and 600 northwest at Dungeness on 18th October 1975. In other autumns relatively few may be recorded.

Numbers remaining to winter also vary considerably from year to year. In most winters though, small flocks can be seen feeding on beech mast, or on weed seeds in fields of stubble, where they mix with other finch species. Flocks of 100–300 have been recorded in all but six winters during the period under review, but usually from only one or two localities, and since 1965 there has been a fairly regular roost of this size at Bedgebury. Flocks of 300–500 are considerably rarer and there were exceptional counts of 1,000 at Littlebourne in February 1965 and at Stockbury in December 1968. However, the highest overall numbers occur in hard winters, when large flocks can be found on coastal marshes and farmland. In February 1954 there were 200 at East Malling, 300 at Motney Hill and 500 at Nagden, in addition to five other flocks of 100 birds. In the arctic winter of 1962/63 there was a peak of 1,400 at Sandwich Bay on 20th January, with 300 at Chetney, 200 at Reculver, and 100 each at Dungeness, Westgate and Shellness between 28th December–3rd February.

There is a small, but often noticeable spring passage, usually indicated by the presence of temporary flocks during March–April, with peak numbers in 1966 involving 200 at Stockbury, 250 at Bicknor and 400 at Shorne between 12th–23rd March. There was also an unusually late influx of 300 at Shoreham and 250 at Ide Hill during 8th–10th April 1973. The latest departure dates occur between mid-April and mid-May, with the mean around 1st May, and the latest at Dungeness on 21st May 1960.

There are three ringing recoveries, two of which show a different choice of wintering area in successive years. One ringed in Belgium in October 1955 was recovered at Hythe in February 1956, another ringed at Stockbury in March 1967 was recovered in Belgium in December 1968, while a third, ringed at Bicknor in January 1966, was recovered in southern France in January 1967.

Serin

Serinus serinus

Rare, but increasingly regular spring vagrant.

Ticehurst includes two winter records, one netted at Dover on 27th January 1879 and two caught there on 16th November 1904.

Of the 20 authenticated records during the period under review, 15 have been at Dungeness, with the first there on 2nd–3rd April 1961. The Serin has subsequently occurred in all but four years. Elsewhere there have been two on Thanet, one at Ash, one at Leigh from 21st–23rd June and a pair at Sevenoaks from 13th–20th July, both in 1969.

J	F	M	A	M	J	J	A	S	O	N	D
		1	2	7	3	4			2	1	

Monthly distribution of Serins 1961–76

The extreme dates are 24th March–29th July and 8th October–12th November. Most sightings concern migrants on one date only, and although a pair and a singing male have occurred there has been no evidence of breeding. On the Continent Serins favour well wooded parks and suburban gardens, and odd birds, even breeding pairs, could easily be overlooked in Kent.

The Serin has a very distinct flight call and a further five records, not accepted by *British Birds*, have come from Dungeness, where singles have been identified mainly by call. Of these there were two each in April and May, and one in October.

Greenfinch

Carduelis chloris

Widespread resident and partial migrant.

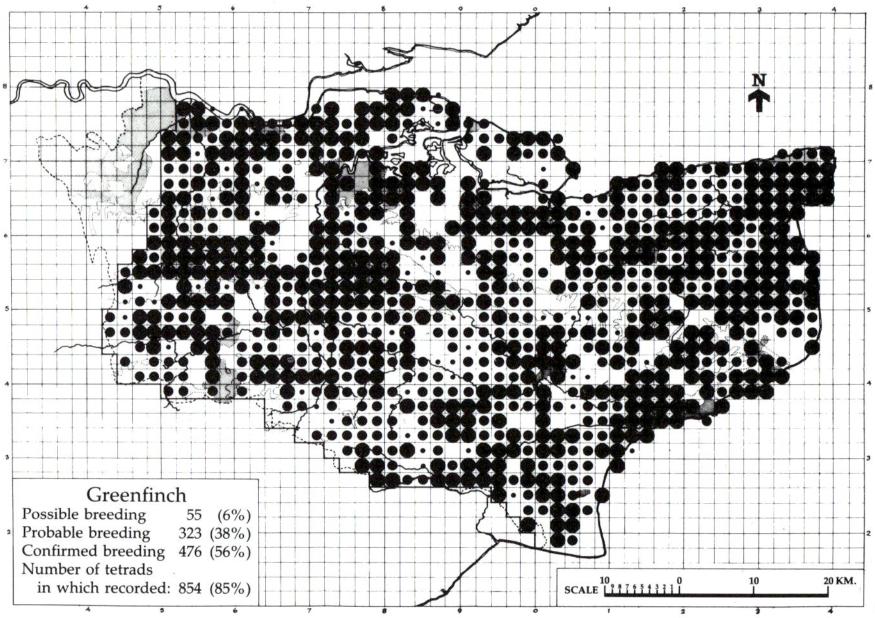

In most parts of the county during the breeding season the Greenfinch is numerous, favouring scrub, open woodland and the hedges and copses of farmland. In recent years more have been found in residential areas, perhaps as a result of food being made available, but the mixed shrubs, trees and lawns of suburban gardens match closely their preferred natural habitat. Not surprisingly, they are scarce in open landscapes with few trees and bushes, and in this respect they differ from Goldfinch and Linnet, which are able to utilise lower vegetation for nesting.

There is no evidence of any major change in the status of the Greenfinch as a breeding species, but there was a temporary decline following the severe winter of 1962/63, when populations throughout the county were reported to be below strength. However, there does seem to have been an increase in numbers present in winter. No flock of more than 600 was reported during 1952–66, but at least one flock exceeding 1,000 has been seen in most winters since. During the winter, Greenfinches are found in a wider variety of habitats than in summer, and some of the largest flocks occur in coastal localities, such as at Dungeness, where they take advantage of the seeds of sea kale. Flocks start to form immediately after the breeding season and even early in the autumn may be quite large. An example of this is the flock of 1,000 feeding on unharvested rape at Langley from August–October 1976. However, the largest numbers are usually seen during October–January, the highest coastal counts recorded being 2,400 at Nagden in December 1967, 3,000 at Capel Fleet in January 1970 and 2,000 there in December 1975, while inland there were 2,000 at Stockbury in December 1968. At Dungeness in autumn, flocks usually build up during October, producing November peaks of 1,000 in 1971 and 1,500 in 1975. In 1976 this flock built up from 2,000 on 10th October to 3,000 later in the month, decreasing to 1,000 on 20th November. A total of 1,600 ringed there during that period showed that there was a continual turnover of birds.

Evidence from ringing suggests that resident Greenfinches are fairly sedentary, but some passage movement is recorded annually, being less evident in spring, during March and April, than in autumn from mid-October to mid-November, but even then counts of more than 100 moving on any one day are rare.

Ringing recoveries show that a good proportion of our wintering birds come from East Anglia and some from the Low Countries and Scandinavia, while locally bred birds have moved to Devon and France. The two most distant recoveries are of birds ringed at Gravesend in December 1972 and Margate in February 1973, which were recovered in southern Norway in August 1973 and January 1975 respectively.

Goldfinch

Carduelis carduelis

Widespread breeding species, but most numerous on spring and autumn passage.

The Goldfinch has been increasing throughout most of this century, and during the 1970s the Common Bird Census shows a further increase in the breeding population. The larger numbers now recorded on migration support this trend.

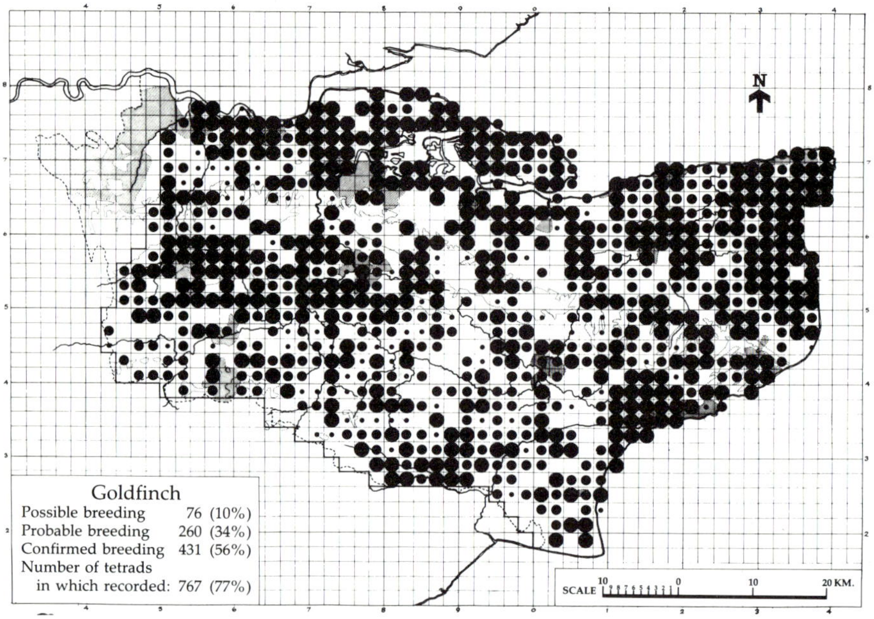

It is obvious that the Goldfinch breeds in a wide variety of habitats, including farmland, parkland, orchards and gardens, scrub and woodland edges, and also in scattered trees and bushes on the more open country of the coastal marshes.

Post-breeding flocks start to form in June and can be found throughout July and August, wherever there is a plentiful supply of weed seeds. In July flocks of up to 250 have been recorded, increasing to an August maximum of 780 at Sandwich Bay in 1968. These later flocks may well be supplemented by migrants.

Autumn migration is most evident between mid-September and mid-November. Like most finches, Goldfinches move largely in the mornings and at favourable coastal sites considerable numbers can be seen, although the peaks vary greatly from year to year. The highest numbers are invariably recorded flying south at Dungeness, where daily counts of 1,000 or more have occurred in seven years during 1960–76. In 1976 peaks of 1,000–1,600 occurred there on five dates in October, with a maximum of 3,000 on 5th October.

Some Goldfinches remain to winter in Kent, usually feeding in small flocks, often with Redpolls and Siskins, again in a wide variety of habitats. Numbers vary considerably and concentrations of 100 or more are unusual, though they have been recorded more frequently in the

1970s. They are generally present in coastal localities, the largest being 400 at Northward Hill in December 1964, 500 at Barksore in February and March 1965, and 300 at Pegwell Bay in February 1973. In very cold weather, as in January 1962 and 1963, there is a further decrease, the birds presumably departing to the west or southwest, perhaps to the Continent.

Spring passage commences in the second half of April and continues well into May. Numbers are smaller than in autumn, and Sandwich Bay generally records the highest numbers, with daily counts of 500 or more coasting north in four years during 1964–76. The largest movement involved peaks of 1,000 on three dates in late April 1975.

Ringing recoveries show that some Goldfinches ringed in this county may winter in western France and Spain, in 1974 no less than seven were recovered in the latter country in April. Spanish and French-ringed birds have also been recovered in Kent, while others wintering, or on passage through Kent, have been recovered further north in Britain in subsequent summers.

Siskin

Carduelis spinus

Passage migrant and winter visitor. Has bred recently.

The first Siskins are usually observed on the coast in early September, with the peak passage in October–November, when inland flocks build up. During the winter, flocks wander in search of seeding birches, conifers and especially alders, and the largest concentrations are recorded in January. Spring passage begins in March, with peak numbers in early April and few records after the third week of this month.

Numbers fluctuate from year to year, presumably as a result of variation in breeding success and food supply in Kent and on the Continent. Favoured sites, such as alder groves in river valleys, regularly hold flocks of 30–50 and there are usually several such flocks and numerous small parties in the county in any one winter. Larger flocks are rare, with 100 at Leeds in February 1964, 160 at Sevenoaks in January 1972 and 100 at Stodmarsh in December 1975 being exceptional. There was a marked increase during 1968–75, with numerous records of Siskins in gardens, feeding especially on peanuts.

Like other finches, Siskins are diurnal migrants, often associating with Redpolls. In autumn they can be observed flying northwest at Dungeness, north or northwest at Sandwich Bay and west along the north coast into the Thames Estuary. The highest day-total was about 100 at Sandwich Bay on 27th September 1957, but numbers vary considerably and autumn peaks of around 30 are more usual. In spring birds pass through on a broad front and flocks often occur inland. The recovery of two Belgian-ringed birds at Sevenoaks in April 1971 suggests a Continental origin for some, perhaps most, of our migrants.

Breeding has been proved once, in 1966, when two young were reared in a plantation of larch and Corsican pine near Canterbury. Summer records have occurred in eight years since 1960. Breeding was again suspected in east Kent in 1969 and 1975, and fledged young were seen close to the Sussex border in 1976. The increase in such records suggests the possibility that regular breeding may soon be established and the extension of conifer plantations is undoubtedly an important factor. Siskins are inconspicuous in the breeding season and usually favour mature conifer plantations where they are easily overlooked.

Linnet

Carduelis cannabina

Widespread breeding species, most numerous on spring and autumn passage.

Like the Goldfinch, the Linnet has increased during the first half of this century, but there is no evidence to show that the increase has been sustained during the period under review. Indeed, the removal of scrub associated with the intensification of agriculture may have reduced the population in some areas.

During the breeding season the Linnet is essentially a bird of scrub, especially hawthorn and gorse. It rarely nests in built-up areas and prefers lower vegetation than the Greenfinch or Goldfinch, even nesting in tussocks of grass on the dunes at Sandwich Bay and in the sea purslane of the Medway saltmarshes.

The build-up of post-breeding flocks and subsequent movements match those of the Goldfinch. Flocks reached over 1,000 by the end of August at Sandwich Bay in 1967 and Wye in 1971, but generally not more than a few hundred occur together. Autumn passage varies from year to year, usually reaching a peak in October, but movement can

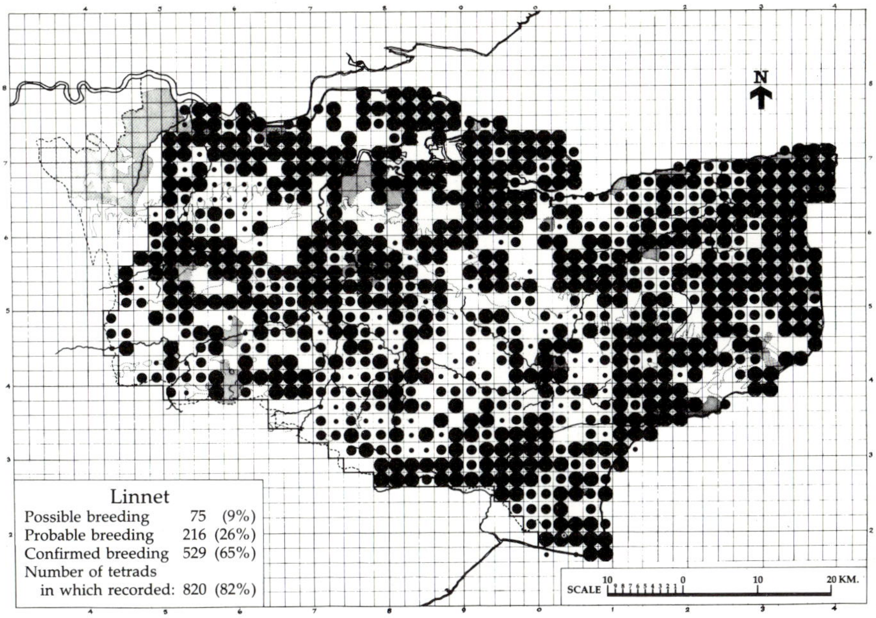

occur from late August through to mid-November. Migration tends to be in fairly small groups and especially in the morning. The largest movements recorded were at Dungeness, where 2,000 moved south on 13th October 1963, while in 1976 there were 1,700 on 29th September, 1,500 on 5th October and 1,100 on 27th October, these birds also flying south. During September–October 1969 there was an exceptional number feeding on seed around the banks of the newly-created Bough Beech reservoir, reaching a peak of 4,000 in October.

The majority of Linnets remaining to winter have probably come from within Kent or elsewhere in Britain. Winter flocks move freely in search of food, but large ones tend to be restricted to coastal localities. Flocks of around 500 are recorded in most years, but larger ones are more irregular, the biggest being 3,000 at Barksore in December 1963 and January 1964, with 4,000 there in February 1965, while inland there were 3,000 near Stockbury in December 1968.

Return passage in spring is also similar to that of the Goldfinch, but is generally earlier, extending from late March to early May. The northerly movement is frequently heaviest at Sandwich Bay, where the largest counts were 1,500 on 7th May 1962 and 1,600 on 3rd April 1967. Elsewhere daily totals may reach 1,000 flying northwest at Dungeness or migrating west along the north coast.

Ringing recoveries reveal a similar pattern of movement to that of the Goldfinch, with Linnets wintering further south and east in Spain. It is assumed that birds from further north in Britain pass through Kent on their way to and from the Continent, but there is curiously little ringing evidence to support this.

Twite

Carduelis flavirostris

Regular winter visitor.

Harrison considered that the Twite was becoming more common, but was unable to record a flock of more than 50.

The Twite favours the saltmarshes of north and east Kent, where wintering numbers began to increase during the 1950s. By the early 1960s flocks of 100 or more were regularly seen in Pegwell Bay and on the Swale and Medway estuaries, but there were no records of such numbers on the Thames marshes until 1971.

Apart from isolated records of four at Sandwich Bay on 26th August 1972 and five on Chetney on 6th September 1970, the first Twite each autumn are generally seen in early October. Numbers build up gradually through October and November, declining again in February and March, with the last birds remaining into April. The latest record was of one at Yantlet on 27th April 1975.

The first really large flock involved 600 on Chetney in the hard winter of 1962/63, these birds feeding on an area of marsh infilled with dredgings, which gave rise to a rich growth of suitable salt-marsh plants. This is still the record number for a single flock, although there were 600 at a similar site at Cliffe Pools in 1971/72, and at Sandwich Bay in 1974/75. During the 1970s the winter populations at these last two localities have varied between 100–600, with average peaks of 400 birds at each. On the Medway and Swale the situation is more confused due to the abundance of suitable sites. On the Medway, for instance, there is usually a flock of 100–300 birds on the south shore between Chetney and Barksore, with relatively few reports elsewhere. However, there were 350 on Nor Marsh in December 1975, while later the same winter probably the same birds were involved in a flock of 440 at Kingsnorth in February 1976. Flocks of up to 100 have occurred along the north shore between Kingsnorth and the Isle of Grain. On Sheppey there is a regular winter population of 100–300 on the saltings between Shellness, Harty and Windmill Creek, often split into several different parties. Numbers on the south shore of the Swale are usually small by comparison, although there was an exceptional flock of 500 at Conyer in November 1973. The figures for 1970–76 give an average winter population of about 1,200 birds in the county.

Away from the main wintering areas this species is most commonly reported during October–November, when small parties of passage migrants may occur anywhere round the coast, especially migrating west along the north shore. Flocks of up to 60 have been seen at

Reculver, with 100 there on 15th October 1967. On the south coast there have been up to 40 at the Wicks, and a maximum of 20 flying northwest at Dungeness on 18th November 1968.

Inland, Twite are recorded very rarely. There was an exceptional flock of 22 at Sevenoaks Reserve on 2nd April 1964, with one remaining on 5th April. One was seen with a flock of Linnets in a hop garden at Langley on 17th February 1974, while at Bough Beech reservoir in 1976 there was one on 21st March and two on 6th November. Closer to the coast, just south of Faversham, a small flock was present from early February 1976, increasing to 40 on 1st April.

Many birds wintering in Kent are believed to breed in northern England and there are two ringing recoveries to support this. The only other recovery concerns one ringed in the Netherlands in November 1972, which was retrapped at Cliffe in February 1975.

Redpoll

Carduelis flammea cabaret

Locally common breeding species, winter visitor and passage migrant.

Both Ticehurst and Harrison considered the British race *C.f. cabaret* a common species in winter, but observed that the summer populations fluctuated considerably. Breeding records were few and very local, mainly from the Weald.

There has been a marked increase in the breeding population since the mid-sixties, associated with the spread of conifer plantations, and another survey now would certainly show an even more widespread distribution.

The first breeding records in the period under review were in 1960 near Canterbury, with increasingly widespread reports in the woodlands of the Weald and around the Stour Valley during the late sixties and early seventies. That large numbers now breed in some years is shown by counts of 250 at Newington in August 1973 and a total of 220 ringed there between mid-July and mid-August 1975. In Farningham and Joyden's Woods 1,200 were ringed between July–December 1975, but many of these would be autumn migrants from further north in the British Isles.

One of the present-day favoured breeding habitats is young conifer plantations. Birch, hawthorn and willow scrub is also favoured, and this

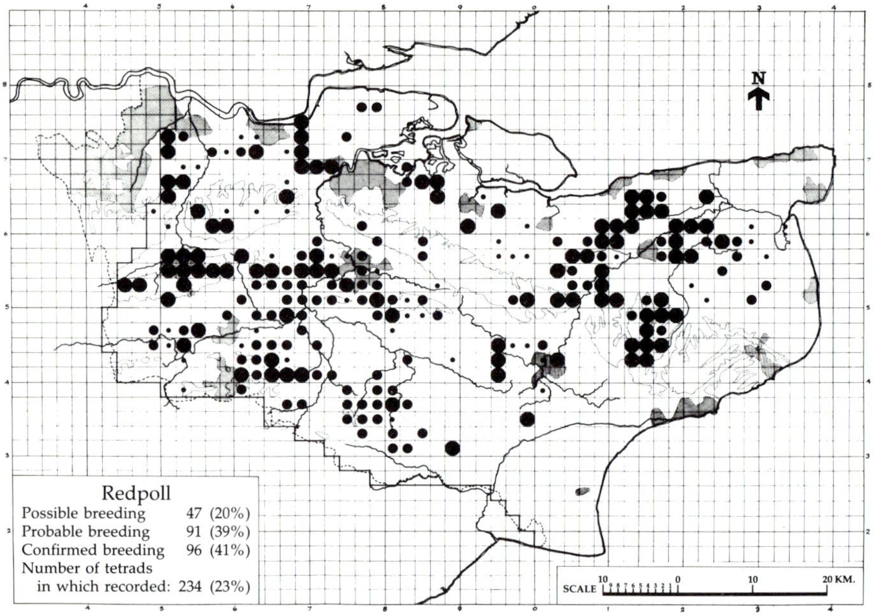

has encouraged the colonisation of well-established gravel pits and waste land. There has also been an increasing number of breeding records from suburban gardens and from orchards. Redpolls breed late and often in loose colonies, so that they may be overlooked and underestimated in many sites.

The increase in the numbers recorded on passage has been equally striking, though the size of the birch seed crop has a considerable influence on the magnitude of movements from year to year. Several ringing recoveries from Belgium confirm that a number of our passage migrants winter on the Continent. Autumn passage is noted mainly on the coast from mid-September to mid-November, with the largest numbers moving southeast at Dungeness in October. Here the peak day-totals increased from 60 in 1957 to 300 in 1964, a year in which extensive movements of British birds were recorded on the Continent. Since then peaks of over 300 have become fairly regular, with 600 in 1967 and 1974 and an exceptionally heavy passage in 1976, peaking at 2,500 on 20th October. Flocks of 100–200 occasionally occur at inland localities at this time, and in some years numbers of this order remain throughout the winter months. Birch and alder trees are especially favoured, but flocks also feed in larch and on weed seeds.

The return passage is much less marked on the coast, but numbers at inland localities may show a noticeable increase in late March and throughout April, with peak counts of 300 at both Pembury and Mereworth in 1976, and flocks of around 100 are not unusual.

Mealy Redpoll

Carduelis flammea flammea

Around the turn of the century Ticehurst recorded several large, late autumn invasions of this northern race, with the most recent in 1910. He and Harrison considered the Mealy Redpoll to be a winter visitor and passage migrant. This status remains true today, though large autumn invasions are unheard of.

J	F	M	A	M	J	J	A	S	O	N	D
7	12	25	140					3	7	19	4

Monthly bird/day totals of Mealy Redpolls 1952–76

Most records in the period under review involve one–three birds at widely scattered localities, but at Sevenoaks in 1970 there was an exceptional movement from 1st–14th April, with 127 bird/days and peaks of 52 on the 6th and 30 on the 8th. On a smaller scale, the next year there were 25 bird/days between 6th March–12th April, with a peak of 19 on 25th March. The only marked autumn influx involved nine birds trapped at Dungeness between 2nd–7th November 1975 and seven at Sevenoaks three weeks later.

[Arctic Redpoll]

Carduelis hornemanni

Although sight records of this rare northern species are not currently accepted by the British Birds Rarities Committee, single birds at Egypt Bay on 8th October and at Dungeness on 21st October 1972 showed the characteristics of pure *hornemanni*, and that autumn there was a marked influx into Britain.

Crossbill

Loxia curvirostra

Almost annual visitor, which breeds following irruptions.

Ticehurst documents records from as long ago as 1593, with occasional evidence of breeding and major irruptions in 1855, 1868 and 1898. Harrison continues with details of an irruption in 1909 following which there were numerous breeding records, and further invasions in 1936 and 1942. Similar behaviour was recorded during the period under review.

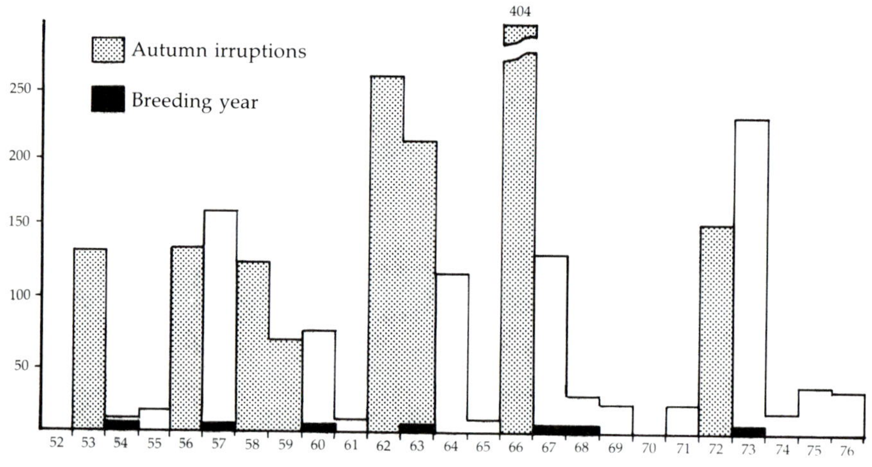

Annual totals of Crossbills, showing years of autumn irruptions and breeding

The pattern of irruptions one year followed by breeding the next is shown quite clearly. It is likely that pairs have nested more frequently, but confirmation is often difficult and thus rare. Even after major irruptions only two or three pairs have been proved to breed.

Most irruptions consist of two waves, the first beginning in late June and reaching a peak in July, followed by a second which normally reaches a peak in October. In 1958 and 1959 there were no second waves, while in 1963 there was no obvious influx until September, following the big irruption the previous year. The numbers involved are difficult to assess with accuracy, but certainly over 400 were present in 1966. During the winter there is usually a decrease and breeding behaviour can be expected to be seen between February–May.

Flocks wander widely looking for ripe cones and are liable to be seen anywhere, including parks and gardens, with mature conifers. In the breeding season there is a preference for Norway spruce, and small copses rather than large stands are favoured. The most-frequented sites include Bedgebury and Hemsted Forest, Lyminge Forest, and parts of the woods around Canterbury and Westerham. There are also regular reports from around the coast, including the Observatories, where the first arrivals are often noted.

Flocks of more than 25 are quite unusual, though there were 50 in Challock Forest on 10th July 1958 and an exceptional count of 109 in Church Woods (Canterbury) on 14th April 1973. This is an unusual date for a large flock and may have involved birds returning to the Continent.

Scarlet Rosefinch

Carpodacus erythrinus

Very rare vagrant.

The first Kent record was of an adult male in song at Dungeness on 2nd May 1966. A female or immature male was seen at Sandwich Bay on 22nd October 1968 and the third record was of a female, trapped at Broadstairs on 19th May 1971.

Records of this species are frequently suspect because of the number of escapes from captivity, however, the dates of these birds are in keeping with those of genuine migrants.

Pine Grosbeak

Pinicola enucleator

Very rare vagrant.

The first Kent record was of an adult male at Charing on 7th April 1955, following an irruption in Scandinavia the previous autumn. A female or immature male was seen at East Malling on 2nd November 1957, and an adult male near Maidstone on 15th May 1971.

Bullfinch

Pyrrhula pyrrhula

Widespread resident and occasional migrant.

Harrison describes the Bullfinch as comparatively rare on Thanet and Romney Marsh, while Gillham and Homes could find no early records for Sheppey.

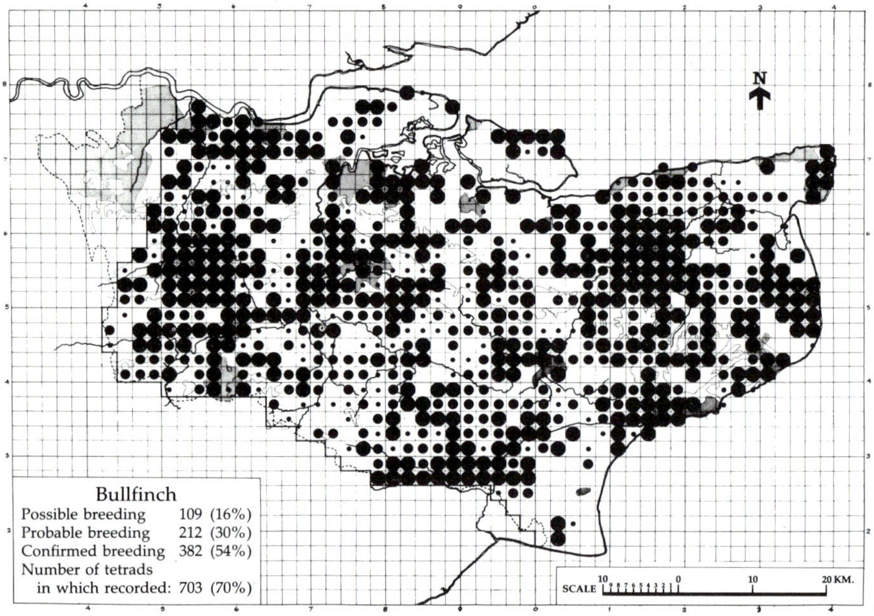

During the period under review the Bullfinch has extended its range in Kent, the first known occurrence on Sheppey being recorded in October 1956. The Breeding Survey provides further evidence of a similar extension of the breeding range, though the Bullfinch is still absent from pure marshland. A wide variety of bushy habitats, including overgrown hedges, gardens and young forestry plantations now provide suitable nest sites.

In the winter months small flocks of up to 12 are usual. Larger numbers are comparatively rare, though frequently a number of small flocks may be found in a limited area, and some of the largest concentrations reported presumably fall into this caregory. These include 120 at Barming on 29th October 1961, up to 80 at Stockbury between 29th October–10th December 1963, 60 at both Appledore on 28th March 1964 and Northward Hill on 28th November 1965, and up to 100 at Elmstone during March 1971. In most winters there are reports of damage to the buds of commercial plantations of pears, plums, apples and blackcurrants. Occasionally the damage is extensive and severe, particularly where orchards are planted adjacent to scrubby woodland.

Although the Bullfinch is scarce at the Observatories, ones and twos occasionally occur in spring and autumn. Unusually high numbers were reported throughout the county in the autumn and winter of 1961/62, and Dungeness had an unprecedented peak of 35 on 29th October. In hard weather, on 1st January, 50 were seen there, with counts of up to 20 being recorded until 4th February. Good numbers have since occurred at Dungeness in two other autumns, with 25 on 29th October 1967 and up to 30 between 27th–31st October 1976, with a peak of 50 on the 30th. In the latter year there were also 48 at Sandwich Bay on 2nd November. The fact that all these autumn peaks have occurred within the same week is noteworthy.

The origins of these apparent migrants remain obscure, but there are two foreign ringing recoveries: one ringed in Holland on 3rd November 1954 was recovered at Mereworth on 14th February 1960, while another ringed at Stockbury on 8th November 1960 was retrapped at Versailles, France on 22nd November 1961.

Hawfinch

Coccothraustes coccothraustes

Resident.

The Hawfinch was considered a rare winter visitor early in the nineteenth century, with a report of breeding at Chelsfield in 1828, but Ticehurst wrote of an apparent increase and gives figures indicating a healthy population by 1876, when as many as fifty nests were found at Cobham. He also cited winter flocks involving several hundred birds at Loddington (Boughton Monchelsea) by the turn of the century. Harrison considered the Hawfinch to be most numerous in the west of the county and included counts of 80–100 at Boxley and Tunbridge Wells around 1920.

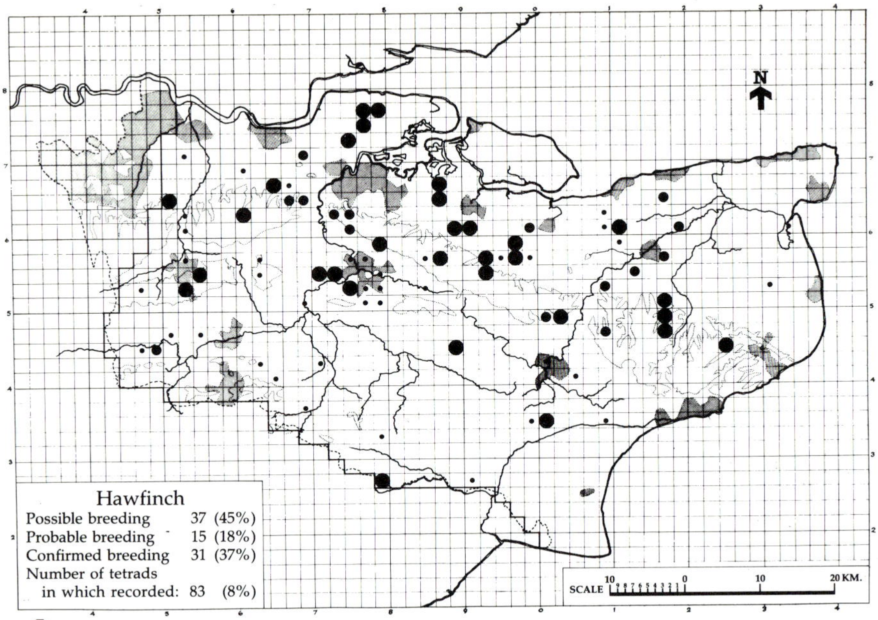

The Hawfinch is a very elusive species and probably better distributed than the map suggests. Since the North Downs were less well covered by observers during the breeding survey than other areas, it would seem that this region is probably the stronghold of the Hawfinch in Kent. A bird of mature deciduous woodland, it prefers hornbeam, beech, sycamore and similar species, the seeds of which are split open by the enormous bill. It is well known in Kent for its partiality to cherry and damson stones and may be associated with such orchards, particularly in the winter months, when it forms relatively large flocks.

The majority of high counts during the period under review come from two main areas, where winter roosts have become established. In the woods between Cobham and Northward Hill concentrations of 10 or more have been reported regularly since 1962, the largest count being 60 in Shorne Woods in March 1971. At Bedgebury the roost has regularly consisted of 20–50 birds since 1966, with the largest numbers during December–February. The highest count there was 100 on 26th January 1975. Elsewhere, flocks of 20 have been recorded at Burham, Maidstone Cemetery and Lyminge Forest, with 30 at Lullingstone in February 1973.

Although indications are that the Hawfinch is largely sedentary in Kent, there have been a number of coastal records, which may possibly refer to Continental immigrants. Singles were recorded at Dungeness in November 1961, January 1966 and on three dates during April–May 1972. Elsewhere round the coast one flew in off the sea at Folkestone in October 1956, and singles were seen at Warden Point (Sheppey) in October 1969, Dumpton Park (Thanet) in November 1973 and Allhallows in May 1976.

Slate-coloured Junco

Junco hyemalis

Very rare vagrant.

A male was trapped at Dungeness on 26th May 1960.

Lapland Bunting

Calcarius lapponicus

Regular winter visitor in small numbers.

Ticehurst lists six records of birds collected towards the end of the last century and Harrison adds three more, two taken near Dover on 8th December 1910, three seen near Stoke on 25th November 1950, and two at the Brooks on 21st October 1951. This species was undoubtedly overlooked before observers learnt to recognise its flight call.

The Lapland Bunting's favourite habitats are coastal saltings and rough pasture behind the sea walls, where they may associate with Skylarks, and occasionally Snow Buntings. Wintering parties have occurred regularly only on the Thames marshes between Egypt Bay and Yantlet, on Sheppey between Elmley and Shellness, at Reculver, and at Sandwich Bay.

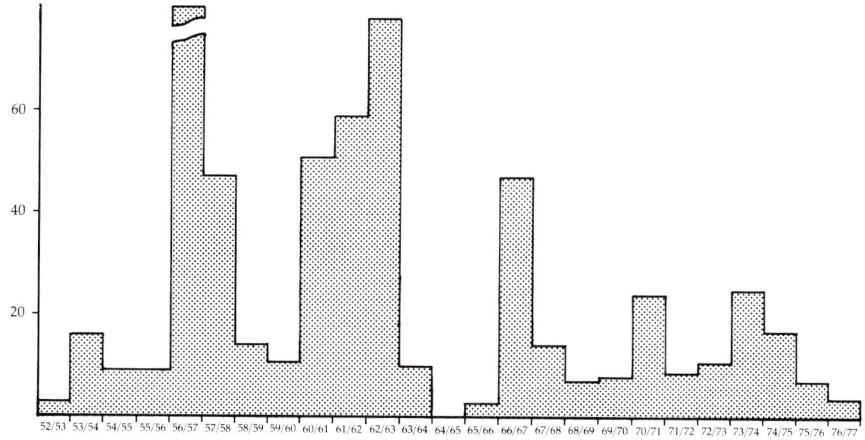

Winter totals of Lapland Buntings

Though recorded annually since 1952, the histogram shows that numbers vary considerably, while none occurred in the winter of 1964/65. In some years there is a small autumn passage of ones and twos in September–October, the earliest being on 9th September 1968, while larger numbers do not usually occur until the second half of November, or during December. In the period under review there were seventeen parties of 10 or more in only nine winters. Flocks greater than 20 birds only occurred in the exceptional influx of 1956/57, when there were 100 at Sandwich Bay on 18th–19th November, 30 at Yantlet on 8th December, and 30 at Egypt Bay on 10th March. Of these larger parties, about half arrive in November–December and then appear to move on, while the others apparently winter. Most leave in February, but some remain during March and there are three April records from the north, with the latest on 25th April 1954.

Inland this species has only been recorded twice, two were caught near Sevenoaks on 19th February 1956 and one was seen at Langley on 5th December 1971.

Snow Bunting

Plectrophenax nivalis

Winter visitor.

The status of this species remains unchanged. The Snow Bunting is an annual winter visitor to coastal marshes and saltings, especially where these are adjacent to shell beaches. The most regular flocks occur along the Thames and Swale, at Reculver and Sandwich Bay.

	Mean Winter Peaks	1959/60	1962/63
Sandwich Bay	88	150	200
Reculver–Minnis Bay	57	130	60
Elmley–Shellness	55	42	300
Nagden–Swalecliffe	35	30	40
Cliffe–St. Mary's Bay	27	130	120
Allhallows–Grain	14		4
Wicks		100	50
Chetney		80	40
St. Margaret's Bay		30	
Greatstone–Dungeness		2	14
Totals		694	828

Mean winter totals of Snow Buntings 1952/53–1976/77 at the six principal localities, with maximum numbers in the peak winters

The total numbers wintering in the county usually vary between 110–430, with an average around 300. However, in 1953/54 there were only 77, while in the winters of 1959/60 and 1962/63 there were exceptional totals, as shown above. The largest flock of 300 was present on Elmley from 3rd–23rd February 1963.

The first birds arrive in September and October, with the mean around 26th September and the earliest at Sandwich Bay on 5th September 1952. In 1966 there was a flock of 33 at Sandwich Bay as early as 25th September, but normally such numbers would only be seen during the main arrival in November–December.

There are a few records of birds seen on diurnal migration at the Observatories and along the north coast. At Ramsgate on 7th October 1966 an exceptional total of about 200, in several parties, flew westwards in off the sea.

Most winter flocks leave during February, while last dates are normally recorded in March and April, with the mean around 31st March. In 1975 there was a flock of 31 at Sandwich Bay as late as 1st April. The last remaining bird from a small party at Reculver in April 1964 stayed until 3rd May, while in 1971 there were exceptionally late singles at Shellness (Sheppey) on 15th May and at Sandwich Bay on 28th–29th May.

Inland records are comparatively rare. There were three singles in the first quarter of 1958, and between 1967–1976 there were almost annual reports, with nine singles between 14th October–11th December, and two on 14th February 1973. All these inland records have occurred west of Maidstone, including six at Bough Beech. Normally this species penetrates no farther inland than Stodmarsh, where odd individuals and exceptionally the whole flock from Reculver may be seen.

Two birds ringed at Sandwich Bay on 6th January 1960 were recovered in Belgium, the first at Zeebrugge only four days later, the second near Knokke on 29th November 1960.

Yellowhammer

Emberiza citrinella

Widespread resident.

There seems to have been little change in the status of this species, though Harrison suggested a possible increase in the 1940s, as more grassland was turned to arable.

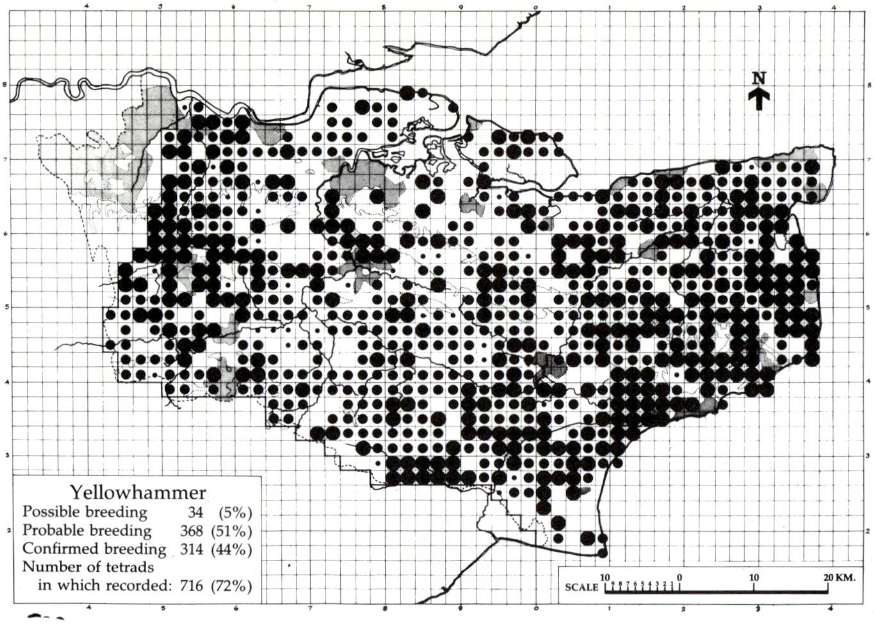

The Yellowhammer is a conspicuous bird of farmland, wherever there are bushes and hedgerows, and along edges of woodland everywhere. It is however, less common as a breeding species on the marshland pasture in north Kent and on Romney Marsh.

Like other bunting species in the winter months, it may sometimes form quite large feeding flocks, wherever its favoured food of grain or weed seeds is available, such as unburnt stubble or places where cattle are fed regularly. Flocks of 40–80 are reported annually from a number of widespread localities, with 100–130 regularly, and occasionally 200, at High Halstow, Mote Park (Maidstone) and Broomfield (Herne Bay) between 1956–59, and at East Peckham in November 1976, with the largest flocks of 250 at Aycliffe (Dover) in December 1969 and Hinxhill (Ashford) in March 1975.

There seems to be little evidence of migration, though records at Dungeness show spring and autumn peaks, and birds have been reported in late autumn arriving off the sea at Warden Point and Shellness on Sheppey, and moving west at Allhallows. The wandering of local birds seems a likely explanation, with some perhaps getting caught up in the diurnal migration of other passerines.

Cirl Bunting

Emberiza cirlus

Formerly a local breeding species, now a very rare visitor.

Ticehurst considered the Cirl Bunting to be locally more numerous than the Yellowhammer on the Downs, and mentions a number of breeding localities near Folkestone and Dover, between Shoreham and Wye, and also to the north at Iwade and Rainham. Harrison also lists several breeding records, including three during the 1940s, two of which were on the Downs at Bredhurst and Charing, the other at Leigh, with a further record at Plaxtol in 1951. The occasional winter records were more widespread.

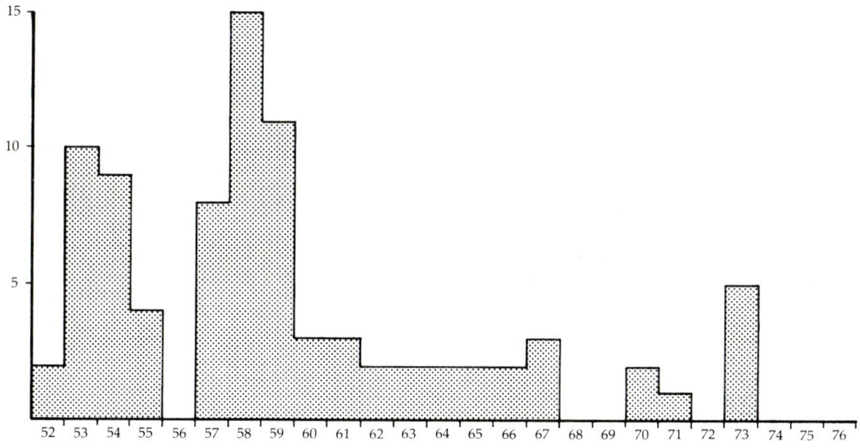

Annual totals of Cirl Buntings

The range of the Cirl Bunting in Britain has contracted considerably in recent years and this has been reflected by the clearly-marked decline in Kent since the late fifties. Single pairs bred near Maidstone in 1952 and 1953, and the last known breeding was nearby at Bluebell Hill in 1958.

The majority of the records in the fifties concern singles, but a flock of eight was seen at Cliffe on 17th December 1954, with four near Northward Hill on 24th August 1958. Apart from a flock of five near Headcorn on 23rd December 1973, the records since 1960 all refer to singles. At St. Margaret's a male was seen annually between 1961–67, on various dates between 1st March–29th August, and once on 17th November.

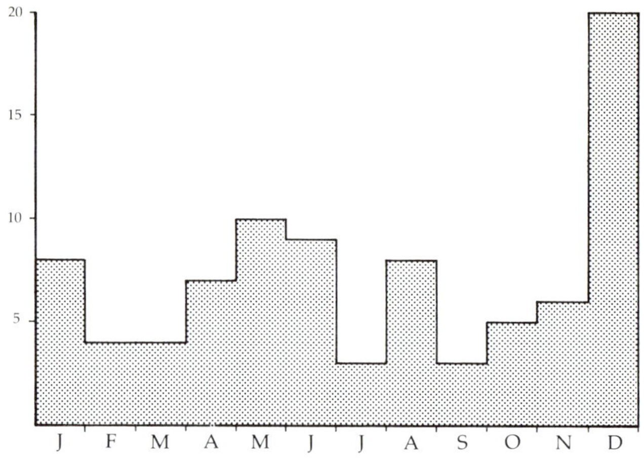

Monthly distribution of Cirl Buntings 1952–76

The seasonal distribution of records shows little change from earlier times, with the majority in the summer months. Reports have come from widespread localities, including three singles at Dungeness.

Rock Bunting

Emberiza cia

The only record is of one caught near Faversham on about 14th February 1905.

Ortolan Bunting

Emberiza hortulana

Rare passage migrant.

Ticehurst describes two definite records, including one caught near Dover on 14th September 1874, while Harrison adds one for Walland Marsh on 10th May 1946.

Since 1952 there have been 20 records involving a total of 28 birds in just thirteen years.

May		September		October		November	
25–8	9–22	29–11	12–25	26–9	10–23	24–7	8–21
2	5	5	6	7		2	1

Fortnightly distribution of Ortolan Buntings 1952–76

The extreme dates for the four spring records, all since 1972, are 1st–19th May, with two males at Reculver on 1st May 1972, two males at Dungeness on 10th May 1974, a female at Dungeness on 16th May 1975 and a pair there on 19th May 1975. The autumn records fall into two periods, with 13 between 2nd September–5th October and three between 26th October–9th November, all referring to singles, apart from three at Dungeness on 2nd September 1956 and two–four at Sandwich Bay between 26th–28th September 1975. The only other records away from Dungeness involved singles at Sandwich Bay on 6th September 1955, Lower Hope Point on 26th October 1959 and Herne on 9th November 1974.

Rustic Bunting

Emberiza rustica

Very rare vagrant.

The only record is of an adult male at Shellness (Sheppey) on 9th April 1962.

Little Bunting

Emberiza pusilla

Very rare vagrant.

Ticehurst records that an adult male was caught near Dover on 16th November 1907.

An immature near Cliffe on 28th October 1956 is the only record during the period under review.

Reed Bunting

Emberiza schoeniclus

Abundant breeding species and passage migrant.

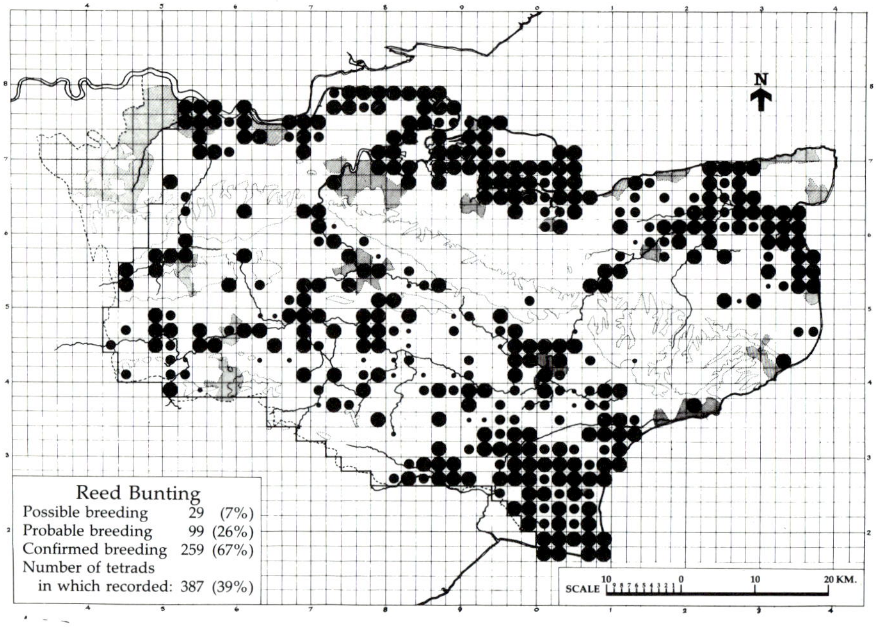

The distribution of this species as a breeding bird is closely linked to the presence of suitably damp, waterside habitats, where it is well distributed. It is virtually absent from the Downs, as one would expect. However, since the 1960s Reed Buntings have been expanding their ecological range into drier habitats, often at quite long distances from water. One pair was observed nesting on an area of downland and scrub near Dover in 1964. In some areas the population is fairly concentrated, with several pairs in close proximity forming loose colonies.

Attempts to assess population densities lack consistency, but during the 1970s small increases were recorded at some localities. At Langley Park Farm there were 14 pairs in 1976 compared with only three in 1971–72. On Dungeness Reserve the population doubled from about 20 pairs in 1971 to over 40 in 1974, while in the Observatory area the numbers fluctuate considerably from year to year, with 5–15 pairs in the early 1960s, 27 pairs in 1971 and 18 pairs in 1974. Some dispersal of the breeding population occurs in late July and August, and winter visitors may appear from late September onwards. In areas with small, isolated breeding populations it is not unusual for none to be seen during late summer.

Numbers on spring passage, during late March and early April, are generally fairly low, the highest counts at Dungeness being 85 on 10th April 1964 and 45 on 3rd April 1965. Peak autumn counts may reach 150 at Dungeness and Sandwich Bay at the height of a good passage, but in other years the maximum may only be 40. Coasting movements observed along the seawall at Reculver occasionally involve large numbers and on 30th September 1971 a total of 210 flew west in 90 minutes.

During the winter months small flocks of 50–70 are frequently found feeding with other finches and buntings in hop gardens and kale fields, or in any site where seeds are in abundance. Flocks of 100–160 have been seen occasionally, with the largest flock of 200 at Pegwell Bay in January 1968, where they were feeding with Linnets.

No particular pattern of movement other than dispersal emerges from the ringing recoveries and there has been none from overseas. A few ringed in autumn have moved westwards into Sussex and Hampshire. One ringed at Dungeness on 16th October 1964 was retrapped at Wolvercote, Oxford on 2nd November and then again at Dungeness on 25th April 1965, 12th March and 29th April 1966. Another ringed at Dungeness moved to Essex and back to Dungeness in the same autumn.

Black-headed Bunting

Emberiza melanocephala

Very rare vagrant.

The two records each concern single adult males, seen at Sandwich Bay on 1st June 1972 and at Reculver on 19th August 1973. Though this is a common cage-bird and occurrences must come under suspicion of being escapes, these dates suggest genuine vagrancy.

Corn Bunting

Miliaria calandra

Resident.

Ticehurst records some isolated breeding records near Tonbridge in the 1890s and Harrison suggests an increase and an extension of the range inland during the first half of this century, as more land was given over to arable farming, but overall there seems to have been little change in Corn Bunting distribution.

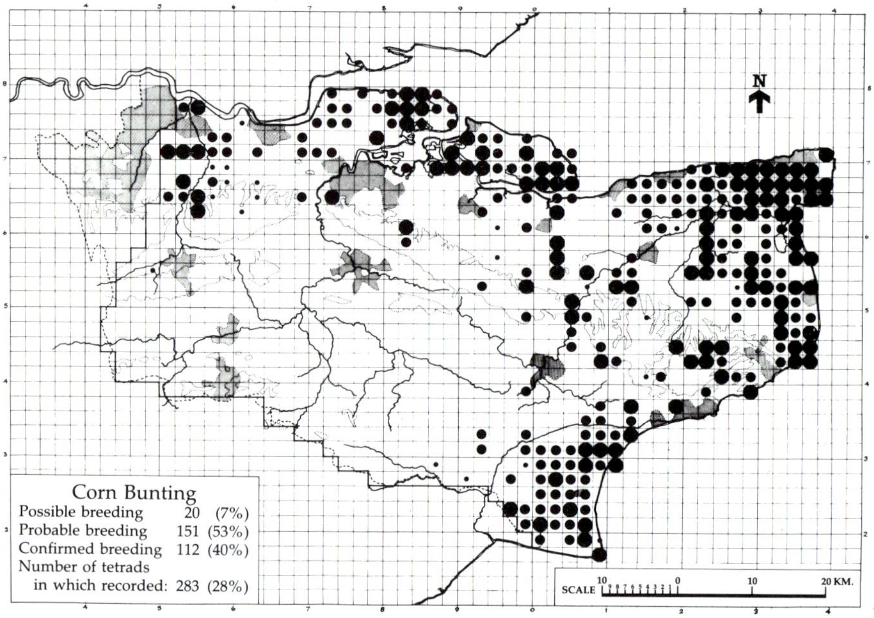

The Corn Bunting breeds predominantly on the coastal lowlands, with a thin distribution along the Downs, but seems to be entirely absent from the Weald. Such a concentration of records in the east, particularly along the Stour Valley between Canterbury and Ashford, has not previously been recorded, but much of this part of the county and the Romney Marsh area away from the coast has in the past been poorly watched.

Fluctuations in the population have been observed, with a decline in some areas. During the 1950s and 1960s, Corn Buntings were recorded more frequently in the Medway Gap and along the Downs to the east and west. Numbers have also dropped in the Darent Valley, and in these two regions urban spread may be partly responsible. In other areas intensive farming has caused the removal of the hedgerows and reduced the number of song posts.

In the winter months this species often forms roosting flocks, particularly in reed beds, and counts of 100–250 have been reported from Swanscombe, Stoke, Broomfield (Herne Bay), Grove, Sandwich, Sandwich Bay, New Romney and Dungeness, with a maximum of 300 at Stodmarsh in December 1971. Further inland in March 1971 a roost of 200 was located at Hinxhill (Ashford), while at Langley (Maidstone) 125 roosted, again in a reed bed, during the winter of 1976/77.

There is little evidence to suggest that the Corn Bunting is anything other than a resident. Out of the breeding season, individuals wander and may occasionally be seen in the Weald. Others seen on the coast during spring and autumn may simply be caught up in the movements of other passerines, though at Dungeness on 23rd and 24th May 1975 counts of 71 and 41 respectively were exceptionally high. Nine flying in off the sea at Sandwich Bay on 24th March 1965 is also most unusual.

One ringed in Essex in May 1957 was recovered at Faversham in January 1958. The only other significant recovery, one ringed on Chetney in February 1963 and found three months later in France, at Arras, Pas de Calais, suggests a cold-weather movement.

Appendix I

The following are listed as Category D species by the British Ornithologists' Union, as there is reasonable doubt that they have ever occurred in a wild state.

Greater Flamingo

Phoenicopterus ruber

Several records given by Harrison between 1873–1943, may have been genuine vagrants. In the Stour Valley from 1928–43 there were regular sightings, including small parties.

One, first seen on 13th October 1962, was found dead in the Stour estuary on 31st December. Another, also of the European race *P.r. roseus* was seen in the same area on 18th August 1967. It is generally accepted that all recent Flamingo records probably refer to escapes, particularly as most are of the nominate, American race *P.r. ruber*, or the Chilean Flamingo *Phoenicopterus chilensis*. Some of these have remained for long periods, particularly on the Thames marshes, with up to five Chilean from September 1975–May 1976.

White Pelican

Pelecanus onocrotalus

Ticehurst includes details of one present at Seasalter from July–October 1906.

There are three records for the period under review. One at the Wicks on 13th October 1971 had been seen the previous week on Walland Marsh, two were seen at Dungeness on 11th–12th November 1972 and one occurred at Fordwich between 8th–11th July 1975.

Wood Duck

Aix sponsa

The three reports, all presumably referring to escapes, concern singles at Sandwich Bay on 2nd November 1968, at Wickhambreaux on 3rd June 1975 and at Faversham throughout 1976.

Ring-necked Parakeet

Psittacula krameri

The first report was of one which frequented the Dungeness/Romney Marsh area from 26th August 1967 into January 1968. A family party was seen near Gravesend in 1969 and since then numbers have increased dramatically. The main populations are centred on the Gravesend area and Thanet, and breeding in the parks there was first reported in 1972. A flock of 30 was seen in Ramsgate in September 1976, by which time reports of ones and twos were widespread throughout the county, and concern was being expressed in fruit-growing areas at reports of damage to ripe fruit.

Red-headed Bunting

Emberiza bruniceps

Harrison includes details of one at Tonbridge on 13th March 1953.

Between 1959–76 a total of 17 was recorded, all but one being adult males. One was seen on 4th March, nine between 2nd–20th May, three between 8th–11th June and four between 21st August–15th September. Seven were recorded at Dungeness, five on the north coast between North Foreland and Sheppey, with singles at Higham, Cliffe, Gillingham, Maidstone and Ashford.

There is little doubt that the majority, if not all of these records refer to escapes from captivity.

Appendix II

The Hastings Rarities

In August 1962, an issue of *British Birds* (Vol. 55, No. 8) was devoted to the controversial subject of the unprecedented quantity of records and specimens of rarities from the Hastings area in the last decade of the nineteenth and the first two decades of the twentieth century. E. M. Nicholson and I. J. Ferguson-Lees listed 542 specimens obtained within 20 miles of Hastings which they recommended should be deleted from the annals of British Ornithology as being frauds, together with a further 53 sight records of rarities.

It is likely that some, at least, of the records from the area during the critical period were genuine, but for the sake of clarity, safety and scientific integrity, Nicholson and Ferguson-Lees erred deliberately on the side of caution when setting the record straight, suggesting rejection wholesale.

Their opinion, backed by complex statistical evaluation of probabilities and some careful detective work, was shared by the majority of ornithologists at that time. There were, however, notable exceptions. Dr. David Bannerman published his views in volume 8 of *Birds of the British Isles*, while Dr. James Harrison gathered dissenting opinion in *Bristow and the Hastings Rarities Affair*, including evidence from Dr. Norman Ticehurst. Research and statistical argument still continues, during which time further unrecorded rarities have been located, and paradoxically a number of those species deleted from the county list have been seen and authentically reinstated.

A considerable number of these 'Hastings Rarities' were from Kent, and in the present state of knowledge, it seems advisable to list all these records in an appendix. All have been omitted from the major text.

In the following list of 110 specimens and seven sight records, the numbers in the left hand column refer to the *British Birds* report, and UR denotes a previously unrecorded specimen.

Part I Specimens

3	Madeiran Petrel	5.12.95	Littlestone
5	Madeiran Petrel	8.11.06	nr. Hythe
8	Little Shearwater	27.11.05	nr. Lydd
17	Great Shearwater	24.10.11	Stone-in-Oxney
21	Cory's Shearwater	21. 1.01	Dungeness
UR	Squacco Heron	9. 6.03	Fairfield
UR	Squacco Heron	9. 6.03	Fairfield

33	Squacco Heron	29. 5.07	Romney Marsh
34	Squacco Heron	29. 5.07	Romney Marsh
36	Squacco Heron	0. 4.14	Romney Marsh
39	Night Heron	4. 6.00	Brookland
41	Night Heron	28. 9.04	Newenden
42	Night Heron	3.10.06	nr. Lydd
45	Little Bittern	8. 6.98	Romney Marsh
49	Little Bittern	0. 5.21	nr. Lydd
UR	Ferruginous Duck		New Romney
UR	Ferruginous Duck		New Romney
UR	Ferruginous Duck		New Romney
61	Ferruginous Duck	10. 1.25	Romney Marsh
62	King Eider	10.11.15	Dungeness
63	Ruddy Shelduck	0. 3.03	Cranbrook
72	Red-footed Falcon	0. 8.95	Dungeness
80	Red-footed Falcon	10. 6.08	nr. Ashford
86	Baillon's Crake	24.11.06	nr. Lydd
96	Little Bustard	2. 1.00	Newenden
106	Sociable Plover	3. 5.07	Romney Marsh
115	Little Ringed Plover	Spring 99	Brookland
UR	Little Ringed Plover	23. 5.13	Lydd
118	Killdeer	20. 4.08	Romney Marsh
119	Killdeer	21. 4.08	Romney Marsh
120	Killdeer	22. 4.08	Romney Marsh
124	Caspian Plover	13. 7.11	Brenzett
125	Caspian Plover	13. 7.11	Brenzett
131	Asiatic Golden Plover	20. 9.15	Romney Marsh
132	Asiatic Golden Plover	20. 9.15	Romney Marsh
133	Asiatic Golden Plover	20. 9.15	Romney Marsh
134	Asiatic Golden Plover	20. 9.15	Romney Marsh
135	Dowitcher	15. 8.07	Littlestone
139	Great Snipe	5.10.06	Brookland
UR	Great Snipe	9. 9.31	Brookland
140	Upland Sandpiper	18. 7.08	nr. Lydd
142	Slender-billed Curlew	21. 9.10	nr. Brookland
143	Slender-billed Curlew	21. 9.10	nr. Brookland
144	Slender-billed Curlew	23. 9.10	nr. Brookland
149	Solitary Sandpiper	15. 8.08	Littlestone
152	Spotted Sandpiper	5. 5.04	Romney Marsh
153	Spotted Sandpiper	5. 5.04	Romney Marsh
166	Marsh Sandpiper	24. 5.15	Romney Marsh
167	Marsh Sandpiper	24. 5.15	Romney Marsh
170	Terek Sandpiper	23. 5.12	Brookland
171	Terek Sandpiper	23. 5.12	Brookland
172	Terek Sandpiper	24. 5.12	Brookland
173	Terek Sandpiper	25. 5.12	Brookland

References

Extensive use has been made of three previous works on Kentish birds, and these are referred to colloquially in the text by the authors' names only:

Gillham, E. H. and Homes, R. C. (1950) *Birds of the North Kent Marshes* Collins, London.

Harrison, J. M. (1953) *The Birds of Kent* Witherby, London.

Ticehurst, N. F. (1909) *A History of the Birds of Kent* Witherby, London.

Other References
(note KBR = Kent Bird Report)

Bonham, P. F. and Robertson, J. C. M. (1975) The spread of Cetti's Warblers in north-west Europe. *British Birds* 68: 393–408.

Cramp, S. (1971) Gulls nesting on buildings in Britain and Ireland. *British Birds* 64: 476–487.

Cramp, S. *et al* (1974) *The Seabirds of Britain and Ireland* Collins, London.

Crick, H., Harrison, J. G. and Jenkins, M. (1978) Sand Martin ringing results from Sevenoaks Reserve 1961–77. *KBR* 25: 103–112.

Fitter, R. S. R. (1965) The Breeding status of the Black Redstart in Great Britain. *British Birds* 58: 481–492.

Fitter, R. S. R. (1971) Black Redstarts breeding in Britain in 1964–68. *British Birds* 64: 117–124.

Fitter, R. S. R. (1976) Black Redstarts breeding in Britain in 1969–73 *British Birds* 69: 9–15.

Grant, P. J. and Scott, R. E. (1969) Field identification of juvenile Common, Arctic and Roseate Terns. *British Birds* 62: 297–299.

Harrison, J. G. (1975) An historical Spotted Sandpiper in Kent. *KBR* 24: 93–94.

Harrison, J. G. (1978) A summary of western European duck wing studies 1974/75–1976/77. *IWRB Bulletin 43/44:* 78–86.

Harrison, J. G. and Grant, P. J. (1976) *The Thames Transformed* Andre Deutsch, London.

Harvey, W. G. (1977) Cetti's Warblers in east Kent in 1975. *British Birds 70*: 89–96.

Hori, J. (1964a) The breeding biology of the Shelduck. *Ibis 106*: 333–360.

Hori, J. (1964b) Parental care in the Shelduck. *Wildfowl Trust Ann. Rep. 15*: 100–103.

Hori, J. (1965) The display flights of Shelduck. *Wildfowl Trust Ann. Rep. 16*: 58.

Hori, J. (1969) Social and population studies in the Shelduck. *Wildfowl Trust Ann. Rep. 20*: 5–22.

Hudson, M. J. (1967) The breeding wildfowl of the North Kent Marshes 1961–64. *KBR 15*: 85–98.

Hudson, R. (1973) Early and late dates for summer migrants. *BTO Guide 15.*

Hudson, R. (1979) Nightingales in Britain in 1976. *Bird Study 26*: 204–212.

Hume, R. A. and Grant, P. J. (1974) The upperwing pattern of adult Common and Arctic Terns. *British Birds 67*: 133–136.

Langslow, D. R. (1976) Movements of Black Redstarts between Britain and Europe as related to occurrences at Observatories. *Bird Study 24*: 169–178.

Latham, J. (1785) *A General Synopsis of Birds* Vol. 3 Part 2, Leigh and Sotheby, London.

Mead, C. J. (1974) The results of ringing auks in Britain and Ireland. *Bird Study 21*: 45–86.

Mead, C. J., Flegg, J. J. M. and Cox, C. J. (1968) A factor inhibiting sub-specific variation in the Lapwing. *Bird Study 15*: 105–106.

Munns, G. F. A. (1978) British Trust for Ornithology National Rookery Survey 1975. *KBR 25*: 100–102.

Parslow, J. (1973) *Breeding Birds of Britain and Ireland* Poyser, Berkhamsted.

Pitt, R. G. (1967) Savi's Warblers breeding in Kent. *British Birds 60*: 349–355.

Prentis, W. (1894) *Notes on the Birds of Rainham* Gurney and Jackson, London.

Prestt, I. (1965) An enquiry into the recent breeding status of some of the smaller birds of prey and crows in Britain. *Bird Study 12*: 196–221.

Reynolds, C. J. (1979) The heronries census: 1972–77 population changes and a review. *Bird Study 26*: 7–12.

Scott, R. E. and Grant, P. J. (1969) Uncompleted moult in Sterna terns and the problems of identification. *British Birds 62*: 93–97.

Sharrock, J. T. R. (1974) *Scarce Migrant Birds in Britain and Ireland* Poyser, Berkhamsted.

Sharrock, J. T. R. (1976) *The Atlas of Breeding Birds in Britain and Ireland* Poyser, Berkhamsted.

Snow, D. W. (1968) Movements and mortality of British Kestrels *Bird Study 15*: 65–83.

Stuttard, P. and Williamson, K. (1971) Habitat requirements of the Nightingale. *Bird Study 18*: 9–14.

Systematic Index of English Names

Accentor, Alpine 298
Auk, Little 226
Avocet 144

Bee-eater 262
Bittern 49
American 50
Little 50
Blackbird 316
Blackcap 340
Bluetail, Red-flanked 304
Bluethroat 303
Brambling 392
Bullfinch 406
Bunting, Black-headed 417
Cirl 413
Corn 418
Lapland 409
Little 415
Ortolan 414
Red-headed 421
Reed 416
Rock 414
Rustic 415
Snow 410
Bustard, Great 141
Little 140
Buzzard 119
Honey 113
Rough-legged 120

Chaffinch 391
Chiffchaff 347
Chough 378
Coot 138
Cormorant 47
Corncrake 136
Courser, Cream-coloured 146
Crake, Baillon's 136
Spotted 135
Crane 140
Crossbill 404
Crow, Carrion 382
Hooded 383
Cuckoo 248
Great Spotted 248
Curlew 179
Stone 145

Dipper 295
Diver, Black-throated 34
Great Northern 35
Red-throated 33
White-billed 35
Dotterel 152
Dove, Collared 244
Stock 242
Turtle 246
Dowitcher 173
Long-billed 173
Duck, Black 89
Ferruginous 99
Long-tailed 104
Ring-necked 98
Ruddy 112
Tufted 99
Wood 421
Dunlin 167
Dunnock 297

Eagle, Golden 121
White-tailed 114
Egret, Cattle 52
Little 52
Eider 103
King 103

Falcon, Red-footed 124
Fieldfare 317
Firecrest 352
Flamingo, Greater 420

Flycatcher, Pied 355
Red-breasted 354
Spotted 353
Fulmar 40

Gadwall 82
Gannet 46
Garganey 91
Godwit, Bar-tailed 177
Black-tailed 175
Goldcrest 350
Goldeneye 107
Goldfinch 395
Goosander 111
Goose, Barnacle 71
Bean 62
Brent 72
Canada 69
Egyptian 75
Greylag 67
Pink-footed 63
Snow 69
White-fronted 65
Goshawk 118
Grebe, Black-necked 40
Great Crested 37
Little 36
Red-necked 39
Slavonian 39
Greenfinch 394
Greenshank 183
Grosbeak, Pine 405
Guillemot 225
Black 226
Gull, Black-headed 201
Common 204
Glaucous 208
Great Black-backed 210
Herring 206
Iceland 207
Ivory 212
Laughing 198
Lesser Black-backed 205
Little 199
Mediterranean 197
Sabine's 200
Slender-billed 203

Harrier, Hen 116
Marsh 115
Montagu's 117
Hawfinch 407
Heron, Grey 52
Night 51
Purple 55
Squacco 51
Hobby 126
Hoopoe 263

Ibis, Glossy 57

Jackdaw 378
Jay 375
Junco, Slate-coloured 409

Kestrel 123
American 124
Lesser 122
Kingfisher 261
Kite, Black 113
Red 114
Kittiwake 211
Knot 158

Lapwing 156
Lark, Crested 270
Shore 273
Linnet 398

Magpie 376
Mallard 86
Mandarin 79
Martin, House 279
Sand 275
Merganser, Red-breasted 110
Merlin 125
Moorhen 137

Nightingale 300
Thrush 300
Nightjar 258
Nutcracker 377

Nuthatch 367

Oriole, Golden 370
Osprey 121
Ouzel, Ring 315
Owl, Barn 249
  Little 251
  Long-eared 254
  Scops 251
  Short-eared 256
  Snowy 251
  Tawny 253
  Tengmalm's 258
Oystercatcher 141

Parakeet, Ring-necked 421
Partridge, Grey 130
  Red-legged 128
Pelican, White 420
Peregrine 127
Petrel, Leach's 45
  Storm 45
Phalarope, Grey 192
  Red-necked 191
  Wilson's 191
Pheasant 133
Pintail 89
Pipit, Meadow 284
  Red-throated 285
  Richard's 281
  Rock 286
  Tawny 281
  Tree 282
  Water 287
Plover, Golden 153
  Grey 154
  Kentish 151
  Little Ringed 147
  Ringed 149
  Sociable 156
Pochard 97
  Red-crested 96
Pratincole, Black-winged 147
  Collared 147
Puffin 228

Quail 131

Rail, Water 134
Raven 384
Razorbill 225
Redpoll 401
  Arctic 403
  Mealy 403
Redshank 182
  Spotted 180
Redstart 306
  Black 304
Redwing 320
Robin 299
  Rufous Bush 298
Roller 263
Rook 380
Rosefinch, Scarlet 405
Ruff 169

Sanderling 159
Sandgrouse, Pallas's 229
Sandpiper, Baird's 163
  Broad-billed 168
  Buff-breasted 169
  Common 188
  Curlew 164
  Green 186
  Least 162
  Marsh 183
  Pectoral 163
  Purple 166
  Spotted 189
  Terek 188
  White-rumped 163
  Wood 187
Scaup 101
Scoter, Common 105
  Velvet 106
Serin 393
Shag 48
Shearwater, Balearic 44
  Cory's 42
  Great 42
  Manx 44
  Sooty 43

Shelduck 77
Ruddy 76
Shoveler 93
Shrike, Great Grey 373
Lesser Grey 373
Red-backed 371
Woodchat 374
Siskin 397
Skua, Arctic 194
Great 196
Long-tailed 195
Pomarine 193
Skylark 272
Smew 108
Snipe 171
Great 173
Jack 170
Sparrow, House 388
Tree 389
Sparrowhawk 118
Spoonbill 57
Starling 385
Rose-coloured 387
Stilt, Black-winged 143
Stint, Little 160
Temminck's 161
Stonechat 311
Stork, Black 56
White 56
Swallow 277
Red-rumped 279
Swan, Bewick's 60
Mute 58
Whooper 61
Swift 259
Alpine 261

Teal 84
Blue-winged 93
Green-winged 86
Tern, Arctic 219
Black 222
Bridled 219
Caspian 213
Common 216
Gull-billed 213
Little 220
Roseate 215
Royal 214
Sandwich 214
Whiskered 222
White-winged Black 224
Thrush, Mistle 321
Rock 314
Song 319
Swainson's 315
Tit, Bearded 356
Blue 363
Coal 362
Great 365
Long-tailed 357
Marsh 359
Willow 360
Treecreeper 368
Short-toed 370
Turnstone 189
Twite 400

Wagtail, Ashy-headed 290
Blue-headed 289
Grey 290
Grey-headed 290
Pied 292
White 293
Yellow 287
Warbler, Aquatic 327
Barred 336
Bonelli's 344
Cetti's 323
Dartford 334
Dusky 344
Garden 339
Grasshopper 324
Great Reed 332
Greenish 342
Icterine 333
Marsh 329
Melodious 334
Moustached 327
Olivaceous 332
Pallas's 342
Radde's 343

Reed 330
Sardinian 336
Savi's 326
Sedge 328
Subalpine 335
Willow 348
Wood 344
Yellow-browed 343
Waxwing 293
Wheatear 312
Black 314
Black-eared 314
Whimbrel 178
Whinchat 309
Whitethroat 338
Lesser 337
Wigeon 80
American 82
Woodcock 174
Woodlark 271
Woodpecker, Great Spotted 268
Green 266
Lesser Spotted 269
Woodpigeon 243
Wren 295
Wryneck 265

Yellowhammer 411
Yellowlegs, Greater 185
Lesser 185

List of Subscribers

To fund the publication of this book it was essential that subscription sales were obtained. Subscribers were given the option of having their names entered in the following list. We hope that many of these subscribers will be active birdwatchers when the next review of Kent's birds is produced, perhaps in 25 years time.

We are especially pleased that H.G. Alexander has subscribed to this 1981 *Birds of Kent*. His name is also included in the subscription list for Ticehurst's *History of the Birds of Kent*, published in 1909: an extraordinary span of active and productive birdwatching.

This edition was limited to 2100 copies.

Abrams, C.D.
Adams, J.K.
Adcock, Maurice A.
Aitken, R.B.
Alder, R.P.
Alexander, H.G.
Alexander, K.
Alexander, Keith N.A.
Allan, D.M.
Allen, C.A.
Allen, P.M.
Allison, Rodney.
Andrews, I.J.
Andrews, Valerie M.
Anson, Mrs. Barbara.
Appleton, Martin.
Archer, Mrs. A.M.
Arnold, Mr. and Mrs. D.C.
Ashby, C.L.
Ashley, T.J., B.Sc.
Ashley, T.W.
Ashworth, S.J.
Atkins, Richard J.
Atkinson, D.N.
Atkinson, Mr. and Mrs. P.A.
Axell, Herbert, M.B.E.

Backhouse, Michael D.
Backhurst, Graeme C.
Baggott, C.J.
Bailey, Anthony.
Bailey, M.P.
Bailey, Roger A.D., M.B.E.
Baker, A.
Baker, Eric K.
Baker, J.A.
Baker, Leslie.
Baldwin, R.A.
Baldwin, T.M.
Ballance, J.K., M.A., M.B.O.U.
Banister, Mrs. R.A.
Banks, Martin.
Barclay, I.J.
Barker, Rosamunde.
Barker, T.R.
Barlow, M.E.
Barnes, Alan.
Barrett, K.
Bartlett, J.L.
Batchelor, D.M.
Bates, W. Terence G.
Baudoin, G.
Bedford, N.R.
Bell, E.M.
Bell, M.A.
Bellchambers, Mrs. B.
Belman, P.J.
Bennett, George C.
Bennett, Jean.
Bennett, Keith.
Bennett, L.J.
Berry, Professor R.J.
Betton, Keith F.
Beynon, Dr. K.I.
Bignal, C.E.
Billett, D.F.
Birchenough, R.F.
Bird, B.J.
Bird, Eric, L.D.S., M.B.O.U.
Bishop, H.G. and J.
Blake, F.W.
Bland, Robert Leslie.
Blase, Peter.
Blowers, Keith.
Boatman, J.L.
Boddy, Michael.
Bollington, K.J.
Booker, Mrs. B.J.
Booker, C.H.
Boorman, John.
Booth, David J.
Bond, C.
Bonneywell, T.L.P.
Borrow, Nik.
Bosworth, Arnold.
Boulton, George.
Boultwood, T.A.
Bourke, D.O'D.
Bovis, G.M., C.Eng., M.I. Mech.E.
Bower, Edward W.
Bowley, J.J.
Bowley, T.E.
Bowman, D.F.
Bown, Ian.
Boxall, P.G., B.A.
Boyes, Michael.
Boyland, Eric D.
Boys, David A.
Bradford, E.S.
Bradshaw, G.F.
Bradshaw, R., C.Eng., M.I.C.E.
Braggs, J.A.
Brawn, Mrs. L.M.
Bray, N.R.
Brenchley, Anne.
Brett, Doris M.
Bridges, D.A.
Brierley, Robert Christopher.
Brighten, John V.
Britton, P.L.
Broad, Miss P.
Brock, Hugh and Eileen.
Brooks, Nicholas.
Brooks, Robert.
Brown, Andrew P.
Brown, B.J.
Brown, P.A., B.Sc.
Brown, S.M.
Bryant, Michael.
Buckham, Andrew.
Buckingham, John.
Buisson, Dennis K.
Bullett, A.W.
Bundock, Brian.
Bunting, K.B.
Burman, G.W.
Burness, R.J.
Burns, D.W.
Burrow, K.J.
Burtenshaw, A.F.
Butcher, A.A.
Butler, Miss D.I.S.
Burton, G.J.A.
Bush, Pamela.
Buxton, Dr. N.E.

Campion, F. Charles J.
Campion, Richard S.J.
Canning, John.
Cantelo, J.
Carden, Dr. R.J.D.
Carr, R.J.F.
Carter, Bertram.
Carter, Magnus.
Carter, W.E.
Casselton, Dr. P.J.
Castle, Ben.
Castle, Dorothy M.
Castle, Miss Nancy.
Castle, Miss Zoë.
Cawkell, E.M.
Cawkell, H.A.R.
Chadder, P.J.
Chambers, Barry.
Chandler, Dr. R.J.
Chaney, B.R. and K.V.
Chapman, K.J.
Cheesman, R.
Chesterman, Sir Ross, Ph.D.
Chesworth, G.J.
Child, Alan K.
Childs, Mr. and Mrs. E.H.
Claringbold, R.G.
Clark, John M.
Clark, Louis M., T.D.
Clark, T.B.
Clarke, Mrs. A.
Clarke, J.V.
Clarke, M.C.A.
Claxton, M.J.
Cleaver, V.J.
Clegg, C.R.A.
Clements, George L.
Clements, J.R.H.
Cluff, N.E.M.
Clugston, David L.
Coates, Brian.
Coath, M.
Coburn, Roberta Olive Clare.
Cochrane, Brian.
Coker, David G., B.Sc., C.P.A.
Coles, Jack, M.B.E.
Coles, M.E., B.A.
Coles, Royston K.
Coles, T.E.J.
Coleman, Mr. and Mrs. E.G.
Coleman, John R.
Collins, Alan N.
Collins, R.E.C., F.R.C.S., M.B.O.U.
Collins, T.
Collis, Dr. Margaret, O.B.E.
Colombé, R.G.
Colston, P.R., B.M.N.H.
Colville, Barry and Sally.
Cookney, A.R.
Copp, Richard.
Corbet, Dr. G.B.
Corbett, John P.
Cordero, Raymond.
Corfield, Colin.
Cornell, Peter.

Corrall, Mrs. Sylvia.
Cottam, E.
Cottam, Peter.
Cottrell, Michael.
Counsell, Major David.
Coutts, Joe and Yvette.
Cowlin, J.A.
Cox, C.J.
Cox, E.W.
Cox, J. Howard.
Cox, M.A.
Cox, Dr. Simon.
Cranbrook, The Earl of
Crawfurd, Miss Betty.
Crawley, D.E.
Cressey, D.
Cressey, G.L.
Crick, H.Q.P.
Crowe, C.J.
Croydon Natural History and Scientific
Society Ltd..
Cullen, D.A.
Cullingworth, John.
Curson, Jon.

Dadson, R.
Dakin, T.M.
Dane Court School Library.
Daniels, M.I.
Dann, Kevin.
Davenport, L.J.
Davey, M.A.P.
Davidson, Michael.
Davies, Barrie.
Davies, Clifford J.
Davies, J.
Davies, N.R.
Davies, Mr. and Mrs. R.H.
Dawes, J.J.G.
Day, Clifford.
Day, Miss J.
Day, J.H.
de Miranda, J.F.
Delve, J.R.
Demar, Grant.
Dengate, M.
Denham, Robert H.
Dennis, M.K.
Dennis, R.R.
Derrett, Keith.
Dey, Dennis.
Dick, J.A.
Dicker, D.S.
Dicker, Tony.
Dickerson, G.
Dighton, K.
Dillon, Brian.
Dimsdale, Dorothy.
Dixon, F. Robert.
Dixon, I., B.A.
Dobbs, Clarice.
Dodd, Peter.
Donnithorne, N.J.
Doughty, H.G.
Douglas, K. Helen S.
Dove, Paul, B.Ed., M.Inst. B.R.M.,
A.R.M.M.
Dowie, M.I.
Doyle, Barbara B.
Draper, Dr. C.C.
Drakeley, Dr. M.J.
Dubbins, R.A.
Dugmore, K.
Dujardin, J.L.
Duke, T., B.Sc.
Dulake, Brenda.
Dulley, Mr. and Mrs. N.J.
Dungeness Bird Observatory.
Dunkley, C.K.
Dymond, J.N.

Earnshaw, K.W. and S.F.
East, J.R.
East Malling Research Station.
Edmead, J.
Edwards, A.T.S.
Eimerl, Mrs. T.S.
Elkins, Donald A.
Ellis, Derek Maurice.
Ellis, Keith B.
Elliott, D.I.F.
Elphick, D.

Ellwanger, Dr. Klaus D.
Else, G.R.
Elvy, R.J.
Emmerson, Keith.
Ennis, Leonard.
Erends, Michael Peter
Erridge, Malcolm W.
Espin, P.
Evans, David.
Evans, Miss Heulwen.
Evans, L.R.
Evans, R.D., L.R.I.C.

Fairless, T.W.
Fahey, Richard Michael.
Faulkner, Derek.
Farnham, Phillip.
Faragher, J.R.
Ferry, Brian.
Ffennell, H. and J.
Finnis, Mrs. Margaret.
Finnis, R.G., M.B.O.U.
Fitch, Philip.
Fitt, R.F.A.
Flack, Bernard H.
Flack, Mrs. Diana W.
Flack, R. Hugh A.
Flegg, M.J.
Flegg, W.J.
Fletcher, Captain H.M.
Flint, Peter.
Flisher, Mrs. Pat.
Flower, Peter.
Foad, J.M., M.B.O.U.
Fontana, P.C.
Foord, Frank G.
Ford, A.T.
Ford, M.J.
Ford, M.T.
Forrester, S.McP.
Forster, R.H.B.
Forsyth, A.
Fowling, R.J.
Fox, R.
Fox, Tony.
Franklin, A.W.L.
Francis, John G., B.Sc., M.B.O.U.
Freeman, Michael S.
Frenken, L.A., O.B.E.
Freethy, Ron, F.L.S.
Frost, D.W.
Frost, Mr. and Mrs. H.M.
Fuller, Dr. H.W.C., F.R.C.S.
Furness, Mrs. M.
Furse, Cdr. J.R. 'Chris'.
Fyffe, D.M.

Gabriel, A. J.
Galey, C.P.
Gallagher, Mrs. E.
Gallop, B.A.
Game, Geoffrey.
Gardner, Mark.
Garner, David.
Garr, J.J.
Gatehouse, Peter.
Gatley, Stephen.
Gayford, Stephen.
Gerrard, Dr. D.L.
Gibbs, A.
Gilbert, C.
Gilbert, D.C., B.Ed.
Gillam, Beatrice.
Gillham, E.H.
Ginger, Dr. Colin D., F.Z.S.
Gladwin, Rev. T.W.
Glover, Mrs. Ann, M.C.S.P.
Godden, R.J.
Golding, Martin.
Goldsmith, Miss D.M.
Gordon, J.Ramsay.
Gordon, P.L.
Gore, G.C.
Goulliart, A.
Grant, S.J.
Gray, M.B.
Green, Graeme, B.Sc., M.B.O.U.
Green, Rémy.
Green, V.A.
Greenham, Dr. David.
Gregory, A.M.
Gregory, B.J.

Griggs, P.M.
Grigson, M.J.
Grimes, Geoffrey.
Grizzell, Roy.
Grottick, H.S.
Groupe Environment –
Protection – Ornitholigie en Picardie.
Guest, A.J.
Guest, Gillian, M.A.
Gullick, Tom.
Guntrip, D.W.
Gymer, Dr. G.E.

Hadley, Mrs. P.M.
Hale, Mr. and Mrs. K.J.
Hale, D.
Hale, Major R.D.
Halliwell, G.
Hambleton, Ian.
Hancock, Mr. and Mrs. Michael.
Hanham, L.E.
Hanlon, W.T.
Harbott, A.G.
Harding, B.D.
Hardman, Miss E.E.
Hardy, Kenneth N.
Harle, Dennis F., S.W.L.A.
Harley, B.H.
Harley, C.G.E.
Harris, R.G.
Hart, J.R.
Hartley, F.R.
Harvey, Bill.
Hasdell, T.A.
Haslam, David V.
Hatcher, David R.A.
Hatton, D.H.
Hawell, John R.
Hawgood, G.J.R.
Hawkes, R.W.
Hawkins, A.D.
Hawkins, M.J.
Hayes, E.T. and M.W.
Hazelwood, R.J.
Headlam, Christopher.
Heaton, Andrew M., M.Sc.
Heathcote, Peter.
Heinzman, K.G.B.
Hemmings, John A.S.
Henderson, A.C.B.
Henderson, A.K.
Hennessy, David.
Hensby, Ronald M.
Henson, Raymond.
Henty, M.V.
Herlihy, Dorothy J., M.B.O.U.
Herringshaw, D.
Heselden, R.G.W.
Hewett, J.W.
Hill, A.P.W.
Hill, Mr. and Mrs. D.
Hindle, Chris.
Hindle, Roy H.
Hinge, R.D. and T.
Hitchon, A., B.Sc.
Hoare, R.
Hobbs, R.N., B.Sc., A.R.C.S.
Hodgson, I.P.
Hogg, Peter.
Holcombe, Anthony J.
Hollingworth, L.N.
Holloway, Stephen J.
Hollyer, J.N.
Holmes, S.C.A., M.A., F.G.S.
Holmes, S.W.
Holt, Christopher.
Holyland, Sidney.
Homer, D.C.
Homer, Ken.
Hooker, Miss J.
Hopkins, A.E.J.
Hori, N.J.
Horn, Ian M.
Houghton, J.W.
Howard, Mr. F.I. and Mrs. E.R.
Howard, Richard.
Howe, Stanley, B.Sc., M.B.O.U.
Hubbard, K.D.
Hughes, W.H.
Hukin, A.T.
Humphreys, Jim.
Hunter-Craig, I.D.

Hutchins, P.D.
Hutton, Keith.
Huxley, The Revd. Keith.
Huxley, M.P.
Hyatt, Keith H.
Hyde, Pamela B.
Hyde, J.M.

Ing, E.G.
Ivens, Mrs. Eleanor.

Jackson, D.I.
Jackson, Dr. Neville C.
Jacobs, Keith.
James, G.C.D.
Jarman, Nigel.
Jarvis, G.N.
Jeffs, L.W.S., T.Eng. (C.E.I.), M.I.Q.A
Jennison, Mr. and Mrs. E.H.
Jervis-Read, S.H., C.B.E., M.C.
Jezzard, Dr. R.G.
Johnson, Alexander F.C.
Johnson, Angharad.
Johnson, Lt. Cdr. D.H., R.N.
Johnson, Major Frederick A., M.A.
Johnson, Miss Katharine A.M.
Johnstone, Rosemary.
Jones, D.B.
Jones, Dr. and Mrs. H.G.
Jones, Philip.
Jones, Walter.
Jones, W.M.
Jordan, Mrs. N.A.
Joslin, R.G.

Keene, Paul.
Kempster, The Revd. Robert.
Kennedy, Dr. C.D.
Kennett, Wendy.
Kent County Libraries.
Kentish, P.A.
Kerry, J.B.
Key, Derek.
Keymer, Faith.
Keymer, Richard.
Kiddie, Roger.
Kim, Dr. Yong-Koo.
Kinchington, John.
King, D.J.
Kingscott, Keith.
Kirsch, Walter F.
Knight, Cedric.
Knight, R.W.
Knott, P.J.
Knox, Dr. Alan.

Lambe, Miss K.D.
Lambert, Roger Unwin.
Landells, Professor J.W., O.B.E., M.B.B. Chir., M.R.C.P., F.Z.S.
Langford, David.
Langford, John.
Lapworth, Andrew.
Larkin, P.
Last, Tod.
Laugharne, Owen.
Law, Mrs. C.S.
Lawn, M.R.
Lawrence, P.A.
Lawrence, R.H.
Lawson, Dr. J.R.
Lea, Stephen.
Leather, Mike.
Lessells, C.M.
Leverton, Roy.
Lewis, Neville.
Lewis V.C.W. and G.I.
Limbert, Martin.
Little, Brian.
Lloyd, A.H.
Lloyd, Peter F.
Lockwood, Frank W.
Lodge, K.W.
Longdon, M.R.
Loseby, T.
Love, G.A., F.C.C.A.
Lovibond, Mr. and Mrs. A.L.
Lowe, A.C.
Lukes, David.
Lurcook, Norman and Betty.
Luxford, C.A.

McAndrew, Paul. B.A.
McAndrew, R.T.
McCanch, N.V., M.B.O.U.
McClintock, D.
Macfarlane, Lt. Col. A.M., R.A.
McGrath, K., B.Sc.
McHenry, Paul and Giles.
McKay, Fiona.
McLean, I.D.
Maclure, Lt. Cdr. E.S.W., R.N.
Macoustra, Neil.
McWilton, I.B.
Magee, John D.
Maidstone Museum.
Mairs, D.
Malins, D.M.
Manger, D.C.
Manship, T.J.
Margerum, Mrs. Daphne.
Markham, Ruth.
Marks, T.R.
Marsh, B.A.
Marshall, Mrs. B.B.
Marshall, W.H.
Martin, Jonathan.
Martin, J.C.
Martin, J.H.
Martin, R.J.
Massey, Michael.
Mather, John R., M.B.O.U.
Manton, Peter W.
May, Matthew.
May, Mr. and Mrs. Maurice.
Mead, Chris.
Meakin, W.J.B.
Meatyard, Dr. B.T.
Medford, J.A.
Medlin, H.A.
Mees, G.F.
Melville, G.F.
Memory, P.R.
Mercer, D.J.
Meredith, P.
Merritt, Andrew.
Messenbird, G.
Metcalf, Geoffrey.
Metherell, Anne M.
Middlemiss, G.R.
Milbled, T.
Milligan, I.
Mills, H.P.
Mills, Keith D.
Mitcham, T.
Mitchell, K.D.G.
Montier, David J.
Moon, A.V.
Moon, J.P.
Moorse, F.R.G.
Moreton, B.D.
Morgan, Phoebe.
Morris, A.J.
Morris, David.
Morton, R.W.
Moss, Dr. A.G.
Mount, S.D.W.
Mountain, G.D., M.Sc., D.I.C., A.R.C
Munns, Christopher.
Munns, Geoffrey.
Murphy, Gerald.
Murray, G.W., C.Eng., M.I.E.E.
Musson, David F.

Nash, D.D.
Nature Conservancy Council.
Naylor, John F.
Neal, D.M.
Neame, Basil.
Neath, Brian.
Nelson, A.W.B.
Newcombe, M.J.
Newman, E.C.B.
Newnham, Dr. John A.
Newton, Eric J.
Nicholls, Graham, B.A.
Nicholson, P.B.
Nightingale, Barry.
Norman, R.
Norman, Steve.
North, Dr. Philip M.
Norton, Mr. and Mrs. K.A.
Novak, John A.
Nyahwa, Paul.

O'Donnell, S.
Offord, T.J.
O'Grady, Ann.
Okines, D.
Oliver, David and Sarah.
Orchard, M.J.
Orton, G.R., B.A., M.B.L.S.
Osborne, Leslie W.
Osborne, T.N.M.

Paine, Gordon J., M.B.E., D.L.
Paine, John, B.Sc.
Palmer, Keith.
Palmer, K.H.
Palmer, Malcolm.
Parker, Alan.
Parker, R.J.
Parmenter, T.W.
Parrinder, Mrs. E.D.
Partridge, T.J.
Paterson, Alan C.
Patten, David E.
Pattimore, R.S.
Payne, A.
Payne, Frank P.
Payne, Kenneth.
Payne, Peter.
Peach, A.N.H., M.B., F.R.C.S.
Pearce, T.A.
Pease, A.G.
Pegrum, Richard M.
Peirce, L.R.
Perrin, D.
Perry, D.F.
Perry, D.T.
Perry, G.C., B.Sc.
Perry, John, M.A.
Pettet, Professor A.
Petty, A.G.
Philp, E.G.
Philps, Dr. J.F.
Pilbeam, D.A.
Plant, C.W., B.Sc., M.B.O.U.
Player, Dr. P.V.
Poole, P.H.
Pope, A.J.
Potter, D.A.
Poulter, Adam.
Poulter, Bruce, B.Sc.
Pratt, J.A.
Price, G.J.
Pritchard, Jan.
Privett, K.C.

Quinnell, R.J.
Quintrell, G.J.

Rackliffe, R.A.
Ratcliffe, Nigel W.
Read, Stephen W.
Redfern, Geoffrey H.
Redman, P.S.
Reid, D.E.
Reid, M.J.
Revell, D.
Riach, Captain J.A.
Richardson, Rev. David M., B.D.
Rigby, Dr. C.H.L.
Rigden, S.
Riley, G.D.
Ripper, Martin S.
Risley, Thomas Joseph.
Rivers, S.L.
Robbins, Peter, B.Sc.
Roberts, F.W.
Roberts, P.
Roberts, R.P.
Roberts, Dr. Theo.
Robinson, H.P.K.
Rollins, C.C., D.F.C.
Roman, Alan J.
Rometz, M.L.R.
Rooke, Miss H.
Rosair, D.B.
Roser, M.P.
Roseveare, Dr. M.P.
Rossor, Dr. M.
Royce, James A.
Rule, Keith W.
Rumley-Dawson, Ian.
Rumsey, G.J.R.
Rusling, D.

Sage, Bryan.
Sampson, David.
Saunders, R.C.
Sayers, J.A.
Saxby, Brian Desmond.
Saxton, Charles E.V.
Scholes, Geoffrey.
Scholfield, C.O.
Scott, Alastair.
Scott, Bob.
Searle, Mrs. Betty.
Searle, Dr. R.J.G.
Seath, R.
Sergeant, Dr. D.E.
Shannon, G.R.
Sharp, Brian J.
Sharp, Philip J.
Sharr, Clifford.
Sharrock, J.
Shaw, Mike.
Shelton, John.
Shepherd, K.G.
Shepherd, Michael.
Shilling, G.A.
Sibson, R.B., M.A. (Oxon.).
Simmons, Mrs. Silvia.
Simonds, L.M.
Simons, Philip.
Simpson, D.A.G.
Simpson, Mrs. I.
Simpson, J.T.
Sinclair, Miss M.J.
Sitters, H.P.
Skinner, P.C.J.
Slater, Martin.
Small, B.R.
Smallshire, D.
Smart, J.H.
Smart, T.
Smeeton, T.R.
Smith, A.J.L.
Smith, Brian and Jean.
Smith, Chas. H.
Smith, D.B.R.
Smith, D.E.
Smith, Donald C.F.
Smith, Donald T.
Smith, Peter.
Smith, Rodney.
Smith, Steven.
Smith, S.G.
Smith, T.H.
Speckmann, Michael.
Spencer, W.I.T.
Spong, Mr. and Mrs. L.G.
Standley, P.E.
Stanley, C.J.G.
Steadman, Major.
Stephenson, M.
Steward, M.M.
Still, E.C.
Stone, P.W.
Stone, R.C.
Stone, W.J.
Stoneham, M.W.
Stoneham, W. R., B.Ed., M.A.
Stoodley, P.E.W.
Street, L.
Sullivan, George.
Summerfield, Dr. B.J.
Sunnuck, Mrs. Jennie.
Sutherland, M.P.
Sutton, B.
Sutton Valence School.
Swales, Paul Richmond.
Swan, George F.
Swan, Mrs. K.J.
Swingland, Dr. I.R.

Tait, Mrs. A.H., B.Sc. Agric.
Tapp, Miss M.S., M.C.S.P.
Tappenden, R.
Tardivel, N.C. and G.M.
Tate, Peter.
Taylor, Bernie.
Taylor, Frank D.
Taylor, Garry.
Taylor, G.J.
Taylor, J.
Taylor, J.H. and D.E.
Taylor, Dr. Moss.
Taylor, Dr. and Mrs. R.
Taylor, R.C., D.R.G.
Templeton, I.C.
Tew, R.P.
Thiel, Marie E.
Thomas, M.B.
Thomas, R.
Thompsett, D.J.
Thompson, A.L.
Thompson, D.
Thompson, Murray J.
Thompson, R.R.
Thomson, Pam.
Thorpe, A.W.
Thorpe, Mrs. B.
Tickner, M.J.
Tilbrook, J.E.
Tilbury, N.R.
Tilley, J.W.
Tinning, J.J. and S.J.
Tinning, P.C.
Tipling, David J.
Todd, Ralph.
Tofts, R.
Tombal, J.C.
Tonkin, A.C.
Tomlin, Miss Freda.
Toohig, T.J.
Took, J.M.E.
Towse, Rev. A.N.B., M.A.
Travers, F.C.
Trobe, W.M.
Trowell, Jotn E.
Trowell, Paul.
Trowell, Sylvia.
Truckle, W.H.
Turk, David Michael.
Tuckey, Mike.
Tunstall Bates, W., F.R.I.C.S
Turner, C.F.
Turner, D.J.
Turner, Mrs. Mary.
Turney, Dr. J.H.
Tutt, Derek.
Tyack, G., L.R.P.S.
Tyas, S.A.

Uhlig, J.
Underdown, I.W.
Utton, Brian.

Vamplew, Sidney W.
Van der Dol, John.
Van Dijk, J.
Vandome, P.
Vaughan, R.J.
Verrall, K.
Vick, Dr. L.L.J.
Vinall, W.J.
Viner, J.E.C.

Wadley, N.J.P.
Waghorn, D.J.
Wakeling, John E.
Walder, W.J.
Waley, Felix, Q.C.
Walker, Jeff.
Walker, J.J.M., M.C.
Walker, R.L.
Walker, S.J.P., B.A.
Walkling, Keith.
Wallace, D.W.
Waller, Mrs. Mary.
Walters, Mrs. David.
Walton, John.
Warburton, M.A.
Wardman, F.A., F.C.A.
Warner, C.R.
Warrington, Michael.
Warry, Simon R.
Warwick, R.G.M.
Washington, Mr. and Mrs. D.
Waters, Professor W.E.
Watson, Dr. E.V.
Watt, The, Family.
Way, Antony.
Weaver, D.J.
Webb, E.H.
Webb, Marcus F.
Websper, J.H.
Welham, M.E.
Wells, Ron.
Welton, F.E.
Wenham, Terry.
Wheeler, A.F.
Wheeler, C.E.
Whewell, Andrew W.
Whitaker, J.
Whittaker, D.N.
White, Dr. D.J.B.
White, G.F.W.
White, Nicholas G.
White, Peter J.
Whiteman, C.A.
Whitworth, Miss Margaret.
Wilcox, Joan.
Wilcox, Malcolm.
Wilkinson, Sir Denys.
Williams, Mrs. B.P.
Williams, C.K.
Williams, R.F.V.
Wilson, David.
Wilson, Mr. and Mrs. D.B.F.
Wilson, David M.
Wilson, Mark J.M.
Wilmshurst, John and Patricia.
Wilton, Rev. Clifford.
Windle, Dr. K.
Windle, Mrs. M.H.
Wise, D., M.D.
Wood, R.
Wood, Roger.
Wood, R.G.
Woodcock, A.M.
Woodcock, Martin.
Woodcock, Stephen.
Woodley, J.A.
Woods, Robin W.
Wooldridge, Mariom and Graham.
Woollard, L.F.
Woollard, Stephen Laurence.
Worsfold, D.C.H.
Wraight, James W.
Wren, J.C.
Wright, Barry E.
Wright, David.

Yates, Mrs. Vera B.
Yates, D.F.
Younl, C.E.

Ziemelis, K.V.